To My Dear Sister

M000202523

anxiously awaiting your book,

Walt

NEGOTIATING LANGUAGES

SOUTH ASIA ACROSS THE DISCIPLINES

SOUTH ASIA ACROSS THE DISCIPLINES

◈ ◈ ◈

Funded by a grant from the Andrew W. Mellon Foundation and jointly published by the University of California Press, the University of Chicago Press, and Columbia University Press

South Asia Across the Disciplines is a series devoted to publishing first books across a wide range of South Asian studies, including art, history, philology or textual studies, philosophy, religion, and the interpretive social sciences. Series authors all share the goal of opening up new archives and suggesting new methods and approaches, while demonstrating that South Asian scholarship can be at once deep in expertise and broad in appeal.

For a list of books in the series, see page 289.

NEGOTIATING LANGUAGES

URDU, HINDI, AND THE DEFINITION OF MODERN SOUTH ASIA

Walter N. Hakala

COLUMBIA UNIVERSITY PRESS
NEW YORK

Columbia University Press
Publishers Since 1893
New York Chichester, West Sussex
cup.columbia.edu

Library of Congress Cataloging-in-Publication Data
Names: Hakala, Walter N., author.
Title: Negotiating languages : Urdu, Hindi, and the definition of modern South Asia / Walter N. Hakala.
Description: New York : Columbia University Press, [2016] |
Series: South Asia across the Disciplines | Includes bibliographical references and index.
Identifiers: LCCN 2015040766 | ISBN 9780231178303 (alk. paper)
Subjects: LCSH: Multilingualism—South Asia. | Language and languages—South Asia. | Historical linguistics—South Asia. | Sociolinguistics—South Asia. | South Asia—Languages.
Classification: LCC P115.5.S623 H35 2016 | DDC 306.442/9143054—dc23
LC record available at http://lccn.loc.gov/2015040766

Columbia University Press books are printed on permanent and durable acid-free paper.

Printed in the United States of America

c 10 9 8 7 6 5 4 3 2 1

Cover design: Jordan Wannemacher

Awarded the

Edward Cameron Dimock, Jr. Prize in the Indian Humanities

by the American Institute of Indian Studies and published with the Institute's generous support.

For Jinhee

CONTENTS

List of Figures *xi*
Acknowledgments *xiii*
Note on Transliteration *xvii*
Chronology *xix*

[1] A PLOT DISCOVERED 1

[2] 1700: BETWEEN MICROHISTORY AND MACROSTRUCTURES 33

[3] 1800: THROUGH THE VEIL OF POETRY 76

[4] 1900: LEXICOGRAPHY AND THE SELF 115

[5] 1900: GRASPING AT STRAWS 155

CONCLUSION 189

Notes *201*
Bibliography *253*
Index *277*

FIGURES

Figure 1.1: Sample pages from *Aḳhbārī Luġhāt* (1915)
Figure 1.2: Detail of the first page of Leyden's *Vocabulary*
Figure 1.3: First page of Leyden's *Vocabulary* (1808), BL MSS EUR B103
Figure 1.4: MS of Thomas Bowrey's *Dictionary of English, Portuguese, Hindostanee, and Malay* (c. 1700), BL MS EUR 192, f. 74
Figure 2.1: Notice of "Hindee" dictionaries employed in Breton's *Vocabulary*
Figure 2.2: *Apwārā* in the *Ġharāʾib al-Luġhāt* (Rampur MS 2543, f. 4)
Figure 2.3: *Apwārā* in the *Ġharāʾib al-Luġhāt* (Rampur MS 2544, f. 4)
Figure 3.1: Northern India (c. 1783)
Figure 3.2: Mirzā Jān 'Ṭapish' and his *silsilah* (chain) of poetic discipleship
Figure 3.3: *Panee pee pee kosna*, from Taylor and Hunter's 1808 *Dictionary*
Figure 4.1: Seal appearing in *Farhang-i Āṣafiyah*: "M. Saiyid Ahmad, Author of New Large Hindustani Dictionary"
Figure 4.2: Topywallas from *The Grand Master; or, Adventures of Qui Hi? in Hindostan* (1816)
Figure 4.3: Sayyid Aḥmad's *silsilah* (chain) of poetic discipleship
Figure 5.1: Title page of *Maḳhzan al-Muḥāwarāt*

ACKNOWLEDGMENTS

IN THE decade I have spent studying Urdu dictionaries I have profited from conversations with many scholars of South Asian literature and history. Frances Pritchett at Columbia University has been my closest mentor and guide. Her intellectual honesty and principled approach to literature has taught me to treat my sources and readers with respect and admiration. In reading multiple drafts and over long conversations she has saved me from innumerable errors in fact and judgment. This project is inspired by, and in many ways is a response to, the work of Shamsur Rahman Faruqi, the colossus of Urdu literary history. Griffith Chaussée introduced me to Hindi and Urdu when I was an undergraduate at the University of Virginia. I first explored the themes that underlie the present project for the thesis I wrote under his supervision. Christi Merrill guided my first forays in Charlottesville into Hindi literature and translation theory and has assisted me at pivotal moments as a mentor and a friend. Professors Khwaja Muhammad Ekramuddin, Muhammad Shahid Husain, and Pasha Anwar Alam trained me as a masters student in the Department of Urdu at Jawaharlal Nehru University. Aditya Behl brought me to Philadelphia to study Urdu and encouraged me to begin this strange and exciting project. Following his tragic death in August 2009, Lisa Mitchell stepped in to help me continue my work. I read her monograph *Language, Emotion, and Politics in South India: The Making of a Mother Tongue* at an important moment in the conceptualization of this project. Its influence, in both form and content, I hope will be apparent in the pages that follow. I am grateful to current and former faculty at the University of Pennsylvania for guiding me at various points in my graduate career: Roger Allen, Daud Ali, Whitney Cox, Jamal Elias, Suvir Kaul, Allyn Miner, Christian Novetzke, Shaheen Parvez, Benedicte Santry, and Harold Schiffman.

In revising this book for publication, I have been assisted by many colleagues and friends. Jerold Frakes and James Holstun carefully read through drafts and contributed valuable insights. Joyce Flueckiger, Brian Hatcher, and Barbara Ramusack shared their collective wisdom during the American Institute of Indian Studies Dissertation-to-Book workshop in October 2012. The Department of English Juxtapositions Lecture Series supported visits to Buffalo by Yigal Bronner and Christi Merrill. I cherish the time I spent with each and the frank advice they shared with me. My prose and arguments have benefitted from participation in writing groups that have included Josh Coene, Rebecca French, Jang Wook Huh, Mark Nathan, and Ramya Sreenivasan. Dave Alff, Roger Des Forges, Jenny Gaynor, and Kristin Stapleton have carefully edited fellowship proposals and book chapters. Kristin Stapleton and EunHee Lee of the Asian Studies Program and Cris Miller and Graham Hammill of the Department of English have provided sage counsel and shielded me from extra obligations. David Bertuca of the University at Buffalo Libraries prepared, with very short notice, the map that appears in chapter 3.

I have had the privilege of presenting portions of what would become chapters of this book at a number of venues, near and far. The encouragement of dear friends and mentors at these meetings has sustained me through a long and sometimes frustrating process. These include Elena Bashir, Indrani Chatterjee, Purnima Dhavan, Jennifer Dubrow, Arthur Dudney, Richard Eaton, Mehr Afshan Farooqi, Katy Hardy, Thibaut D'Hubert, Sumit Guha, Abhishek Kaicker, Pasha M. Khan, Hawon Ku, Barbara Metcalf, Traci Nagle, Francesca Orsini, Margrit Pernau, A. Sean Pue, Ryan Perkins, Yael Rice, Katherine Butler Schofield, and Nathan Tabor. Closer to home, Emera Bridger-Wilson, Hope Childers, Filomena Critelli, Ananya Dasgupta, Michael Fisher, Shaman Hatley, Ayesha Irani, Ashima Krishna, Shaanta Murshid, Elen Turner, and Ian Wilson have saved me from my self-imposed isolation. The advice and friendship of Audrey Truschke has been especially valuable as I prepared the manuscript for final submission. Paul Beattie, Hans Harmsen, Farhana Hasan, Prabha Manuratne, Joseph Stadler, Matt Zaslansky, and other members of the UB Foundations of South Asian Studies Research Workshop generously read through and commented on the second chapter of this book. With the range of disciplines they represent, they were ideal readers on whom to test my arguments. Hasti Pir-Moradian and Niyaz Pordel devoted hours to reading passages in Persian with me. The book is enriched by their insights, though all mistakes in interpretation are my own. My students

Kevin Roth and Sushmita Sircar have challenged many of my assumptions about the functions of language in society. I am grateful to them for involving me in their own literary and linguistic investigations.

There are numerous people working at various libraries in India and England who patiently tolerated my often unreasonable requests for assistance and special dispensation. I wish in particular to thank Dr. Siddiqi, Dr. Abusad Islahi, Mr. Isbah Khan, and Mr. Irfan Khan of Rampur Raza Library; Dr. Abu Muzaffar Alam (Manuscripts In-Charge, Khuda Bakhsh Oriental Public Library); Mr. Syed Gul Hasan (Jamia Millia Islamiya, Dr. Zakir Husain Library); and Dr. Mukherjee (Manuscripts Section) and Dr. Chatterjee (Assistant Librarian) at the Asiatic Society of Bengal in Calcutta. I owe special thanks to Dr. Abusad Islahi, Mr. Isbah Khan, and Mr. Irfan Khan of the Rampur Raza Library for generously providing access to the Persian and Urdu Manuscript collections. My fieldwork in India and England involved my consultation not just of texts but of expert scholars: Wahajuddin Alvi, Ravinder Gargesh, Rehana Khatoon, Gopi Chand Narang, Alok Rai, Abdur Rashid, and Chandar Shekhar in Delhi; Shireen Moosvi, Irfan Habib, and Iqtidar Alam Khan in Aligarh; and Sâqib Bâburî, Javed Majeed, P. J. Marshall, Christopher Shackle, and Ursula Sims-Williams in London.

Several organizations have generously funded my research and writing: the American Institute of Pakistan Studies, the U.S. Department of Education Fulbright-Hays Doctoral Dissertation Research Abroad Program, and the Library of Congress Florence Tan Moeson Fellowship Committee. Research leave from the University at Buffalo College of Arts and Sciences, Humanities Institute, and Office of the Vice Provost of Research and Economic Development provided the time I needed to prepare a complete draft in early 2014. Erik Seeman, Libby Otto, and Carrie Bramen of the UB Humanities Institute deserve special praise for fostering a vibrant intellectual community in Buffalo and pressing me to consider different kinds of readers for my work. *Negotiating Languages* has been enriched by the comments and trenchant critiques of the South Asia Across the Discipline series editors and anonymous readers who reviewed the manuscript. One could not ask for more sympathetic and capable interlocutors than Wendy Lochner, Cathy Felgar, and Christine Dunbar at Columbia University Press. Robert Fellman's great care in editing the manuscript saved me from many embarrassing errors. Philip Lutgendorf, Brian Hatcher, and the members of the American Institute of Indian Studies Publications Committee have been eloquent champions of this project.

The University at Buffalo College of Arts and Sciences Julian Park Publication Fund provided generous assistance toward the cost of indexing.

Nearly all the anxiety I experienced in my separation from my wife and friends while carrying out research in India during the spring of 2008 was balanced out by the joy of spending four months with my sister-in-law, *sāṛhū*, nephew, and niece. I will forever treasure my time with Jimin and Jihong. Their parents, Bochan Shin and Jiyeon Song, opened their home to me and showered me with love. During trips to London, I relied on Randy and Kathy Hoffman's hospitality. During a second four-month stay in Delhi, my wife and I enjoyed the kindness of our dear friends Minjoon Park and Taehee Kwon and were pleasantly distracted by their adorable children, Seongwon and Yeonsu.

My family has provided every manner of support to me, and it is to them that I owe the most profound and enduring debt. Laura Lucille Hakala has been more a friend than a grandmother. In hours of conversation over coffee she has shared her perspective and wisdom, and I have learned much about myself in the process. Linden Nuri Hakala arrived four years ago on a cold December evening, and we have celebrated each day since with laughter and joy. I am overwhelmed by the sacrifices my mother, Susan Hakala, continues to make for her children. Not only has she given this manuscript her careful attention, but, by being such a constant companion to Linden, she has also given me the time I needed to bring this project to a close. Convention dictates that the final words of thanks go to that person who, in reality, deserves first billing. As we celebrate ten years of marriage, Jinhee, I hope that our love and friendship will continue growing stronger and deeper.

NOTE ON TRANSLITERATION

South Asian terms commonly seen in English, including the names of some places, languages, and famous figures, are transcribed without diacritics. The system I employ for Urdu is modified from that used by Professor Frances Pritchett in her *Nets of Awareness*[1] and John T. Platts in his *A Dictionary of Urdū, Classical Hindī, and English*.[2] My transliteration of postvowel *iẓāfat* is also somewhat different. No modifications, however, are made to transliterations contained in English translations of Urdu or Persian texts quoted from other sources. I have followed the Indian pronunciation of Persian texts. In sum, I have striven to remain faithful first to the orthography of original texts and second to pronunciation (hence my occasional use of *ĕ* for *i* and *ŏ* for *u*, following Platts). Single quotation marks surround the *taḳhalluṣ* (pen name) of poets in the first instance where they appear.

The letters of the Urdu script are thus rendered as follows:

ا	آ			
a, i/ĕ, u/ŏ	*ā*			
ب	پ	ت	ٹ/ٿ	ث
b	*p*	*t*	*ṭ*	*ṡ*
ج	چ	ح	خ	
j	*ć*	*ḥ*	*ḳh*	
د	ڈ/ڐ	ذ		
d	*ḍ*	*ż*		
ر	ڑ/ڙ	ز	ژ	
r	*ṛ*	*z*	*zh*	
س	ش	श	ष	
s	*sh*	*ś*	*ṣ*	

ص	ض		
ṣ	*ẓ*		
ط	ظ		
ṭ	*ẓ*		
ع	غ		
ʿ	*ġh*		
ف	ق		
f	*q*		
ک/ك	گ		
k	*g*		
ل	م		
l	*m*		
ن	ں	ञ	ण
n	*ṅ*	*ñ*	*ṇ*
و			
w, ū, o, au			
ھ/ہ			
h			
ی	ے		
ī	y, e, ai		
ء	iẓafat (ِ)		
ʾ	-*i* and (when following *ye*) -*yi*		

CHRONOLOGY

1220	*Niṣāb al-Ṣibyān* (Capital-stock of children) by Abū Naṣar Farāhī in Afghanistan, oldest extant Arabic–Persian vocabulary in verse, in sections organized by meter, inaugurates *niṣāb* genre of multilingual vocabularies in verse
c.1275–1325	*Ḳhāliq Bārī* (Measurer, Creator) by Amīr 'Ḳhusrau' of Delhi, a Hindvī–Arabic–Persian vocabulary modeled on the *Niṣāb al-Ṣibyān*
1526	Establishment of the Mughal Empire in India
1553	*Ajay Ćand Nāmah* (Book of Ajay Ćand): a Hindvī–Arabic–Persian vocabulary in verse, with sections named for rooms in a palace
1608	Completion by Mīr Jamāluddīn Ḥusain Injū Shīrāzī (d. 1626) of the *Farhang-i Jahāngīrī*, a dictionary originally commissioned by Akbar and ultimately dedicated to the Mughal emperor Jahāngīr
1654	Publication of *Farhang-i Rashīdī*, a Persian dictionary by ᶜAbdul Rashīd, dedicated to the Mughal emperor Shah Jahan; its introductory essay is the basis for ᶜAbdul Wāsĕᶜ's *Qawāʾid-i Luġhāt-i Furs* (Grammar of the languages of Persians)
c.1656–1707	Reign of the Mughal emperor Aurangzeb; approximate period in which ᶜAbdul Wāsĕᶜ of Hansi was active
1739	Sack of Delhi by Nadir Shah
1743	*Nawādir al-Alfāẓ* (Rarities of terms), a revision of *Ġharāʾib al-Luġhāt* (Wonders of words) by the philologist Sirājuddīn ᶜAlī Khān-i 'Ārzū' (1687/8–1756)

1754	Publication by Shāh 'Ḥātim' (1699–1783) of his *Dīwān-zādah* (Son of the *dīwān*), where he claimed to have purged his four previous *dīwāns* (volumes of poetry) of verses in which appeared "unliterary" vocabulary
1777	John Richardson's *A Dictionary, Persian, Arabic, and English* is perhaps the first European work to include terms from *Ġharāʾib al-Luġhāt*
1784	Mirzā Jawān Bakhsh Jahāndār Shāh (c. 1740–88), heir apparent of the Mughal emperor Shāh ʿĀlam II, escapes captivity in Red Fort, seeks refuge in Lucknow
1788	Mirzā Jān 'Ṭapish' (c. 1768–1816) arrives at the court of the nawāb nāẓim of Bengal, Mubārak al-Daulah (r. 1770–1793), in Murshidabad; enters service of Shams al-Daulah, Mubārak al-Daulah's son-in-law and the younger brother of the nāʾib naẓīm of Dhaka
1792	First recorded date of completion for the *Shams al-Bayān* (Sun of clear discourse)
1794	Date of completion of the *Shams al-Bayān* as recorded in the British Library manuscript
1796	(March) The governor general in Calcutta resolves to remove Shams al-Daulah from the court of Nuṣrat Jang, citing interference in the management of Nizamat stipends
1797	Shams al-Daulah retires from Murshidabad to Dhaka
1797	(May) Muḥammad Ẓahīruddīn 'Aẓfarī' first arrives in Murshidabad and meets with Mirzā Jān
1798	(February 28) Shams al-Daulah seeks permission to come to Calcutta from Dhaka "for a short time for change of air and medical advice," which is rejected in a letter dated March 8
1799	(March 22) Barlow directs Douglas to apprehend "Mirza Jaun or Jaun Mirza"
1799	(April 22) Fendall reports that "Mirza Jaun Tuppish has been apprehended"
1799	(August 22) Shams al-Daulah tried by a special tribunal
1800	Shams al-Daulah convicted
1802–3	Ṭapish composes *Maśnavī-yi Bahār-i Dānish* (Springtime of knowledge)
1803	Shams al-Daulah released on a security pledged by his brother, Nuṣrat Jang

1806	Shams al-Daulah granted a full and free pardon in 1806 by the acting governor general, Sir George Barlow, with a restored stipend
1806 or 1807	Mirzā Jān released from prison
1807	Completion of *Daryā-i Laṭāfat* (Sea of delicacy) by Inshāʾallāh Ḳhān 'Inshā' (1753–1817)
1808	Verses by Ṭapish appear in *A Dictionary, Hindoostanee and English*, prepared by Captain Joseph Taylor
1811	Ṭapish edits collected works of Muḥammad Mīr Taqī 'Mīr' (1722–1810)
1812	(September) Reward distributed for the "Kooliyati Ṭupish; the poetical works of Mirza Jan, a living poet," as part of the "11th Public Disputations" of the College of Fort William
1812	(November) Mirzā Jān in Patna
1812	(December) Hunter dies, leaving a *Collection of Proverbs and Proverbial Phrases in Persian and Hindustani, with Translations* incomplete; completed by his friends Thomas Roebuck (1781–1819) and Horace Hayman Wilson (1786–1860) and published in 1824
1813	Mirzā Jān in Benares
1814	Last entry in the *bayāẓ* (notebook) of Mirzā Jān Ṭapish
1817	Birth in Calcutta of Samuel William Fallon
1825	Peter Breton, *A Vocabulary of the Names of the Various Parts of the Human Body and of Medical and Technical Terms in English, Arabic, Persian, Hindee, and Sanscrit for the Use of the Members of the Medical Department in India* lists "Ghura, eb ool Loghāt" as a "Dictionary of Mystical Words by Khan Arzoo"
1837	Act XXIX approved by the Presidency of Bengal permitting the replacement of Persian with other languages (including Urdu) for official documents
1845	Publication of Sir Henry M. Elliot's *Supplement to the Glossary of Indian Terms*
1845	Niyāz ʿAlī Beg 'Nakhat' publishes *Maḳhzan-i Fawāʾid* (Treasury of benefits)
1846	Sayyid Aḥmad born in Delhi
1849	Publication of first lithograph edition of the *Shams al-Bayān* in Murshidabad

1855	Publication of Horace Hayman Wilson's (1786–1860) *Glossary of Judicial and Revenue Terms*
c. 1856	Publication of *Qādir Nāmah* (Book of the Almighty), a versified Urdu–Persian–Arabic vocabulary by Mirzā Asadullāh Ḳhāṅ 'Ġhālib' (1797–1869)
1869	Publication of second edition of Elliot's *Supplement*, revised by John Beames and renamed *Memoirs on the History, Folk-Lore, and Distribution of the Races of the North Western Provinces of India: Being an Amplified Edition of the Original Supplemental Glossary of Indian Terms*
1869	North-Western Provincial Government awards Sayyid Aḥmad Rs. 200 for his primer *Kanz al-Fawāʾid* (Treasure of benefits)
1869–1911	Reign of Maḥbūb ʿAlī Ḳhān, sixth Aṣaf Jāhī Niẕām of Hyderabad, India's largest princely state
1871	Sayyid Aḥmad publishes *Muṣṭalaḥāt-i Urdū* on Urdu idioms
1871	North-Western Provincial Government awards Sayyid Aḥmad Rs. 150 for *Waqāʿīʾ-i Durāniyah*, a history of the ruling Durrānī dynasty of Afghanistan
1873	Sayyid Aḥmad begins approximately seven-year apprenticeship under S. W. Fallon
1874	Sayyid Aḥmad completes but does not publish *Luġhāt al-Nisāʾ*, a vocabulary of the speech of the women of Delhi
1878	Sayyid Aḥmad's *Armaġhān-i Dihlī* (A souvenir of Delhi) first published in installments; it is later incorporated into the *Farhang-i Āṣafiyah* (Dictionary of the Aṣaf Jāhī dynasty)
1875–9	Fallon publishes his *Hindustani–English Dictionary* with assistance from some fifteen Indian apprentices including "Munshī Chiranjī Lāl, [and] Munshi Sayad Ahmad" of Delhi
1880	Fallon dies in England "of mental exhaustion, leaving his work incomplete"
1883	An "efficient staff" of Indians "under the supervision of Revd. J. D. Bate" complete *A New English–Hindustani Dictionary* following Fallon's death in 1880
1884	Publication of *A Dictionary of Urdū, Classical Hindī, and English* by John T. Platts (1830–1904)
1886	Munshī Ćiranjī Lāl publishes *Maḳhzan al-Muḥāwarāt* (Treasury of idioms)

1888 Sayyid Aḥmad's *Luġhāt-i Urdū* (*Ḳhulāsah-yi Armaġhān-i Dihlī*) (Dictionary of Urdu, an abridgment of A souvenir of Delhi) published in Shimla

1888 First two volumes of Sayyid Aḥmad's *Hindūstānī Urdū Luġhat* (Hindustani–Urdu dictionary) published

1898 Death of Ćiraṇjī Lāl; second revised edition of *Maḳhzan al-Muḥāwarāt* published; third volume of Sayyid Aḥmad's *Hindūstānī Urdū Luġhat* published

1900 Sir Anthony MacDonnell, lieutenant governor of the North-Western Provinces and Oudh, permits use of *devanāgarī* script in official court documents

1901 Fourth (and final) volume of Sayyid Aḥmad's *Hindūstānī Urdū Luġhat* published

1902 *An English–Hindi Vocabulary in Verse or Vallabhkoṣ* by Pandit Braj Vallabh Mishra, a Hindi-English vocabulary in verse

1903 Founding of *Anjuman-i Taraqqī-yi Urdū* (Society for the Advancement of Urdu) in Aligarh

1906 *The East and West Khaliq Baree* by Munshi Ahmeduddin Khan, an Urdu–English vocabulary in verse

1912 Fire destroys Sayyid Aḥmad's home, including an entire run of the first, second, and third volumes of the new edition of the *Farhang-i Āṣafiyah*, and kills his nine-year-old daughter

1912 Anjuman-i Taraqqī-yi Urdū moves, under ʿAbdul Ḥaq's leadership, to Hyderabad

1914 Anjuman-i Taraqqī-yi Urdū begins receiving a regular stipend from the government of the niẕām of Hyderabad

1915 Sayyid Aḥmad's son granted a pension of Rs. 50 per month from the government of the niẕām of Hyderabad

1916 Nawāb of Hyderabad gives an additional award of Rs. 500 to Sayyid Aḥmad for his son's circumcision and *bismallāh* ceremonies

1917 Sayyid Aḥmad publishes *Luġhāt al-Nisāʾ*

1918 Revised and expanded edition of *Hindūstānī Urdū Luġhat* republished as *Farhang-i Āṣafiyah*

1918 Sayyid Aḥmad dies at age seventy-two

1951 Lithograph edition of *Nawādir al-Alfāẕ & Ġharāʾib al-Luġhāt*, edited by Sayyid ʿAbdullāh

1961 Death of ʿAbdul Ḥaq, called the *Bābā-i Urdū*, 'Grand Old Man of Urdu'

1973	Publication of the first volume of the *Luġhāt-i Kabīr-i Urdū* (Great dictionary of Urdu), a dictionary intended by ʿAbdul Ḥaq to be modeled on the *Oxford English Dictionary*
2010	Publication of the twenty-second and final volume of the *Urdū Luġhāt: Tārīḵhī Uṣūl Par* (Urdu dictionary: on historical principles), a continuation of the *Luġhāt-i Kabīr-i Urdū*

NEGOTIATING LANGUAGES

[1] A PLOT DISCOVERED

This is a very interesting and useful book, my son. I have studied it often, but I never could discover the plot.

— Mark Twain, on awarding *Webster's Dictionary* to a grammar-school student

IN THE spring of 2008, I visited my favorite bookshop in Urdu Bazaar, a neighborhood in Old Delhi adjacent to the Jāmʿĕ Masjid, the massive Friday Mosque built in red sandstone during the reign of the Mughal emperor Shāh Jahān. I had come to India to work at various libraries and universities, gathering materials on the lexicographers who shaped the Urdu language from just one of many North Indian dialects into the national language of Pakistan. I was seeking to understand a constellation of genres that range from multilingual vocabularies in verse, to glossaries of terms drawn from classical Persian texts, to comprehensive dictionaries published in multiple volumes and, more recently, on the Internet. On an earlier visit, I had told the owner of the bookshop that I was looking for *luġhāts* and *farhangs* (two words that are frequently used in Urdu to mean a defining dictionary), telling him the older the book, the better.

On this particular visit, the owner of the shop produced a thin book published in Delhi during the summer of 1915, at the height of what the author, Munshī Ẓiyāʾ al-Dīn Aḥmad Barnī (1890–1969), in his introduction called the "European War." While thumbing through the text—whose title, *Aḳhbārī Luġhāt (maʿrūf bĕh Kalīd-i Aḳhbār-Bīnī)*, translates as *A Newspaper Dictionary (also known as The Key to Newspaper Viewing)*[1]—I came across the following entry (translated here into English from the original Urdu):

Dīmākraisī (DEMOCRACY [in English]) This is a form of government in which all decisions (*iḳhtiyārāt*: 'elections', 'powers') are universally in the hands of the aggregate population (*majmūʿī jumhūr*) or in the hands of their appointed officers. This is the sort of government that is done for the people, by the people (*logoṅ ke liye logoṅ ke żarīʿah*). Executive decisions are in the hands of publicly elected individuals. The republic (*jumhūriyat*) is the most perfect (*mukammal*) kind of government. This government is instituted in France, America, Brazil, Switzerland, Mexico, Portugal, and China, etc. The basis for this sort of government has been established from the Islamic era. Both a republic and a nobility are parts of England's government.[2]

There was a certain poignancy to this definition: beneath the author's claim, written across the title page, to have gathered "all those [English] words in alphabetical order that are used in Urdu newspapers" and to have explained them "in easy, simple, and clear Urdu," there was surely a story hidden within. Or, rather, it is hidden in plain view in the final pages of the book. "At the end of these pages," so explains the author in his introduction, "I have given a concise sketch of the 'Organization of the Government of England' and 'Organization of the Government of India [Hind]' with this aim that the ordinary observer should become aware of . . . how England and Hindustan are governed."[3] His motive for compiling this work, he explains, stemmed from the feeling that "it is our duty to be more familiar with the form of governance of our country in comparison with other countries."[4]

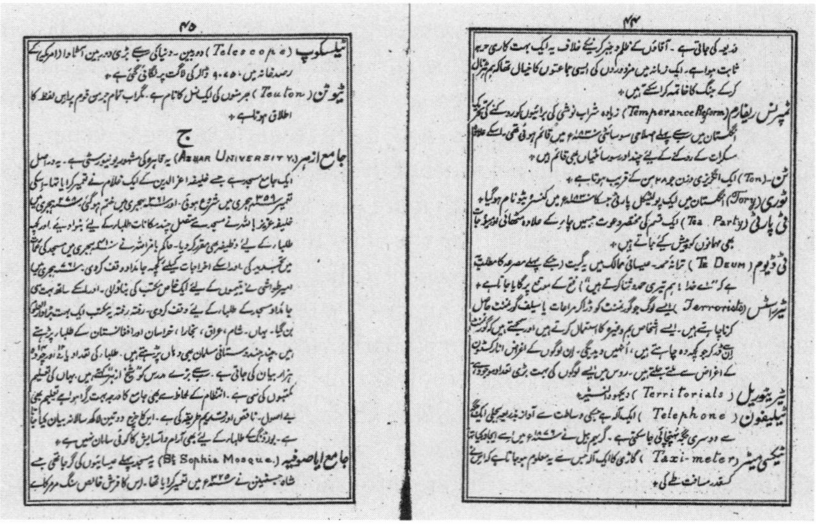
۴۴

ٹمپرنس ریفارم (Temperance Reform)

ٹن (Ton)

ٹوری (Tory)

ٹی پارٹی (Tea Party)

ٹی ڈیوم (Te Deum)

ٹیررسٹس (Terrorists)

ٹیریٹوریل (Territorials)

ٹیلیفون (Telephone)

ٹیکسی میٹر (Taxi-meter)

۴۵

ٹیلسکوپ (Telescope)

ٹیوٹن (Teuton)

ج

جامع ازہر (Azhar University)

جامع ایاصوفیہ (St. Sophia Mosque)

FIGURE 1.1 Sample pages from *Akhbārī Lughāt* (1915)

Born into a prominent Delhi family of Urdu-language newspaper publishers, Munshī Ẓiyāʾ al-Dīn in 1915 was a vocal pan-Islamist and advocate for Home Rule. He would later work in the Oriental Translator's Office in Bombay from 1918 to 1947 before finally settling in Pakistan.[5] As is clear from his definition of democracy, Munshī Ẓiyāʾ al-Dīn's *Key* is permeated with a sense of self-conscious distance, as though the author was all too aware that simply defining a term did not in and of itself guarantee full political participation and self-determination. He defines *impīriʾyalizam* (imperialism) as either "to completely conquer through domination or in an effort to situate colonists (*nau-abādiyāṅ*)."[6] The distinction between the two was not lost on him or, he hoped, on his readers. By being selective in his definitions, he could bring emphasis to some matters while avoiding potential pitfalls as, for example, when in his definition of the American Declaration of Independence (*Ĕʿlān-i Āzādī*) he elides the armed conflict that preceded England's acceptance of it:

> *Ĕʿlān-i Āzādī* (Declaration of Independence) On 4 July 1776 delegates (*delīgaiṭoṅ*) of American colonists (*nau-ābādiyoṅ*) wrote a declaration of self-authority (*ĕʿlān-i ḳhwud muḳhtarī*), of which this is a passage: "We, the Representatives (*numāyande*) of the united states (*riyāsat-hāʾe muttaḥidah*) who are gathered in this Congress (*kāngres*), appeal (*apīl karte haiṅ*) to the Supreme Jurist (*aʿlā ḥākim*) of the world for the validity (*durustī*) of our intentions and publish this declaration that the united states are free and independent (*ḳhwud muḳhtār*). And the right of these [states] is that they ought to be independent." England accepted this declaration.[7]

His definitions make reference to universals, such as when he implies that India, too, might make a similar appeal to a "Supreme Jurist" in framing her political aspirations. The very form his entries take, with prose definitions following headwords arranged alphabetically from first letter to last, was itself emblematic of the author's—and by extension his readers'—mastery of a thoroughly modern and increasingly widespread mode of reference.

Our interactions with a dictionary can be both very intimate—as when we embarrassedly consult it when unfamiliar with a term that a public figure or acquaintance treats as common knowledge—and very collective. The zealous attorney who quotes a definition from the dictionary to clinch an argument is a figure familiar from many courtroom dramas. To argue against the definition given in the dictionary is to mark ourselves somehow as not belonging to the collectivity, as existing beyond the pale of a community of legitimate language users designated by the text. A dictionary, more than any other object, is the most concrete modern material artifact of a community that shares a common language. It now seems natural to us that all words should find a place in some sort of dictionary and that for every person there is some dictionary that best describes his or her mother tongue. We pity as primitive those peoples who, lacking dictionaries, are threatened with the extinction of their language and the assimilation of their culture into larger, more successful *cultures with dictionaries*. Those of us who live with dictionaries cannot imagine what it would be like not to have recourse to *some* dictionary, and we assume that those who do not possess—or, rather, are not themselves possessed by—dictionaries are doomed to disappear from history altogether.

Lydia Liu, in her classic study of the passage between China and the West of concepts that have been associated with modernity, describes the "thriving industry of bilingual dictionaries" in East Asia as dependent on the almost universal and perduring "illusion" of languages as commensurate entities composed of actually or potentially equivalent terms and ideas.[8] Like Ernest Gellner and others, she argues that the analytical categories through which these grounds for equivalence are asserted are the products of the unequal power relationships enacted through the long history of European and Asian cultural encounters.[9] Rather than taking these grounds for equivalence as a static quality inherent to language, Liu argues that this "hypothetical equivalence" is a process that is continually "established, maintained, or revised among languages so that meaning, which is always historical, can be made available or unavailable to the translator."[10] A history of inequity on a global scale always undergirds any individual act of asserting intercultural equivalences. As individual sites of contest, each semantic equation is also a narrative of the victories, capitulations, and, especially, adaptations that produced the conditions of their articulation: "In thinking about translatability between historical languages, one cannot but consider the actual power relations that dictate the degree and magnitude of sacrifice that one language must make in order to achieve some level of commensurality with the other."[11] For Liu, the processes of cross-cultural comparison share the same illusory premise of all bilingual dictionaries, the notion that "a word in language A must equal a word or a phrase in language B; otherwise one of the languages is lacking."[12]

Recent scholarship on South Asia has complicated these formulations by revealing sustained forms of cultural exchange among the region's multilingual communities during—but also well before—South Asia's experiences of European imperialism. Sheldon Pollock's pathbreaking work examines the cultural influence of a Sanskrit "cosmopolis" across much of Asia more than a thousand years prior to Vasco de Gama's arrival on the western coast of India. The impact of Sanskrit literature upon a bewildering variety of South Asian, Central Asian, and Southeast Asian languages is only beginning to be documented.[13] The success of this *translatio studii* (the transfer of knowledge from one person or culture to another) was not always accompanied by a parallel process of *translatio imperii* (the imposition or transfer of power from one entity to another):

> There is little evidence that [Sanskrit] was ever used as the language of practical rule. . . . The work Sanskrit did do was beyond the quotidian and the instrumental; it was directed above all toward articulating a form of political consciousness and culture, politics not as transaction of material power . . . but as celebration of aesthetic power.[14]

The extent to which these inter- and intracultural transfers were carried out, even in the absence of marked differentials of political and military power, material resources, and technology, calls into question many of the assumptions regarding the uniqueness of modern European encounters with its "others." Inspired in part by Pollock's work, scholars of Persian have traced broadly analogous processes of cultural diffusion in South Asia through literature, works about literature, and state power.[15] The imprint of cosmopolitan Asian literary cultures is apparent not just on the modern languages of South Asia—the so-called vernaculars—but also upon Arabic, Persian, and Chinese—all languages that Liu would consider to be both "historical" and decisively shaped by their extended encounters with European imperialism.[16]

The contemporary South Asian linguistic landscape is characterized by a process of what Pollock, drawing on Mikhail Bakhtin, calls *hyperglossia*, "a relationship of extreme superposition (hyper-) between two languages that local actors knew to be entirely different."[17] In practice, this entailed the deployment by individuals of multiple more or less distinct means of expression in order to perform felicitously the variety of social interactions they encountered in their daily lives. An individual's choice of one language or distinct style (or register) of a language over another often appears uneven: one's use of a particular language or form of language was usually limited to certain activities, with that individual facing various obstacles to the acquisition of the means to perform additional linguistically delimited activities. Individuals who mastered multiple, and often linguistically quite disparate, registers also had the opportunity to gain entrance to and successfully function within a greater range of social situations. As much as dictionaries, grammars, and other didactic texts could legislate the boundaries between registers, by subjecting linguistic forms to systematization, these texts also provided the means by which individuals could gain access to new linguistic repertoires. They often permitted one generation to share knowledge with the next: a Central Asian physician émigré, to cite one example, prepared the *Qaṣīdah dar Luġhāt-i Hindī* (An ode on Hindi terms), a Persian–Hindi medical vocabulary, for his sons in early sixteenth-century India. By identifying local analogues for the Central Asian medicinal plants with which he was familiar (sometimes on the basis of shared color or other properties), he had also found a practical means to sustain his family's practice in the markedly different cultural and ecological climate of northern India.[18]

Lisa Mitchell has traced the nineteenth-century emergence in South India of a faith in the commensurability of language—the assumption, at least at a lexical level, "that a word in any language must have a ready equivalent in each and every other language."[19] She contends that prior to the nineteenth century, South Indians associated certain forms of knowledge with particular languages, or to phrase it more precisely, particular linguistic registers were appropriate for the performance of a very limited set of social actions. Mitchell documents how new forms of technology, when combined with disruptive intrusions of European forms of knowledge, governance, and modes of patronage, compelled South Indian intellectuals to consider for the first time the possibility of a single linguistic structure—a so-called mother tongue—as capable of fulfilling *all* the social functions that had previously been carried out by linguistically diverse registers and, increasingly, by English.[20] Dictionaries played a key role in these transformations. In their most schematic form, the materials examined in *Negotiating Languages* depict, first, how a language comes to be written down; then, second, how it comes to be made literary; and, finally, how it comes to be repositioned as the "mother tongue" of a community with political aspirations. For inasmuch as dictionaries may serve as guides to potentially unfamiliar communicative situations, they also permit a person or a people to stake their claim to a lexical realm by marking out the boundaries that separate one dominion (or community) from another.

Returning to the so-called *Key to Newspaper Viewing*, there is a clear message, if not a fully developed "plot," embedded between the lines of Barnī's entry on democracy. Munshī Ẓiyāʾ al-Dīn asserts that the republic is the "most perfect" or "most complete" form of government, a system in place not just in advanced imperialist nations like France, America, and Portugal but also in developing countries like Mexico, Brazil, and even China. In Ẓiyāʾ al-Dīn Aḥmad's account, even the government of Britain at the height of its power—upon whose empire the sun was said never to set—was an antiquated system in which a landed nobility coexisted as part of an imperfect or incomplete republic. By semantically linking English terms with Urdu equivalents, Ẓiyāʾ al-Dīn Aḥmad is also implying, not as subtly as one might expect, that there may be some political equivalence between the colonizers and the colonized.

If a single dictionary entry offers clues about a message, what emerges from reading multiple works intertextually is precisely the sort of "plot" that would have interested Mark Twain. The lexicographic works that are introduced in *Negotiating Languages* tell several interrelated stories. One of the "plots" this book tells is the story of a language—or rather, what would become a language through the course of several centuries. Scholars, politicians, and ordinary native speakers alike have struggled to explain how *hindwī*—a term used in Persian scholarship until the eighteenth century to describe a spectrum of unwritten dialects spoken from the Indus River eastward to the Bay of Bengal—evolved into two competing linguistic registers: Urdu and what is sometimes called Modern Standard Hindi.[21] Through the later nineteenth and twentieth centuries, advocates for Hindi and Urdu increasingly associated their "language" with competing religious and nationalist projects, each group vying to install one or the other as the official language of, first, British South Asia and, later, postindependence India and Pakistan. To cite Christopher King's memorable formulation, lexicographic texts contributed to the transformation of the equations Urdu = Muslim + Hindu and Hindi = Hindu + Muslim into Urdu = Muslim and Hindi = Hindu. The result was a powerful "three-fold assertion of the identity of language, religion, and motherland."[22] *Negotiating Languages* demonstrates how proponents of the two styles of a single, mutually intelligible language—which shared a common grammar and serves as the mother tongue of a combined population that is surpassed only by Mandarin Chinese and Spanish—inscribed through dictionaries, children's vocabularies, and administrative glossaries a lexical division that contributed to the bloody partition of the Indian subcontinent in 1947.

"YOU CAMPAIGN IN POETRY. YOU GOVERN IN PROSE."

To explain the differences between the passionate rhetoric of his 1984 keynote speech to the Democratic National Convention and the more moderate policies he pursued as governor of New York, Mario Cuomo was reported to have said: "You campaign in poetry. You govern in prose."[23] This is a surprisingly apt representation of the way that South Asian languages developed written literary traditions. *Negotiating Languages* deals in particular with dictionaries and other lexicographical works appearing in three languages—Persian, Hindi-Urdu, and English. It also explores the relationships, usually complementary but sometimes competitive, of dictionaries with poetry. In the sixteenth and seventeenth centuries, literacy in the Persian language promised gainful employment across an expanse of territory that extended from Eastern Europe to Southeast Asia.[24] Persian was spoken by few in South Asia as a first language, though it was used by many more as a second, largely written, language of education. It was this fact—Persian's status as a second language equally accessible to speakers of a variety of India's so-called vernacular languages—that contributed to its cosmopolitan character. A similar process enabled English to replace Persian in the nineteenth century as the preeminent language of statecraft across much of South Asia. The bilingual dictionaries through which speakers of Hindi and Urdu gained access to Persian- and, later, English-language texts served as vessels carrying cultures across both physical and cultural divides. As such, they offer valuable insights into the ways in which those who aspired to participate in the apparatus of government collaborated in generating new forms of knowledge by grafting them onto preexisting structures. In the South Asian context, this process entailed the circulation of scholars among Iran, Central Asia, and India, and, beginning in the second half of the eighteenth century, between the Mughal capital in Delhi and the seat of the British East India Company's governor general in Calcutta.

In the early colonial period, written Urdu was largely limited to a literary register styled on Persian models and based on the spoken dialect of Delhi Khaṛī Bolī. As a literary register it was substantially influenced by other regional literatures, incorporating to varying degrees both lexical and morphosyntactic elements of Braj, Awadhī, and Punjābī.[25] Beyond a few stray examples, it had not been widely cultivated as a literary language in the Delhi region until the early decades of the eighteenth century, at which point it became very closely tied to the prestige of the Mughal court. Prior to the eighteenth century, however, it was largely a phenomenon of central and western India, especially in the once-independent Bahmani sultanates of Golconda and Bijapur (where the style is now called Dakanī Urdu) as well as in various centers in present-day Gujarat (known as Gujrī Urdu).[26] By the turn of the nineteenth century, British colonial authorities had identified Urdu (then known as Hindoostanee) as a potential lingua franca that could be understood by many, if not most, of northern India's urban population. The spread of lithograph technologies and the sulfite pulp process, as well as of a postal service and educational institutions established upon European models, set the conditions for a proliferation of inexpensive periodicals that used prose forms closely replicating the syntax and diction of spoken language. These technological changes and colonial educational reforms led not only to the rise of literacy in a multitude of South Asian "mother tongues" but also to their inclusion into social domains that had previously been reserved for such cosmopolitan languages of prestige as Persian and Sanskrit.[27] By the 1840s, voluntary associations like the Vernacular Translation Society in Delhi were commissioning textbooks in the fields of medicine, law, science, economics, and history as part of a larger project to transform Urdu prose into a medium that was sufficiently capacious to accommodate translations of scientific terminology from English.[28] Poetry is increasingly absent from later twentieth-century colonial language textbooks.

Munshī Ẓiyā' al-Dīn, the author of the *Key to Newspaper Reading*, continues a long tradition common to Persian dictionaries of listing the sources both for his lexical corpus—that is to say, the foreign-language headwords—and for the information he used to provide definitions of these terms. Three centuries earlier, Mīr Jamāluddīn Ḥusain Injū Shīrāzī (d. 1626), in the introduction to his monumental *Farhang-i Jahāngīrī*, a Persian dictionary dedicated in 1608 to the Mughal emperor Jahāngīr, listed forty-four Persian dictionaries that he had consulted in compiling his work. Since poetry was seen as the touchstone of the Persian language, Injū often offered verses by authoritative poets as prooftexts, citing in total about one thousand verses by some four hundred poets.[29] This symbiotic relationship of dictionaries with poetry is an example of the *supplementarity* of premodern Persianate lexicography. The credibility of the precolonial South Asian lexicographer rested entirely upon his ability to select out the most eloquent poets from the middling ones. Conversely, the dictionary, as an anthology of authoritative poets, could itself reinforce the canonicity of these poets and their verses in the literary tradition.

In the sources cited by Munshī Ẓiyāʾ al-Dīn, however, prose reigns supreme over poetry. He lists standard reference works from which he took assistance, and some, like the *Encyclopædia Britannica*, *Whittaker's Almanac*, Walter Bagehot's *English Constitution*, *Pears Cyclopedia*, and *The Essays of Elia*, continue to this day to appear in print, serving as useful sources of general information. The periodicals from which Munshī Ẓiyāʾ al-Dīn drew the bulk of his terms, however, are texts that are more topical—even ephemeral—in nature, reflecting the author's stated aim to describe "those political idioms and explanations that are regularly mentioned in the newspapers."[30] In the early decades of the twentieth century, it was no longer necessary for an Urdu lexicographer to confine himself to citations from previous lexicographic or poetic sources. He instead drew upon sources completely beyond the performative context of a literary register, and he preserved them in a prose medium that was increasingly expected to convey any information, be it literary or mundane. This new tendency to provide prose citations within definitions signals a broader shift beginning in the second half of the nineteenth century in the modes through which South Asian lexicographers could assert their linguistic and even political authority. The basis for this change lies in part in increased efforts of the colonial state to quantify aspects of its subjects' lives by such means as the decennial census, linguistic surveys, district gazetteers, standardized examinations, and records submitted by printers detailing the circulation and content of the materials they produced.[31] This change can also be attributed to a decline in the status of the professional poets whose personal authority had once guaranteed the spread of the Persian culture that dominated much of northern India.

C. M. Naim describes how the great Urdu poet Mīr Muḥammad Taqī 'Mīr' (1722/3–1810) would copy obscure Persian idioms from the *Ćirāġh-i Hidāyat* (Lamp of wisdom)—a lexicographical work produced by the Indo-Persian poet (and Mīr's maternal uncle) Sirājuddīn ʿAlī Khān-i 'Ārzū' (1687/8–1756)—into his autobiographical *Żikr-i Mīr* (Memorial of Mīr). These idioms would appear only once in Mīr's Persian prose and are followed in most manuscripts by a Persian gloss. As Naim explains:

> The glosses supplied by Mir are themselves very close to Arzu's glosses, and in some instances, even identical. On the other hand, quite a few times Mir seems to have misread Arzu's gloss and used the idiom incorrectly. If one simultaneously reads the text and consults [the *Ćirāġh-i Hidāyat*], one frequently feels that Mir could have had a copy of the dictionary open before him as he composed his text, often incorporating in one paragraph several words from the same page in the dictionary.[32]

Naim goes on to note that it was during an eleven-year period of extended exile from Delhi that Mīr produced the "bulk of his Persian poetry and the two [Persian] books." In his exile, away from the Urdu-saturated literary culture of Delhi, Mīr could focus on his Persian literary output as a means to secure for himself panregional literary legacy. Writing in Persian, however, also served a very practical purpose:

> Mir may have first written [the *Faiẓ-i Mīr*][33] out of the need to provide a book for his son's education. He had with him a copy of Arzu's dictionary (or found one in Raja Nagar Mal's [his patron while in exile] collection) which he used the way he did for some private reason—the addition of glosses in [the *Faiẓ-i Mīr*], however, makes perfect sense in a student's textbook.[34]

This particular example illustrates what occurred time and time again throughout much of South Asia in the midst of what we might, following Sheldon Pollock,[35] call the "Persian cosmopolis." Persian, for all its ubiquity as a literary register in South Asia, still had to compete in the realm of oral discourse with a variety of South Asian languages. Despite several notable exceptions, Persian tended to be the mother tongue only of those who had recently emigrated or whose parents had emigrated from the Persian-speaking areas of present-day Iran and Central Asia.

The case studies included in this book demonstrate that the act of equating terms often follows an event of personal displacement of an author from his linguistic home. This physical and cultural separation has the effect of giving the lexicographer an unusual perspective on his spoken language, often providing the impetus to reproduce and explain aspects of that language in written form. The challenges faced by authors during the gradual integration of the European colonial economy across the Indian subcontinent ranged from acute degradations, like those that followed in the wake of the so-called Mutiny of 1857, to a more endemic decay of traditional patronage networks and a corresponding increase in competition for state largesse.[36] In response to this competition, authors produced works like *The Key to Newspaper Viewing* to render the language of the colonial power legible for a class of people who aspired to comprehend and participate in the functioning of the state.

EMPLOTTING THE COSMOS

The central premise of this book is that lexicographic works reflect dominant cosmographies: the means by which a people understand the organization of the universe about them.[37] Frederic Jameson has argued that the form an individual text or cultural artifact takes is suggestive of broader social processes, what he terms the "ideology of form," or the mode of interpretation through which the historical systems of production and reception, or the social bases underlying a given work, are correlated with the formal elements through which that individual work is expressed. By engaging with an ideology of form, "it has become possible to grasp such formal processes as sedimented content in their own right, as carrying ideological messages of their own, distinct from the ostensible or manifest content of the works."[38] The generic form of a given work thus represents for Jameson an ossification of certain power structures inherent in the cultural artifact under consideration. For Tzvetan Todorov, the presence of recognizably distinct genres suggests a consistency in social response or, more boldly, the copresence of mechanisms for the elicitation of consent: "A society chooses and codifies the acts that correspond most closely to its ideology; that is why the existence of certain genres in one society, their absence in another, are revelatory of that ideology and allow us to establish it more or less confidently."[39]

Rather than seeing genres as ideal or "pure" types and the genre-bending work as the product of literary miscegenation, formalist theorists have depicted genre as dynamic, fluctuating "systems." Ireneusz Opacki introduces the concept of the "royal genre," the dominant conventional form of literature within a specific set of sociopolitical conditions at a particular place and time in history. These royal genres "stood at the peak of the contemporary hierarchy of literary genres; they best rendered the aspirations of the period; they were the most appropriate 'language of translation' for socio-political phenomena into 'the internal tasks and problems of literature.' "[40] Opacki hypothesizes: "A literary genre, entering, in the course of evolution, the field of a particular literary trend, will enter into a very close 'blood relationship' with the form of the royal genre that is particular to that current."[41]

This formulation might be best described using an analogy from physics. The royal genre is analogous to a dominant body in a gravitational system. It influences the other bodies in that system, which experience a centripetal attraction to that dominant body. In the course of the system, however, mass may become transferred, potentially from the orbiting bodies to the dominant body, or vice versa, so that over time certain elements from the dominant and subordinate bodies may coalesce to form a new dominant body, or royal genre.

For all the advantages of treating genres as dynamic entities in a complete system, one observes in it a strong echo of Ferdinand Brunetière's crude application of Darwinian precepts in his 1890 work *L'evolution des genres dans l'histoire de la litérature*, a work that Benedetto Croce criticized for underemphasizing the roles played by individual creativity, authorial agency, or (to use Croce's romantic terminology) "artistic spirit."[42] Barbara Fuchs, in her work on romance, treats genre as a set of mobile and adaptive strategies exploited by authors and readers to produce certain results.[43] Treating genre as a set of strategies allows a genre to "retain some of its historical commodiousness" and anticipate its adoption into a potentially unlimited range of communicative forms. Johannes Fabian, in his classic study of the colonial adaptation and promulgation of Swahili in French and Belgian central African colonies, likewise argues that any study that uses texts to make sense of changes in communicative fields must be attentive to corresponding shifts in genre.[44] Genre can then become, in John Frow's formulation, "a set of conventional and highly organized constraints on the production and interpretation of meaning"[45]—constraints that do not restrict but rather "shape and guide" the processes of making meaning. This approach is premised on the human need to organize knowledge so that it may be efficiently accessed and indexed in a variety of discursive situations. These arrangements take the form of cognitive schema, or patterns that one's brain employs to comprehend and explain the phenomena encountered in life.[46] Genre, then, is not merely the set of schema or the background knowledge necessary to make sense of the world but also the set of skills in making reference to these schema in our representations of phenomena. To conduct comparative studies of genre across cultures and time is to study the institutions through which genre is sustained. This is the intention of the studies contained in the chapters that follow.

Many of the earliest works to contain Hindi and Urdu terms are multilingual vocabularies in verse that arrange their content thematically. An example is the *Ajāy Ćand Nāmah*, a vocabulary in verse containing Persian and Hindvī terms organized under section headings named for the rooms of a nobleman's household.[47] Completed in AD 1553 near Aligarh, it anticipates by several decades the technique Matteo Ricci would employ to train aspiring Chinese bureaucrats in the art of memory and to promulgate his Christian faith.[48] Other works conformed to the Ptolemaic "Great Chain of Being" featured in the philosophical systems of Islamic thinkers like Ibn Sīnā (known in the West as Avicenna, d. 1037).[49] They also map onto the circuit of the "emanation of the ten higher substances" outlined by ʿAlāʾ al-Daulah al-Simnānī (1261–1336): a path that takes the Sufi novice "from the divine presence in the Realm of Divinity to the Human realm" with a subsequent return to the Realm of Divinity.[50] These notions are themselves analogous to mnemonic technologies employed in ancient Greece[51] and classical Sanskrit lexicons, with the *Nighaṇṭu* and Amarasiṁha's *Amarakośa* providing early examples of a lexical cosmography.[52] Audrey Truschke has recently surveyed the numerous bilingual Sanskrit–Persian glossaries produced during the Mughal period. This "continuous tradition of intellectual responses" of India's traditional Sanskrit-language elite "to the political, social, and cultural changes associated with the rise of Indo-Persian polities" relied upon shared notions of the hierarchical structure of the lexical universe to carry the meaning of individual terms across languages.[53] The importance of poetry as an organizing force is apparent in other lexicographic works. Some versified vocabularies are organized by poetic meter,[54] and many comprehensive Indo-Persian dictionaries compiled before the nineteenth century arranged terms alphabetically not by initial letter but by last, to serve as rhyming dictionaries to aid in the composition of poetry, particularly the *qaṣīdah* genre of encomia that use a single rhyme throughout.[55] Solomon Baevskii explains:

> The early [Persian] farhang was at the same time a defining dictionary, an encyclopedia, an onomasticon, a dictionary of rhymes, and a thesaurus of synonyms. All these functions were determined by its purpose, which explains the great demand for a lexicographic work in medieval society: the farhang was designed above all as a manual, a *vade mecum* of commentary upon the products of poetry and belles-lettres.[56]

It is not until the nineteenth century that we see a flattening of the lexical hierarchy. Words no longer are organized by their denotational content, and the rationale for their inclusion no longer depends upon their presence in a canonical literary work. Instead, it is a single seemingly arbitrary (at least to preprint encyclopedists) attribute of the lexical item—its graphic written form—that comes to determine the macrostructural means of arrangement, from first letter to last.[57]

SHARED COSMOGRAPHIES: LEYDEN'S VOCABULARY

The thematic arrangement of terms persisted well into the colonial period and was even adopted by British officials in their own work. Arriving in the South Indian city of Madras (now Chennai) on August 19, 1803, the twenty-seven-year-old Scottish poet John Leyden (1775–1811) quickly set out to establish, among other things, an efficient means of learning the languages of India. He was ambitious: he vowed to surpass the famous eighteenth-century Orientalist William Jones (1746–1794) "a hundredfold" in learning, to become a "furious Orientalist, *nemini secundus*," second to none.[58] Within two years of his arrival in India, he listed the languages that attracted his attention as "Arabic, Persic, Hindostani, Mahratta, Tamal, Telinga, Canara, Sanscrit, Malayalam, Malay, and Armenian." At his death, he was said to have command of some forty-five languages. Despite his quick rise to become the judge of the twenty-four parganas of Calcutta, his friend Sir Walter Scott (1771–1832) described how his passion for learning language consumed his earnings and his health:

> The expense of native teachers, of every country and dialect, and that of procuring from every quarter Oriental manuscripts, engrossed his whole emoluments, as the task of studying under the tuition of the interpreters, and decyphering the contents of the volumes, occupied every moment of his spare time.[59]

Another friend, John Malcolm (1769–1833), described the method that Leyden employed in reading these manuscripts:

> When he read a lesson in Persian, a person near him, whom he had taught, wrote down each word on a long slip of paper, which was afterwards divided into as many pieces as their [*sic*] were words, and pasted in alphabetical order, under different heads of verbs, nouns, &c., into a blank book that formed a vocabulary of each day's lesson. All this he had in a few hours instructed a very ignorant native to do; and this man he used in his broad accent to call "one of his mechanical aids."[60]

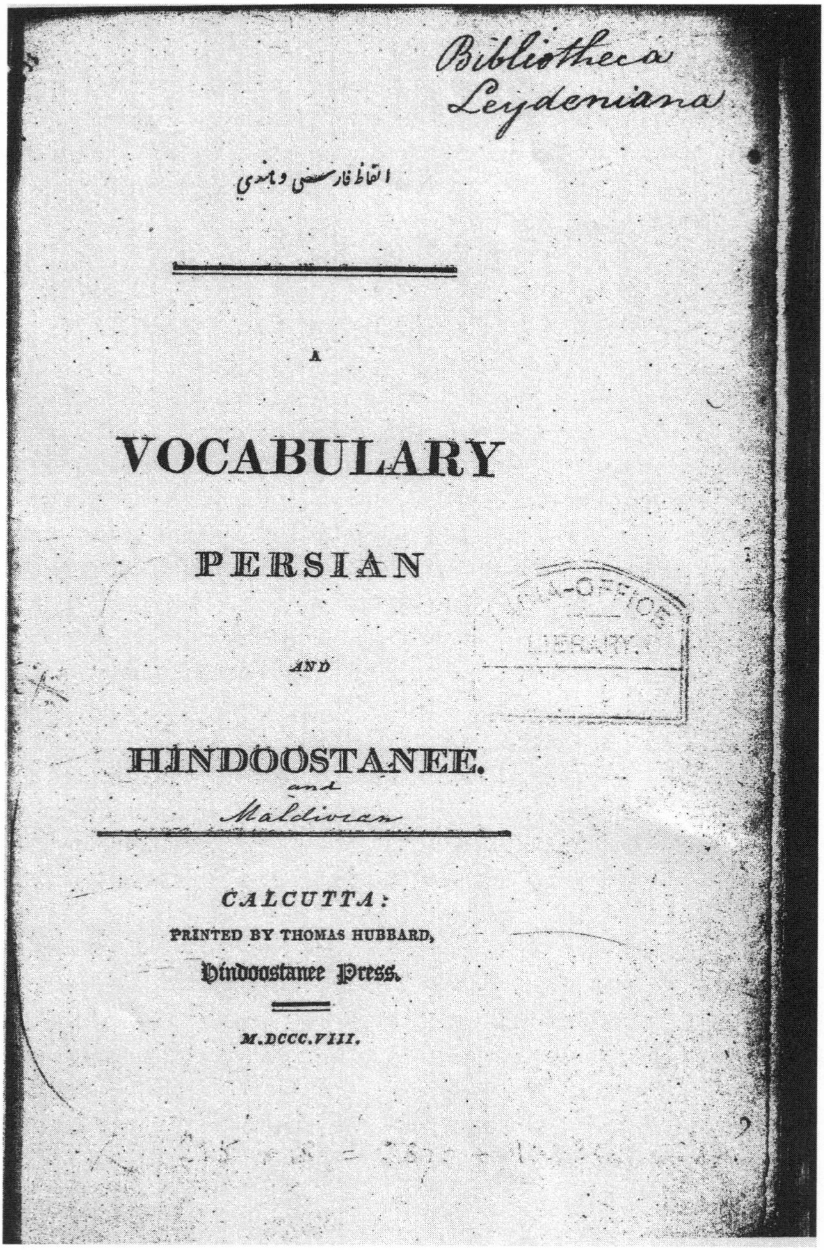

Bibliotheca
Leydeniana

الفاظ فارسی و هندی

A

VOCABULARY

PERSIAN

AND

HINDOOSTANEE.

and

Maldivian

CALCUTTA:

PRINTED BY THOMAS HUBBARD,

Hindoostanee Press.

M.DCCC.VIII.

FIGURE 1.2 Title page from Leyden's *A Vocabulary Persian and Hindoostanee* [*and Maldivian*] (1808). © The British Library Board, BL MSS Eur B103

The title "mechanical aid" that Leyden applied to his assistants betrays more than European bigotry—it also indicates just how pervasive print culture, and how normal the mechanical reproduction of texts, had become.[61]

In 1808, Leyden published *A Vocabulary Persian and Hindoostanee*. In the copy housed in the British Library, the words "and Maldivian" are added in pencil below the title.[62] The first page of the vocabulary, forgoing any prefatory material, abruptly begins with Persian and Hindi terms for God: *ḳhudā* and *īsar*. The next set of terms, *ḳhudā'ī* and *iśvaratā*, both are abstract nouns denoting "divinity." The third pair of terms is composed of the Arabic *ḳhāliq* and Sanskrit-derived *sirjanhār*, both meaning "creator."[63] When the manuscript was prepared for publication, a wide space to the right of the terms was left intentionally blank. In this particular copy of the work, the third column lists equivalent terms in Arabic and the Dhivehi language of the Maldives handwritten in Arabic-script transliteration (figure 1.2). In the margins to the left of the printed-text equivalent, Dhivehi terms are written in the Thaana writing system typically used in the Maldives. Starting from the third page, however, the Arabic transliteration of the Dhivehi terms stops, and only Thaana script equivalents are provided.

In a note at the end of the work, the individual responsible for providing the Dhivehi equivalents is identified as one "Hasan bin Adam, of Himithi Island in North Nilandhe (now Faafu) Atoll." Hasan bin Adam had probably arrived in Calcutta in a trading vessel and had been convinced to stay to help Leyden with linguistic investigations—and, from 1810, with a translation of the Gospel of Mark commissioned by the Serampore Bible Society. In 1811, Leyden accompanied Governor General Lord Minto on an expedition to Java; following a visit to an "unventilated native library," he fell ill with a fever and died three days later, aged only thirty-five years. Hasan is believed to have returned to his home island when Leyden's successor in the Bible translation project himself died suddenly ten months later.[64] It is clear that the 1808 vocabulary was not merely the result of Leyden's early lexicographic labors but was itself designed to be a tool, indeed a "mechanical aid," for the acquisition of additional languages.

The order in which Leyden lists the terms in his vocabulary does not correspond to their component letters. To put it another way, this is not an alphabetically arranged list. Instead, the terms appear to be arranged according to common themes in what is known as an onomasiological arrangement, where the user goes from concept to word, rather than the more familiar arrangement found in most modern dictionaries, which

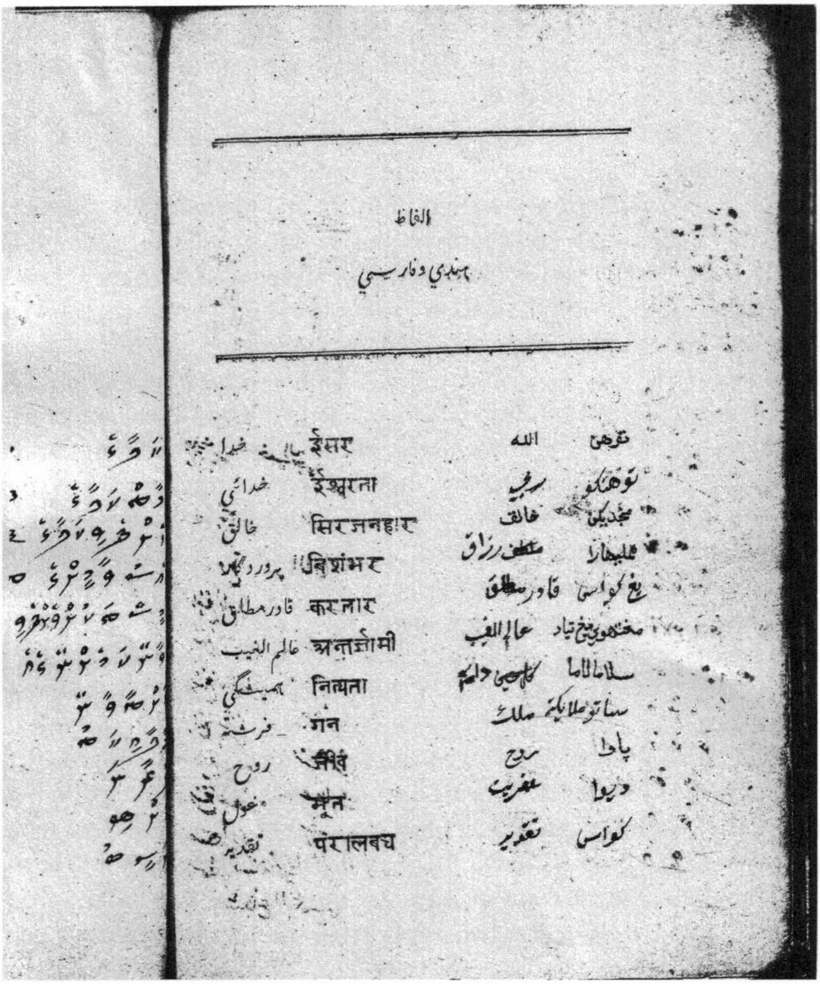

FIGURE 1.3 First page of Leyden's *Vocabulary* (1808). © The British Library Board, BL MSS EUR B103

enables the user to go from word to concept. When setting up linguistic equivalences among terms from multiple languages and sometimes with multiple writing systems, script is often not the most useful means of organization. By deploying an onomasiological arrangement, multilingual vocabularies were able to draw upon a more stable and universal structure of reference than any offered by the graphical representation, that is to say the orthography, of the terms contained therein.[65]

The relative stability of thematic macrostructures across languages is surprising in light of the potential for textual interpolations in many preprint lexicographic works. In trying to trace the source of John Leyden's list of terms, I discovered that they corresponded with the *Lughāt-i Hindī*, a handwritten list of Persian terms with their Hindvi equivalents housed in Calcutta at the Asiatic Society of Bengal[66] and formerly in the collection of the College of Fort William, where Leyden taught as professor of Hindustani from 1806 until his death.[67] While it is impossible to determine whether this work was commissioned prior to Leyden's *Vocabulary* or indeed whether Leyden ever possessed this manuscript, there is no question that the two works are identical: both list Hindi equivalents to the same list of Persian terms. There are surprising similarities between Leyden's 1808 vocabulary and another prepared eight years earlier by Francis Gladwin, professor of Persian, also for his students at the College of Fort William.[68] Lest one believe that this is merely a product of their having both been produced by two Englishmen living in close proximity in Calcutta, it should be noted that there is remarkable convergence in the arrangement of Leyden's 1808 vocabulary and one appearing in a draft vocabulary of English, Portuguese, Indostanee, and Malayo prepared around 1700 by Thomas Bowrey (c. 1650–1713), a prominent London merchant and occasional lexicographer.[69] Both lexicographers saw fit to begin their works with terms related to divinity, saints, spirits, and the structure of the universe. This arrangement is repeated in an English–Chinese vocabulary that Bowrey prepared.[70] These and other texts examined in *Negotiating Languages* show that at the turn of the nineteenth century, South Asian "traditions of the state, of social dominance, and [especially] of human communication" were not as far apart from their European counterparts as has been argued.[71]

Prior to the widespread adoption of print in South Asia, and a concomitant shift away from a craft literacy associated with manuscript production and toward the literacization of new social groups, the conceptual hierarchies embedded within shared South Asian cosmographies served as the most effective means of facilitating the serial recall of lexical information. The onomasiological basis of multilingual vocabularies could serve to reduce the cognitive load required in the memorization of these works, enabling vast mnemonic compression in the storage of lexical content. It also had value for the lexicographer in his interactions with a

English	Portuguese	Indostanee	Malaya
God	Deos	Allah, or Coodah	Allah
Lord Christ	Christou	Eissau	Eissau
Holy Ghost	Spirito Santo		
Virgin Mary	Virge Maria	Bibee Mariam	
Saints	Santos	Peere	
Angels	Angelos	Peeree	
Prophets	Prophetas	Nubbe	Nubbe
Heaven	Ceos		
Hell	Inferna	Honnum	Hannum
Divell	Diabolo	Shittan	Shittan
World	Mundo		
Earth	Terra	Xeimein	Tana
Sea	Mar	Durrea	Laut
Skie	Ceos		
Sun	Sol	Dupe	Mata Aree
Moon	Luna	Chaund	Bulong
Star	Estrella	Terra	
Clouds	Nuvoes	Baddal	
Raine	Chuva	Bursaut	Oodjong
Wind	Vento	Bau	Angin
Light	Lume	Oodjalla	Seriung
Dark	Escuro	Andul	
Day	Dia	Deen or Roes	Aree
Night	Anoite	Raut	Maulum
Year	Anno	Bans	Toun
Month	Meis	Miena	Bulong
Week	Somana		Jumahout
Man	Home	Adame	Oran
Woman	Mulhe	Jurru	Parampuan
Husband	Marieda	Mard	Lacki
Wife	Mulhe	Ourut	Binne
Son	Filho	Chocura	Anac
ughter	Filio	Chorre	Anac
er	Pai	Baup	Baupa
	Mai	Maa or Maa	Amak or Maum

FIGURE 1.4 Manuscript of Thomas Bowrey's *Dictionary of English, Portuguese, Hindostanee, and Malay* (c. 1700). © The British Library Board, BL MS EUR 192, f. 74.

linguistic informant. The serial encoding of conceptual hierarchies served as conceptual cues for the elicitation of semantic equivalents in a target language, especially when a linguistic informant was unable to recognize one or more terms proffered by the lexicographer. It was thus possible for Leyden's linguistic interlocutors and target users to be familiar with the contents and order of the denotations presented in an onomasiological vocabulary without themselves possessing any prior facility with the script in which those terms were represented on the page. In spite of this, however, Dhivehi (or Maldivian) equivalents are not always indicated for each corresponding Persian-Hindvi lexical pair. As a vocabulary, Leyden's work does not purport to represent the entirety of the total lexicon of either Persian or Hindvi. It instead represents a stable set of concepts with cultural significance embedded within a shared cosmographic representation of the universe.

Encyclopedists and lexicographers in many cultures, from antiquity to well into the twentieth century, rejected—often deliberately—an alphabetical arrangement of knowledge in favor of logics specific to individual classes of objects that were themselves perceived to follow a precise hierarchical arrangement within the universe.[72] The encyclopedias of Pliny the Elder, Cassiodorus Senator, and Isidore of Seville, along with Old English "catalogue poems," are the products of long-established "didactic strategies for ordering large quantities of material."[73] Important recent advances in our understanding of cognition have enabled modern lexicographic studies to draw insights in the field of what is known as *Listenwissenschaft*, or "list science."[74] This "science" is motivated by the need to make the comprehensive comprehensible: it imposes a structure upon the world's diversity, dividing the cosmos into sets governed by a universal organizational logic.[75] European encyclopedists, much like Indo-Persian and Sanskrit lexicographers, perceived the world as following sensible laws and considered their task to be to one of discovering the logic by which that world is organized.[76] For Nicholas Howe, a scholar of medieval European literature, the reliance of modern encyclopedists on alphabetization signals a "loss of nerve" and "announced their inability to contain in a more satisfactory form the increasingly diverse 'circle of knowledge' necessary for their culture."[77] The stability of the preprint lexicographic cosmography across languages (as much as across oceans and continents) should thus be interpreted not as proof of intellectual stagnation but rather as evidence of the dynamism of cultural and material exchanges across immense distances. The lexicographic preference for thematic over alphabetical organizations indicates, first, the extent to which South Asia was (and remains) a multilingual society; second, the limited social functions performed by languages—what really amounts to their being distinguishable as socially appropriate and context-dependent registers—prior to the advent of print; and third, a mutual ideological framework shared by a class of people, sedimented in the arrangements of preprint multilingual vocabularies.

The eventual dominance of alphabetical arrangements in various forms of reference—dictionaries as well as encyclopedias—was a consequence of an emerging perception that all forms of knowledge could be reduced to their orthographic elements.[78] This ontological development was brought about through shifts in the study of numerous areas of knowledge and the unprecedented complexity of early modern bureaucratic structures, enabled through the spread of new technologies of the written word and a correspondingly rapid expansion of literacy. New technologies of language and governance had the effect of flattening earlier structures of knowledge, and, of equal importance, these technologies reimagined existing social hierarchies as communities sharing a single language capable of expressing the total social life of individuals and the complete political life of nations. The monoglot ideology of nationalism, I contend, reduces a vast complex of shared cosmographies to a flat orthographic logocentrism.[79] Lexicographic genres like the multilingual vocabulary in verse are subsumed within the totalizing logocentric logic of the comprehensive dictionary.

When diglossic uses of language gave way, at least in theory, to a monolingual ideal embodied in the concept of a "national language," the social capital once demonstrated through command of the prestige language reappeared in the value attached to new forms of linguistic distinction *within* the nationalized language. In northern India, the replacement of Persian with Urdu as the official language of the courts led to the oft-repeated complaint about the continued superabundance of Persian forms in court documents. A frequently cited example appears in the following "Circular Order of the Sudder Adawlut, N.W.P," no. 33, dated April 19, 1839:

> It is the wish of the Government that care should be taken that the pleadings and proceedings be recorded in clear intelligible Oordoo, (or Hindee where that dialect is current), and that the native ministerial officers, hitherto accustomed to write a somewhat impure Persian, do not merely substitute a Hindoostanee for a Persian verb at the end of a sentence under the mistaken

> idea that such a practice will be considered as fulfilling every object in view in making the change.[80]

The assertion of linguistic commensurability—the one-to-one equivalency of one term to another—is not a new phenomenon in South Asia. Nevertheless, the potential for total commensurability, a lexicographic reconfiguration that attempts to discover the entire corpus of a given language, including the stock of terms with neither a precedent in literature nor any conceptual significance within a belief system, becomes possible when languages lose their cultural specificity and are instead viewed, like Leyden's native informants, as mere "mechanical aids."

FROM CHARISMA TO CURRENCY

An important corollary to lexicographic articulations of dominant cosmographies is the contention, also essential to this book, that lexicographic works derive their legitimacy from models of political authority and textual authentication available at the time of their compilation. Precolonial South Asian Islamicate states and Sufi orders operated through parallel modes of clientelism that privileged the direct interpersonal transfer of authority, cash, and other privileges[81]—a system wherein even "corporate" entities such as caste associations, rather than the fixed categories presented in colonial documents, are best understood as ephemeral, context-dependent solidarities.[82] Linguistic authority was conveyed analogously through the direct interpersonal transfer of knowledge and charisma among individuals in *silsilahs* (chains) of ritually sanctioned users. South Asian lexicography before the nineteenth century described and, in turn, reproduced discrete linguistic registers serving sharply demarcated social functions, especially those related to poetic composition and appreciation. As such, these works tell us about the social frameworks that brought these people into contact with one another in specific ritualized contexts within broader society. Participation in these activities entailed the acquisition of a set of social skills, the command of which offered a certain degree of mobility—both spatial and socioeconomic. Lexicographic works functioned as guides to the acquisition of a courtly culture: as portable objects, these texts could offer those on geographical and social peripheries of the Mughal Empire a glimpse into the linguistic and literary habits of the residents of its cultural center.

From early fourteenth-century Persian works to the current efforts of India's National Council for the Promotion of Urdu Language (NCPUL) and Pakistan's National Language Authority, South Asian dictionaries of Persian and Urdu have served a practical role as pedagogical tools in the education of a class of individuals who both consumed and themselves produced the elite culture of the Mughal state as well as its regional and colonial successors. The extension of Persian to all levels of the Mughal administration in the late sixteenth century was accompanied by an increase in the number of Persian lexicographical projects undertaken throughout India and a corresponding expansion of a distinctively South Asian Persian literary culture to include new social groups.[83] With their command of Persian, a language privileged in both the political and literary spheres, scribal groups produced not just administrative documents but poetry and belles-lettres as well. Dictionaries, grammars, and other works about language concretely link pedagogical practice to the formation of literate classes and ultimately to the literature produced by these groups.[84] Dictionaries and affiliated lexicographic genres are key documents detailing not just the development of the political, literary, and linguistic concepts contained within them[85] but also changes, often dramatic, in material culture[86] and modes of literary transmission. This emphasis on lexicographic works as a historical archive thereby provides fresh insights into the eighteenth-century formation of Urdu in Delhi as a literary register and its subsequent nineteenth-century deployment as a language of administration, demonstrating the local interactions of a South Asian elite class with a cosmopolitan Persian literary culture that was a model for much of Asia.

By the nineteenth century, however, lexicography, much like cadastral mapping and census taking, became part of larger European colonial and South Asian nationalist projects to render subject populations—and for these populations to render themselves—socially and politically legible.[87] With an ever-greater proportion of the population becoming subject to direct assessment and thus gaining access to state services, so too did the scope of lexicographers expand to include hitherto unexamined lexical data. As the state adopted sophisticated tools to classify and quantify its population in corporate groups, these groups increasingly came to use these tools to demand a proportionate share of state largesse and political representation. Language reformers began to use dictionaries to shape language into a central marker capable of motivating political movements.[88] The rise of a political ideology of representational commensurability in South Asia was partly enabled by ruptures in the structures of patronage and innovations in the technologies of mass printing, including lithography in the 1820s and sulfite pulping a few decades later.[89] Drastic changes in the educational system, particularly the introduction of government-sponsored competitive examinations, helped foster expectations of the commensurability of languages and, ultimately, of political representation, in South Asia.[90] As discussed above, this universalizing ideology required the conceptualization of language as a medium capable of expressing the total social life of individuals and the complete political life of a nation. As David Washbrook has argued, a new nation was thought to require its own language,[91] and various competing South Asian political movements of the period regarded the "modern" comprehensive dictionary, compiled "scientifically" on "historical principles," as a concrete expression of a nation's arrival on the world stage.

The ambiguous relationship of Urdu lexicographic works with literature, especially classical Urdu and Persian poetry, has confounded scholarly efforts to explain the development of an Urdu lexicographic tradition. Urdu-language lexicographers would cite verses of canonical poets in their definitions, and the dictionaries they compiled occasionally preserve the only record of otherwise forgotten poets and poetry. While aspiring poets might prepare bilingual Persian–Urdu glossaries to help make sense of centuries-old Persian classics, professional poets could consult dictionaries that arranged terms by final letter (or "rhyme order") to assist them in identifying rhyming terms for the challenging *qaṣīdah* genre.[92] Doting grandfathers even adapted a famous thirteenth-century Arabic–Persian vocabulary in verse to ensure their grandchildren gained access to the languages of empire and social advancement.[93] Today, libraries across South Asia preserve hundreds of these *niṣāb* primers containing Indic equivalents of Persian terms and, in the colonial period, of English ones.[94] Insofar as lexicographers would cite poetic verses as prooftexts in support of definitions, thereby invoking the literary authority and collective memory of canonical poets, the Urdu lexicographic work may also represent meaning through peculiarly literary modes of ambiguity. Early Urdu lexicographers were often not content to provide straightforward listings of synonyms or interpretive definitions of the denotative content of terms. The dictionary before print was intended not to introduce new information but to remind the user of knowledge already acquired. As vital contributors to literary production and consumption, lexicographers could indulge in forms of verbal play, suggesting meaning only to those whose educational training had paved the way for them to distinguish between the explicit and implicit (*ẓāhir* and *bāṭin*) meanings of words in their literary context. Effective interpretation of lexicographic works thus requires one to straddle important disciplinary divides, avoiding the literary tendency to indulge in ahistorical aesthetic analysis and the historical proclivity to mine texts purely for their content.

The great variety in the metalinguistic terminology that the authors of these works apply to the expressions they gloss often raises the question whether, from word to word, a single author is describing the same language within the same text. The linguistic diversity of South Asia is proverbial,[95] and the contents of these works exemplify this heterogeneity. The question naturally arises as to whether one text may be appropriately included in the same lexicographic tradition as another. The answer, thankfully, comes in the works themselves: authors of lexicographic works often justify their labors in an introductory essay, offering insights into not just the original impetus to begin collecting terms and expressions but also the corpus from which their lexical data is drawn and the function of that work among its intended users. Of course, one cannot always trust that the author is being honest, especially when rationalizing a project ex post facto. Moreover, it is often difficult to extract the actual functions of a text from the highly conventionalized formal constraints of the prefatory material appearing in the Mughal-Persianate and, as in the case of the aforementioned *Key to Newspaper Viewing*, British colonial contexts.[96] As one observer has noted: "Borrowing—even plagiarism—is no sin to lexicographers."[97] This lexicographic tendency to appropriate the research of others into one's own work is an oft-repeated truism, sometimes presented with a positive connotation (indicated with such terms as "borrowing," "palimpsest," "reproduction," etc.) but more often a negative valuation ("plagiarism" and even "daylight robbery"). What is undeniable is that dictionaries, glossaries, and other works belonging to allied lexicographic genres hardly if ever appear, as one colonial educator phrased it, ex nihilo, that is to say, from nowhere. Though they are a product of their times, they also both look back to earlier works for inspiration and themselves inspire use and abuse by later authors. They may illuminate the genius (and failings) of an individual but also reflect the labors and the aspirations of larger communities, be they fellow compilers or the vast laity of potential users.[98]

Rather than a passive reflection of a dominant cosmography, Munshī Ẓiyāʾ al-Dīn used the dictionary format to critique subtly the British government. He was able to take advantage of the scientific rhetorical stance of objectivity required of the twentieth-century lexicographer, one typified in the statement of the important German linguist Berthold Delbrück (1842–1922):

> A dictionary . . . is not a work in which a man's mind reveals itself fully, nor does it have an impact on others' minds similar to that of, say, a philosophical system. On the other hand, it is perhaps possible to say that dictionaries usually last [that is, are valid] longer than philosophical systems.[99]

While this occlusion of the author may have become the ideal in the twentieth century, an examination of lexicographical works, including dictionaries, glossaries, word lists, and vocabularies in verse, reveals that much of the authority of Urdu and Persian lexicographers was founded upon their assertion of charisma, usually conveyed through a carefully cultivated poetic persona in verses scattered throughout their works.

If this project seeks to discover a plot where none had been anticipated, the main character is surely the language whose adventures are depicted, at times dramatically, on the pages of a disparate set of texts. Unlike a typical dramatic personage, however, this character does not have a single name. Indeed, far from being a static figure—a mere plot device—this protagonist is continually molded by surrounding events. Early on, its role seems vague and undefined: with little direction, it took whatever appearance the lexicographer would give to it. Later it finds its home in courtly milieus, an eloquent witness to the political tragedy of the later Mughal Empire. In the nineteenth century, our protagonist is robed afresh in a new costume, this time in service of a vast country and, increasingly, the entire population contained within it. In any narrative, be it a dictionary or a staged drama, authors can draw upon a range of techniques to depict events with such verisimilitude that it becomes difficult to distinguish the actors from their stage presence. As a "science" of lexicography developed under colonial patronage in the nineteenth century, the literary conceit of the lexicographic work gave way to expectations of a transparent realism: the character depicted in the modern standard dictionary was "language itself" and not the literary projections of a single author. The primary object of this book is thus to explode the belief that any lexicographic work, be it a children's glossary or a multivolume dictionary, is merely a mimetic representation of an underlying linguistic reality and not a carefully constructed product of human labor.

SCOPE OF THE STUDY

Drawing on the foundational work of Gustave Lanson and Pierre Bourdieu,[100] *Negotiating Languages* outlines the history of Urdu literature as a sociological phenomenon. The authority of the lexicographer had long been founded upon the compiler's mastery of and participation in social circles of poetic production and appreciation. Even when compiled by a single individual, the dictionary persisted as a collective effort. Its genius lay in the logic of its organization, which must identify and exile idiosyncrasy to achieve value as a reference work. Hardly static, these idiosyncrasies—appearing particularly in error-prone handwritten manuscripts—beg their readers to interpolate, improve, and erase. Lexicographic genres are an especially compelling set of material sources for the history of South Asia precisely because of their ability both to construct a social class and to carry the range of ideologies that served to make this class aware of itself. Lexicography's reflexive characteristics, its ability both to construct and reflect a reality—indeed its capacity to map out a comprehensive *cosmography*—endows this set of materials with a unique set of potentialities. Much of the sociological and historical value of these works lies in their very conventionality: we learn as much about the *social* conditions of their production and circulation as we do about any individual genius working in isolation.

Negotiating Languages documents the role that dictionaries and other lexicographic genres have played in educating and defining the bureaucratic and literary classes of the Mughal and colonial periods and shows how these groups have contributed to the creation and standardization of the languages of North India. Following this introduction, subsequent chapters loosely follow the innovative arrangement adopted by Friedrich Kittler in his important (and occasionally disorienting) *Discourse Networks 1800/1900*.[101] The following chapters each treat particular moments in the development of the Urdu language as emblematic. They are each centered around a key work and author whose career coincided with the turn of a century—in this case the eighteenth, nineteenth, and twentieth of the Christian calendar. Each chapter examines the sources of that work, the relation of its author to contemporary political, economic, and social developments, and the afterlife of the work through its critical reception and reformulation in subsequent lexicographical projects. Moreover, each chapter employs a more or less distinct historiographical method:

"1700" requires a sociological approach, "1800" reveals the contours of the colonial archive, and the two "1900" chapters provide opportunities to reflect on the limits of self-representation in light of increasingly communitarian conceptions of the nation-state. Because of the broad historical range of the present study, I have been selective in my choice of texts to analyze. As such, *Negotiating Languages* is intended to serve not as a comprehensive history of either Urdu lexicography or literature but as a historical survey of the Urdu language documented through a largely unstudied set of materials.

Chapter 2, "1700: Between Microhistory and Macrostructures," is devoted to the first dictionary with significant coverage of the Urdu language. ᶜAbdul Wāsĕᶜ 'Hāṅswī' is usually (if rarely) acknowledged as having produced this dictionary, entitled the *Ġharāʾib al-Luġhāt* (Marvels of words), which became an important source for later lexicographic works, including the *Nawādir al-Alfāẓ* (Wonders of words), compiled by the great eighteenth-century philologist Khāṅ-i Ārzū, and Sir Henry M. Elliot's *Supplement to the Glossary of Indian Terms* (1845). Writing in the provincial fort town of Hansi (located 130 kilometers to the northwest of Delhi) during the latter half of the seventeenth century, the Mughal-era educator ᶜAbdul Wāsĕᶜ declared that he compiled his *Ġharāʾib al-Luġhāt* to help his friends gain access to "nonunderstood meanings, the meanings of words meant in opposition to ordinary dictionaries, and for the sake of correction—so that the discovery of a word for a meaning may be easy for everyone." Through the *Ġharāʾib al-Luġhāt* and later adaptations of ᶜAbdul Wāsĕᶜ's work, Urdu lexicography developed from a limited set of lexical curiosities and technical vocabulary glossed in Persian dictionaries to include a broader set of terms.

In his critical study of the *Ġharāʾib al-Luġhāt* carried out in the middle of the eighteenth century, the famous polymath Ārzū derides ᶜAbdul Wāsĕᶜ's language as "not of the knowing ones of the imperial camp (*mutaᶜarrif-i urdūʾe bādshāhī*) and of the language of Akbarābād [Agra] and Shāhjahānābād [Delhi]," being instead merely "the language of the native land of the author of the treatise (*zabān-i waṭan-i ṣāḥib-i risālah*)." ᶜAbdul Wāsĕᶜ presents his linguistic material as belonging within a spectrum of dialects all more or less mutually intelligible. What changes at the midpoint of the eighteenth century is the effort, led by such figures as Ārzū and others, to develop this spoken language into a literary register possessing not just regularized orthography but all the trappings that attend the coalescence of a class of professional poets and critics supported by a healthy population of amateur appreciators. It was in this period that this register came to be known as *reḵhtah* (poured out, scattered, mixed), famously defined by the poet Mīr Taqī Mīr as "poetry of the Persian style in the language of the exalted city of Shāhjahānābād in Delhi."[102] Originally a musical term, its denotation was later extended to describe a form of poetry that mixed Indic and Persian vocabulary, themes, and formal elements.[103]

Chapter 3, "1800: Through the Veil of Poetry," details the inclusion, beginning at the turn of the nineteenth century, of new sets of linguistic data within lexicographic works, including folksongs, the speech of women, proverbs, and the argots of particular occupational groups. Lexicographic works that included spoken proverbs represent a shift in the lexicographic data away from the poetic register and toward a prose of speech. Mirzā Jān 'Ṭapish' (c. 1768–1816), a native of Delhi, composed the *Shams al-Bayān* (c. 1794) in the eastern province of Bengal for his patron at the court of the nawāb of Murshidabad. This work purports to represent the native speech of Delhi's residents, defines idiomatic expressions with Persian glosses, and attests to their usage through reference to verses by poets who actively composed and recited in that city. While the author's reliance on highly mediated literary representations of idiomatic speech may be cited as evidence of the incomplete development of descriptive lexicographic methods, it also signals the extension into Urdu of preexisting techniques of authentication from the Persian lexicographic tradition.[104] This work, however, cannot be identified as belonging entirely within a "native" Persianate tradition. Within a few decades the contents of the *Shams al-Bayān* were incorporated into early nineteenth-century English dictionaries of Urdu, the result of the author's confinement in a Calcutta prison and subsequent recruitment by East India Company officials for their own lexicographical projects. For the subimperial Persianate court of Murshidabad as much as for colonial Calcutta, the *Shams al-Bayān* served as a portal through which nonintimates could gain access to the linguistic charisma and authority of Delhi's courtly culture.

The final two chapters explore the reception of dictionaries produced by figures who, for different reasons, have been dismissed as unqualified or otherwise lacking credibility as lexicographers. "1900: Lexicography and the Self" explains the discomfort felt by early twentieth-century language reformers with the projection by a prominent nineteenth-century lexicographer, Sayyid Aḥmad Dihlawī (1846–1918), of a poetic persona and his cultivation of a poet's madness. The assertion of a literary persona derives from Persianate modes of poetic participation, the preeminent domain in which an individual could establish his linguistic competence. This charismatic self-presentation had once been essential not just for the practice of composing and critiquing poetry but also lexicography. Though it became an anachronistic liability for the twentieth-century lexicographer, the development of print technologies and corresponding legal systems of copyright recommended the insertion by authors of a surfeit of subjectivity into their dictionaries to inhibit plagiarism in what was becoming an increasingly competitive market of pedagogical works.

The obscure career of Ćiraṇjī Lāl (d. 1898), the Hindu author of an important nineteenth-century Urdu dictionary *Makhzan al-Muḥāwarat* (A storehouse of idioms), is the focus of the final chapter. Like Sayyid Aḥmad, Ćiraṇjī Lāl was from Delhi and had assisted S. W. Fallon, a prominent British educational official and folklorist, on at least two dictionary projects. Ćiraṇjī's useful dictionary, however, has languished alongside Sayyid Aḥmad's more illustrious *Farhang-i Āṣafiyah*. An early essay prepared by the prominent Urdu poet Alṭāf Ḥusain 'Ḥālī' declared two conditions to be necessary for the compiler of a "national" dictionary of the Urdu language: the author must be from Delhi, where the purest form of the language was spoken, and he must be Muslim.[105] In the midst of the increasingly communalized linguistic environment of late nineteenth-century northern India, Hindu lexicographers like Ćiraṇjī Lāl could no longer fit neatly into the emerging Islamicized Urdu literary culture.

Ultimately, the collation of dictionaries by solitary lexicographers was unsustainable in a new corporate economy that required the cooperative financing, compilation, and mechanical reproduction of texts intended to benefit not individual patrons but the "imagined communities" enabled by what Benedict Anderson calls "print capitalism."[106] Corresponding with a diffusion of ideologies of representative governance, lexicography thus is remobilized as a reflection of the total social life of a speech group. As space and people become increasingly reimagined as homologous units entirely contained within a universal system of state formations,[107] languages are expected to fill an analogous role, completely filling the space of the nation and fulfilling a total set of linguistic needs. The modern standard dictionary of a "national language" becomes a document that both affirms the totality of functionality and asserts the linguistic independence of the nation.[108]

The history of Urdu lexicography reflects processes both of *assimilation*, by which different regional, social, religious, and ethnic groups integrate into a single polity through use of a more or less common language, and of *differentiation*, by which previously unified polities disintegrate, in part through the promulgation of linguistic differences. In the case of South Asia, early multilingual works enabled contacts between populations, with linguistic equivalences facilitating communication among different ethnicities, occupational groups, and material and literary cultures. Later monolingual dictionaries helped transform ethnic groups into nations by providing symbols of group identity, etymological myths of origin and destiny, and "discoveries" of forgotten elements of the past. In the South Asian context, elites have deployed dictionaries to align symbols of secondary importance (for example, language, script, region, social condition) with what has become the preeminent and most visceral symbol of South Asian political identity: religion.[109]

[2] 1700: BETWEEN MICROHISTORY AND MACROSTRUCTURES

THE LATE seventeenth-century *Ġharā'ib al-Luġhāt* (Marvels of words/languages) has been described by its twentieth-century editor, Sayyid ʿAbdullāh, as "Urdu's oldest dictionary" (*urdū kā qadīmtarīn luġhat*).[1] Little is known, however, about the life and career of its author, ʿAbdul Wāsĕʿ 'Hāṅswī'—a schoolteacher with origins in a provincial fort town northwest of Delhi who was active during the reign of the Mughal emperor Aurangzeb.[2] Despite this dearth of information, I will argue, building on the work of such sociologists as Pierre Bourdieu and Susanne Janssen, that ʿAbdul Wāsĕʿ's life and work is emblematic of those lexicographers who occupied a special intermediate position between, on the one hand, an autonomous, aesthetic, "reputational" field of "restricted production" and, on the other, a market-driven, utilitarian, commercial field of mass cultural production. ʿAbdul Wāsĕʿ's dictionary is an early demonstration of the late Mughal transition in lexicography toward the inclusion of a broader and more representative corpus of terms that more closely resembled the spoken language. His dictionary would reemerge from obscurity as an important source for later lexicographic works, including the *Nawādir al-Alfāẓ* (Wonders of words), compiled by the great eighteenth-century philologist Ḳhān-i Ārzū, and Sir Henry M. Elliot's *Supplement to the Glossary of Indian Terms* (1845).

The *Ġharā'ib al-Luġhāt* is among the earliest South Asian works to document the generally unwritten language of a largely illiterate hinterland.[3] ʿAbdul Wāsĕʿ's use of Persian, an international language of culture and administration, as the language of explanation left his work prone to criticism from elites in Delhi, the Mughal capital. In his 1743 revision and expansion of the work, the eminent Indian philologist Ārzū rejected

ʿAbdul Wāsĕʿ's terms and definitions as unfamiliar and "not of the knowing ones of the imperial camp and of the language of Akbarābād [Agra] and Shāhjahānābād, [but instead merely] the language of the native land of the author of the treatise."[4] British officials in the nineteenth century would nevertheless find its very rusticity to be its greatest virtue: the regional specificity of the speech ʿAbdul Wāsĕʿ's dictionary recorded could be adapted for glossaries intended to assist colonial officials in producing more accurate assessments of land holdings and agricultural surplus. In collecting examples of rustic speech, ʿAbdul Wāsĕʿ in his own limited way anticipated by nearly two centuries the projects that would be carried out in the nineteenth century by European lexicographers and folklorists.

Despite his obscurity in the historical record, he is thus generally acknowledged as having compiled the first dictionary devoted to terms that would come to be associated with the Hindi and Urdu languages. In the introduction to the 1951 printed edition of Ārzū's revision of ʿAbdul Wāsĕʿ's dictionary, the work's editor, Sayyid ʿAbdullāh, a prominent literary historian, declared, "although with regard to intention and purpose it was not a dictionary of Urdu, nevertheless in light of form and utility, we may certainly accept it as the first Urdu *farhang* (dictionary)."[5] ʿAbdullāh here usefully distinguishes among three elements in dictionary production—intention, language, and genre. The three are qualities whose determination, he implies, is not an entirely straightforward process. Identification of the work as a "dictionary" (*luġhat* or *farhang*) of the Urdu language, leaving aside the claims of it as the *first* Urdu dictionary, proved controversial nearly from the moment of its (preprint) publication. The value, however, of assigning temporal priority to this or any work is perhaps of less importance than is a more complete evaluation of the text's influence upon later lexicographers.[6] One may fruitfully ask, then, whether the *Ġharāʾib al-Luġhāt* was indeed a dictionary (or at least a functional analogue), and if so, of what language? More vital is the question—hitherto ignored—of why ʿAbdul Wāsĕʿ even went to the effort of compiling this particular work at all.

EX NIHIILO ET VIVA VOCE: GILCHRIST'S DICTIONARY

In 1785, some hundred years after ʿAbdul Wāsĕʿ completed his *Ġharāʾib al-Luġhāt*, John Borthwick Gilchrist (1759–1841), a Scottish assistant surgeon with the East India Company's Bengal Army, obtained leave from his post "for the express purpose of giving a Hindoostanee Grammar, and Vocabulary to the community."[7] His extended leave of absence would result in the production of two works, *A Dictionary, English and Hindoostanee* (1798) and *A Grammar of the Hindoostanee Language* (1796), cementing Gilchrist's reputation as the foremost Hindustani-language pedagogue in British India. Appointed the first professor of Hindustani at the College of Fort William in 1800, Gilchrist would be instrumental not just in advancing South Asian–language pedagogy among East India Company officials but also in establishing Hindi and Urdu as fields of academic study for Europeans. Through his patronage, the Indian scribes employed by the College of Fort William prepared *devanāgarī*- and Arabic-script adaptations of earlier works in an unadorned and simple—even, according to critics, austere—style of prose using the Khaṛī Bolī dialect of Hindi-Urdu spoken in and around Delhi.[8]

Following the approval of his request for leave Gilchrist settled in Faizabad, the former capital of Avadh (Oudh). There he set about acquiring (in addition to a "long black beard" and "the dress of the natives") the services of a number of "learned Hindoostanees" from whom he hoped "to extract *viva voce*, every known word in their voluminous tongue."[9] These "Hindoostanees," he explained, consisted of "both Hindoos and Moosulmans [Muslims], as the latter have been naturalized by many generations to this name, when applicable to them as mere natives of India," referring here to the claims of many South Asian Muslims to foreign ancestry and reinforcing the notion of Islam and Persian as foreign impositions.[10] His first order of business was to seek out earlier dictionaries of the language and use them as a basis for his own more "compendious" volume. Much to his surprise, he discovered that

> not a dictionary or grammar could be procured for me, those from whom I required them stared with astonishment, and answered interrogatively, if it was ever yet known in any country, that men had to consult vocabularies, and rudiments for their own vernacular speech. This was to be sure a puzzling response, and set me a ruminating, amidst some retrospective glances upon the former state of our own tongue, which long before it had a grammar *visible to the vulgar*, was nevertheless no more a jargon, than the object of our present enquiries. I insisted, that in the extended succession of five or six centuries, some thing or other must have been produced on the modern Hindoostanee philology, by the Moosulmans who introduced it.[11]

It is worth considering the perspectives of the different figures represented in Gilchrist's account. For Gilchrist, it was difficult to imagine that a language like Hindustani, "current over mighty civilized empires,"[12] could lack something so fundamental as a comprehensive dictionary. His Indian interlocutors must have been equally baffled by the idea of someone wishing to study a language or a spectrum of languages—what Gilchrist called "Hindoostanee"—comprising a variety of dialects and registers that lacked a single standard for the representation of the ordinary prose of speech. Even if the Khaṛī Bolī dialect of the Delhi region was at that time the most prestigious form of "Hindoostanee" used in northern India, its high status was attributable to the quality of its poets and only to a very limited extent to that of its prose authors.[13] Moreover, there seemed at that time little scope for "Hindoostanee" to displace Persian in the production of official state documents, including court records of testimony and thus little financial incentive for Indians not already familiar with Khaṛī Bolī Hindi-Urdu to study that language for financial gain.

Of the two works that were eventually presented to him, he writes:

> My coadjutors at last produced a Tom Thumb performance, called from its initial words the *Khaliq baree*, which they dignified with the title of vocabulary, though on inspection I discovered only the shrivelled mummy of an old meagre school glossary, handed down since the time of *Khoosro* the poet, about the year 1300, and like the Tohfat ool Hindi, explanatory of the ancient Hinduwee alone.[14]

The *Ḳhāliq Bārī* was the most popular South Asian example of the *niṣāb* genre of multilingual vocabularies in verse. Comprising synonymous or near-synonymous terms and phrases drawn from Arabic, Persian, and early Hindvi, it was commonly attributed to the celebrated fourteenth-century Persian poet Amīr 'Ḳhusrau' of Delhi (1253–1325). The question of whether it was originally intended to teach Central Asian immigrants Hindi through Persian (as was the case of an early sixteenth-century *niṣāb*, the *Qaṣīdah dar Luġhat-i Hindī*) or native Hindi speakers Persian has been hotly debated,[15] but it is clear that for most if not all of its existence it had been deployed to teach Indian children Persian through a Hindi-Urdu medium. And, regardless of its provenance, the *Ḳhāliq Bārī* has inspired legions of imitators, including several inexpensive works printed in the early twentieth century that provide Hindi and Urdu equivalents for English terms.[16]

Mirzā Ḵhān's "Tohfat ool Hindi" (*Tuḥfat al-Hind* 'The gift of Hind') is an important late eighteenth-century study of Braj Bhāṣā grammar and poetry written in Persian in approximately 1675. It includes in an appendix a vocabulary of approximately three thousand Braj terms with Persian explanations.[17] This work, with its focus on Sanskritic vocabulary, was intended for members of Persianate Indo-Muslim society who as "devotees of Braj bhāṣā poetry . . . wanted to understand the Sanskrit terms used in poetry." Rather than a bilingual dictionary of a "foreign language," the Hindi scholar Stuart McGregor suggests that a better analogue might instead be found in early modern English dictionaries of "hard words."[18] It serves as a portent of the later nineteenth-century differentiation of Hindi and Urdu on the basis of the sources—Sanskrit and Persian, respectively—from which they would draw and mint their lexical stock.

Gilchrist's difficulty in obtaining formal texts on language had led, he felt, to the misunderstanding among his own countrymen that "the grand popular language of Hindoostan" was a mere "jargon," relegating it in their estimation to a "catechismal pedlars speech, or cant," unbound by regular rules and without reference to a written literature.[19] Elsewhere, Gilchrist anticipates criticism of his use of the epithet "grand" in connection with a so-called vernacular, adding his own alliterative twist:

> Should any sapient sneerer cock his nose at the term *grand* or *popular*, which I apply to the Hindoostanee, let him recollect, that I have an equal right to raise the dignity and renown of this important tongue, which others have who talk of the *divine* Hebrew, the *sacred* Sanskrit, the *sublime* Arabic, the *celestial* Persian; or who reverence the name of a *heaven-born* premier, a *grand* Turk, or the *great* Mooghul. All this is a matter of mere taste, and when I prefer the *utile dulciae; de gustibus non est disputandum*.[20]

One hears in this sardonic passage echoes of the rhetoric that Gilchrist's Orientalist contemporaries had used to elevate the classical languages of what Sir William Jones (1746–1794) called the "five principal nations, who have peopled the continent and islands of Asia," bringing them to the attention of the broader European scholarly community. In his "Third Anniversary Discourse" of 1886, Jones famously extolled Sanskrit's "wonderful structure" as "more perfect that the Greek, more copious than the Latin, and more exquisitely refined than either,"[21] and Nathaniel Halhed's (1751–1830) 1778 grammar of Bengali reinforced common perceptions of "Hindoostanee" as a pidgin characterized by a disordered and irregular grammar and seemingly "ungoverned by rules."[22] Gilchrist's statement anticipates a rift that would grow between, on the one hand, those like Jones, whose pursuit of comparative philology gave prestige to India's classical languages, and, on the other, promoters of vernaculars like Gilchrist, who saw in them a more expeditious means of administering Britain's growing South Asian dominions.[23] These differences can, however, be overdrawn: Gilchrist was himself content to select a Latin phrase (*de gustibus non est disputandum*) over an English equivalent ("there is no accounting for taste") to conclude this remarkable statement of cultural relativism.[24]

According to Gilchrist, what was lacking in the "Hindoostanees" was sufficient "retrospection" upon one's own language: earlier, he claims that it is the absence of adequate "reflection" that had caused "the grand living popular speech of all Hindoostan . . . to languish in very unmerited, and most unaccountable neglect."[25] Things had come to such a state that

> the Hindoostanee spoken by the Gipseys in Europe, seems from the accounts lately published there, to be more the language of rational creatures, than the monstrous clack now prevalent among us in Bengal, which is called Moors, but it is luckily confined to those only, whom the natives presume are ignorant of any other.[26]

Gilchrist criticized native speakers of Hindustani for an underdeveloped sense of linguistic detachment, that is to say, a disinclination to treat one's own spoken language as an object of research through a cultivated distance between subject and linguistic object. This attitude was not entirely incomprehensible to Gilchrist, for he only cast "retrospective glances" upon his own unreflexive relationship with English when confronted with his linguistic frustrations in faraway Faizabad.[27] Upon further reflection, however, he wondered how it escaped the notice of the Muslims of India who, ostensibly as outsiders, "introduced" Hindustani to India.[28]

Gilchrist's perception of language use in South Asia and his vigorous demarcation of "Hindoostanee" ("a comparatively recent superstructure, composed of Arabic and Persian") from "Hinduwee" ("the exclusive property of the Hindus alone . . . the old language of India, which prevailed before the Moosulman invasion") was inextricably linked to his own experience as a Scotsman serving in an official British capacity.[29] His identification with and fervent advocacy on behalf of "Hindoostanee" as a link language[30] was an artifact of his own desire to be accepted as a social equal in English society. Following the 1707 Acts of Union, certain de jure structural barriers Scotsmen had previously faced in their interactions with London-based mercantile financial ventures disappeared. John MacKenzie notes, for example, that "the Scots' infiltration of the East India Company's marine and medical establishments was notorious."[31] Although Scots only comprised about a tenth of the total population of the British Isles during the rule of Warren Hastings, the first governor general of Bengal (from 1772 to 1785), they contributed nearly half of the East India Company's writers and a similar proportion of the company's army officers and surgeons.[32] Despite Scots' numeric overrepresentation among the professional ranks of the East India Company, de facto barriers remained, not least of which was the matter of acquiring not just the English language but its "proper" usage and pronunciation in the capital of the new union.[33] With regard to politics, the relatively liberal attitudes prevailing among these Scots during the 1760s and 1770s in Calcutta contrasted sharply with the xenophobic and whiggish predilections of the company's London-based directors.[34]

As outsiders to English culture, Gilchrist and other Scots who taught South Asian languages shared with antecedent Indian linguists and lexicographers like ʿAbdul Wāsĕʿ and Ārzū a heightened awareness of the lingua francas spoken in their respective imperial capitals as potential objects of linguistic study.[35] As a Scotsman growing up in Edinburgh during the clearing of the Highlands, Gilchrist was probably exposed from birth to a multilingual environment.[36] Those like Gilchrist whose origins afforded them a slightly distanced position from the language of the imperial center could also recognize that it was partly through language that one could begin to engage with a broader imperial cultural economy. Gilchrist claimed that this distance from standard English provided him and his northern compatriots with certain linguistic advantages. For example, he considered "the only very difficult sounds" among those consonants used in Hindoostanee and derived from the Arabic and Persian to be "*ghu*, *khu*, and *qu*," corresponding with the letters غ, خ, and ق. The first two of these, he claimed, "are easy enough to people from the north."[37] It was thus outsiders to London's dominant culture like Gilchrist who most acutely felt the incentive to systematize language and other social codes associated with the imperium as a means of gaining access to other social and financial opportunities.

One would expect that in seeking to raise "Hindoostanee" above the status of a mere "jargon" to one "current over mighty civilized empires,"[38] he would make some effort to extol the virtues of the written form of the language. Yet while "Hindoostanee"—the language that Gilchrist claims to be interested in—is at times the "the grand popular speech of India," at others "the grand colloquial speech of all India," and still others "the grand popular tongue," he at the same time argued that the spoken language needed to be liberated from the pedantry and insipidness of its written forms, which he perceived as the result of the stylistic dominance of poetry over prose.[39] Thus, in describing the technique he developed for discovering words for his lexicon, he claims to have discarded the mass of works by "Hindoostanee writers" and instead created his dictionary entirely ex nihilo (from nothing) and viva voce (with living voice):

> To select words from the Hindoostanee writers, as they occurred in their compositions seemed so endless a task, that I at once took the alphabet regularly so. My auditory were severally instructed to furnish me with every signification they could possibly attach to such sounds or words as *a, ab, abab, ababa, abach, abad, abada, abaf,* &c. &c. so on, ringing the changes in this manner progressively, with every letter. One or two syllables commonly led the way to a numerous tribe of words, till I at last in this manner compiled, in the space of a few months by incessant application, the whole of the Hindoostanee Dictionary noticed hereafter, with more ease, and precision, and probably much sooner than I could have accomplished it by any other mode, in a living speech of which neither a vocabulary nor grammar existed.[40]

Gilchrist, who did not wish to remain beholden to the literary past of "Hindoostanee," limited though it may seem when juxtaposed to the "copiousness" of classical Arabic, Persian, and Sanskrit, nevertheless found the extant compositions significant enough to make selecting terms from them seem "so endless a task." Yet, "with more ease, and precision, and probably much sooner than . . . by any other mode," he claimed to be able to create a lexicon of this "living speech of which neither a vocabulary nor grammar existed" and populate it with meanings, taking the alphabet "regularly so" and reconstructing words from their constituent letters.[41]

By establishing the lexis of a language partly through this method of oral elicitation, Gilchrist anticipated that his critics would object to his prejudice against the existing written corpus of the language. In defense of his technique, he wrote:

> The persevering efforts which I have made to banish all learned lumber from the Hindoostanee, will not, at this period, I flatter myself, be misconstrued into any wish for the expulsion also of all concord, propriety, accuracy of speech, and pronunciation, by those men who, not having at first acquired the grammar of that language, wisely affect afterwards to undervalue and despise it. . . . That Arabic and Sunscrit are the grand sources of profound oriental literature; I never was silly enough to deny; on the contrary, I respect them in the higher regions of science, as they richly deserve.[42]

By according respect to Arabic and "Sunscrit" as "grand sources of oriental literature," Gilchrist is able at the same time to exile them safely to the realms of the higher—that is to say, largely impractical—"regions of science." Gilchrist, by documenting the grammar and vocabulary of a language that had circulated previously as a spoken "tongue" and in verse compositions, is able to have his cake and eat it, too: spoken universally throughout India, "Hindoostanee" nevertheless has no prose history (at least none acknowledged by Gilchrist)[43] to limit its future or to challenge Gilchrist as its premier—that is, its very first and greatest—authority.

BETWEEN MICROHISTORY AND MACROSTRUCTURES

The typical sources of information about the lives of poets and authors in Mughal India, the vast *tażkirah* tradition of biographical anthologies describing the lives, works, and qualities of an immense number of Urdu and Persian literary figures, are remarkably silent in their treatment of ᶜAbdul Wāsĕᶜ. The only *tażkirah* to have made any mention of Hāṅswī is the nineteenth-century *Gulshan-i Be-Ḳhār* (Flowerbed without thorns) by Muṣṯafā Ḳhān 'Sheftah' (1806–1869),[44] whose entry on ᶜAbdul Wāsĕᶜ is extremely laconic, neglecting to provide even a *taḳhalluṣ* (nom de plume):

> ᶜAbdul Wāsĕᶜ
> The name is ᶜAbdul Wāsĕᶜ. His history (*ḥāl*) is not known.[45]

Sheftah's entry is noted in the monumental biographical compendia compiled by the influential French Orientalist Joseph Heliodore Garcin de Tassy (1794–1878). De Tassy's entry on ᶜAbdul Wāsĕᶜ makes brief mention of two works attributed to the author: a dictionary, the *Ġharāʾib al-Luġhāt*, and a treatise on Persian grammar, the *Risālah-yi ᶜAbdul Wāsĕᶜ* (Treatise of ʿAbdul Wāsĕʿ). He provides bibliographic details for an 1851 print edition of the grammar and explains that the *Ġharāʾib al-Luġhāt*, while cited by Peter Breton as a source for his 1825 medical vocabulary, is misattributed to "Khan Arzoo."[46] Writing for a European readership, he expands on Sheftah's entry by offering in footnotes first a gloss of the author's name ("Slave of the Immense One") and, second, a brief discussion of Hansi, situating the town in terms of latitude and longitude, noting its eleventh-century founding by the Ghaznavids, and relating its recent significance as a base of operations for the late eighteenth-century European adventurer George Thomas (1756–1802).[47]

By the nineteenth century, constructing a narrative of ʿAbdul Wāsĕʿ's life had already become impossible. The best that scholars like Garcin de Tassy could do was to make inferences based on the author's name and hometown. Seen in this light, the verse attributed to ʿAbdul Wāṣĕʿ by Sheftah seems especially poignant:

bajuz rafāqat-i tanhāʾī āsrā nah rahā
siwāʾe be-kasī ab koʾī āshnā nah rahā

Besides the companionship of solitude, no security remained
Except for Friendlessness, now not a friend remained[48]

While the works of ʿAbdul Wāsĕʿ enjoyed moderate success, the *ḥāl* (condition, history, state) of ʿAbdul Wāsĕʿ was never memorialized by contemporaries. The lack of a pen name suggests the absence of a developed poetic persona, ostensibly the object of study for such biographical compendia. The great popularity of the works attributed to ʿAbdul Wāsĕʿ thus stemmed not from the charisma of their author: unlike poetry, these eminently useful works did not require an author of equal eminence.

If ʿAbdul Wāsĕʿ's toponymic *nisbat*—a term literally meaning "reference" or "relation" and here denoting the author's toponymic title Hāṅswī (of Hāṅsī)—tempts us to identify the man with the place, the lack of biographical details for the individual demands that we treat this individual's lexicographic contributions sociologically.[49] Microlevel analyses, according to the cultural sociologist Susanne Jenssen, "by more or less bracketing the societal and institutional levels of analysis . . . have been able to detail how the norms and conventions of aesthetic judgment and collaboration allow artists of all types to create and build careers in the process." Yet what is gained in biographical texture signals a potential loss in broader relevance: the data "verges on the anecdotal and results in decontextualized cases," the broader implications of which "teach us little about the historical and structural conditions" in which the cultural products are produced, transmitted, and consumed.[50] In short, the sociological approach to creative production is not merely a position of convenience: the lack of individuated biographical information on ʿAbdul Wāsĕʿ prods us to bridge micro- and macrolevel analyses through comparative longitudinal studies.

The ambiguous relationship of Urdu lexicographic works with literature, especially classical Urdu and Persian poetry, has confounded scholarly efforts to explain the development of an Urdu lexicographic tradition. Early Urdu lexicography is generally assumed to be an outgrowth of literary production, one secondary to and contingent upon the primary and essential processes of literary production. The sociologist Pierre Bourdieu turns this formulation on its head by arguing that it is through the shift toward the commodification of art (as items corresponding to definite monetary values), effected through the diminishing role played by direct patronage and the rise of a "market of symbolic goods," that the notion of art for art's sake—which appears in our discussion as the sharp demarcation of literary genres of poetry from lexicography—becomes fetishized and subsequently becomes generally accepted as fact.[51]

Lexicographic works do not so much stand at the frontiers as straddle the borders shared by a range of creative human activities. Far from being marginal in terms of a hierarchy of creative production, lexicography was and remains a "middle-level occupation" situated between what too easily may be imagined as the extremes of the "purely" aesthetic and the "purely" utilitarian. As a result of industrialization and in light of an increasingly dominant "bourgeois" public culture, Bourdieu argues that the "field of production and circulation of symbolic goods" developed an emphasis upon an opposition between the field of "restricted production"—"a system producing cultural goods (and the instruments for appropriating those goods) objectively destined for a public of producers of cultural goods"—and the field of "large-scale cultural production"—"the production of cultural goods destined for non-producers of cultural goods, 'the public at large.' "[52] Following Bourdieu and Dimaggio,[53] Janssen has noted:

> The former field (for instance poetry) tends to evolve toward the model of a "reputational" profession (where professional hierarchy is based on reputation), with the ultimate reward of becoming part of the "canon." On the other hand, large-scale production is similar to "market" professions, where hierarchy is based on market success.[54]

Insofar as dictionaries and allied lexicographic genres did not enjoy the benefit of widespread print production in South Asia until well into the nineteenth century, any distinction that can be drawn in the precolonial period between, on the one hand, an autonomous, aesthetic, "reputational" field of "restricted production" and, on the other hand, a market-driven, utilitarian, commercial field of mass cultural production quickly breaks down on closer examination. From their perspectives in the middle of the nineteenth century, however, ᶜAbdul Wāsĕᶜ's pedagogical work fits only uncomfortably in Sheftah and de Tassy's biographical anthologies of literary figures. ᶜAbdul Wāsĕᶜ Hāṅswī in Garcin de Tassy's *Histoire* acquires the questionable honor of deriving his importance not from the "reputational" field of "restricted production" but from the utilitarian value of his work. What matters for de Tassy is the availability of the work in print, not the availability of the author's *ḥāl* (situation).

MARGINAL REFERENCES: HĀṄSWĪ'S PROVINCIAL ANTECEDENTS

The obscurity that shrouds the life and times of ᶜAbdul Wāsĕᶜ extends beyond an absence of biographical notices within the *tażkirah* tradition. The town of Hansi, from which ᶜAbdul Wāsĕ acquired his toponymic title, or *nisbat*, has suffered two major calamities in the centuries that separate his life from our own. Both resulted in the wholesale dispersion of the greater section of the city's population, the result being that Hansi—both the author and the city—are joint heirs to a long history of amnesia. The general tendency toward desertification and the rise of new cities in the region has further curtailed the cultural influence of its residents. Historically, the greatest factor in the peripheralization of Hansi—indeed, of the poet as much as the place—is, ironically, its proximity to the city of Delhi, which served as the capital of the Mughal Empire throughout much of the eighteenth century.

Hansi is situated on the ancient trade route that connected Delhi and points east with Khorasan and Central Asia.[55] Architectural and inscriptional evidence indicate the importance of this city as a center of Islamic power from the early eleventh century if not earlier, with the Ghaznavid king Masᶜūd conquering the town in AD 1038.[56] Its importance as a military outpost (protecting the main route to Delhi from Mongol and other incursions) and a religious center[57] came in part from its strategic location and the strength of its fort. The fourteenth-century Moroccan traveler Ibn Baṭūṭah declared it "one of the best, strongest and most prosperous of cities," and Tīmūr spared the city out of respect to the descendants of a prominent Chishtī saint whose *ḳhānaqāh* (lodge) and tomb complex continue to serve as an important religious site.[58]

Even with the shift of the administrative center of gravity to the newly established town of Ḥiṣār-i Fīrozah in the latter half of the fourteenth century, later evidence indicates that the town held its own against its nearby neighbor and may have supported a large population well into the Mughal period.[59] For in addition to being well connected through a network of roads, the construction during the reign of Fīroz Shāh Tuġhlaq (r. 1351–1388) of a canal linking the town with the Yamuna River allowed for the further development of agriculture in the surrounding region.[60] This canal is traditionally remembered as having been extended and further improved during the reigns of the Mughal emperors Akbar (r. 1556–1605) and Shāh Jahān (r. 1628–1658).[61] The presence of an extensive canal system enriched the city and region and linked its finances closely to those of the broader Mughal imperium. During the reign of Aurangzeb (r. 1658–1707), for example, market dues levied within the Hansi and Hisar *parganahs* (district subdivisions) were directly appropriated by the crown rather than assigned as *jāgirs* (assigned land grants).[62]

The city thus seemed to enjoy significant prosperity throughout much of the Mughal period, its political and economic condition tightly integrated with the Mughal heartland. The author of the 1892 district gazetteer notes, "Hánsi . . . is both the richest, most irrigated and most developed tahsíl in the district [and] has far the largest rural density."[63] In the two decades that followed the death of Emperor Aurangzeb in 1707, the region as a whole seems to have been affected by the uncertainty that attended the tumultuous succession struggles. Hansi returned to prosperity under the stewardship of Shahdād Ḳhān, a fascinating figure who had been appointed *niẓām* (governor) of Hisar district by Emperor Muḥammad Shāh (r. 1719–1748).[64] By 1748, however, and within a decade of Shahdād Ḳhān's death in battle at Karnal and Nadir Shah's infamous sack of Delhi, the authors of the *Maʿāṡir al-Umarā* depict Hansi and Hisar as "wilderness."[65] The failure of the monsoon in 1782 and its late arrival in 1783 precipitated the deaths of untold numbers in the so-called *ćālīsā kāl* (famine of *sambat* year 1840), leading to the exodus of a large portion of the population east and south in search of food and work.[66] While certainly affected by the massive economic disruption and human tragedy of the famine, Hansi seemed to have fared better than other parts of the region.[67] Indeed, following the historian C. A. Bayly's observation that it was typical during bad seasons for populations to "drift from the unstable to the surplus areas," accounts of the famine suggest that many residents, upon their return to Hansi, discovered their land to have been occupied and cultivated in their absence by migrants from Bikaner and more severely affected points further west.[68]

The effects of the famine, however, extended beyond the destruction and displacement of human populations, labor, and agricultural infrastructure. The author of the 1892 district gazetteer poignantly notes the desolation that famines could inflict upon the social landscape:

> The fatal year is the era from which every social relation of the people dates. Few villages have a history which goes back uninterruptedly to a period before the famine, and there probably is not one which does not date its present form of tenure from the time when cultivation was resumed.[69]

This dislocation of memories from built structures and landscapes is reflected in the frustrations encountered by a team of architectural historians in the 1980s as they endeavored to carry out their survey of Islamicate architecture in the Hisar district. With the partition of India and Pakistan came the emigration of nearly the entire Muslim population of the district to the new state of Pakistan and, subsequently, the decay of many built structures that had ritual, cultural, and historical links to that population. A less obvious form of dilapidation was that which afflicted the memories of the communities that remained, or had themselves immigrated to, the district from afar: "most of the traditions associated with these buildings have also been lost. . . . In some cases even the traditional names of the monuments are no longer known locally."[70]

A LIFE IN LETTERS

The *Ġharā'ib al-Luġhāt* is one of five works attributed to ʿAbdul Wāsĕʿ.[71] The second work is a Persian grammar in prose form known variously as the *Risālah-i ʿAbdul Wāsĕʿ* (Treatise of ʿAbdul Wāsʿĕʿ)[72] and *Qawā'id-i Luġhāt-i Furs* (Grammar of the Persian language),[73] and it is based upon the preface of an important Persian dictionary entitled *Farhang-i Rashīdī*, compiled by ʿAbdul Rashīd in 1654 and dedicated to Shah Jahan.[74] It appears to have enjoyed great popularity: writing in 1868, the German philologist Heinrich Ferdinand Blochmann (1838–1878) depicted it as "a book which is read in most Indian schools."[75] Hāṅsī also prepared commentaries on two important Persian works, Saᶜdī's *Būstān* and Jāmī's *Yūsuf Zulaiḳhā.*[76] Regarding the *Sharḥ-i Yūsuf Zulaiḳhā*, the Indian scholar of Persian Sayyid ᶜAbdullah is rather dismissive:

> Clearly he has made great efforts in the demonstration of knowledge, but in this, too, his accomplishment is not permitted to surpass the height of the school walls: there is no debate regarding the graces of poetry and that he absolutely does not attempt to raise questions of literary qualities.[77]

ᶜAbdul Wāsĕᶜ is also known to have produced a very popular *niṣāb*, or multilingual vocabulary in verse, entitled *Risālah-i Jān Pahćān* (The treatise of the familiar friend), alternatively known as the *Ṣamad Bārī.*[78] The second title is derived from the first word in the text, *ṣamad* (Arabic, 'The Most High, The Creator'), and by the generic affix *bārī* (Arabic, also 'Creator'), which appears as the second word in the famous *niṣāb*, known as the *Ḳhāliq Bārī*, attributed to Amīr Ḳhusrau.[79] This text, when read in parallel with the *Ḳhāliq Bārī*, is differentiated by its regularity in syntax[80] and a more systematic arrangement of terms into thematically related clusters.[81]

In many ways, the *Ṣamad Bārī/Jān Pahćān* is, from a pedagogical standpoint, far superior to its better-known generic antecedent, Ḳhusrau's *Ḳhāliq Bārī*. Nevertheless, Sayyid ᶜAbdullah's evaluation of this work is, as one might expect, especially damning:

> There cannot even be an expectation of any capacity or loftiness since it is written for young children; the result of this pedagogical objective (*madrasānah muṭmaḥ-i naẓar*) of Hāṅswī is that his definitions—even in the *Ġharāʾib al-Luġhat*—are superficial.[82]

Sayyid ᶜAbdullāh's blanket condemnation of ᶜAbdul Wāsĕᶜ's work as excessively pedagogical or, literally, "schoolish" (*madrasānah*), stems from what Janssen and others have described as an anxiety regarding occupational control—"the collective capability of members of an occupation to preserve unique authority in the definition, conduct and evaluation of their work"[83]—in the evaluations of cultural products. Insofar as the skills shared by precolonial lexicographers did not necessarily distinguish them from poets or chancellery officials (and many lexicographers performed these roles and more), Janssen's claim that artists did not possess "a monopoly of access to the knowledge that is needed to perform their tasks" applies equally to premodern lexicographers.[84] Moreover, while lexicographers, like artists, are certainly qualified and rarely hesitate to critique the work of other compilers, they do not possess (be it in the past or, indeed, in the present) the sole authority to evaluate lexicography. Readers, patrons, and a range of critics have all contributed to the evaluation of lexicographic products, both in ways that are obvious (for example, the monograph or journal article detailing "problems" with a particular work or lexicographic tradition)[85] and more subtle. For instance, each time a reader selects a particular lexicographic work for consultation from among others, and each time a user cites a particular definition as either correct or incorrect, that reader is evaluating the authority (or lack thereof) attributable to a particular text and, by extension, lexicographer. Likewise, the very presence of a lexicographic work in written form in a classroom or library reading room is a projection of that institution's authority onto that text.[86]

This lack of apparent "occupational control" among precolonial lexicographers suggests that instead of asking who in particular had the right to produce and publish a dictionary, a more fruitful line of inquiry would examine how a particular lexicographic text could accrue authority in the eyes of the broad range of potential evaluators, be they individual lexicographers, students, teachers, poets, British colonial officials, or various cultural and pedagogical institutions, and how the "stock" (reputational or commercial) of a particular work increases or decreases over time. Complicating this task, however, is the peculiarly intense intertextuality that characterizes both lexicographic works and the role of the lexicographers themselves as linguistic gatekeepers. Despite depictions of Hansi as a cultural backwater, ʿAbdul Wāsĕʿ did not produce his dictionary or *niṣāb*s in the "wilderness." Haryana and western India produced several notable literary figures during the seventeenth century. Mīr Muḥammad Jaʿfar 'Zaṭallī' (1659?–1713?), to cite just one, an early Urdu poet from nearby Narnaul (and a near contemporary of ʿAbdul Wāsĕʿ), was notorious for his satirical verse.[87] Despite complaints about being unable to acquire dictionaries, ʿAbdul Wāsĕʿ was aware of works that preceded his—though which works in particular, we cannot fully determine[88]—and understood himself as belonging within a broader Persianate lexicographic tradition.

As will become clear from a discussion of the prefatory material in both the *Ġharāʾib al-Luġhāt* and Ārzū's *Nawādir al-Alfāẓ*, from a sociological perspective, this textual community of lexicographers lacked (at least at the turn of the eighteenth century) many of the characteristics of a modern institution, and thus its professionalization may be deemed incomplete.[89] In spite of the absence of "occupational controls," Hāṅswī's own cultivation of lexicography as an occupation was far from accidental. As Janssen notes: "The question of how people become artists, in more than one respect, is and always has been a structured affair, and this was particularly true in earlier centuries."[90]

ʿAbdul Wāsĕʿ offers some indication of what brought him to write his dictionary in the unpublished preface to the work.[91] Following a formula of praise in Arabic, ʿAbdul Wāsĕ begins his brief introduction with several formulaic statements of humility as one who is "perfectly ignorant of the suitability of arrangement and appropriateness of composition." The author, in explaining his reasons for penning the work (*sabab-i taṣnīf*), suggests that while his companions requested the compilation of these "obscure names, a plenitude of things, and unfamiliar words," the benefits would extend beyond these "companions" and "intellects" to include a public of "ordinary ones" at large:

> Since it was desired by [his] companions and the abundant enthusiasm of many primary intellects, for these reasons the meanings of obscure names, a plenitude of things, and unfamiliar words mentioned among mankind shall be explicated through clear explanations and evident indications so that ordinary people (*ʿāmm*) can benefit from it and its advantage be realized.

ʿAbdul Wāsĕʿ's complaints about lacking resources—textual, temporal, monetary, and (most interestingly) interpersonal—may not be entirely attributable to the conventions of the Persianate preface, wherein authors preemptively deflect criticism through self-deprecation:

> Because of that—and despite the loss of advantage and the nonexistence of the aid of time and the nonacquisition of dictionaries and the unavailability of a facilitator of proficiency on which explanations and the forms of the names of things and the meaning of words should be derived—in these folios a line [would be taken] from authoritative dictionaries and some from the mouths and the discourse of trusted friends.

If one can assume that he compiled this work in Hansi, the question arises as to what access a scholar like ʿAbdul Wāsĕʿ would have had to the broader Persianate textual and social spheres, what C. A. Bayly has called a Persian "ecumene of Hindustani-writing literati, Indo-Islamic notables and officers of state (which included many Hindus)."[92] According to ʿAbdul Wāsĕʿ, "these [folios] together appeared in a text for limited distribution." Yet he also seems to anticipate a broader set of readers, including those who may not be familiar with the dialect of Hindi described in this text:

> Since the essence of words is extensive (*wāsĕʿ*: ample, large)[93] and knowledge of all details and trifles is reserved for the Wisest One, I expect from impartial intellects that, in the study of vowels and diacritical marks of the meanings [and] before delving deep into the dictionary and seeking the explicit meaning, if they notice any faults in meaning, they consider it as a variant of the word and not oppose it.

The last portion of the introduction further explains how the particular words that appear in this text were selected, namely for "meanings that are not understood," those "that are in opposition to ordinary dictionaries," and those that might serve "for the sake of correction":

> Hence the reason for the darkening of these folios is to arrive at words for the meanings—meanings that are not understood, which are in opposition to [those in] ordinary dictionaries, and [also] for the sake of correction—so that the discovery of a word for a meaning may become easy for everyone.

The final clause suggests that these words had been collected not so that their meanings may be easily discovered, as we might expect today, but rather so that a user might find particular "words for meanings."

To use the terms coined by Roland Barthes, ʿAbdul Wāsĕʿ's dictionary positions itself as a writerly (*lisible*) text, one that makes "the reader no longer a consumer, but a producer of the text." Barthes contrasts the writerly text with "its countervalue, its negative, reactive value: what can be read, but not written: the *readerly*." Readerly texts, he suggests, are those whose form is fixed and status in the canon is well established: "We call any readerly text a classic text."[94] The point of this dictionary, ʿAbdul Wāsĕʿ explains to us, is not as an aid to reading an already extant text (for he himself apologizes for being unable to acquire and cite these in his research) or as a means by which to determine the meaning of a particular arrangement of lexical items written on a page. It is rather to be used as a tool in producing *new* texts. ᶜAbdul Wāsĕᶜ's preface does not position the dictionary as the product of his own readings—for do these words exist yet in writing?—but rather introduces it for the user's *lexeographical* (literally "the writing of reading") use. When Hāṅswī declares the *Ġharāʾib* to be a sui generis work, it is not a vain boast or a Gilchristian denigration of past "Tom Thumb performances." ᶜAbdul Wāsĕᶜ apologizes for any faulty application of diacritics and indications of vowels, believing that these terms have never "blackened these folios" or graced any other writing surface before.

ĀRZŪ AND THE ORIGINS OF URDU TEXTUAL CRITICISM

In contrast to the uncertainty that attends any definitive statements about the life of ᶜAbdul Wāsĕᶜ, in the case of Ḳhān-i Ārzū (1687/8–1756) we are overwhelmed not merely by the abundance of works authored by him but also by the mass of materials written about him by his contemporaries and subsequent biographers.[95] Ārzū played an indispensable role in the history of Urdu literature, serving as tutor to a number of the most famous eighteenth-century poets of that language. While he did not himself compose much verse in the literary language of Delhi, then called *reḳhtah* (mixed, poured), he is acknowledged as among the greatest precolonial linguists of South Asia.[96] Ārzū has been credited as having been the first to discover the linguistic affinity between Old Persian and Sanskrit—this several decades prior to the essays on similar subjects by the famous Welsh Orientalist William Jones.[97] He compiled, in addition to the *Nawādir al-Alfāẓ*,[98] three other dictionaries: one minor work covering Persian verbs,[99] a second covering terms used in the Persian poetic canon to the year 1492,[100] and a third, the *Ćirāġh-i Hidāyat* (Lamp of wisdom), that covered Persian terms many of which more recently coined and therefore not appearing in extant dictionaries.[101] In this, the latter work may have resembled the *Bahār-i ᶜAjam* (1162/1748–1749) of Tek Ćand 'Bahār' (1687/8–1766/7), said to have been prepared with the assistance of native Persian speakers who had accompanied the invading Nadir Shah from Iran and Central Asia.[102] Far from lacking a "retrospective" linguistic gaze, Indian scholars—"Moosulman and Hindoo" alike[103]—were obsessed with categorizing, documenting, hierarchically ordering,[104] and improving the literary languages of Delhi.

Having secured, with the help of his friend Ānand Rām 'Muḳhliṣ' (1699–1751), a minor post in the imperial government and the patronage of some important noblemen, Ārzū had abundant time to devote to his research into lexicography and linguistics.[105] Ārzū took a liberal view with regard to the authority of Indian-born Persian poets and specifically argued for the acceptability of including Indic terms in Persian writing. This pitted him against the Iranian poet Mīr Muḥammad Bāqar 'Ḥazīn' (d. 1752) in a linguistic battle fought out over numerous tracts and treatises.[106] This debate would reemerge in the nineteenth century, beginning in a polemic tract by the celebrated poet Mirzā Asadullāh 'Ġhālib' (1797–1869), in which he criticized several dictionaries compiled by Indian-born lexicographers, though at that time, comparatively few Persian dictionaries had ever been compiled inside Iran.[107] Ġhālib denied the authority of any Indian-born Persianist on linguistic matters while at the same time claiming authority for himself through a combination of a "natural affinity" with Persian and his having studied as a youth with a Persian emigré.[108] Faruqi sums up the debate neatly: "Khān-e Ārzū and his friends regarded the Iranians as human, and liable to error. Ghālib regarded all Iranians . . . as little short of God."[109]

We know the date Ārzū published his revisions to ᶜAbdul Wāsĕᶜ's *Ġharāʾib* from information he provides in his entry for the Sanskrit-derived term *baisākh*, denoting "the first of the twelve months constituting the Hindū solar year," equivalent to April–May:[110]

> Yet the distinction between *baisākh* and *farwardī* [the first month of the Persian year, corresponding with March][111] is coincidental, such that this year the New Year (*nau-roz*) took place on the 24th of Muḥarram 1156 [March 21, 1743], and that is the new moon of *farwardī*, and in *baisākh* there must be nineteen or twenty days.[112]

Ārzū, like ᶜAbdul Wāsĕᶜ, provides a preface in which he explains the reasons for compiling his revisions, beginning:

> Says the poor wretch Sirājuddīn ᶜAlī with the pen name Ārzū that one among the fortunate learned men and famous scholars of Hindustan (the vision of Paradise) compiled a book in the art of lexicography entitled *Ġharāʾib al-Luġhāt*, and Hindi words, which became [part of] the Persian or Arabic or Turkish of that, the everyday talk of the people of lesser homes, those [words]

> are spelled out with their meanings such that in [ʿAbdul Wāsěʿ's] explanation of the meaning of words, careless expressions or defects (*tasāhule yā suqum*) came into view, and with this, having brought the pen to the manuscript in this chapter, in the places where he [Ārzū] discovered omissions and errors, an indication was made on it, and then those things which in diligent pursuit of the deficient he [Ārzū] wished to complete this and improve upon this.[113]

At this point, one would feel that Ārzū is showing great restraint in his criticism of his predecessor's work. By introducing "Hindi terms" as entering into the "everyday talk of the people of lesser homes [or regions, *ahl-i diyār-i kamtar*]," we may see that he is at best ambivalent about their inclusion in the Arabic, Persian, and Turkish of these people. Indeed, the "intruder" depicted here is Hindi, as opposed to the typical colonial-era depictions of Persian, Arabic, and Turkish as "foreign-imposed" languages of "invaders."

This is somewhat surprising in light of his statements in another work regarding the permissibility of Indic terms appearing in Persian poetry. In the following translation of a chapter entitled "An Exposition on the Use of Non-Fārsī Terms in Fārsī" from the *Muśmir*, his pathbreaking work on linguistics, Ārzū justifies the use of Indic terms in Persian poetry, arguing that if Arabic, Turkic, and even Armenian terms could find a place in the Persian language, surely Indic terms, by dint of a long shared history, could do the same. He sought to prove this by demonstrating that a great master of Persian poetry like 'Sanāʾī' (fl. late eleventh–early twelfth centuries) writing outside India could still include the Indic term *pānī* in his poetry:

> The importation of not just Arabic and Turkish terms, but also the Armenian language into Fārsī is accepted (*musallam*), but [the question still] remains [for] Hindi terms, and that is still not established in a familiar way (*běmażhab-i muʾlif*) in this language, though in the writings of the teachers it happens in this way that if a Hindi term appears in writing it is without any trouble considered to be correct by the general consensus of the people of poetry (*bijtimāʾ-i ahl-i naẕm*), [for according to] 'Sanāʾī':

nah darān maʿidah ḳhadrah-yi maidah	There was nary a bit of flour in that stomach
na darān dīdah qaṭrah-yi pānī	Nor a drop of water in that eye[114]

> And this I have written in the *Mauhbat-i ʿUẕmā*[115] that logically, if the Arabic and Turkish terms exist in the idiom of most, and everyone accepts it, then why should the importation of Hindi terms not be permitted? At the same time in a connected investigation . . . the Arabic language, because of the exercise of dominion by the Arabs over Persia (*ʿajam*), the faith of the Arabs alongside the companions of Islam, and the entanglement of the ancient Fārsī books, appeared mixed and mingled with the Fārsī language to this extent that most ancient usages of this language left its speech. . . . The importation of Arabic words in this language is certainly correct, and moreover the use of Arabic words is most eloquent (*afṣaḥ*) in spite of the [existence of] ancient Persian words, and [it is] on this analogy that Turkish words because of vicissitudes of time (*taqallab o taṣarruf*) became blended with Fārsi. It is true that many of the meanings of Persian words also came from Turkish, for example: *qurch* ['armory'], *pāshī* ['a diffusion', 'irrigation'], and *īshīk aġhāsī*[116] *bāshī* ['chief usher'], and all other things meaning the ranks of the people in the military, and those of management and supervision of the cavalry, and in the house in the service of them, and what they called at first in Hindustan Mīr Baḳhshī, and second Mīr Tozak, and both of these terminologies (*iṣṭilāh*) of the kings are in this place [i.e., in Hindustan]. Why then cannot the analogy of Hindi with these two languages be made to the extent that it is heard [in India]? And this must be cut short, and whatever this poor one (*wāshilah*) desires, God most high willing, the Divine will apportion according to the capacity of each.[117]

We might then ask why Indian lexicographers were so hesitant to write definitions of Hindvi vocabulary in either Hindi or Urdu. The answer to this is related, no doubt, to the perceived superiority of Persian and Sanskrit as "classical" languages particularly suited to prose expositions of scholarly material.[118] This preference for Persian prose over Urdu was by no means unique to the field of lexicography. As Frances Pritchett has noted:

> Like almost all other Urdu literary genres, the *tazkirah* tradition [sometimes glossed in English as "biographical dictionaries," typically of poets or Sufi saints] was taken over from Persian; in fact, until well into the nineteenth century most *tazkirahs* of Urdu poetry were themselves written in Persian. . . . Just to complicate the picture, however, it should be kept in mind that the first *tazkirahs* of Persian poetry itself were Indian: they were composed in Sind, in the early thirteenth century.[119]

Here, one could easily replace the term *tażkirah* in every instance with *farhang* (typically used in modern Urdu as an equivalent to the English "dictionary"). Indeed, just as Arabic lexicography was by and large developed by Persians, Persian lexicography was by and large the product of Indian philologists.[120]

The lack of completely monolingual works should not be taken as proof of the complete absence of Hindi/Urdu as a glossing language.[121] When the first monolingual dictionary of Urdu was finally published in 1849 it was several centuries after the proliferation of versified multilingual glossaries of the late fifteenth and early sixteenth centuries,[122] not to mention works from the previous two centuries, like Hāṅswī's *Ġharāʾib al-Luġhāt* and the early European glossaries of Hindi-Urdu.[123] The literary historian Ḥāfiẓ Maḥmūd Sherānī has shown that almost every premodern Persian dictionary produced in South Asia would occasionally provide an Indic synonym for especially difficult Persian terms.[124] These dictionaries, produced in places as diverse as Bengal, Bihar, the Deccan, Malwa, Gujarat, Delhi, and the Punjab, all use more or less the same language, namely what was called Hindvi. Lest one believe, warns Sherānī, that this was merely the result of Persian lexicographers' supposed penchant for uncritically copying the work of their predecessors,[125] the stock of terms glossed in Hindvi by these authors is by no means consistent, and where Indic terms recur from text to text, interesting variants appear.[126] As Sherānī put it, "It should also be remembered that the original intention of giving currency to Hindi terms in Persian dictionaries was to explicate difficult or ambiguous terms which could be done in a concise and easy way that otherwise were felt to require long and difficult explanations."[127]

From this interesting observation, Sherānī then draws a conclusion that is more an indication of his own Muslim nationalist objectives than a reflection of the uses to which the texts were subjected. He thus claims with great aplomb, "for this reason, such a language [i.e., Hindi-Urdu], spoken and understood by Muslims, was necessary" for glossing Persian terms. Continuing, he adds, "from this evidence, we come to the correct conclusion that these words are connected with that general shared language that in our time is known *as Urdu* and those words which are found in the *farhang*s of the eight and ninth centuries AH are the earliest materials (*sarmāyah*) of the Urdu language."[128]

By explicitly identifying the common language of these works as Urdu (and not as Hindi, Hindvi, etc.) and as the language "spoken and understood by *Muslims*," he is eliding two important further considerations that, having examined a broader set of materials, one cannot ignore. First, the more deeply one examines the history of literary Hindi-Urdu, the more inextricably it seems bound to the Persian language. Thus, Ārzū deserves credit for enriching the lexical stock of both Hindi-Urdu *and* Persian in his own time through his various lexicographic, linguistic, and poetic productions. Second, Persian was a language that was (and, to a more limited extent, even now continues to be) studied and produced by non-Muslims.[129]

Hindus were so successful in acquiring Persian that by the end of the seventeenth century bilingual Sanskrit–Persian vocabularies were promulgated with the ostensible purpose of teaching Hindus new clerical terms to curtail the widespread use of Persian.[130] Sumit Guha has argued that as the cultural and political confidence of the Maratha successor state rose to new heights in the late seventeenth century under Shivājī, the linguistic policy (though "policy" might suggest an undeserved coherence and legality to what might better be termed a more vague "intentionality") pursued through the emerging bureaucracy sought to replace not so much the *language* of the Mughal imperium but rather its *vocabulary*. One of the means by which this substitution was achieved was through the preparation of "a thesaurus of official usage" entitled *Rājavyavahārakośa*, purportedly produced as a guide to the young Maratha leader Shivājī, around or somewhat after his coronation in 1676. Valerie Ritter describes what she believes to be a similar process at play in Mahārājā Pratāp Nārāyaṇ Singh's publication of a Braj-medium exposition on Sanskrit poetics at the turn of the twentieth century:

> In addition to glosses throughout, a glossary rephrases poetics terms like *upamā* as *tashbīh*, suggesting that the audience for this text was undergoing a transformation and perhaps that the Maharaja was consciously reintroducing Bhasha specifically instead of current Urdu poetic practices.[131]

The British incorporation of Mughal administrative terms is well documented in numerous official glossaries and dictionaries of administrative vocabulary. Efforts to de-Persianize the language of administration continue in India to this day. Notwithstanding the efforts of the Indian government to limit Persian-, Arabic-, Turkish-, and English-derived words in its official glossary of administrative terms, the Standing Commission for Scientific and Technical Terminology was nevertheless compelled to include the occasional "non-Hindi" word: for example, *ghairhājirī* (*ġhair-ḥāẓirī*) for "absence," *ṭeṅdar* for "tender," and *hisāb* (*ḥisāb*) for "account." The primary objectives of the project, "to maintain as far as practicable a uniform all-India character" and "to achieve the maximum possible identity of terms in Indian languages," were evaluated against the "simplicity, precision, and easy intelligibility besides the currency that some of these terms have already gained in the various regions." It seems, however, that the latter considerations were considered only in the absence of Sanskrit-derived equivalents.[132]

In Ārzū's introduction to the *Nawādir*, the author, having concluded his discussion of the reasons for compiling the dictionary, presents an impressive display of literary fireworks in praise of potential patrons. These include the hope that "that the ray of favor of the addressee may have the shadow of the wing of the *Humā* [a bird of happy omen, prognosticating a crown to every head it overshades]" and that through "the shade of his [patron's] favors, the preface of the book may have every beauty of the seal of the imperial signature (*ḥusn-i k̤hātimah-i tuġhrā*)." Aware that "excessive and habitual self-applause is the livelihood of wicked poets," he nevertheless offers two verses that show the unique power of the lexicographer. The first verse may be translated literally as:

luġhat nawīsh k̤hirad dar ṣaḥāh himmat-i ū
ba-maᶜnī-i luġhat-i andak āwarad bisyār

[For] the writer of words, [there is] wisdom in his perfect power
To the meaning of a small word, he brings forth multitude (*bisyār*)

The phrase *luġhat nawīsh*, understood generically, literally means the "writer of a language/word"; it also serves as a technical term denoting a lexicographer (an English term that itself means a "writer of words") and thus announces a new set of denotations attached to the other terms that appear in this verse. Thus, the term *ṣaḥāḥ*, translated in the verse above as "perfect," is also the title of a famous Arabic dictionary of the fourth/tenth century.[133] Likewise, the term *k̤hirad* (wisdom) appears identical to its homograph *k̤hurd* (minute, small). This verse, reinterpreted in light of its lexicographical subject matter, offers up a far richer tribute to his craft:

[For] the lexicographer, his power in the *Ṣahāh* [is] wisdom/minute:
To the meaning of the word *andak* ['small'] he brings forth *bisyār* ['abundance', 'multitude']

In the verse that follows, he adds:

> *wa gumān-i faqīr 'Ārzū' miṣraᶜah-i s̈ānī īn qism*
> *ba-maʾnī-i luġhat-i kam biyāwarad bisyār*

> And the fancy of the *faqīr* 'Ārzū' in the second hemistich is of this nature
> [That] to the meaning of the word *kam* ['little'] he brings forth a multitude (*bisyār*)

As Ārzū explains, this ability to make the word for "little" appear as "great" is not magic, for "originally, according to the *Ṣaḥāh,* the term *kam* [in Persian, 'a little', 'less'] in Arabic means *bisyār* ['much', 'a multitude'] . . . and it is most proper (*alyaq*) with that meaning."[134]

The arrangement of terms in the *Ġharāʾib al-Luġhāt* gives some indication of the technique by which ᶜAbdul Wāsĕᶜ compiled his work. Headwords are arranged only with regard to their first letter. Ārzū noted this in his introduction the *Nawādir:*

> It should also not remain hidden that since in the *Ġharāʾib al-Luġhāt* there is no observance of the second letter, it was difficult to bring order to the words . . . it is hoped that from the generous gentlemen that this will be acceptable to the knowers of the language (*maqbūl-i zabān dānān*).

Ārzū sought to improve upon this scheme by arranging them alphabetically with regard to each letter. ᶜAbdul Wāsĕᶜ's method of arrangement by first letter only conforms to what one expects to find in a "paper poor" social setting. Lloyd Daly noted in his survey of the history of alphabetization in the Greek and Latinate traditions:

> Early examples of alphabetization do not fully exploit the possibilities of the principle. It is applied only to the first letter of words or, at most, to the first two or three letters. It may well be supposed that this degree of systematization was an entirely satisfactory achievement. The time and effort it would save would not be inconsiderable. And if fuller alphabetization was contemplated at this stage it must be remembered that the pains it would have taken to achieve absolute order would probably not have repaid the effort. Without slips on which to set down individual items so that they may be re-sorted the process is not easy and I know of no evidence that such an extravagant use of writing material was ever made in antiquity.[135]

Allowing, mutatis mutandis, for a change in the medium of inscription from papyrus to paper or parchment, the same situation also obtained in seventeenth-century Hansi as that which prevailed in the Mediterranean region in antiquity and throughout the medieval period in Europe, when "alphabetization was carried out by means of sheets with fixed allowance of space for entries under each letter of the alphabet, and that the items to be alphabetized were then transferred to these spaces."[136] ᶜAbdul Wāsĕᶜ's method of arrangement thus demonstrates a significant differential in resources available to a figure like Ārzū in the imperial center from those obtainable by ᶜAbdul Wāsĕᶜ in the imperial hinterland, including in their access to earlier dictionaries produced by others. Indeed, it is no accident that the most famous "monumental" dictionaries of Persian were often copied in imperial and subimperial ateliers and commissioned by emperors, independent *sulṭāns*, and wealthy noblemen.[137]

Ārzū effectively writes ᶜAbdul Wāsĕᶜ out of the tradition. He is only referred to in Ārzū's introduction as "one among the fortunate learned men and famous scholars of Hindustan," and the *Ġharāʾib al-Luġhāt* is denoted throughout the body of the *Nawādir* merely by the generic term *risālah* (treatise). Ārzū did not hesitate to cite the celebrated Persian poet Amīr Ḳhusrau by name as an authority in several entries, even going so far as to cite an apparently nonexistent verse by Ḳhusrau in support of his definition of *ćakāwak* (ruddy goose).[138] In contrast to this, Ārzū only makes reference to the author of the *Ġharāʾib* as an individual on those occasions when he judges the definition provided in the earlier "treatise" to be doubtful *because* of its author's provincial origins. To cite an especially evocative example, Ārzū begins his entry on the term *ḍabbā* in a way that is typical for the work, quoting ᶜAbdul Wāsĕᶜ's definition in full:

> *ḍabbā*[139]—in the treatise (*risālah*): "a piece of flesh which a camel takes out from the mouth during the rutting season, *shiqshiqah*[140] the *shīn* diacritically marked with a *kasr*, and the *qāf* clipped (*zadah*) and *shīn* and *qāf* both with *fatḥah*."[141]

This rather obscure definition refers to a phenomenon known in English as the "exteriorization of the soft palate," which occurs in male dromedary camels.[142] In his discussion of the definition, however, Ārzū takes great pains to differentiate himself from Hāṅswī:

> But the mentioned term is not of the knowing ones of the imperial camp (*mutaᶜarrif-i urdūʾi bādshāhī*) and of the language (*zabān*) of Akbarābād and

> Shāhjahānābād, [but] is the language of the native land of the author of the treatise (*zabān-i waṭan-i ṣāḥib-i risālah*).[143]

This passage is fascinating not merely for Ārzū's disdain for the language of "the native land of the author" of the treatise—which remains unworthy of specific mention—but also for the interesting use of the term *urdū*. Though Iqtida Hasan has claimed that Ārzū is the first to use this term to denote a language,[144] the literary historian Shamsur Rahman Faruqi argues that this instance of the term *urdū* properly refers to a particular place: "Ḳhān-e Ārzū, in the *Navādir*, constantly uses both *urdū* and *urdū-i muʿallā* to mean Delhi."[145] The entry in the *Nawādir al-Alfāẓ* that Faruqi cites in support of the supposed equation of the *urdū-i muʿallāh* with Delhi corresponds with the term *ćhanīl*, which Ārzū believes to be a corruption of *ćhināl*, "a courtesan":

> *ćhanīl* in the treatise (*risālah*): "a woman who brings her head out from the home and who, when looking out, returns back again, *ṯulaʿah*; with the unmarked *ṯāʾ* [i.e., ط] with a *ẕammah*, and the *lām* [ل] and unmarked *ʿain* [i.e., ع] carrying *fataḥ*." But it is unknown where this word *ćhanīl* is from. We who are the people of Hind and who live in the *urdū-i muʿallā*, we have not heard [this word]. And it is clear that it is *ćhināl*, with the connected meaning of "an evil-doing woman" which they call in Fārsī *rūspī* ['courtesan'] . . . and *jalab* ['courtesan'] . . . and *ḳhushnī* ['harlot'].

Sayyid ʿAbdullāh points out in his 1951 introduction to the printed edition of the work that Ārzū subjected this definition to particular scrutiny:

> One of the peculiarities of the *Ġharāʾib* is that its Urdu terms bear the mark of a Haryānī pronunciation and accent. That is to say, we see that Ḳhān-i 'Ārzū' in critiquing the *Ġharāʾib* in the *Nawādir al-Alfāẓ* severely objects to Hāṅswī's rustic (*gaṅwārī*) pronunciation and accent. Such words which are peculiar to Hāryāna appear in great number in the *Ġharāʾib*.[146]

Ārzū believes—with good cause, it must be admitted—that ʿAbdul Wāsĕʿ's definition ("a woman who brings her head out from the home and who, when looking out, returns back again") is misattributed to this word, belonging more properly to the synonym ʿAbdul Wāsĕʿ proffers immediately after, that is, *ṯulaʿah*, which the nineteenth-century German lexicographer Francis Steingass defines as "a woman who now peeps out and anon withdraws"[147] and which John Richardson, one century earlier, presents as "(a woman) now peeping out, and then withdrawing herself."[148] It is clear from the similarity of ʿAbdul Wāsĕʿ's Persian definition of the Hindvi *ćhanīl* to the English definitions from Richardson and Steingass of the Persian *ṭulaʿah* that they are derived from a common source. Since the term *ṭulaʿah* does not appear with this definition in any of the great seventeenth-century Persian dictionaries—the *Farhang-i Jahāngīrī* (1607), *Burhān-i Qāṭĕʿ* (1651), and the *Farhang-i Rashīdī* (1654)[149]—ʿAbdul Wāsĕʿ is the probable source for the later Persian–English dictionaries of Richardson and Steingass in which it does. Indeed, further support for this view comes from the absence of this term even in Ārzū's own *Ćirāġh-i Hidāyat* (1147/1734–1735) and other important dictionaries of the eighteenth century. More immediately, this view supports ʿAbdul Wāsĕʿ's claim in his preface to the "nonacquisition of dictionaries (*kutb-i luġhāt*)" in preparation of his work.

Significantly, it gives us some insight into ʿAbdul Wāsĕʿ's method of composition: rather than seeking only to define those Hindvi terms "for nonunderstood meanings, the meanings of words meant in opposition to common dictionaries, and for the sake of education [or 'correction', *tarbiyat*]," he may have been projecting onto his intended readers the method that he deployed himself, namely that of discovering "a word for a meaning." Stated another way, ʿAbdul Wāsĕʿ's aim was not necessarily to provide Persian equivalents and definitions for Hindvi terms but also to offer Hindvi terms as equivalents for Persian terms. Much as we might wish to imagine ʿAbdul Wāsĕʿ wandering the fields that surround Hansi, collecting the speech of the "common folk" he met along the way and, returning home, defining them in Persian, his impetus appears to have been quite different.

South Asian readers and writers—these were not always one and the same—participating within the "Persian ecumene" were familiar with two or more languages, possessing sometimes subtly different, sometimes dramatically divergent competencies in each. Hindvi was probably widely understood in its spoken form and accommodated a great deal of diversity in pronunciation. The orthography of Persian and Arabic, inasmuch as they existed primarily as written languages in South Asia, were relatively fixed and stable across regions. Ārzū does not fault ʿAbdul Wāsĕʿ with equating that particular Persian definition ("a woman who brings her head out from the home and who, when looking out, returns back again") with the Persian equivalent that follows it (*ṭulaʿah*). If he had, then no doubt Richardson and Steingass would not have uncritically reprinted ʿAbdul Wāsĕʿ's definition in their own works. Rather, he vehemently disagrees with the association of these two elements from ʿAbdul Wāsĕʿ's original entry with a particular Hindvi headword, *ćhanīl*. Ārzū does not deny that there may be a Hindvi word with the meaning of "a woman who brings her head out from the home and who, when looking out, returns back again" or that this particular denotation is associated with the Persian *ṭulaʿah*. He merely says that the vocable *ćhanīl* is unknown to him (and people like him) and that a similar term, *ćhināl*, corresponds more properly with certain other Persian terms (that is, *rūspī*, *jalab*, and *ḳhushnī*).

Embedded within Ārzū's criticism is a reference to his own place within an authoritative group of language users ("*We* who are the people of Hind and who live in the *urdū-i muʿallā*") and, by implication, ʿAbdul Wāsĕʿ's apparent exclusion from it. It is quite clear from his phrasing—the use of the locative *dar urdū-i muʿallā* (in the exalted camp)—that this is a reference to the royal, sometimes peripatetic, encampment of the Mughal-Timurid emperor. For Shamsur Rahman Faruqi,

> It is thus obvious that in the 1750s, the terms *urdū*, *urdū-e muʿallā*, and *zabān-e urdū-e muʿallā* did not, at least among the elite, mean the language which is known as Urdu today. When used alone, *urdū* would, more often than not, mean "royal city" (therefore, Delhi). We just saw Ḳhān-e Ārzū freely using *urdū* in this sense, without the least hint that he was using a neologism or that he was using the word in a special sense.[150]

Be this as it may, the use of the term *urdū* in Ārzū's entry on *ḍabbā* as "not of the knowing ones of the imperial camp (*mutaʿarrif-i urdūʾe bādshāhī*) *and* of the language (*zabān*) of Akbarābād and Shāhjahānābād" (emphasis added) suggests that the term *urdū* was employed more generically than Farurqi suggests. The copresence of both phrases—*urdū-i bādshāhī* (imperial camp) and *zabān-i* (language of) *Akbarābād o Shāhjahānābād*—within the same sentence demonstrates that *urdū* did not possess, by itself or in enclitically joined compounds like *urdū-i bādshāhī* or *urdū-i muʿallā* (exalted camp), the toponymic specificity of denoting a particular city, whether it may be Agra (Akbarābād), Delhi (Shāhjahānābād), or some other place. It would not, however, be unreasonable to assume that if Ārzū was employed in compiling his work over an extended period,[151] the denotation of the term *urdū* may, by 1743, have acquired a topographic specificity that it did not possess a few years earlier.

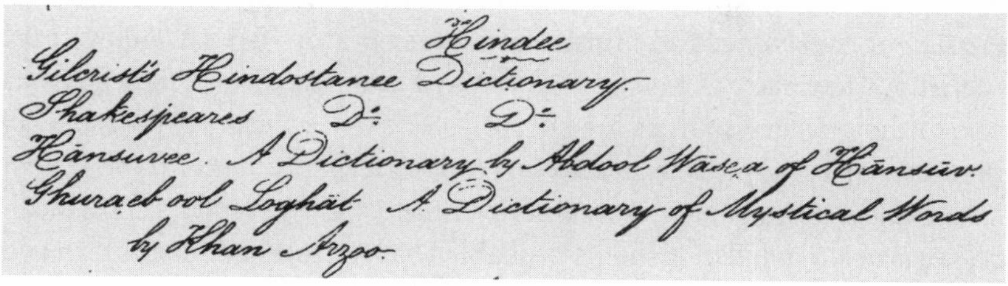
Hindee
Gilcrist's Hindostanee Dictionary.
Shakespeares D: D:
Hānsuvee. A Dictionary by Abdool Wāsea of Hānsūv.
Ghuraeb ool Loghāt A Dictionary of Mystical Words
by Khan Arzoo

FIGURE 2.1 Notice of "Hindee" dictionaries employed in Breton's Vocabulary

As Faruqi himself remarks, the imperial camp could not have referred to Delhi any earlier than 1648, when Shāh Jahān formally invested the "new" city of Shāhjahānābād with imperial status.[152] From Ārzū's position in Shāhjahānābād during the middle of the eighteenth century, identifying the city in which he currently resided with *urdū-i bādshāhī* may not have seemed entirely natural: Aurangzeb had established a new capital in the Deccan and called it Aurangabad, Bahādur Shāh spent much of his short reign (1707–1712) in Lahore, and Shāh ʿĀlam II (r. 1759–1806) spent many years exiled in Allahabad. The imperial treasury had been traditionally located in Agra (Akbarābād), and that city continued to enjoy a special imperial status well into the eighteenth century.[153] Ārzū himself would depart for Lucknow two years after completing the *Nawādir*, his body being returned to Delhi only after his death in 1756 to be buried in Vakilpura, a neighborhood to the north of Delhi's Jāmĕʿ Masjid. Regardless of whether the *urdū-i bādshāhī* referred to Delhi, Agra, or the abstract notion of the site of the imperial camp, wherever it might be, it certainly was not located in Hansi.

A DICTIONARY'S ADMINISTRATIVE AFTERLIFE

ʿAbdul Wāsĕʿ, who received so much criticism from Ārzū and who might with justification complain from the grave of enjoying only the companionship of solitude and the friendship of friendlessness, was nevertheless dutifully read by scholars at the end of the eighteenth century. Beginning perhaps with John Richardson's (1740/41–1795) *Dictionary, Persian, Arabic, and English* (1777),[154] European lexicographers ardently studied the *Ġharāʾib* and *Nawādir* in search of terms that might assist them in understanding both the "grand speech" of Hindustan and the classical Persian of government administration. Peter Breton listed a "*Ghura,eb ool Loghāt*, A Dictionary of Mystical Words by Khan Arzoo" (see figure 2.1) as one of the primary sources for his 1825 work, *A Vocabulary of the Names of the Various Parts of the Human Body and of Medical and Technical Terms in English, Arabic, Persian, Hindee, and Sanscrit for the Use of the Members of the Medical Department in India.* It seems probable that Breton had misunderstood the *Ġharā᾽ib* to be the title of Ārzū's revision, having, like most, accessed the content of the former through the latter.[155]

The title page of the National Archives of India manuscript copy of the *Nawādir al-Alfāẓ* indicates that it was copied "through H. Blochmann by a Kátib attached to the Calcutta Musalmán Madrassah 1870."[156] Heinrich Ferdinand Blochmann (1838–1878), a German-born professor of Arabic and Persian who was principal at the Calcutta Madrassa, was best known for his translations of the first volume of the *Ā᾽in-i Akbarī*, an important document of the reign of the Mughal emperor Akbar.[157] This copy of *Nawādir al-Alfāẓ*, originally part of the College of Fort William Collection, was copied after Blochmann's reappointment as professor of Persian at the Calcutta Madrassa in 1865. In 1868, Blochmann published a seminal essay, "Contributions to Persian Lexicography," which remains among the most useful works on the topic available in English. It also served as an early prospectus for a project ultimately overseen by another German, Francis Joseph Steingass (1825–1903), who compiled a revised and expanded edition of Richardson's Persian dictionary for a work that was ultimately published in 1892.[158] Blochmann also wrote an 1877 essay on the history, inscriptions, and famous individuals of Hansi in which he lists ᶜAbdul Wāsĕᶜ as the fifth (and last) Hansi "celebrity" hailing from that city. In that entry, he writes,

> His Persian grammar, entitled *Risálah-i-᾽Abdul-Wási᾽* is read in every Madrasah in India. He also wrote in Persian an Urdú Dictionary of Technical (chiefly Agricultural) Terms, which he entitled *Gharáib-ullughát*. This book, copies of which are very rare, was criticized by Siráj-uddín ᾽Alí Khán Árzú in his *Nawádir-ul-Alfáz*, likewise a rare Urdú Dictionary of Technical Terms. Sir H. Elliot used the latter work extensively for his "Supplemental Glossary."[159]

The importance of the *Ġharā᾽ib al-Luġhāt*'s to later colonial lexicographical projects is also hinted at in a note on the title page of the National Archives of India manuscript copy of the *Nawādir al-Alfāẓ*. This note identifies Ārzū's dictionary as "the source of Sir H. M. Elliot's Glossary."[160] This particular copy of *Nawādir al-Alfāz* intersperses blank pages between folios of the original text in Perso-Arabic script, a clear indication of Blochmann's intent to translate or transcribe in Roman script Ārzū's text on the blank facing pages. The only material that appears in translation, however, is the opening formula, "In the name of God," appearing between the pages numbered 3 and 4.

The "glossary" that Blochmann mentions in his note on the manuscript's title page and, again, in his 1877 essay, refers to the *Supplement to the Glossary of Indian Terms* compiled by Henry Miers Elliot (1808–1853) and first published in 1845.[161] It originated in 1842 as a "rough glossary" circulated to British East India Company officers employed throughout South Asia.[162] These company officials were requested to return the glossary after noting in a blank right-hand column local equivalents for revenue terms printed on the left. They were instructed by the prominent Sanskritist and project superintendent, Horace Hayman Wilson (1786–1860), to record these terms in "the native characters of the district in which the words were current" and, further, to "subjoin full, careful, and accurate explanations of their meaning."[163] The response of these officials to this project, however, proved unsatisfactory.[164] In his 1870 review of the expanded second edition, E. B. Cowell stated: "The scheme on the whole proved a failure; little interest was taken in it in India, and few of the returned papers added much to our previous knowledge."[165] Wilson remarked in the introduction to his own 1855 *Glossary of Judicial and Revenue Terms* that "so little interest was felt in India in the subject, such was the unwillingness to devote any time or trouble to the task," with even those who flattered themselves as possessing an aptitude for Oriental languages neglecting this duty.[166] Some even seemed to mock the exercise: "More than one . . . in Upper India," Wilson complains, "turned to Shakespear's [1834] Hindustani Dictionary, and deliberately covered the blank pages of the Glossary with words taken at random from the Lexicon."[167] With obvious disappointment, Wilson concedes, "the fate which has attended a measure so judiciously conceived, and so well calculated to have brought together a large body of valuable information of the most authentic character, is far from creditable to the public zeal and philological proficiency of the East-India Company's Civil Service."[168]

The lone "honourable exception" among the otherwise desultory contributions was that of Sir Henry Elliot, praised by Wilson as "a most zealous and accomplished Oriental scholar, and an enlightened and efficient public officer."[169] The Sudder Board of Revenue, North-Western Provinces, encouraged Elliot to publish his glossary, considering its focus on terms in use throughout the North-Western Provinces (comprising parts of present-day Uttar Pradesh, Uttarakhand, Haryana, and eastern Rajasthan) to be "a highly valuable addition to the original *Glossary*."[170] Limiting himself to terms that had little coverage in "the common Dictionaries" and drawing heavily upon Ārzū's *Nawādir al-Alfāz*, Elliot modestly describes his research as comprising only "a few notices respecting the tribes, the customs, the fiscal and agricultural terms" of the North-Western Provinces. In 1845, he had completed the first volume of his *Supplement to the Glossary of Indian Terms* to the letter *J*. The second volume remained incomplete at his death in 1853. Copies of the first edition of the *Supplement to the Glossary of Indian Terms* had become difficult to obtain, however, within a few years of its first printing.[171] Though much of its content was incorporated by H. H. Wilson into his 1855 *Glossary of Judicial and Revenue Terms*,[172] a second edition of Elliot's *Supplement* was brought out in 1869 after undergoing significant enlargement and revision by the Indian Civil Service officer John Beames (1837–1902).

The title of this second edition, *Memoirs on the History, Folk-Lore, and Distribution of the Races of the North Western Provinces of India: Being an Amplified Edition of the Original Supplemental Glossary of Indian Terms*, reflects the more encyclopedic and descriptive scope Beames envisioned for the revised *Glossary*. He modified the basic alphabetical arrangement (by Roman transliteration) of Wilson's 1842 *Glossary* and Elliot's 1845 *Supplement* by reverting to Elliot's original plan of providing definitions only for "the tribes, the customs, the fiscal and agricultural terms." To this end, Beames separated the list of terms into four sections: (1) castes and their subdivisions; (2) customs, rites, and superstitions; (3) revenue and official terms; and (4) terms illustrative of rural life. A large portion of the third section of Beames's revised edition had already appeared, as mentioned above, in H. H. Wilson's 1855 *Glossary of Judicial and Revenue Terms*. Though Beames justified these modifications as having been "already hinted at by the author [i.e., Elliot] in the Memorandum prefixed to the first edition,"[173] the historian Shahid Amin has argued that it was also enabled by other epistemological trends that emerged in the latter half of the eighteenth century. For Amin, the shift in macrostructural arrangement from a single alphabetical list into multiple lists based on thematic categories fits within a pattern of allied colonial projects—most notably, the decennial census—that relied upon elaborate classification schemes: "the systematic counting of heads and the arrangement of agricultural terms were both part of the same late-nineteenth-century movement from a descriptive to a classificatory representation of colonial India."[174] However, a tradition of classifying lexical material thematically extends well beyond the South Asian experience with European colonialism. If anything, the classificatory system employed by Beames was less elaborate than that observed in Breton's medical *Vocabulary* or the glossaries prepared at the turn of the nineteenth century by Gladwin and Leyden (see chapter 1).

Amin contends that the significance of Elliot's work lies in its having "created a field, encouraging others to report rustic terms." The importance of Elliot's glossary to later colonial lexicographic projects, including those prepared entirely through the agency, initiative, and capital investments of South Asians, cannot be overstated except in this regard: Amin represents Elliot as compiling his dictionary, in Gilchristian fashion, ex nihilo and viva voce. Elliot makes no such claims: his 1845 edition is a modestly titled *Supplement to the Glossary of Indian Terms*; that is to say, his additions to the 1842 India House glossary are "taken chiefly from a list of words collected by the late Mr. Warden during his residence at Bombay" and circulated to government officials.[175] Lexicographers suffer far less from the "anxiety of influence" than one might expect: successive texts derive their authority in part through the citation and incorporation of previous works.[176] These intertextual borrowings at times include the wholesale absorption of one text into another. At the end of this chain of reference, which extends from ʿAbdul Wāsĕʿ in the seventeenth century through Ārzū in the eighteenth to Breton, Elliot, and Wilson in the nineteenth, are two late nineteenth-century projects by William Crooke (1848–1923) and George Abraham Grierson (1851–1941). Grierson's 1885 *Bihar Peasant Life* hewed so closely to Crooke's 1879 *Glossary of North Indian Peasant Life* that the former admitted to have "not scrupled to use his very words":[177] "Not only the 'general system and arrangement,' but also hundreds of words and entire sentences, are common to the *Materials* and *Bihar Peasant Life*: Grierson seems to have incorporated Crooke's work so completely as to have almost consumed it."[178] Amin's observations, however, would apply equally as well to Elliot's influence on Crooke, not to mention that of ʿAbdul Wāsĕʿ on Ārzū and, in turn, Ārzū on Elliot.

To illustrate this chain of reference with a concrete example, the term *aiwārā* (ایوارا) can be traced from its first appearance in ʿAbdul Wāsĕʿ's dictionary to its nineteenth-century renditions in works produced during

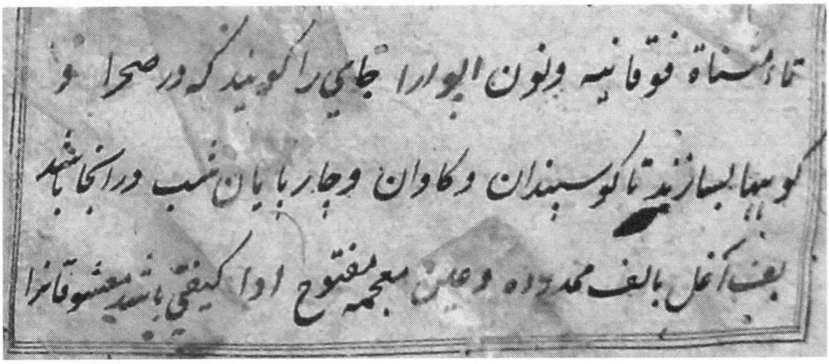

FIGURE 2.2 *Apwārā* in the *Ġharāʾib al-Luġhāt* (Rampur MS 2543, f. 4)

the colonial period. Two of the Rampur manuscripts (2543 and 2544) depict the text of the entry identically (see figures 2.2 and 2.3):

> *Apwārā* they call a place that they construct in the wilderness (*ṣaḥrā*) and in the mountains (*koh-hā*) so that sheep and cows and quadrupeds may stay in it. In Fārsī: *āġhal*, with *alif mamdūdah* ['long ā', آ], the pointed *ʿain* [i.e., غ] with *fataḥ*.

The spelling of term *apwārā* (اپوارا) is probably a scribal error for the more correct *aiwārā* (ایوارا, through the addition of a third dot below the second letter). That it is reproduced in the later Rampur MS 2544 (copied in 1865) is somewhat surprising since the standardization of Urdu orthography had greatly advanced by the middle decades of the nineteenth century.[179] Ārzū represents the term in its more familiar form as *aiwārā*.

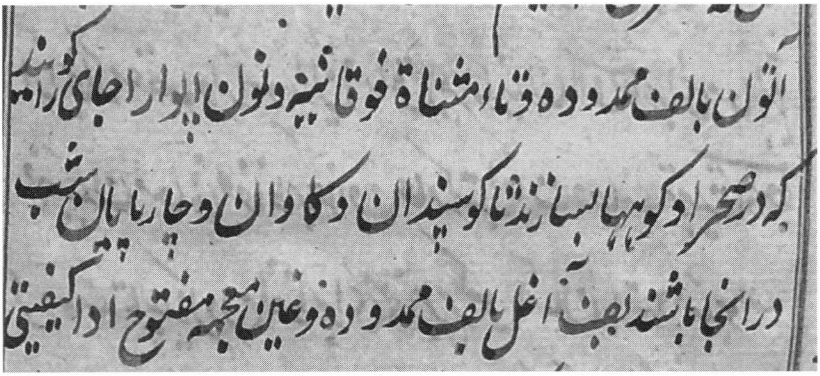

FIGURE 2.3 *Apwārā* in the *Ġharāʾib al-Luġhāt* (Rampur MS 2544, f. 4)

Ārzū proves himself as unwilling to reproduce slavishly his predecessor's work as he is to grant it any validity. While claiming to quote from "the treatise" (that is, the *Ġharā'ib*), he has made significant modifications to the original, mostly in the form of deletions, and he adds his thoughts on the "original" entry in a few sentences that following it:

> *Aiwārā* in the treatise (*risālah*): "a place that they construct in the wilderness (*ṣaḥrā*) and in mountainous areas (*kohistān*) for quadrupeds so that at night they may stay in it, *āġhil*, with *alif mamdūḥ* [*sic*],[180] the pointed *ġhain* [i.e., غ] and *lām* [i.e., ل]," however in reliable books (*muʿtabarah kutub*) [there] is *āġhil* with the meaning of a place of cows and sheep, so this is most common, and likewise, *aiwārā* would be the language of the homeland of the author of the treatise (*risālah*), and in the language of Braj and Gwāliyār which is the most eloquent (*afṣaḥ*), they call it *kharak*.[181]

Ārzū thus disapproves of both the Hindvi *aiwārā* and the Persian equivalent, *āġhil*. With regard to *aiwārā*, it was impossible to discount Hāṅswī's definition on the basis of written texts, as the term did not occur in any dictionary that Ārzū could cite. With regard to *āġhil*, Ārzū was on somewhat firmer ground. Ārzū argues that ʿAbdul Wāsĕʿ confused the *genus proximum*, or more general category meaning "a place for quadrupeds," for a more specific term signifying "a place for quadrupeds *in the wilderness for them to stay at night*." By the time Steingass had published his *Comprehensive Persian-English Dictionary* in 1892, however, the "most common" general meaning which Ārzū argues to be more correct had given way to an intermediate term, *āġhil*, defined by him as "a sheep-cote in a mountain."[182]

Unable to call upon the authority of "reliable books" in his criticism of ʿAbdul Wāsĕʿ's choice of *aiwārā*, Ārzū must forgo textual evidence in favor of claims resting upon his own identity as a speaker of the "most eloquent language" of Hind, namely that of Braj and Gwalior. Ārzū was born in Agra but had spent some of his early life in Gwalior, where his maternal grandfather, Muḥammad Ġhauṡ Gwāliyārī, was revered as a Sufi saint.[183] Ārzū makes striking use of two Arabic-derived superlative adjectives in his entry: *aʿamm* (the most common) and *afṣaḥ* (the most eloquent). Implied, of course, is that the language of Hāṅsī is not *the most* eloquent language and that therefore ʿAbdul Wāsĕʿ, composing under suboptimal conditions, was not qualified to offer either correct definitions of "the most common" Persian terms or examples of "the most eloquent" Hindvi terms as equivalents.

In spite of the admittedly compelling weight of Ārzū's personal authority and his skillful manipulation of textual evidence, Elliot not only included the term *aiwārā* in his glossary but, like Breton, (mis)attributed the definition to Ḳhān-i Ārzū! Beames's 1869 version of Elliot's original entry is reproduced below, with the deviations from the original 1845 edition indicated in brackets:

> Aiwára, ايواره ऐवारा[184]
>
> A cow-shed in the middle of a jungle, according to the "Gharíbu'l-lughat" ["Gharaib-òòl-Loghat" in 1845 ed.] of Khan Arza [*sic*, his name appears as "Arzoo" in the 1845 edition]. The "Tuḥfatu'l-lughát" ["Tohfut-òòl-Loghat" in 1845] does not notice it.—E[lliot].
>
> The common words are Arár अड़ाड़ and Bathán बथान q.v.—B[eames].[185]

One of the many surprises of this particular definition is that Elliot highlights two specific features—its presence "in the middle of the jungle" as a shelter of cows—while Steingass, in his entry for ᶜAbdul Wāsĕᶜ's original Persian "equivalent" *āghil* foregrounds that structure's mountain location and ovine inhabitants. Ārzū would no doubt express similar exasperation with the similarity of their shared fallacy of pars pro toto, that is, of confusing the part for the whole.[186] Elliot was not oblivious to regional variations in Hindi, however: in his definition of a term with a similar meaning, باکھر *bākhar*, he notes this word in Delhi is specifically "applied to cattle sheds."[187] It should be noted moreover that this constellation of semisynonymous terms—whose association to agriculture and animal husbandry is irrefutable even while its appropriateness in polite company is not—does not appear where one would most expect them in Crooke's 1879 *Glossary of North Indian Peasant Life*. Perhaps Crooke had, unlike his predecessors, become aware of the disapproval Ārzū had expressed toward ᶜAbdul Wāsĕᶜ's definition and was sufficiently convinced to leave the term out of his *Glossary* altogether.

"SLAVE OF THE IMMENSE ONE"

The Dutch trader and lexicographer Joan Josua Ketelaar, near the end of his 1698 Hindi grammar and glossary, devotes an entire section of his book to explaining the meanings of Islamic names.[188] Beginning this section, entitled *Beduijding eeniger moorse namen* (Explaining Moorish names), with the pair *gods/godschenk—allabaa*, the rest of the names he reproduces appear like a long list of acquaintances encountered during his travels. There is a *piar chan* (Piyār Ḳhāṅ), a *gulam alie* (Ġhulām ᶜAlī), a *nettoe* (Naṭṭū), a *bhoola* (Bholā)—these are figures from everyday life in South Asia, individuals with whom one easily imagines Ketelaar to have endeavored to communicate and trade. Later nineteenth-century texts would betray colonial anxieties regarding the state being, at one moment, overwhelmed by the superabundance of recorded Indian proper names and, in the next, unable to associate those names uniquely with individuals. This, Javed Majeed argues, was the result of a philological emphasis on discovering the "meanings" of words, thereby demonstrating that "Indian names are not proper at all, they are [all] common."[189]

Gilchrist, too, in his 1825 work *The General East India Guide and Vade Mecum*, represented names as, if not a window into the soul, at least a means by which to distinguish Hindu from Muslim:

> Finger-rings and particular insignia of state are almost the only ornaments worn by the Moosulmans. In other apparent or obvious circumstances of counting rosaries, the form of the hair, turbans, &c., it is no easy matter always to discriminate them from the Hindoos: their names however being all significant, as I have explained in the Guide [i.e., Gilchrist's *British India Monitor, Guide, and Story Teller*], can hardly ever be confounded by a Hindoostanee scholar.[190]

De Tassy likewise begins his memorial of ᶜAbdul Wāsěᶜ Hāṅswī with brief notes on the meaning of his given name and *nisbat*, or toponymic surname, grasping for clues in the absence of substantive data on the identity of this lexicographer with no *ḥāl* (situation). In the midst of this abundance of minutia, trivia, and arcana—all manner of tangential information but precious little that could help one "know him from Adam"—the question naturally arises: who is this figure, this "Slave of the Immense of Hāṅsī"?

Despite protests against those who would collapse ᶜAbdul Wāsěᶜ into his *nisbat*, I have employed the appellation "Hāṅswī" throughout this chapter as an alternative to the lexicographer's given name. An assumption of this chapter has been that the production and indeed the reception of ᶜAbdul Wāsěᶜ's dictionary were significantly shaped by his residence in a provincial town, Hansi, located eighty-two miles to the north and west of Delhi. There is, in fact, reasonable internal, even lexical, evidence to support this. His twentieth-century editor, Sayyid ʿAbdullāh, has identified several dozen examples that "we should call 'the words of the spoken speech of the ordinary folk and townspeople' (*ʿawwām aur qaṣābatīyoṅ kī bol cāl ke alfāẓ*)" and that "bear the stamp of Punjabi pronunciation."[191] In one of his more generous moments, ʿAbdullāh even grants faint praise to ʿAbdul Wāsěʿ:

> The *Ġharāʾib al-Luġhāt* in spite of its defects retains immense importance for research in the history of the Urdu language. The *Ġharāʾib al-Luġhāt* throws valuable light upon many of the peculiarities of the state of language in northern India during the reign of ʿĀlamgīr Aurangzeb. As has already been explained, Mīr ʿAbdul Wāsěʿ was associated with Haryana and Haryana itself is the region in which we find in northern India a literary movement prior even to in Delhi. Having looked at the literary work of this period, this impression may be established that the influence of the Haryānī language reaches well beyond the borders of Haryana. In this manner, even Delhi's language appears to be influenced by Haryānī. In the *Nawādir al-Alfāẓ*, which was written in Delhi, the words have many written and spoken forms which are present in the *Ġharāʾib al-Luġhāt*, although many words of Ḳhān-i Ārzū and Hāṅswī are established by external mints [i.e., sources of authority], though there are many such words that are commonly accepted which later reformers of the Urdu language, once they asserted them to be improper (*makrūh*) and rustic (*gaṅwārī*), excluded from the language.[192]

Despite this evidence, the *Ġharāʾib al-Luġhāt* makes no explicit mention of ʿAbdul Wāsěʿ's place of residence—in Haryana or elsewhere.

This mattered very little when, hardly half a century later, perhaps the greatest Persian philologist that India ever produced concluded that "the author of the treatise" whom he undertook to critique and revise was neither conversant in the Persian lexicographic tradition nor qualified to decide what Hindvi terms deserved to be written down and associated with the language of the Mughal capital. Shamsur Rahman Faruqi has interpreted Ārzū's occasional references to the *urdū-i muʿallā* as evidence of the mid-seventeenth-century coalescence in Delhi of a standardized literary dialect and the subsequent redeployment of *urdū*, the "(military) camp," from its service as a toponym to that of a glottonym.[193] An examination of the actual use of that term by Ārzū would indicate that in 1743 *urdū* continued to lack an association with a single topographic feature: one could speak, as Ārzū himself recorded, of the "knowing ones" of the *urdū-i bādshāhī* and Akbarābād and Shāhjahānābād in a single statement.

In a quotation cited at the beginning of this chapter, Sayyid ʿAbdullāh questioned whether the *Ġharāʾib al-Luġhāt* could really lay claim to being the "first dictionary of the Urdu language" on the basis of intentionality, language, and genre. His distinction between *luġhat* and *farhang*, both of which I translate as "dictionary," does not hold much analytical weight. Inasmuch as ʿAbdul Wāsĕʿ's work offers definitions, equivalents, and guides to pronunciation for a list of terms arranged according to an alphabetical order (at least of the first letter), it would seem to fulfill all the formal requirements of that lexicographic genre. The question of whether it is a dictionary of *urdū* is a more debatable proposition. For Ḳhān-i Ārzū, it clearly contained many terms that were not known to the people of "the *urdū*."

Rather than rehearsing a debate regarding a notoriously slippery term, one might simply cite ʿAbdul Wāsĕʿ's own claim to have explained "nonunderstood meanings, the meanings of words meant in opposition to ordinary dictionaries, and for the sake of education [or 'correction']—so that the discovery of a word for a meaning may be easy for everyone (*har kas*)." Why, then, did he write a work in this format, and why did he include the words he did? ʿAbdul Wāsĕʿ's dictionary, unlike his vocabulary in verse, the *Ṣamad Bārī/Jān Pahcān*, does not explicitly identify the language of the headwords in his text as Hindvi, let alone by the anachronistic terms *haryānvī*, *reḳhtah*, or *urdū*. He was not aiming to produce either a standard dictionary of a literary language or a glossary to a defined literary corpus of terms. If Ārzū had acknowledged ʿAbdul Wāsĕʿ's preface to be a sincere statement of intent, he should not have been surprised if the definitions provided were either "nonunderstood" or "in opposition to ordinary dictionaries," even if he did doubt the value of the dictionary's having been produced "for the sake of education" or "correction." ʿAbdul Wāsĕʿ's own statement that he compiled this work "so that the discovery of a word for a meaning may be easy for everyone" suggests the *Ġharāʾib* to be intended as a "writerly" text: this is a work one consults to find a word and not a meaning—rather more like a modern thesaurus than an encyclopedic dictionary. When ʿAbdul Wāsĕʿ writes "everyone" (*har kas*), he is nevertheless referring to a specific set of people participating in this Indo-Persian "ecumene" and not to our modern conceptions of a "populace at large" contained within a geographic region or borders of a state. What, then, were the words that were meant to be discovered?

The alphabetical arrangement of the terms, rudimentary though it may be, indicates that this was a text intended for nonsequential visual consultation. Stated another way, to interact effectively with this dictionary, one would have to possess a general conception of the orthographic form taken by the Hindvi terms contained within it.

The pedagogical nature of the other titles attributed to Hāṅswī (the author) are consistent with statements that the *Ġharāʾib al-Luġhāt* was intended as an aid to those studying under him in "discovering" the right Persian word for a particular meaning. Here, however, the common notion of what constitutes a "word" is contaminated by a belief that every spoken utterance is composed of *inscribable*, that is, *written*, "words." While the Arabic triliteral root *l-f-ẓ* (لفظ) denotes the process of "ejecting (something) from the mouth,"[194] an artifact perhaps of a long tradition of oral literature in pre-Islamic Arabic that owed little to the written word, by the time this term arrived in South Asia and came to mean "word," the Arabic from which it was derived was very much a written language. The presence of Hindvi terms in an Indian dictionary devoted ostensibly to the Persian language was by the seventeenth century, as Sherānī argued, nothing new. Hindvi terms, like those that appear as headwords in the *Ġharāʾib al-Luġhāt*, were, in light of this tradition, not even considered "words" but were rather denotations (or, reversing ʿAbdul Wāsĕʿ's phrasing: "meanings for words") of the *true* "words" collected, culled, and collated from Persian texts.[195]

Intentionality is thus the most important aspect in explaining the use and abuse of the *Ġharāʾib al-Luġhāt*. In the half-century that separated it from the *Nawādir al-Alfāz*, the *zabān-i urdū-i muʿallā* (language of the exalted *urdū*) had become, to the *people* of the *zabān-i urdū-i muʿallā*, a literary language. During Hāṅswī's lifetime, to produce a literary work on Persian models in the spoken language of the townsfolk of Delhi (to say nothing of those of Hansi) would have seemed at best a highly eccentric project. By 1743, however, the new (at least in North India) literary language *reḳhtah* was not only flourishing as a broad-based social phenomenon; it was also perceived to require extensive pruning to become a language of prestige in the vacuum created by a receding Persian literary culture. The importance of Persian as a cosmopolitan language and medium of transregional communication was severely curtailed by the dramatic constriction of the Mughal Empire as a political entity. For ʿAbdul Wāsĕʿ, however, writing at a time when the Mughal Empire, under Aurangzeb, was at the apogee of its territorial extent, to have stated that he was compiling a dictionary "for the sake of educating" or "correcting" students' use of *Persian* was too obvious to have warranted any comment.

By 1743, when Ārzū was casting a "retrospective gaze" over his predecessor's dictionary, some had begun making the writing of poetry and even prose in Hindvi into a viable career, if not a full-fledged profession. One can hardly blame Ārzū for confusing ʿAbdul Wāsĕʿ's intention as being to explain Hindvi terms *in Persian*. Hāṅswī's real intention, however, had been to create a dictionary of Persian terms—"nonunderstood meanings, the meanings of words meant in opposition to ordinary dictionaries," but Persian terms nonetheless—to be "discovered" through their Hindvi equivalents. The Hindvi content, was, in a very real sense, incidental: if Hāṅswī's toponymic *nisbat* had instead been Lāhorī, Aurangābādī, or Bījāpūrī, he might well have organized his text using a different glossing language. By the middle of the eighteenth century, composing poetry in *reḳhtah* had become a very real option: indeed, poets who had studied under Ārzū were entering into lucrative relationships of patronage by virtue of their mastery of a poetry composed in this "new" literary register.

The collective effort, beginning in the middle decades of the eighteenth century, to prune *reḳhtah* of unliterary usages and to evaluate (often critically) the poetry of the current and previous generations was inspired by a need to establish "occupational controls" in an effort to professionalize what was becoming, financially, an increasingly remunerative business.[196] That this was occurring just as the most famous "professional" poets of *reḳhtah* were seeking patrons in new regional centers is no coincidence—it may well have been the original impetus for the establishment of a "standard" literary Urdu and, subsequently, heated debates over who had the right to define what that "standard" was.[197] A work like the *Ġharāʾib al-Luġhāt*, whose literary ambitions were strictly confined to the use of Persian, was an easy straw man against whom a figure like Ārzū could express his own vision of what form this "new" literary language should take. In the final analysis, Hansi, the town, and Hāṅswī, the man, were limited by their status as intimate outsiders: in time, in space, and in language, they were far enough away to be excluded yet just close enough to cause discomfort.

[3] 1800: THROUGH THE VEIL OF POETRY

In 1799, the Urdu poet Mirzā Jān 'Ṭapish' was arraigned by British authorities under charges of having conspired to overthrow East India Company rule in Bengal and Bihar. This plot was alleged to have involved Shāh Zamān of Afghanistan, the viceroy of Muscat, and dozens of disaffected feudal landlords. Having left his home in the Mughal capital, Delhi, some fifteen years earlier, Ṭapish had entered the service of the deputy niẓām, or governor, of Dhaka (the capital of present-day Bangladesh), Nawāb Shams al-Daulah. It was for Shams al-Daulah that Ṭapish compiled in 1792 his important Urdu dictionary, *Shams al-Bayān fī Muṣṭalaḥāt al-Hindūstān* (The sun of speech, on the idioms of Hindustan), which he named for his patron and through whose Persian definitions he provided "explanation of the idioms of the houses of Delhi and the colloquial speech of the eloquent men of the Exalted Court, arranged in numerous verses, and the understanding of distant ones . . . situated in cities far away." This chapter discusses the first efforts of Urdu lexicographers to record the idiomatic speech of Delhi in alphabetical form, a project with which they were to become increasingly occupied from the late eighteenth century onward. Ṭapish appears to have continued his lexicographic activities both while in custody in Calcutta and later in collaboration with British philologists. The increasing professionalization and geographic dispersal of poets like Ṭapish who could claim a connection with the erstwhile Mughal imperial capital resulted in the production of works like the *Shams al-Bayān*, which conveyed the literary authority of their authors to new centers across the length and breadth of South Asia. It enabled the participation by new social groups in an elite literary culture, a process that led eventually to the promotion of a language, Urdu, as an ethnic marker of political identity.

Lexicographers were forced to contend with two major conceptual shifts that accompanied the nineteenth-century rise of Urdu as a language of political authority and its subsequent decline in India over the course of the twentieth century. First, it becomes increasingly difficult by the early decades of the nineteenth century to identify an independent Persianate tradition that does not in some way draw upon analogous European colonial forms of knowledge. In the pages that follow, I will explore the first direct interactions of Urdu lexicographers with colonial power. In the closing years of the eighteenth century it was by no means obvious to the actors involved that the methods of each camp would soon begin to converge, much less that the traditional forms of Urdu lexicography would soon be completely subsumed in a monological mode of dictionary compilation based upon an increasingly standard set of principles. Far into the twentieth century and beyond, both traditions would continue to coexist and even symbiotically thrive.

A second and closely related shift relates to the double reference function of lexicography: its ability both to define and reflect social groupings, mediating political and cultural expressions. Lexicography is both a documentation of language—as it exists, existed, or potentially should exist—and a guide to the felicitous performance of certain forms of social interaction. Through the nineteenth century, as the colonial government extended political patronage and financial support to new elite communities, Urdu, primarily as a language of education,[1] military use,[2] and government administration,[3] likewise shifted from a written medium largely confined to poetic craft to an expansive set of codes associated through prose genres with a rapidly expanding literate public sphere. In such a setting, the means of political legitimation transmitted through Urdu, and the political institutions upon whose continued support writers' cultural and economic viability depended, were destined to change dramatically. As the modes of documentation deployed in lexicography expanded to reflect both the functioning of the Urdu language in new social domains and the participation of new language users, so too did the performative reach of dictionaries, affecting the lives and social interactions of an ever-expanding set of literate (and, increasingly, illiterate) language users. In short, the political and linguistic structures reflected and enacted through nineteenth-century lexicography are symptomatic of broader social and political changes. In the same way that political elites were compelled to rearticulate the basis of their authority using the rhetoric of representative governance, so too did the authority of lexicographers shift from a mode of legitimation conferred by membership in a charismatic lineage to more institutional forms of accreditation.[4] The corporate form of this emerging mode of authority relied upon the rapid improvements in the capacity of states and lexicographers alike to observe, classify, and quantify their subjects. The varied career of Mirzā Jān Ṯapish, a product of the ancien régime and a comprador in the nouvelle, serves as both an emblem of these shifts and a portent of what was to come.

COMPILING AND CONSPIRING

On April 22, 1799, John Fendall, the acting Murshidabad district collector and magistrate,[5] shared with Henry Douglas, magistrate of Patna, the happy news that he had apprehended a "Mirza Jaun Tuppish" and had sent him to Calcutta.[6] Exactly one month earlier, on March 22, 1799, Douglas had received a letter from his superior, George Hilario Barlow in Fort William, directing him to apprehend this "Mirza Jaun or Jaun Mirza supposed to be an Armenian, or possibly a Mogul . . . employed by Shems ud dowlah in certain intrigues in Behar."[7] The instructions that followed suggested that "Mirza Jaun" was under suspicion for crimes somewhat more involved than those befitting an ordinary petty criminal:

> You will endeavour at the same time to secure [his and others'] papers . . . keeping the contents of them secret, and forwarding the originals to Calcutta after keeping copies of them. You will not disclose these or any other orders you may receive respecting the conspiracy of Vizier Ally and Shems ud dowllah farther than may be necessary for the guidance of the Agents you may employ in carrying them into execution.[8]

From the lack of detail provided by way of description of the suspect (he was "supposed to be an Armenian, or possibly a Mogul"), it would seem that the British knew little to nothing about this "Mirza Jaun." His name had first emerged that March in connection with the plot discovered between two disaffected noblemen in their alleged efforts to secure the military support of the king of Afghanistan, Zamān Shāh, and the viceroy of Muscat in overthrowing British rule in eastern India. The British were nevertheless able to take advantage of an extensive and quick postal service to mobilize a broad intelligence network to identify and apprehend this figure.[9]

The arrest of Mirzā Jān now appears as but a minor episode amid a broader rash of rebellions confronting the British in South Asia during the final years of the eighteenth century. Recent historians of the events of 1798 and 1799 seem compelled to apologize for a revolt that seems never to have really been able to get off the ground. In spite of being acknowledged by the Lucknow nawāb as the sole legitimate son and heir to the throne, the governor general John Shore in a visit subsequent to the nawāb's death would rebuke Wazīr ʿAlī Ḳhān as a low-born servant who had been adopted by the childless nawāb.[10] Shore successfully orchestrated in January 1798 a nearly bloodless coup by adhering to what he called "the principle of Justice" in pursuing his resolution to appoint Wazīr ʿAlī Ḳhān's long absent uncle as the "rightful successor to the late Nabob."[11] By making reference to the universality of "Laws of Justice" he was also able to bypass centuries of South Asian custom and Islamic probate law. Barun De characterizes the "forgotten" rebellion as being "nowhere as militant" and "not as heroic" as the anti-British efforts of some near-contemporaries like Tipu Sultan.[12] Aniruddha Ray, the author of a book-length monograph on the subject, conjectures it to have been a derivative rebellion modeled on the more celebrated 1781 insurrection of Chait Singh,[13] the "significant difference" being that "Vizir's revolt . . . was tucked away in a corner of Oudh without the expansion of the revolt of Chait Singh."[14] And while Wazīr ʿAlī may not be featured as prominently in Indian nationalist and "anticolonial" (defined broadly) historiographies,[15] De does make the important observation that Wazīr ʿAlī Ḳhāṅ represents "new tendencies of subalternity to a new type of ruling class,"[16] the result of increasing anxieties among higher-status groups as they faced a new social and economic order engendered by the expansion of East India Company participation—or interference—in the various political and administrative systems obtaining in South Asia at that time.[17] The British response to the supposed machinations of Wazīr ʿAlī and his coconspirators was characterized by a peculiarly internationalist paranoia,[18] imagining an unprecedented international axis that would join Wazīr ʿAlī and eastern Indian *zamīndārs* with Tipu Sultan, the maratha Scindias, and "French Revolutionary Imperialists" in battle against British hegemony. While the entire affair may thus be disparaged as being but a "mare's nest,"[19] one cannot help but be impressed with the speed with which the British were able to gather information about a plot—real or imagined—from a wide variety of intelligence sources and take action at once to apprehend, try, and convict the individuals they deemed responsible.[20]

A mere three days after Barlow's original directive was penned, a new piece of information regarding the whereabouts of "Mirza Jaun" came to light in a letter from William Camac, magistrate of the city of Dhaka, to Henry Douglas, dated March 25, 1799. We must assume Camac to have received a similar letter from Fort William enjoining him to exercise the greatest care and secrecy, and so while he regretted being "uninformed of the family resident [*sic*, read as "residence"] of Meerza Jaun Tuppas," he was able to add the vital clue that Tuppas (or, variously, Tuppish) "has been for several years in the service of the Nabob Nuzim at Moorshadabad and is well known at that place."[21] John Fendall, magistrate and acting collector of Murshidabad district, was thus duly notified that a "Mirza Jaun" was probably residing in his district. By April 2, it would seem that Fendall had secured the personal effects of a "Mirza Jaung Tuppuh," having captured and dispatched him to Calcutta at some point prior to April 22, when Fendall penned the above-quoted letter to Henry Douglas.

The general lack of surviving secondary source material on the lives of all but a few prominent classical Urdu literary figures is in stark contrast to the vast amount and variety of written documents that accumulated whenever an individual had the misfortune of interacting with the East India Company judicial apparatus. A very different image of an individual might thus be formed from the examination of colonial records without recourse to non-English materials. The reverse also applies: existing Urdu-language scholarship does not account for the vast amount of correspondence, testimony, and other official documentation prepared by officials in the employ of the British East India Company in connection with the capture, trial, and sentencing of "Mirza Jaun Tuppish" (or, variously, "Tuppuh" or "Tuppas"). This is, in part, a simple matter of inconsistency in transcribing the Arabic script in Roman letters. While an online search for the phrase "Mirzā Jān" or terms *tapish* and *ṭapish*, representing the poet and convicted rebel's title and nom de plume[22] reveal very little, similar searches for "Mirza Jaun" and "Tuppish"—antiquated and idiosyncratic representations though they may be of the Arabic-script originals—reveal a vast trove of information of whose existence few Urdu literary scholars appear to be aware.[23]

Born in Delhi, Muḥammad Ismāʿīl, better known by his title, Mirzā Jān, and *taḳhalluṣ* (nom de plume), Ṭapish, was the son of Mirzā Yūsuf Beg Buḳhārī, a soldier of Central Asian descent. The biographical accounts in *taẕkirah*s note that Ṭapish was himself also familiar with the military sciences.[24] He had acquired training in the art of rhetoric from Mirzā Yār Beg 'Sāʾil'[25] and in the art of poetry from Shāh 'Hidāyat' (d. 1805?)[26] and Ḳhwājah Mīr 'Dard' (1722–1785). Dard was a prominent Delhi Naqshbandī sufi leader famously described as "one pillar among the four pillars of the Urdu language."[27] T̤apish was also trained in Persian belles-lettres, a skill that enabled him to find employment both before and after his imprisonment.[28] As a young man, he entered into the service of Mirzā Jawān Baḳht Jahāndār Shāh (c. 1740–1788), heir apparent to the Mughal emperor Shāh ʿĀlam II (r. 1759–1806), in whose company he was retained at an officer's rank.[29] Court intrigues compelled the crown prince in 1784 to make a daring escape from Delhi to Lucknow to seek the protection of Nawāb Āṣaf al-Daulah and Warren Hastings and, subsequent to that, in 1786, to Benares.[30] In accompanying his patron, T̤apish had probably given up hope of ever returning to Delhi.[31] Following the death of the prince in Benares in 1788,[32] he sought his fortune at the court of the Nawāb Nāz̤im of Bengal, Mubārak al-Daulah (r. 1770–1793) in Murshidābād. He was able to gain employment in the company of Nawāb Shams al-Daulah, Mubārak al-Daulah's son-in-law and the younger brother of the nāʾib naz̤īm or

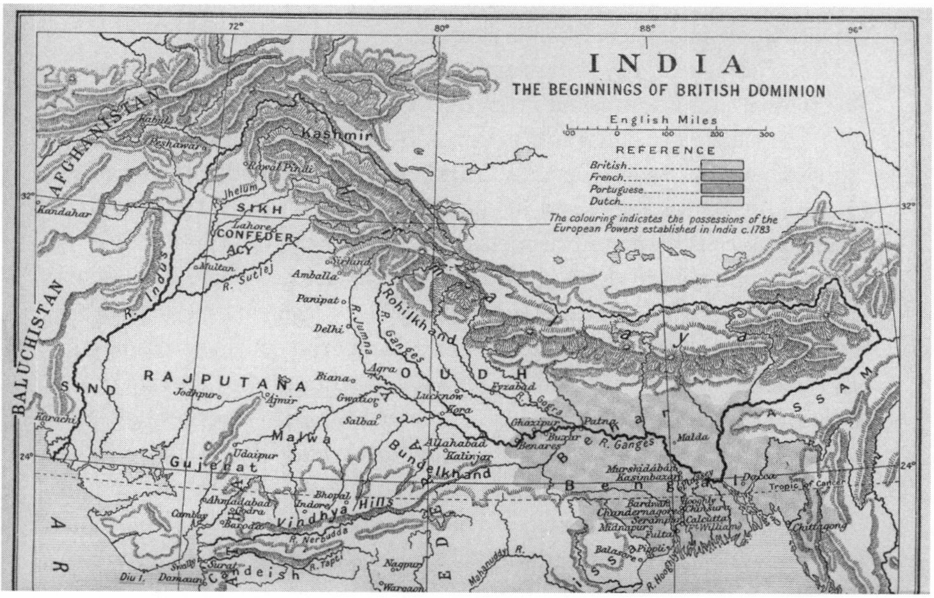

FIGURE 3.1 Northern India c. 1783. "Map 64: India: The Beginnings of British Dominion," in *The Cambridge Modern History Atlas*, edited by A. W. Ward et al. (New York: Macmillan, 1924).

deputy governor of Dhaka.[33] It was during his residence in Murshidabad that he prepared his first major work, an alphabetical collection of idiomatic expressions from *reḳhtah* (as the literary register of Urdu was at that time called) with Persian glosses, giving it the Arabic title *Shams al-Bayān fī Muṣṭalaḥāt al-Hindūstān* (The sun of speech, on the idioms of Hindustan) in honor of his patron, Shams al-Daulah.

In light of a variety of manuscript evidence, it is not possible to state conclusively when, if ever, the *Shams al-Bayān* was completed. It may have remained an open-ended work to which the author continued to make additions following its initial "publication" in the last decade of the eighteenth century. In a manuscript copy preserved in the British Library (Add. 18,889) dated Nāgpur 26th Rabīᶜ I, AH 1215 (c. August 17, 1800), the author is represented as having written that his dictionary "was brought to completion in 1208 after the flight of the Prophet (Peace be upon him!), in the month of Żī-i Hijjah, on the 17th date [i.e., July 16, 1794], in the city of Murshidābād."[34] The date of completion that appears in the author's preface in a recent print edition of the work, itself based on the 1849 lithograph edition,[35] is represented as 22nd Muḥarram al-Ḥarram, AH 1207, that is, nearly two years earlier, on or around September 9, 1792.[36] The most probable explanation for this discrepancy is that the *Shams al-Bayān* remained very much a work in progress.

After the *Shams al-Bayān* appeared in the forms in which it is now available to us in manuscript and lithograph editions, ostensibly in 1792 and 1794, our next notice of Ṭapish occurs in the travelogue and autobiography of another Mughal prince, Mirzā ᶜAlī Baḳht Bahādur Muḥammad Ẓahīruddīn, better known by his poetic sobriquet 'Aẓfarī' (most triumphant). Aẓfarī had been imprisoned as a Mughal prince (and potential aspirant to the throne) in the Red Fort, and like his cousin, friend, and fellow prince Mirzā Jawān Baḳht Jahāndār Shāh,[37] he arranged an escape from his confinement, sojourning at various subimperial courts across northern India before settling finally in June 1798 at the court of the nawābs of Arcot in South India.[38] Prior to his voyage by boat down the coast of eastern India, Aẓfarī traveled from Lucknow to Murshidabad—where, after encountering an impostor fraudulently posing as himself,[39] he sought introductions to the leading figures of the Bengal court. He applauds himself for having "performed all stages of service in an extremely appropriate manner" for Nawāb Nāṣir al-Mulk, who ascended the *masnad* (throne) at Murshidabad after the death of his father Nawāb Mubārak al-Daulah in 1793.[40] He then sent a notice of his "deepest wish and desire" to meet

Shams al-Daulah, the son-in-law of the late nawāb and youngest surviving brother of the then-governor of Dhaka. Shams al-Daulah was a charismatic figure whose star was in the ascendant during that final decade of the eighteenth century.[41] In response to his letter of intent, he received "a very faith-filled message sent orally by an individual worthy of favor and kindness whose pen name is 'Tapish.'" He continues with an extended account of his association with the poet:

> He is famous by the name of Mirzā Jān. He is a very vigorous Mughal-born youth with roots in Bukhara. He has spent time with nobles and has acquired the art of the manners and methods of the poetic assembly. He is a very affable person . . . we were connected and joined to the blessed Timurid family through a paternal relationship. For some time during these days I was included among the dear friends of Mīrzā Jān. This verbal message of Mīrzā 'Tapish' only fanned the flames of the desire of the author [to meet Shams al-Daulah]. But at this time *on the basis of several reasons, whose explanation at this place is unnecessary*, the aforementioned nawāb [Shams al-Daulah] was bound for Jahāngīr Nagar [Dhaka], and the desire to meet was unfulfilled. However, having in a suitable manner explained and given instruction in pure friendship (*ik̤hlāṣ*) and in the allurement of discipleship (*targ̣hīb-i irādat*) along with the author [i.e., Az̤farī] to the Dignity of the Government and Administration Nāṣir al-Mulk Bahādur [the young nawab of Murshidabad], [he] begged to take his leave. Following his departure, the named one carried out service to me with all dignity. True God, oh this Remover of grief! Wherever he, distinguished by sincere friendship, may be, may you keep him in eminence and dignity! Amen![42]

Az̤farī's prose incongruously combines certain limited details—most notably in individuals' titles and epithets—with an extreme laconicism in delineating the motivations of those characters. Thus, in the sentence that follows the passage, Az̤farī provides the exact date and location at which these observations of Ṯapish were first noted down:

> [At] the time when I am writing these events, it is the 25th date of the month of Muḥarram al-Ḥarām, year AH 1212, and on the day of Friday [corresponding with the evening of Thursday, June 20, 1797], in the *rang maḥal* of G̣hulām Ḥusain K̤hān ʿArẓ Begī, situated by the banks of the river in the neighborhood of Kalhaṛiyā, and seeking to travel to the countries of the Deccan, I am with my feet in the stirrup.

The image evoked by the author penning these lines—"feet in the stirrup" at the banks of the river—is seemingly at odds with the lacunae of the previous paragraph, proffering a real stirrup instead of the figural "spur" that brought our author to that particular place at that particular time. The careful reader is left asking: what exactly was the reason "whose explanation at this place is unnecessary" for Shams al-Daulah to be "bound for Jahāngīr Nagar [Dhaka]"?

Additional circumstantial evidence may be gleaned from the colonial record. Among the papers seized for the investigation of Shams al-Daulah was a letter composed by "Shaikh Khalifun, Vice-roy of Muscat." Recent scholarship has shown that these letters were composed in October 1796 and made reference to "verbal negotiations" with a deputy "who it appears is not at Moorshedabad."[43] An abstract of the findings of the advocate general at Fort William prepared on July 3, 1799, at Fort St. George sheds additional light on the identity of these figures: "the agents employed upon this occasion were adventurers who had resided a considerable time within the Company's territories and at Lucknow and thro[ugh] the means of Shaikh Alli, himself an Arab and connected with Muscat, had been introduced to Shums oo Dowla."[44] This "deputy" who had "resided a considerable time" in Lucknow and the company-controlled Benares was probably Mirzā Jān Ṭapish. He had been sent by his employer to negotiate terms with agents of disaffected landholders and other entities.

In the absence of any direct insight into the motivations of the characters Aẕfarī describes, we are compelled to draw inferences from the dates he provides. We may assume that Aẕfarī first arrived in Murshidabad in early May 1797,[45] shortly after the departure of Shams al-Daulah for Dhaka. Citing the nobleman's interference in the management of Nizamat stipends, the governor general in Calcutta resolved, on March 5, 1796, to remove Shams al-Daulah from the court of Nawāb Nāṣir al-Mulk Nuṣrat Jang.[46] Official responsibility for administering these funds had been placed in the hands of Munni Begam, widow of the former nawāb Mīr Jaʿfar (r. 1757–1760, reinstated 1763–1765) and stepmother of Nāṣir al-Mulk's father, Mubārak al-Daulah. She had enjoyed this privilege, in addition to serving as the English-appointed guardian to the male heirs to the *masnad* (throne) at Murshidabad,[47] after the death of her husband in 1765. With the rise of Nāṣir al-Mulk to the throne, Shams al-Daulah attempted to wrest control of the stipend from Munni Begam through his influence on the young nawāb and his minister, Raʾī Mānik Ćand. He was able to postpone leaving another year until the spring of 1797, by which point

Aẓfarī had already noted the nobleman's departure from Murshidabad. While it has been speculated that this forced expulsion was the cause of his alleged discontent with East India Company rule, a letter received by the governor general on February 28, 1798, indicates that Shams al-Daulah sought permission to come to Calcutta from Dhaka "for a short time for change of air and medical advice," a request that was rejected in a letter dated March 8 of the same year.[48] One year later, his wish would be granted, albeit under far from ideal circumstances: an order was issued for his arrest, and he was duly sent to the jail at Fort William.

Ṭapish was a close confidant and the "principal agent"[49] of his employer, Shams al-Daulah; as a member of Delhi's sophisticated émigré literati, his influence as an arbiter of taste in the Bengal court would have been quite substantial. From the introduction to the *Shams al-Bayān*,[50] Ṭapish draws upon the cachet of his literary apprenticeship in Delhi. The passage begins with a praise of the divine as the "Lord of Speech-Creation" (*haẓrat-i suḳhan-i afrīn*) and his prophet as having "turned the weighers of words to delicate essences with [his] bounties of speech and with [his] exalted rhetoric." The author then introduces himself in a conventionally self-deprecating manner as an "ignorant one" who, despite possessing but "a minuscule measure" of eloquence, still presents "an opinion of the idioms [that] the eloquent knowers of the language and the subtlety [which] the correct knowers of speech keep." The bulk of the introduction comprises a list of epithets in praise of his patron, Shams al-Mulk, several of which laud his literary and critical faculties as "the weigher of poets, the most honored nightingale of the rose garden of rhetoric, the flower of the basket of the flower garden of eloquence, the assayer of all the people of the language (*ahl-i zabān*), the touchstone of all the possessors of speech."

The statements that follow belong to the traditional *sabab-i taṣnīf* (reason for composition) typically included in the author's preface of Persianate texts. The author found in the manuscripts "explanation of the idioms of the houses of Delhi and the colloquial speech (*rozmarrah*) of eloquent men of the Exalted Court (*urdū-i muʿallā*), were arranged in many verses" according to "the understanding of distant ones (*dūr-dastān*) all of whom are situated in cities far away." The listing of the verses, however, was haphazard, and students could not "arrive at the genius of their kind." He adopted an arrangement by key terms, thus allowing composition to be "ornamented with gems so that the study of that sort of allusion (*kināyat*) was given perspicuity," thereby making "this art easy for students." The author professes to have composed this work not for "the acquisition of wealth" but rather to give "precedence to [offering] direction" to those scattered in distant cities like Murshidabad so that "clarification of the idioms of *reḳhtah*" might be achieved to "the increase of the delicacy of meaning." In explaining the contents of the text, Ṭapish differentiates between two sorts (*nauʿ*) of idioms: "a variety from the daily speech of the noble classes (*ḳhawāṣṣ*) and a variety of the ordinary ones, differentiated in every manner." His inclusion of both types is justified by the claim that these idioms are "in use by distant ones in the ordinary speech of those homes" and that they are "current in the speech of those cities." The British Library manuscript qualifies the "distant ones" (*dūr-dastān*) as *mustanad* (authenticated), a term that shares the same Arabic root as *sanad* (deed, certificate) and *isnād* (chain of transmission).[51] In both cases, he signals that the idioms are of value because of their place of origin: they "have the seal of distant dear ones." For each Hindi verse there is "an expression from the dialect from the measured language of Delhi, so that for each [it may be determined] which are according to them correct, and those which in their opinion are mistakes and deformed." He concludes by stating, "in sum, quite a few words appear," and by seeking assistance from the divine "Loving King" (*al-malik al-wadūd*).

Several structural similarities between this and the original preface of ʿAbdul Wāsĕʿ's *Ġharāʾib al-Luġhāt* are apparent, most notably the similar statements regarding the lack of commercial profit attending lexicographic composition (a reflex among scholars concerned that overtly pedagogical texts might diminish their literary standing), the desire to make language "easy" for "students" and "dear ones," and assertions of the credibility of their linguistic sources. On closer examination, however, significant differences emerge. While it is not entirely clear what sources ʿAbdul Wāsĕʿ consulted in his text—he bemoans his "nonacquisition of dictionaries (*kutb-i luġhāt*) and the nonarrival of a facilitator (*muyassir*) of proficiency"—he does refer to himself as a "collector of senseless speech" and describes amassing terms, some from "authentic manuscripts of words [or 'dictionaries', *luġhāt*] and some from the mouths and the tongues of trusted friends." We know that ʿAbdul Wāsĕʿ had access to dictionaries like *Farhang-i Rashīdī* (1654) because the latter text, itself based on the *Farhang-i Jahāngīrī* (1607), formed the basis for another composition of his, a grammar of Persian. As regards Ṭapish, he makes no reference to any dictionaries as being physically in his possession during the compilation of the *Shams al-Bayān*. The two sources he does specifically mention are the "daily speech" of both the noble and common folk of Delhi and collections of "Hindi verse" (*shiʿr-i hindī*)[52] showing the "idioms of *reḳhtah*." Neither of these would have been available to ʿAbdul Wāsĕʿ: the former because of his location in the Haryana hinterland and the latter because *reḳhtah*, as a literary term and a widespread phenomenon of eighteenth-century Delhi, postdated the compilation of the *Ġharāʾib al-Luġhāt* by as much as half a century.

Beyond shared structural elements within their prefatory materials, the most obvious similarity between the content of the two works is an artifact of the "paper-poor" conditions of their production. Both lexicographers resorted to a macrostructural arrangement listing headwords alphabetically only by first letter, a result of their having employed similar methods of compilation through the listing of terms (or, in the case of Ṭapish, idioms and expressions) sharing a common first letter. Both texts lacked a final step of a recopying the draft copy according to strict alphabetical order. Most obviously, both authors gloss Indic terms and expressions using Persian and include brief notes on usage. Ṭapish does not usually include remarks on pronunciation in his dictionary entries. Beyond this, there is little other similarity in the micro- or macrostructures of the two texts.

AUTHORITY AND AUTHENTICATION

Ṭapish includes poetic verses to explain and support almost all of his definitions of the *kināyāt* (allusions) and is generally quite scrupulous in his documentation of the authors of these verses. The following entry for the phrase *rafū cakkar meṅ ānā or ā-jānā* (to be taken in the meshes [of], to be entangled [in]; to be lost in astonishment),[53] is typical of the *Shams al-Bayān*:

> *rafū cakkar meṅ ānā*: To remain in astonishment upon witnessing a strange occurrence, and the ordinary folk of the bazaars use this. Sirājuddīn 'Sirāj' Dakanī has said:
>
> *rafū-gar ko kahāṅ ṭāqat kĕh zaḳhm-i ʿishq ko ṭāṅke*
> *agar dekhe mirā sīnah rafū cakkar meṅ ā jāve*
>
> Where is the darner with the power to stitch up the wound of love?
> If he were to see my breast, he would become darned up in meshes[54]

The entry consists of the expression, indicated in red ink in the British Library manuscript, followed by a definition with a note on the usage ("the ordinary folk of the bazaars [*ʿawāmm-i bāzārī*] use this"). He concludes with a verse by the poet Sirāj (1714–1763). His choice of authenticating verse seems, on the face of it, to be rather surprising: Sirāj, who despite being considered to be among the more excellent and mystically inclined eighteenth-century poets, is strongly associated through his toponymic *nisbat*, Aurangābādī, with the Deccan, more than six hundred miles (almost one thousand kilometers) south of Delhi. The choice of Sirāj as an authority may have been attributable in part to the obscurity of the phrase and the likelihood of its having already fallen out of usage by the time Ṭapish noted it.[55] Others have remarked at how catholic Ṭapish was in his selection of authenticating verses, especially those by Deccan poets[56]—this despite his claims in the preface to have selected those "Hindi verse[s]" that express "the dialect from the measured language of Delhi, so that for each [it may be known] which are according to them correct."

The methods of authenticating linguistic usage employed in Urdu lexicography derive quite directly from the science of *ḥadīs̤* (usually transliterated from the Arabic as *ḥadīth*),[57] be it in terminology or in the actual practice of evaluating the transmitters themselves. Both the science of *hadīs̤* collection and lexicography relied on a corpus of discourse that was limited in theory if not in practice,[58] the limits of which were established by authority of the transmitters of that discourse. The most direct generic link between the two is to be found in *taẕkirah*s, whose inclusion of *reḳhtah* poets, beginning in the middle of the eighteenth century, was integral to the establishment both of a literary canon and the increasingly standardized form that the literary language would take by the end of the eighteenth century.[59] In Arabic literature, the term *taẕkirah* "occurs not infrequently in the titles of . . . two different "genres" of text presentation: (1) handbooks and (2) notebooks."[60] The earliest examples of its being used to describe a written work of the second sort appear in the form of "collections of text snippets that the compiler found of interest to himself and gathered mainly for his own use." The term was rapidly adopted to describe Persian-language works, and it came to represent a specific genre of biographical anthology.[61]

In 1967, Najmul Islām prepared an essay in Urdu for the Pakistani journal *Nuqush* in which he described a manuscript on loan to Ġhazālī College in Hyderabad (Pakistan) for an exhibition held during May of that year.

The work described in the article is a *bayāẓ* (notebook)[62] belonging originally to Ṭapish and in the possession of Professor Dr. Ġhulām Muṣṭafā Ḳhāṅ, head of the Department of Urdu at Sindh University.[63] The unpublished text of this notebook, according to the excellent summary offered by Najmul Islām, contains an astonishing variety of material, in the form of excerpts from other authors as well as compositions by Ṭapish himself.[64] Following the death of Ṭapish in approximately 1816,[65] the notebook passed into the hands of several other owners, including a person whose name is effaced in the notebook and who appeared to have used it to excerpt articles from various newspapers during the 1850s.[66]

Najmul Islam has documented how at one place in the notebook several *hadīṡ* are written in a different hand.[67] At the conclusion of these *ḥadīṡ* one of the students of Ṭapish explains:

> These *aḥādīṡ* [pl. of *ḥadīṡ*] on the art of poetry on this page are written by order of my teacher, that is His Excellence and Lordship Mirzā Jān 'Ṭapish'. May his days of bounty remain forever illuminated. The writer of these words is the sinner of the two worlds (*ʿāṣī al-kaunain*) Sayyid Munīruddīn Ḥusain Riẓvī, may the forgiveness of Allāh be upon him![68]

These *aḥādīṡ* correspond with the lexicographer's method both in format and content. *Aḥādīṡ*, in their most basic form, combine a chain of transmission (*isnād*) with the text (*matn*) of the tradition itself. Scholars frequently append their own interpretations and commentary (*sharḥ*) to the *matn* as a means of explaining the application and signification of the tradition to the community of believers. There is a convergence between the functions of *matn* and *sharḥ* in the Arabic and Persianate commentarial traditions and those of the headword (or lemma) and definition in the respective lexicographic genres. The implementation of various technologies of authentication (*isnād*) to Urdu lexicography in a text like *Shams al-Bayān* makes the homologous relationship of the component parts even more apparent. The collection and evaluation of *aḥādīṡ* dealing with a particular subject, like that prepared by Sayyid Munīruddīn on the "art of poetry," may even be viewed as an application of the methods of lexicography upon a particular corpus, namely that of the *ḥadīṡ* traditions, rather like seeking out authoritative usage of a term or phrase in the poetic corpus of a literary register.[69]

It is the term *sanad* (authority) that the poet Inshāʾallāh Ḳhāṅ 'Inshā' (1753–1817) would use to describe the means by which eloquence is to be judged in the Urdu language. Near the beginning of his critical treatise on the Urdu language, the *Daryā-i Laṭāfat* (Ocean of subtlety),[70] he writes in a section titled "The Birth, Origin, and Center of Urdu" that "in every country it is a rule that its consummate men and eloquent ones are gathered in some such city in which the pillars of state of the government reside and people from all directions keep on arriving in search of securing livelihoods." As with Isfahan for the Safavids and Istanbul for the Ottomans, he argues that the "eloquent writing and discourse" of the Mughal capital in Delhi likewise acquired distinction over "Lahore, Multān, Akbarābād [Agra], and Allahabad," which, despite "being the place of residence of kings, yet . . . may not be called the equals of Delhi since this place remained more often the abode of kings." For Inshā, it is the centripetal quality of a political capital, drawing as it does people from distant regions and of all walks of life "in search of securing livelihoods" that permits not just the language and literature of that city but its entire culture of urbanity to achieve distinction. Quite unlike the exodus of the latter half of the eighteenth century, "in times past, the men of each city would come to this city, and acquire both manners and urbanity." Indeed, Delhi's residents "did not used to go off to other cities" except when, "out of necessity," they were compelled to leave the capital in order to "perform a pilgrimage (*ziyārat*) to the grandees (*shurafā*) of that [other] place." From these forays beyond the capital, those in far-flung subimperial centers "learned the form and fashion and manners of the assembly of the form of etiquette (*nishast o barḳhwāst*, 'sitting and rising up') and conversation."[71]

Inshā, in defining the true Dihlawī (or person of Delhi), claimed that this social distinction was acquired not automatically through birth—for this would make even the lower classes potential equals of the nobility—but rather through education. Regardless of whether "their descendants live in Shāhjahānābād or in some other place, they will be Dihlawīs" so long as "their education and upbringing took place in the company of their parents, or maternal or paternal uncles, or big brother or some other elder" who had acquired their habits in Delhi.[72] The Urdu language, Inshā very clearly states, was not a recent byproduct of interactions between "invading" Mughals and indigenous commercial classes, as it had been described in the nearly contemporaneous account of Mīr Amman Dihlawī in *Bāġh o Bahār* (1802/3).[73] Instead, it was, like the "form and fashion and manners of the assembly," something cultivated from a range of Indian speech forms and written literary traditions. Indeed, the cultivation of this "new language" was an explicitly lexicographic process: "The excellent speakers of this place having agreed, picked out various good words from numerous languages and in applying for their purpose several expressions and terms, created a new language separate from others that was named *urdū*."[74]

Going by the statements of Ṭapish in his introduction to the dictionary, it would seem that he anticipates Inshā in privileging the speech of Delhi above that of other places.[75] It is thus surprising that he selects a relatively insignificant poet of Lucknow as an authority for the following entry for the idiom *pānī pī pī kosnā*, meaning "to curse excessively, to heap curses (upon)" or, more literally, "to curse so much that the throat, becoming dry, must be moistened by drinking":[76]

> *Pānī pī pī kosnā = kunāyah az kas̤rat-i bad duʿā-st kĕh dar hīć ḥāl faut nakanad. Mirzā ʿAlī Naqī Maḥshar kā shiʿr:*
>
> *kyā ẓulm hai dil meṅ bas masosā kī jaye*
> *jab yād-i lab-i jām kā bosah kī jaye*
> *īẕā hai saḳht mŏḥtasib ke hāthoṅ*
> *pānī pī pī ke us ko kosā kī jaye*[77]
>
> *Pānī pī pī kosnā* = idiom; an abundance of ill-will from which one cannot in any condition ever escape. A verse of Mirzā ʿAlī Naqī 'Maḥshar':
>
> What oppression in the heart! Let it be endured!
> When there is the memory of the kissing of the lip of the cup.
> It is a difficult trial at the hands of the censor
> He should be cursed repeatedly.

Mirzā ʿAlī Naqī Beg 'Maḥshar', a Kashmīrī native to Lucknow, was assassinated in Muḥarram AH 1208 (August 1793), aged about thirty years, by the relatives of the poet Mirzā ʿAlī 'Mŏhlat' in retaliation for his having killed the latter poet in a duel.[78] The charm of Maḥshar's verse lies in its ironic application of the idiom in connection with the sanctimonious inspector of public morality (*mŏḥtasib*): one must drink repeatedly in order to heap curses on him, presumably for separating the poet from the wine cup. For Ṭapish to have acknowledged the authority of Maḥshar as a poet and master of idiomatic speech—despite his primary associations with Kashmīr and Lucknow—may be attributed to their both having been among the students of Ḳhwājah Mīr Dard at Delhi, Ṭapish during his discipleship and Maḥshar while residing in Shāhjahānābād for two years as a fugitive.[79] It is possible that the two interacted during that time at the *mushāʿarah*s organized in the home of Dard before that famous sufi's death in 1785 and Ṭapish's flight to Lucknow in 1784.[80] In this particular case, and despite statements to the contrary, Ṭapish was in practice willing to recognize the authority of figures with whom he was personally connected or through whom he could demonstrate a direct relationship to a readily accepted Delhi-based master, implicitly accepting Inshā's self-serving claim that "being a *Dihlawī* is not restricted to an individual who is born in Delhi."[81]

As David Lelyveld has deftly argued,[82] the trouble with identifying in Inshā a theory of linguistic authority for Urdu is that one can never be entirely certain when the author is having a joke at his readers' expense. In fact, Inshā was not himself born in Delhi, having instead been born in Murshidabad in 1753 after his father, Mā-shāʾ Allāh Ḳhān 'Maṣdar', had left Delhi to seek out new opportunities in the capital of the Mughal province of Bengal.[83] Inshā spent most of his life in Avadh, first in Faiẓābād and then in Lucknow.[84] In the *Daryā-i Laṭāfat*, he describes visiting Delhi with his father, seeking out the poet and mystic Mirzā Jān-i Jānāṅ 'Maẓhar' (1699–1781) for his "fluency and eloquence" (*faṣāḥat aur balāġhat*).[85] In his description of the meeting, Inshā is primarily concerned with demonstrating his mastery of the social protocols of appropriate dress and gesture: he was, after all, seeking out Mirzā Jān-i Jānāṅ for the polished language of an authentic Dihlawī.

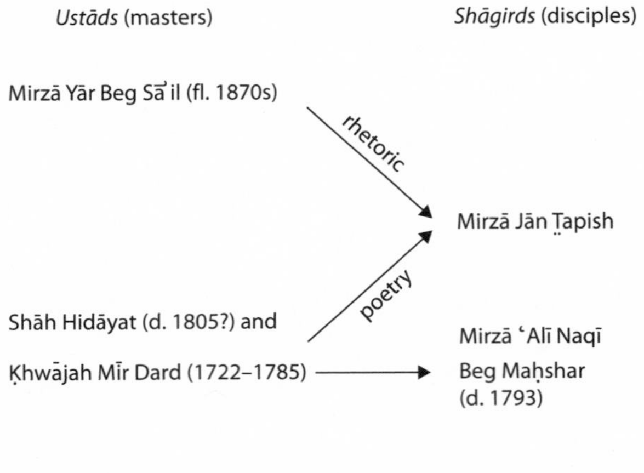

FIGURE 3.2 Mirzā Jān 'Ṭapish' and his *silsilah* (chain) of poetic discipleship

It thus comes as a surprise to read, in a later section entitled "The Authority of Poets" (*shuʿarā kī sanad*), Inshā's unequivocal rejection of the lexicographer's stock-in-trade, the citation of poets as authorities of linguistic usage. "According to the people of discernment," begins Inshā, "those people who take from the works of poets the authority of a word's eloquence are mistaken." Continuing, "this answer is also mistaken," so Inshā asserts,

> that poets are the most eloquent among all people: there are several such terms which having been constrained to the necessity of verse are generally bound within poetry [and] which are contrary to the language of their city. . . . Poets doubtless know the language of their city well, and it is not out of ignorance that they use unfamiliar words in their works (that is to say, they only use them out of poetic necessity).[86]

Eloquent poets may use a particular term, knowing full well that its usage is appropriate to a poetic context (perhaps for purposes of rhyme or scansion), though it would be out of place in spoken discourse. Inshā's claim is remarkable because it draws a clear distinction, unfortunately lost to polemicists like Amrit Rai, between the literary register of *rekḥtah* and an increasingly standardized Urdu of prose and speech. Instead of representing Urdu as a language slavishly adhering to Persian usages, as Rai argues,[87] what Inshā is documenting is the divergence of a literary register (*rekḥtah*) from a spoken language (Urdu) increasingly being called into service as a link language in an unprecedented range of social contexts.[88] Instead of doing "a lot of hair-splitting on the question of the *fasīh* and the *non-fasīh*,"[89] the anxiety, if it may be termed that, is more a matter of establishing which among the many spoken forms of the language would become the standard for Urdu literary prose. Inshā was able to anticipate that this linguistic standard need not be located in Urdu's most prestigious social domain, the realm of poetic usage.

EXILED FROM THE GARDEN OF *REKḤTAH*

Inshā and Ṭapish were both witnesses to a new era for the Urdu language, one in which Urdu as a language of prose was emerging as an important and by no means identical counterweight to a well-established poetic register. While disagreements regarding usage in the poetic register continued to be debated and, as in the aforementioned example of two students affiliated with rival *ustāds*, violently contested, the universal respect afforded to, and influence exercised by, a small group of individuals, the so-called pillars of classical Urdu poetry, provided models for literary production that were by and large universally accepted. These figures were able to wield their authority as poets, critics, and *ustāds* to turn the production of Urdu poetry into a true profession. Inshā challenged a literary culture that placed a premium upon devotion to one's *ustād*. In acknowledging the prerogative of skillful poets to use idioms that appear to run contrary to spoken usage, he warns about the potential of their students and admirers to mistake the skilled poet's self-conscious manipulation of idiomatic speech or dialect as possessing universal purchase:

> However, what can their students and imitators who live in other places know about whether this belongs to Urdu or the language of somewhere else, when Urdu-knowing Delhi poets have used these words in their poetry; and whether this [usage] has purposefully out of necessity been made permissible in their own works, or out of unnecessarily exertion. It may even rather be that in the poetry of that poor *ustād*, whatever one will see, all of it will be perceived to be good, and his companions will perform tortuous reasoning and will ultimately be forced to be embarrassed, in the manner in which we people who look in the works of any Mughals [i.e., Persian-speaking Tajik Turānīs from the Trans-Oxus region of Central Asia] understand it to be Fārsī, though we come across [Indic] terms like *sar-pānī*, etc.[90]

Inshā is not unique in expressing his skepticism about privileging "book learning" over that which is acquired through interpersonal guidance from an authoritative master.[91] Indeed, his example of the apparently misinformed Indian poet of Persian employing the so-called *istĕʿmāl-i hind*, deriving, as some have claimed, more from the "Turānī" or Mughal Persian of the trans-Oxus than from the "standard" modern Persian of Isfahan, evokes a criticism frequently leveled against South Asian poets of Persian.[92] Here, in fact, the familiar anxiety about the potential for students to be misled by the unsupervised reading of texts is combined with the possibility of the *ustād*'s lexical and syntactic choices in poetry being misapprehended as constituting a standard Urdu of speech and, potentially, prose. As *reḳhtah* poetry came to be appreciated in ever more diverse social and geographic contexts, it was increasingly becoming a diglossic register of prestige among populations whose mother tongues diverged quite significantly from that of the Delhi region.

Continuing, it is clear that Inshā disagrees not so much with those misapprehending of the character of Persian in India but rather with the thorny matter of Hinduwī's other literary registers, especially Braj:

> From this debate my private opinion is not that the most eloquent of Urdu poets, that is to say that the high status of the late Mirzā Rafīᶜ ['Saudā'] Dihlawī [1706?–1781] and 'Mīr' Ṣāḥib Mīr Muḥammad Taqī Ṣāḥib [1722–1810], should be reduced, although the seeker of sources of the mentioned one [i.e., Mīr], because of [his] having been born in Agra brought into his conversation the accent of that place and the vocabulary of "Braj" and Gwalior, and I even get the sense of these gentlemen that they abandoned several inappropriate terms (*nā-maᶜqūl alfāẓ*) . . . [93]

By stating that they abandoned several "inappropriate terms," Inshā is making the very provocative claim that *reḳhtah* did not come "naturally" to those two celebrated poets of the eighteenth century, Sauda and Mir, but was rather something they cultivated—perhaps even imperfectly—over the course of their creative careers. He goes on to connect these poets to the even more Braj-inflected poetry of the generations before them through a hemistich by Shāh Mubārak 'Ābrū' (c. 1683–1733?), whose origins in Gwalior situated him squarely in the middle of the Braj cultural region.[94] He cites the following examples of Braj usages as appearing in the verses of all three poets: "*dakho* [Braj for 'look!'] in place of *dekho*, and *dasā* [Braj past participle, 'appeared'] in place of *dekhā gayā* . . . are found in their works." Not surprisingly, examples of nonstandard usage can also be found among even the most storied Delhi families:

> Ḳhwājah Muḥammad Mīr Ṣāḥib [1735/6–1794], with the *taḳhalluṣ* 'Aṡar', who is the younger brother of Ḳhwajah Mīr 'Dard', used *dasā* in his *maṡnavī*, in this there must be some sort of good cause, just as in *tarwār* (sword), a word which his bigger brother in language used fluently instead of *talwār*.[95]

In short, Inshā demonstrated that the use of linguistic elements diverging from the spoken language of Delhi could be found in the *reḳhtah* poetry of both those born in Delhi and those from the hinterland. Even Ṭapish, a poet and lexicographer who had earned his way in distant Bengal through his command of the language of Delhi, was an appreciator—or even, as some have speculated,[96] himself an author—of Braj poetry.[97] Clearly, even the most famous poets of *reḳhtah* still broadly appreciated Braj as a literary register.

Inshā concludes with a statement, deceptively succinct in its phrasing, that, if taken out of the broader context of the work as a whole, can only be understood as a non sequitur: "In short, these [poetic] masters are, for the garden of *reḳhtah*, the cleaners of the thorns, rubbish, and debris of faults." Up to that point, the argument forwarded by Inshā would appear to make the case for precisely the opposite claim: that true masters (*aṣḥāb*) possess the skill to manipulate the lexical, morphological, and syntactic code of the poetic register, arranging the garden's "thorns, rubbish, and debris" in such a way that they *do not* appear as faults but rather as proof of their "fluency" in *reḳhtah* composition. To understand the true import of this statement, though, one must understand the distinction Inshā is making here between, on the one hand, *reḳhtah* as a linguistic register functioning within the limited social domain of poetic composition and, on the other, the *zabān-i urdū* (language of [the] Urdū), that is to say, the spoken language associated with particular places like Shāhjahānābād and other centers aspiring to replicate the courtly culture of the Mughal capital. Inshā is acknowledging that one cannot always use poetry as the standard by which to distinguish, in speech *and* prose, *faṣīḥ* (polished) from *ġhair-faṣīḥ* (unpolished).[98] In other words, whatever occurs linguistically within the garden of *reḳhtah* is all well and fine, so long as it remains safely hidden from view and away from the ordinary folk residing outside. However, the moment one wishes to carry the contents of this garden beyond its walls and into the broader world of speech and prose, one would do well to leave its "thorns, rubbish, and debris" behind.

Following his chapter on "The Description and Distinction of Being Born in Delhi," in which he makes the by now familiar argument that being a true Dihlawī depends more on the acquisition of *ādāb*—a word connoting elegance both of manners *and* of speech[99]—through education rather than birth, Inshā concludes his discussion of linguistic authority (*sanad*) with a chapter devoted to "the authority of Urdu." "In short," he begins, "the authority of Urdu should come from emperors and noblemen (*bādshāhoṅ aur umrā*) and their courtiers and companions." The cause for this is not what we might expect—their high or noble birth and access to power[100]—but rather their exposure to the best and the brightest of all walks of life:

> Because in their gatherings are present the theologian and poet, mathematician and accountant, singer and doctor, sufi and beautiful women; and the jargon (*iṣṯilāḥeṅ*) of various classes all come to be heard; and the words that they make into a jargon (*iṣṯilāḥ*), in accepting them the disapproval of both

> the great and insignificant ones is not possible, [for these three reasons] those *iṣṭilāḥ*s will with all haste come into currency. The words that come out of the mouths of very articulate and eloquent individuals in their company have been deeply considered, and if one has spoken correctly, then *amīr*s and their courtiers will like it. . . . And at the moment of speaking, this thought occurs to every consummate gentleman: "God forbid any such term should emerge from my tongue which should give rise to laughter at me in this full gathering!"[101]

If Shāhjahānābād, the capital city of Mughal emperors, drew ambitious social and economic entrepreneurs, the court of the emperor, in turn, engaged the most successful among them. He connects the authority of a courtly jargon (*iṣṭilāḥ*) with other social phenomena: "the tying of the turban, the fashion of the cut of tunic and under-robe (*qabā aur zer jāmah*) and slipper."[102] This authority, according to Inshā, explains the strangeness of the customs and speech of earlier monarchs,[103] whose ability to effect great changes in the codes of courtly performance was brought about through the consensus of the imperial assembly. Indeed, Amrit Rai is correct in identifying in Inshā a valorization of selectivity in the Urdu lexical corpus. But what Rai neglects to notice is that Inshā celebrated this selectivity precisely because it drew from a variety of linguistic sources and registers far beyond that of the Persian literary tradition. Urdu, according to Inshā, makes no claims to purity. Urdu's authority, instead, rests upon its appropriations from the Babel-like multitude, embodied in the felicitous conflation of *urdū* as place and *urdū* as language.

However much talent may have once been drawn to Delhi in previous centuries,[104] it is clear that by the middle of the eighteenth century Delhi was struggling to retain its most prominent literary and political figures. As we have seen, *urdū* denoted *a* royal camp, not just *the* royal camp of Shāhjahānābād, and likewise, Inshā's fixation on identifying for the "authority of Urdu (*urdū kī sanad*)" a standard "touchstone (*mĕʿyār*) [in] the language of Delhi" belies the supposed success of efforts by the "great ones" in the preceding decades to cull a literary register of its basilectal, or low-status, variants. Lexicography may reflect the rich diversity of the linguistic reality, but it does so within the walls of a well-tended garden in which the only visible weeds were those left intentionally. When ʿAbdul Wāsĕʿ was compiling his *Ġharāʾib al-Luġhāt* at the end of the seventeenth century, the spoken language of Delhi (not to mention that of Hāṅsī) was not yet fully codified: its value was limited to its novelty as a linguistic curiosity and its convenience as a medium through which to gloss Persian and other prestige languages for non-native speakers. If, however, by 1743 the term *urdū* could refer to the "*urdū* of Akbarābād" as naturally as to that of Shāhjahānābād (see chapter 2), so, too, could the language of the *urdū* be carried to new centers of power and talent. For Ḳhān-i Ārzū in his final years, this new center may have been at the Awadhī court of Ṣafdarjang in Faiẓābād; in 1792, it was for Ṭapish the Bengali court of Nawāb Nuṣrat Jang in Murshidābād. If *urdū* evolved gradually in usage from the place of the royal court to the name of a language, *urdū* as "language" would prove more portable and protean than even the tents and stakes of the original *urdū* "camp."

We would, however, be denying Inshā his due as a brilliant observer and satirist of social mores if his characterization of Delhi in the previous century were reduced to mere fantasy. Inshā was keenly aware that individuals are the carriers of culture and as such cannot be limited, as Rai claimed them to be, within the confines of a single class, neighborhood, or ethnic group:

> The language of Shāhjahānābād was that language of courtly people and those in the society of the worthy occupations (*muṣāḥibat-i peshah-yi qābil*), the beautiful beloveds, Muslim artisans (*musalmān ahl-i ḥirfah*), coolies (*shahd*), and the student-followers and servants of *amīrs*, even their sweepers.[105]

The charisma of the court thus extended through its many attendants and—perhaps controversially—even its lowest servants: "These people, wherever they go, their children are called 'Dillī-wāle,' and their home neighborhood is famous as the 'neighborhood of Dillī-wāle.' And if they are spread through the entire town, then that town is called 'the *urdū*.' "[106] The medium through which this court charisma was conveyed was the broad framework of social rules known as *ādāb* (plural of *adab*), whose most obvious manifestation was in the dress and speech of its initiates.

The *ādāb* of the Delhi court was, however, just one among many throughout the empire, and as Inshā acknowledges, these traditions were themselves constantly in flux over the course of time. Few could make a stronger claim to representing the legacy of Delhi's courtly tradition than Aẓfarī, a scion and former prisoner of the Mughal royal family. Yet throughout his account, Aẓfarī is frustrated by the apparent inability of others to recognize this distinction,[107] blaming it in part on the loss among the Mughal princes of their command of the Turkish language and, by extension, of a Turkic linguistic "whip to keep the populace in subjection" (*turkī zabān cābuk-i salṭanat-i hind ast*).[108] Through his eyes, Bengal appears as a wild, exotic, and dangerously enchanting land. Following his stay in Murshidabad and his meetings with Ṭapish, Aẕfarī continues his account with complaints about the insalubrious climate and geography of Bengal. Having fallen ill, he describes the exotic preparations of anise seed (*sauṅf*) and black pepper prescribed as remedies. While praising the quality of the local mangoes and bananas, he condemns the women as extremely bold, saucy, and cunning (*bisyār be-bāk va shok͟h-ṭabʿ va cālāk*) and belittles their husbands as weak and submissive.[109] On the road from Murshidabad to Calcutta, in the nearby city of Burdwān (contemporary Bardhaman in West Bengal), he complains about the paucity of "Shāhjahānābād folk" (*dar īn baldah kamtar az ahl-i shāh jahān ābād yāftah mī shavad*) and the ugliness, bad breath, and odor of its men—while at the same time admiring the beautiful teeth and long hair of its women. He reports that the town was populated by descendants of Yazīd (r. AD 680–683), a much-maligned figure associated with the martyrdom of ʿAlī's son and the Prophet Muḥammad's grandson Ḥusain, and he marvels that Muslims should take pride in this. Betraying his own frustrated (sexual) efforts, he decries the refusal of its people to marry their daughters to outsiders.[110] Not only are these people oblivious to the status of Aẕfarī as a descendant of the great Mughals and heir to their courtly culture, but they themselves incorrectly esteem their own descent without realizing how abhorrent it may be to the broader Persianate, or indeed Islamic, community.

It is thus this very lack of people from Delhi that relegates Murshidabad and other centers of South Asian Persianate culture in the judgment of Aẕfarī and Inshā to second- or third-tier status, if not complete irrelevance. According to Inshā, "the residents of Murshidābād and ʿAẓīmābād [Patna] consider themselves to be 'Knowers of Urdu' (*urdū-dān*) and call their towns *urdū*, because in ʿAẓīmābād [Patna] a quantity of Dillī-wāle must be living in a neighborhood." However, what is missing everywhere beyond Delhi—with the notable exception of Lucknow, Inshā's adopted home—is a critical mass of Dihlawīs, something that could develop in Lucknow because of the "proximity" of those two cities. The result is that "this city did not remain as Lucknow, but has become a Shāhjahānābād."[111] What emerges in this analysis, crude and anecdotal though it may be and despite the vociferous protests of Inshā's other interlocutors,[112] is an acknowledgment that self-proclaimed Shāhjahānābāds had begun to crop up by the 1750s in *qaṣbah* towns throughout northern India.[113] Certainly, they could not all thrive or draw Dihlawīs to the same extent, nor could they ever hope to match the splendor of the Delhi court of yore. Lucknow was clearly in a class apart, and ʿAẓīmābād (Patna) and Murshidābād a step below, "and the people of Muġhalpūrah [Lahore] and other Shāhjahānābādis are excluded from this discussion."

The inferior status of Murshidabad and ʿAẓīmābād was attributable not merely to the small numbers of true Dihlawīs settling there. It was also a function of the quality of persons attracted to a place so distant, insalubrious, and, by Delhi's standards, unrefined:

> You should know that during the time of Sirāj al-Daulah [r. 1756–1757], some few *manṣab-dārs* and several actors (*naqqāl*), who are called *bhāṇḍ* ['jester,' 'buffoon,' 'strolling player'], two or three singers and courtesans (*kasbīyāṅ*), one or two dancing boys (*bhagete*), two or three bakers (*nān-bāʾī*), ten or twelve elegy-reciters (*marśiyah ḳhwāṅ*), one or two greengrocers (*kunjṛe*) and grain-parchers (*bharbūṅje*) seeking profit arrived in Murshidābād from Shāhjahānābād, for which reason in that era even a chickpea roaster would not proceed toward Murshidābād from Delhi without [the promise of] ten thousand rupees.[114]

Despite mentioning the "some few" (*baʿẓe*) men of rank (*manṣab-dars*, including, presumably, Inshā's father), who made their way to Murshidabad, the impression the reader comes away with is of Delhi's flotsam and jetsam floating downstream toward greener pastures. How could such a motley crew of such low birth and occupational disrepute possess the ability to influence the customs of the original inhabitants to the extent that the character of the entire city could, as had occurred in Lucknow, be completely transformed into a new Shāhjahānābād?

Ṭapish, in producing a dictionary of idiomatic expressions for his patron Shams al-Mulk, and Inshā, by outlining a history, theory, grammar, vocabulary, and manual of rhetoric for the language of Delhi, produced guidebooks enabling those not blessed by birth or birthright with exposure to Delhi's culture of courtly *ādāb* to obtain them through study. As the economic and political importance of Delhi declined in the latter half of the eighteenth century and the poets of Delhi fanned out to Avadh, the Punjab, Hyderabad, Bihar, Bengal, and other regions, they acquired students who wished to emulate, first, a poetic register (*reḳhtah*) in their poetic production and, second, the speech and manners of the elite residents of Shāhjahānābād in formal spoken situations and (increasingly) in their prose writing. Ṭapish, writing in the Bengali court in Murshidabad, claims to be reproducing the idiomatic speech of Delhi, ostensibly to give the elite of the Bengal court access to the language of the Mughal capital. The dictionary's entries, however, are supported not with the quoted speech of Delhi's inhabitants (thereby approximating prose) but rather with poetry. About fifteen years later, Inshā argued that people who wish to know Urdu should not take the usage of poets as authoritative since the poetic register, *reḳhtah*, allows certain lexical and syntactic usages that are *contrary* to the *speech* of Delhi. As Inshā points out, these prestige "registers" are not identical: *reḳhtah poetry* permits vocabulary, expressions, and grammatical elements deriving from Braj, not to mention Persian usages that appear ostentatious when incorporated into Urdu *speech.*[115] I do not, however, wish to draw too fine a terminological distinction between *reḳhtah* as a poetic register and *urdū* as an elite dialect conforming to the speech of the courtly culture in Shāhjahānābād. I am using them as terms of convenience, fully aware that they were applied to a wide variety of poetry, speech, and prose, not all of which adhered linguistically to the speech of Shāhjahānābād, and that both *reḳhtah* poetry and Urdu speech, as documented by Inshā, had both undergone significant changes (at least lexically) over a short period of time.

CULTIVATING A "SENSE OF DISPLACEMENT"

The *Shams al-Bayān* appears to document a linguistic situation wherein a prestige dialect, the language of Delhi, coexisted with a vernacular lacking official status, that is, whatever the Bengal courtiers might have spoken in their homes.[116] The diglossia of the Murshidabad court was thus characterized by the coincidence of multiple registers specific to certain limited social domains. It also was influenced by the continued presence of Persian as both a language of poetry and a ubiquitous medium of prose among the educated elite (including many British). Arabic and to a far lesser extent Turkish were also familiar, if not universally comprehended, the first primarily as a language of ritual and scholarship and the latter as an expression of ethnic solidarity. A range of vernaculars, including dialects of what is now called Bengali and forms of eastern Hindi, may also have been present in courtly situations. While Bengali (or Bhojpuri or Awadhi) might be "genetically related" to the Delhi dialect of western

Hindi, the situation at regional courts corresponds more with Fishman's "extended" diglossia (occurring among grammatically distinct languages) than the "classic" diglossia occurring in the early part of the eighteenth century, when Delhi poets were learning to write in a new poetic register (*reḳhtah*) that approximated but was not always identical to the spoken language of their own city, that is, Shāhjahānābād (Delhi).[117] Abstract notions of diglossia, however, rarely account for the range of linguistic repertoires that an individual acquires and deploys over his or her lifetime: microanalytic studies that document individual language use over a career usefully complement the longitudinal historical method of literary production introduced in the previous chapter.[118]

Another explanation for the linguistic situation obtaining at the court at Murshidabad is that Urdu, like Turkish, as the language of Delhi's émigré community, had become a symbolic means of maintaining social and political solidarity among this linguistic diaspora. Travel provided a very strong incentive for the codification of linguistic forms—that is, the repertoires over which one had active command and those observed in others. The eminent historians of early modern South Asia Muzaffar Alam and Sanjay Subrahmanyam have documented the importance in Persianate travelogues of a rhetoric of authenticity that emphasizes an "empiricism" of lived experience lacking the "exaggerations and diplomatic statements . . . one finds in the history books."[119] Autobiographical works likewise combine authenticating elements from both Arab-Persianate biographical and travel genres and, in the case of well-traveled authors, are themselves often indistinguishable from travelogues. Geographic and linguistic displacement forces the traveler to make sense of cultural and material differences through analogies, recorded in literary form through the travelogue and memoir or the grammar, dictionary, and phrasebook.

Travel, as often undertaken through compulsion as by choice, created a sense of displacement among some prominent members of the Persianate elite during the eighteenth century. While perhaps not as drastic as the displacement experienced by those working in close proximity to the British, it nevertheless brought certain aspects of language—both within and beyond one's repertoire—into sharp relief. It was travel that provided the impetus for Āz̤farī to produce a Persian translation of a Chaghatay Turkish treatise on prosody prepared more than two centuries earlier by another inveterate traveler, Z̤ahīruddīn Muḥammad Bābur (1483–1530), the founder of the Mughal dynasty in India and Āz̤farī's own direct ancestor.[120] For Ṭapish, command of Turkish, the native language of the earliest and most vigorous Mughal emperors, proved to be a skill that was both portable and readily convertible into social status and economic advantage in the regional courts. For both men, language, through its objectification in such explicitly didactic genres as the Persianate grammar and dictionary, was inextricably and (for them) felicitously bound with *ādāb*, the dominant international social code of courtly behavior.

The cosmopolitan nature of Persian scholarship in South Asia cut across traditional ethnic, religious, and economic groupings; C. A. Bayly argues that it constituted an "ecumene" defined by the literary and linguistic competence of its users. For increasingly dispersed language communities the deployment of Persianate modes of metalinguistic objectification through genres like dictionaries and grammars contributed not so much to the preservation as to the gradual spread of vernacular languages into new social domains hitherto reserved solely for Persian and Sanskrit. Rather than a cosmopolitan ecumene that self-consciously cultivated a myth of universality, these diasporic or displaced languages of limited social domain had, at least in the final years of the eighteenth century, no illusions of achieving the same transregional ubiquity enjoyed by Persian and Sanskrit in their roles as prestigious link languages of literature and statecraft. Speakers of the various Turkish languages prided themselves in being heirs to a long tradition of literature and political successes. As was the case with Persian, they would be unlikely to claim that the "standard" of their language derives from any particular place in India,[121] with authors like Aẕfarī especially critical of the Mughal descendants residing in the Red Fort. Nor would they want to make such a claim: Turkish (unlike Persian) persisted in India primarily as a marker of genetic identity, a link between foreign-born ancestors and Indian-born descendants, and only secondarily as a marker of class identity—theoretically, in the case of Persian, available to anyone able to obtain fluency in it.

With Urdu, the situation at the turn of the nineteenth century was quite different: inasmuch as its cachet derived from an association with a particular place—Shāhjahānābād—the language relied upon an increasingly nostalgic creation myth located in a glorious Mughal past. For Inshā, Urdu made no claims to purity, for its quality derived from a broader horizontal, that is to say, areal, integration of the best parts of all languages, coming together to form a vertically (that is, socially) integrated whole in a single place, Shāhjahānābād. Inshā celebrates (perhaps with tongue in cheek) "the language of the courts and the society of the occupations of competent individuals, the beautiful beloveds, Muslim artisans, coolies (*shahd*), and the student-followers and servants of *amīrs*, even their sweepers"[122] precisely because of the association of language with a place—the Mughal capital—that drew charismatic interlocutors from afar and from both high and low. Transported away from Delhi, either in written literary collections or in the form of their physical persons, the charisma of the most celebrated pillars of *reḳhtah* was proving to be a valued commodity in the regional courts of India.[123]

Subjected to the same reproducible and conventionalized methods of objectification (through genres such as the *niṣāb* primers, grammars, and dictionaries), certain languages like Turkish and Urdu became increasingly (or, in some cases, for the first time) pedagogically viable. The experience of acquiring familiarity with a language could be detached from prior participatory frameworks, whether of poetic discourse, domestic usage, or particular forms of knowledge preserved in writing, and made available to new groups of learners seeking to fulfill social functions once exclusively performed in Persian. Instead of literate groups deriving their authority from access to distinct languages and scripts associated with various elite social domains, it was becoming feasible by the turn of the nineteenth century to imagine a single language fulfilling the broad spectrum of social functions that an individual could expect to encounter on a daily basis. Indeed, the rapid spread of the literary culture of *reḳhtah* among traditionally illiterate and nonelite groups caused anxiety among traditional elites. The poet Mīr, to give but one example, began writing, in response to this development, savage satires against what he perceived as the explosive growth of a class of poetasters.[124]

This objectification of language into pedagogical materials was enabled by the eighteenth-century geographical displacement of certain elite speech groups away from their homes. For Turkish and Persian speakers from more distant climes, this came about through war, slavery, and the search for financial and social gains. Similar causes compelled an increasingly self-aware Urdu language community to relocate away from more proximate centers of Mughal culture to towns across the length and breadth of the subcontinent. The languages of displaced elites enjoyed affiliations with cultures of distinction, and at this early stage in the deracination of language from social domain, the linguistic prestige that sustained their continued cultivation traveled with them. They were received in distant courts precisely because of their association with an elite cosmopolitan culture. The social historian Lisa Mitchell neatly explains the development of linguistic commensurability in this way:

"Once content became free-floating, available equally via every language, the only thing left that appeared unique about any particular language was its ability to signify 'culture.' "[125] Unlike later nineteenth-century language movements, at the turn of the century, Urdu did not need to justify its worth by an enumeration of its constituent speakers or by mapping out their distribution within certain geographic boundaries. Instead, Urdu was valued for the culture that it signified—an elite Persianate culture for which authority was derived not by popular mandate but rather by the individual influence of exemplary, usually literary, figures. In short, Urdu derived its authority from charisma, not currency.

Despite the disparity in the respective language communities of Turkish and Urdu, both represented political formations that were increasingly in competition with the new political dispensation emanating from Calcutta. Ṯapish participated in an Indian intellectual vanguard that confidently engaged with new and increasingly global regimes of knowledge. He was perceptive enough to codify the language of his own home, thereby helping turn the linguistic charisma he possessed by dint of his elite Delhi upbringing into a fungible commodity. Indeed, it was Ṯapish who reputedly encouraged Aẕfarī to set his recollections down in the *Wāqiʿāt* (Events), nine years after the latter had escaped from the Red Fort and arrived in Murshidabad in May 1797.[126]

More than to Aẕfarī, credit for realizing the potential for Urdu to expand into new social domains and include new social participants goes to Inshā, whose creative output demonstrates a recognition of the radical potential of the total commensurability of language. He viewed language as a vessel capable of carrying any content: his experiments include a *dīwān* (poetic collection) composed of words lacking dotted letters, a lengthy grammatical note and incomplete diary in Turkī, poetry in Pashto, and what may be the first *ġhazal* to incorporate English terms. Most celebrated of all is *Rānī Ketakī kī Kahānī* (The story of Rānī Ketakī), in which he set upon the task of "composing a story in which no other language than Hindi would be used" by eschewing "foreign" terms drawn from Arabic and Persian:

> One day as I was sitting about I had the idea of composing a story in which no other language than Hindi would be used (*hindī ko chuṭ aur kisī bolī kī puṭ na mile*). On deciding this my heart expanded like a flower-bud. It should contain no foreign language (*bāhar ki bolī*) or local dialect (*gaṁvārī*). A certain literate, conservative, shrewd old fellow of my acquaintance protested at this, and with shaking head, screwed-up face, raised nose and eyebrows, and rolling

> eyes said, "This can never come off. Your story will neither lose its Hinduī character nor take on *bhāṣā* character? You will simply write just as worthy folk generally talk among themselves? Using no admixture of language? It won't succeed!"[127]

As will be clear from the passage above, Inshā's intent was as much to entertain as it was to innovate. Scholars will no doubt continue to debate the impact, if any, that this particular work (like the Persian *Daryā-i Laṭāfat*) may have had upon the subsequent development of Hindi and Urdu prose.[128] What, however, is most remarkable about this passage is how clearly Inshā illustrates through his incredulous interlocutor how great the perceived distinction was between the language spoken among "worthy people" and that actually deemed worthy of being recorded on paper, presumably combining both "foreign language" *and* rustic "dialect."

It is this very distinction between the literary register of *reḳhtah* poetry and that spoken among "worthy people" that is effaced in the *Shams al-Bayān* of Ṯapish. Despite his claims to document the variegated idioms of both "the daily speech of the noble classes (*ḳhawāṣṣ*) and a variety of the ordinary ones . . . in use by authenticated distant ones in the ordinary speech of those homes and . . . current in the speech of those cities," it is clear that this work belongs more properly to the function of the glossary, assisting readers as they wade their way through difficult texts. Ṯapish says as much himself.

> In the manuscripts were arranged in many verses and the understanding of distant ones (*dūr-dastān*) all of whom are situated in cities far away, employed in explanation of the idioms of the houses of Delhi and the colloquial speech (*rozmarrah*) of eloquent men of the Exalted Court (*urdū-i muʿallā*). [But students] could not arrive at the genius of their kind. [This] composition was ornamented with gems so that the study of that sort of allusion (*kināyat*) was given perspecuity, making this art easy for students.[129]

It would be a mistake to conclude that the *Shams al-Bayān* is simply a document of either "the daily speech of the noble classes" or of the "ordinary ones" of Delhi. Instead, it is a commentary, organized alphabetically, on the poetic texts that were making their way along the length of the Gangetic river system, serving as a guide to those seeking to participate in Delhi's *reḳhtah* literary culture from the distant court in Murshidabad.

Moreover, his stated intent, to add to "the clarification of the idioms of *reḳhtah* to the increase of the delicacy of meaning," signaled that this participation entailed not merely passive readings of texts by novices but also the active contributions of mature authors seeking to add their own meanings to those already recorded in the poetic lexicon.

Like Hāṅswī's *Ġharā'ib al-Luġhāt*, the author of the *Shams al-Bayān* was unable to stare directly at the stuff of spoken language. He was instead compelled to view language through the veil of poetry. This was the case even when, as will be shown in the following chapter, an already extant authenticating verse was not immediately available. Mirzā Jān's tendency to provide his own verses when no others were forthcoming later in the nineteenth century proved to be a controversial method of providing authentication. In retrospect, it served as a functional compromise between the requirement, first, that the idiomatic phrase be authenticated through the citation of a text and, second, that the author of this text belong to what he calls variously the "people of the tongue" (*ahl-i zabān*) and "authenticated distant ones." By the end of the nineteenth century, South Asian lexicographers were coming under increasing scrutiny as they began to fashion their craft into a profession. It was thought that in order to establish a objective "scientific" perspective, all connections with one's meticulously cultivated poetic persona would need to be severed. While few could question the right claimed by Ṭapish to present *as a lexicographer* "an opinion of the idioms the eloquent knowers of the language and the subtlety the correct knowers of speech keep," should the lexicographer also endeavor to carry out the work of the poet, his objectivity could no longer be assured.

PRISON, PATRONAGE, AND PENSIONS

Within ninety days of his arrest, the British had already submitted a preliminary report on the conspiracy that Ṭapish was alleged to have helped perpetrate between Shams al-Daulah and Wazīr ʿAlī. A Special Tribunal indicted Shams al-Daulah on August 22, 1799.[130] On January 16, 1800, Shams al-Daulah composed a letter to Governor General Wellesley, in which he criticized the British for confining him "while his degradation had continued since his transfer to Dacca." In this letter, he also confessed to having been forced into writing a letter to "Agha Muhammad Khan, King of Persia and Zaman Shah [amīr of Afghanistan], in a state of mental agony and degradation." He begged permission to leave India "in consequence of the vexation, despondency and sorrow" when he was "persuaded by [an] ill-disposed designing man, of whose character I was ignorant and who for his own advantage practiced his artifice and cunning upon me." Citing a letter written to the governor general in December 1798 several months prior to his arrest, he outlines how he suffered with his wife and child in Murshidabad on account of that unnamed individual.[131] A little more than a week after Shams al-Daulah penned his letter to the governor general, on January 25, 1800, a special court held at the latter's Belvedere Estate announced that the nobleman had been "convicted of attempts to enter into League with the Sovereigns of other Countries for the purpose of destroying the sovereignty, of endeavouring to convert[132] himself with the Zamindars of Zilla Bihar, with a design of exciting internal connections and of keeping up a treasonable correspondence."[133] He was sentenced by the Special Tribunal on February 25, 1800, to confinement "until the Governor General in Council shall be satisfied with the sincerety [*sic*] of his repentance."[134] Shams al-Daulah composed another letter to the governor general appealing his sentence and promising that he "will never act contrary to the British Government."[135] It would seem that this letter was to little avail since his sentence was approved by the governor general in council on December 18, 1800.

Though considerably less space is devoted in the histories of the conspiracy to Mirzā Jān Ṯapish, we know that just two days prior to the approval of his former employer's sentence Ṯapish was himself tried under the same procedure and, after having been charged with and convicted of treason, was handed a similar sentence.[136] The following *fatwā* was issued by Chief Qāẓī Sayyid Mŏʿaẓẓam Ḥusain:

> Mirza Jan Tuppish became associated with Shams-ud-daulah for creating troubles and induced him to send letters to Zaman Shah and his courtiers. He is also charged with inciting the Bihar *zamindars* to Join. But this *Mukhtarnama* [a power of attorney alleged to have been written to incite almost two dozen Bengali *zamīndārs* to rally against the British] is a forged document. There is no foundation for the second charge.
>
> The Governor of the province is to prevent this nobleman's pursuing his rebellious endeavours. Mirza Jan Tuppish is to be put into prison till he repents.
>
> Mufti's fatwa—The defendant after his confession will remain in prison till the signs of repentance become evident.[137]

While the identity of the "unnamed individual" that Shams al-Daulah alleges to have "practiced his artifice and cunning upon" him remains unclear, it is interesting to note that the council on December 30 of that year instructed the registrar of the Nizamat Adalat to continue to keep Ṭapish jailed separately, in the charge of a different authority (the officer commanding the town guard) than that of his former employer (the sheriff of Calcutta).[138] Ṭapish was represented to the court during his trial as "the chief adviser and confidant of Nawab Shams-ud-daulah," and drafts of the correspondence sent with the seal of Shams al-Daulah were, according to the testimony of several witnesses, discovered in a pen holder belonging to Ṭapish.[139] Ṭapish, in his defense, claimed that it was he who suggested a departure from Bengal, not wishing his master to experience the shame of being humiliated by being removed from Murshidabad to Dacca: "I suggested Iran . . . I made a draft of a letter to the ruler of Iran . . . I also expressed my desire to accompany him [Shams al-Daulah]."[140]

Whether or not Shams al-Daulah blamed Ṭapish for his predicament, the distance between the two during their confinement only grew upon their release. Shams al-Daulah was released in 1803 on a security pledged by his brother, the nāʾib niẓām of Dacca, Nuṣrat Jang.[141] The nawāb was eventually granted a full and free pardon in 1806 by the acting governor general, Sir George Barlow,[142] with a restored stipend of Rs. 1000 (£66 13s. 4d.) per month.[143] It remains unclear from published records when exactly the British authorities released Ṭapish. Ṭapish documented the year of his release in a chronogram. Preserved in his notebook, it appears in a verse set written in praise of Muftī 'Ṣabīḥ' al-ʿĀlim, a Calcutta-based legal scholar to whom Ṭapish owed his release:

mirzā jān ṭapish ānkĕh yad-i qadrat ḥaqq
gil-i ḥasmish hamĕh az āb-i nijābat bĕsarast
bĕhar tārīkh rihāʾish 'ṣabīḥ' az khāmah
"ṭapish az qaid-i alam yāft rihāʾī" bĕnosht[144]

Mirzā Jān 'Ṭapish' who by the omnipotence of God
The clay of his marking [*ḥasm*, A. 'cutting'] is the limit of all waters of generosity
On every date, from the writing-reed, [comes] liberation from 'Ṣabīḥ' ['beautiful']
[So that] he wrote " 'Ṭapish' obtained release from the prison of grief"

The simple sum of the *abjad* values of the words comprising the final hemistich of the verse set comes to AH 1221, corresponding with the period of March 1806 to March 1807. Given the proximity of that date to Barlow's pardon of Shams al-Daulah, it is quite possible that Ṭapish was able to gain his release through the intercession of Muftī Ṣabīḥ al-ᶜĀlim once the government had forgiven his erstwhile employer.

When he was released, Ṭapish chose not to return to the service of Nawāb Shams al-Daulah, instead selecting to join the retinue of Rājah Lab Kishor. Najmul Islām believes that this change was motivated by the courtier's desire to continue living in Calcutta.[145] Contrasted with this, we can cite the example of Mirzā Muḥammad ᶜAlī, alias Nanko Miyāṅ, another imprisoned nobleman attached to the retinue of Shams al-Daulah. Nanko Miyāṅ had served as overseer of the nawāb's household establishment prior to the trial of his master. In the account of Najmul Islām: "Due to devotedness, Nawāb Shams al-Daulah, after release, esteemed Nanko Miyāṅ even more than before and established him as the chief business manager of his retinue."[146] Ṭapish, in contrast, elected to try his luck in the city of his captivity—the new capital of the Bengal Presidency.

It is at this point that the colonial record on Ṭapish becomes silent except for a few stray references, including one from September 1812, when a reward was distributed for a copy of the "Kooliyati Ṭupish ['Collected Works of Ṭapish']; the poetical works of Mirza Jan, a living poet" as part of the "Eleventh Public Disputations" of the College of Fort William.[147] Unnoticed by historians of Urdu literature were the contributions by Ṭapish to the compilation of the collected works of Muḥammad Mīr Taqī Mīr, published for the college at Calcutta in 1811 and "edited by Meerza Kaẓim Ulee Juwan, Meerz Jan Tupish, Muoluvee Mooḥummud Uslum and Moonshee Ghoolam Ukbar."[148]

Equally neglected is the assistance that Ṭapish may have provided to British lexicographers working at the College of Fort William. Verses by Ṭapish are cited on numerous occasions in *A Dictionary, Hindoostanee and English* prepared by Captain Joseph Taylor "for his own private use . . . [and] Revised and prepared for the press, with the assistance of learned natives in the College of Fort William, by W. Hunter, M.D." in 1808.[149] From the presence of verses selected by Ṭapish for his *Shams al-Bayān*, including many attributed to "Mirza Jan Tupish," reproduced in this *Dictionary*, it would appear that either Taylor or Hunter or both had access to a manuscript of the *Shams al-Bayān*. Compare, for example, the entry for the phrase *panee pee pee kosna* (figure 3.3) in the first volume of the 1808 *Dictionary*[150] with

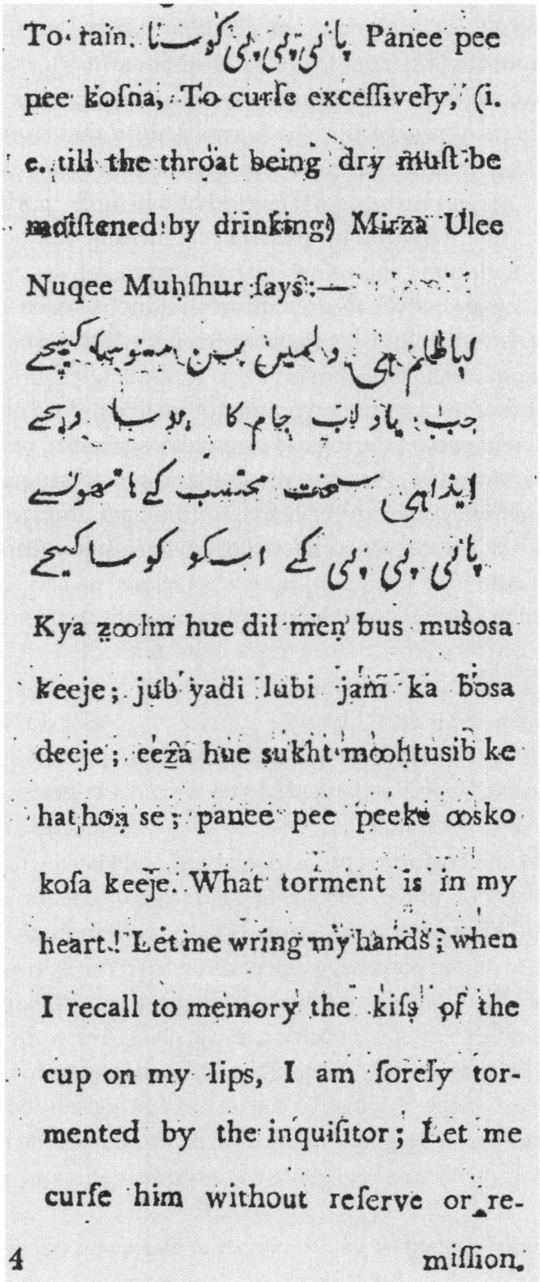

To rain. پانی پی پی کوسنا Panee pee pee koſna, To curſe exceſſively, (i. e. till the throat being dry muſt be moiſtened by drinking) Mirza Ulee Nuqee Muhſhur ſays:—

کیا ظلم ہے دل میں بس مسوسا کیجے
جب یاد لب جام کا بوسا دیجے
ایذا ہے سخت محتسب کے ہاتھوں سے
پانی پی پی کے اسکو کوسا کیجے

Kya zoolm hue dil men bus musosa keeje; jub yadi lubi jam ka bosa deeje; eeza hue sukht moohtusib ke hathon se; panee pee peeke oosko koſa keeje. What torment is in my heart! Let me wring my hands; when I recall to memory the kiſs of the cup on my lips, I am ſorely tormented by the inquiſitor; Let me curſe him without reſerve or remiſſion.

4

FIGURE 3.3 *Panee pee pee kosna* from Taylor and Hunter's 1808 *Dictionary*

that in the *Shams al-Bayān.* William Carmichael Smyth, who prepared a revised second edition of the *Dictionary* in 1820, moved "numerous elegant quotations from the different Hindoostanee poets" (originally drawn by Taylor and Hunter from the *Shams al-Bayān*) to an appendix at the end of his single-volume octavo edition. He acknowledged that these quotations, "though elegant in themselves, [are] still of no use to a mere beginner, who could not understand them, or who would be satisfied . . . without requiring the authority."[151] Writing from distant England without the benefit of either Taylor or Hunter (both of whom had died in the intervening years), Smyth may have prepared his appendix—in effect a verbatim transcription and translation of Ṯapish's *Shams al-Bayān*—without any clear awareness of its original Indian authorship.

The sum of evidence, however, points to the likelihood that Ṯapish had been consulted in person during the original compilation of the 1808 first edition of the *Dictionary.* It is conceivable that the relationship between Ṯapish and William Orby Hunter (1755–1812) began during the former's captivity. Hunter had served as sheriff of Fort William from 1790 to 1791 and as such would have been familiar with the jails in Calcutta.[152] As a regular examiner in Persian and Hindustani at the college from 1801, Hunter must have been aware of the presence of so respected an Urdu poet as Ṯapish during his long imprisonment.[153]

Ṯapish composed his most famous literary work, *Maśnavī-yi Bahār-i Dānish* (Springtime of knowledge), in AH 1217 (1802–1803), while in captivity.[154] After his release, Ṯapish rededicated the work to Captain Joseph Irwin Taylor (1765/6–1811) and appended several verses in praise of the British government at the beginning of the narrative in the *sabab-i tālīf* (reason for composition) section of the preface. Scholars agree that Ṯapish must have made these additions after his release (AH 1221), perhaps in the hope that he would be able to obtain patronage or a pension from the British government or serve in an official capacity within the College of Fort William.[155] Whether or not he was able to obtain a position at the college or work directly with Taylor, it is clear that both Taylor and the institution were familiar with his work and at least engaged Ṯapish in the task of editing the abovementioned collected works of Mīr Taqī Mīr. Najmul Islām also makes the briefest mention of a section of the notebook devoted to the "usage of poets":

> Ṯapish included quotations and summaries of many books from which one may obtain a good sense of Ṯapish's scholarly interests. At several places, one suspects that these are the foundations for some sort of composition by

> Ṭapish, but for which he did not have the opportunity to bring to completion. For example, several pages are marked up with the titles of "the usages of poets" (*taṣarrufāt-i shuʿarā*), on which in some places one sees corrections, additions, and alterations from the pen of Ṭapish himself, and in these very folios, some space has been left in the spaces in-between.[156]

His continued interest in compiling lists of the usages of poets (*taṣarrufāt-i shuʿarā*), replete with blank spaces, provides strong evidence that Ṭapish continued to be engaged in lexicographic projects well after his release from jail, possibly contributing these "usages" to the lexicographic projects of Taylor and Hunter.

The chronology of the notebook's contents generally corresponds with the period in which Taylor and Hunter were occupied with the compilation of their own *Dictionary*. The earliest date mentioned in the notebook appears in a memorandum written about two years after his release from prison on 10 Rabīʿ I AH 1223 (c. May 6, 1808).[157] The text of the memorandum (*sih rūpiyah cahār ānah dar sarkār dārad*, '3 Rupees, 4 Ana received by *sarkār*') probably refers to his post within the household establishment of Rājah Lab Kishor, as corroborated by Maulvī ʿAbdul Qādir's account of Ṭapish in a description of the renowned men of Calcutta:

> Among the famous poets of Calcutta was Mirzā Jān 'Tapish' [*sic*] Shāhjahānābādī, the *shāgird* of Ḳhwājah Mīr Dard. 'Tapish' remained in Murshidābād as a companion of Nawāb Shams al-Mulk and in the companionship of his own Āqā ['master'] many afflictions were created, after liberation from these calamities, Rājah Lab Kishore provided surety for his livelihood.[158]

The last date appearing in the notebook corresponds with July 1814, some two years after the death of Hunter in 1812. While the first edition of Taylor and Hunter's *Dictionary* appeared in 1808, Hunter continued to labor on another work, a *Collection of Proverbs and Proverbial Phrases in Persian and Hindustani, with Translations*, until his death in 1812.[159] As was noted above, Ṭapish was awarded a prize for the publication of his collected works in 1812 and had been involved in editing the collected works of Mīr published under the auspices of the college in 1811. A memorandum in the notebook dated ʿAẓīmābād (Patna) 27 Shawwāl 1225 (c. November 3, 1812) places Ṭapish in Bihar approximately one year after Hunter's departure for Java and one month prior to Hunter's death there in December 1812.[160] This would suggest that Ṭapish had indeed found patronage through Hunter and Taylor but that once Hunter had left Calcutta his situation there became untenable, compelling him to seek out new opportunities in Patna and Benares, the latter place being indicated in another memorandum dated 20 Rabīᶜ al-Ṡānī 1225 (c. April 22, 1813).

It was British rather than Indian lexicographers who would take the innovative work of Ṯapish and incorporate it, almost wholesale, into their own lexicographic endeavors. And while Ṯapish is not given any explicit credit for having contributed to—or even provided the basis for—the compilation of Taylor and Hunter's *Dictionary*, he was granted more authority as a poet and witness of lexical usage by these contemporary British lexicographers than was later conceded to him by fellow Indians. Taylor and Hunter were by and large content to copy without attribution his lexical corpus and often reproduced his selection of prooftexts from canonical eighteenth-century poets. When, however, Ṯapish saw fit to append poetic prooftexts by his own hand to his definitions, these were almost always rejected by later Indian lexicographers and replaced with authenticating verses of their own selection (or fabrication). Indeed, an Urdu lexicographer would be surprised to find "Tupish" depicted as one of the "celebrated poets" included among the most "well-known of Hindoostanee poets . . . equally well-known [as] Meer, or Souda, or . . . Taban" in *The Orientalist; or, Letters of a Rabbi*, an 1831 English work on Indian literature.[161] Already, his lengthy contact with the British, first in captivity and later as a lexicographic collaborator, afforded Ṯapish certain social advantages, albeit ones that proved difficult for his Indian peers to accommodate even a century after his death. Whether it was because of his contact with the British or his lengthy exile from the Mughal heartland, Ṯapish earlier than anyone had come to experience and embody the struggle in Urdu between past and future modes of authority, be they political, literary, or lexicographic.

[4] 1900: LEXICOGRAPHY AND THE SELF

Like a banyan tree in whose shade saplings could sprout but not thrive, let alone grow to equal, the author of the Farhang-i Āṣafiyah *casts a shadow across the field of lexicography. In the entire history of Urdu, there is no other dictionary that has surpassed it.*

— Sayyid Ḳhwājah Ḥusainī

Persian lexicographers are not original in their compositions. They are mostly borrower [sic] and immitator [sic] and they copy from their predecessors so closely that they may be accused of plagiarism.[1]

— Nażīr Ahmad

THE "NEW" URDU LEXICOGRAPHY

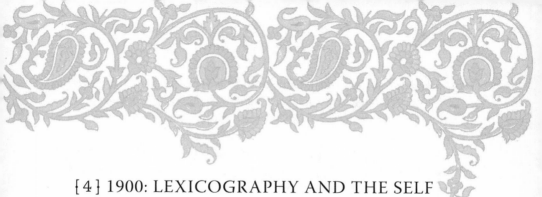

In 1888, Sayyid Aḥmad Dihlawī (1846–1918) published the first two volumes of what would eventually become for many scholars the single most useful dictionary of the Urdu language. The title that Sayyid Aḥmad chose for his dictionary, *Hindūstānī Urdū Luġhat*, with its indication of the language covered (Hindustani with Urdu definitions) and genre (*luġhat*, 'dictionary'), signaled a new era of Urdu lexicography, one that drew as much from the work of contemporary British linguistic and ethnographic methods as it did from existing traditions of South Asian Persianate lexicography. Published in the midst of contentious Hindi-Urdu debates that were taking place during the late nineteenth and early twentieth centuries,[2] his goal to define in Urdu both the spoken and written forms of language in use across a vast region (Hindustan) must be interpreted as part of a strategic effort to prove his language as capacious enough to represent the diverse populations that came under his expansive purview. Ultimately facing financial difficulties, however, Sayyid Aḥmad would seek and secure support from the sixth Aṣaf Jāhī Niẓām of Hyderabad, Maḥbūb ʿAlī Ḳhān (1866–1911) to publish the third (1898) and fourth (1901) volumes of his dictionary. In recognition of his patron's generosity, he renamed the revised and expanded 1918 edition of the entire work the *Farhang-i Āṣafiyah* (*Farhang* of the Āṣaf [Jāhī Dynasty]).[3] It is by this title that the text is best known today. With its associations to a precolonial Persianate genre of lexicography (the *farhang* versus the modern, unmarked term *luġhāt*) and precapitalist modes of patronage that glorify an individual rather than a nation, the title of the 1918 edition suggests its author had retreated from the ambitious, even imperious, vision of his *Hindūstānī Urdū Luġhat* toward increasing nostalgia for happier days in a distant past.

The modern comprehensive dictionary has become, and remains, a most concrete means by which to demonstrate the arrival of a linguistic community upon the international stage. The commensurability of the modern comprehensive dictionary as a genre refers to a consistency in its means of production, distribution, and consumption: ideally, a modern comprehensive dictionary's formal structure and layout should be determined entirely by a writing system and independent of semantic content. Its arrangement conforms so closely to that of other dictionaries (including those in other languages) as to be unnoticeable. The modern comprehensive dictionary gains its authoritative purchase in large part through the homogeneity and ubiquity of its generic conventions, irrespective of region or language. The stubborn persistence in past and contemporary lexicographical projects of artifacts associated with precolonial generic forms continues to be a source of great consternation to nationalist advocates of official status for Urdu in present-day Pakistan and India. Later critics have denigrated Sayyid Aḥmad's dictionaries for failing to represent the Urdu language with sufficient objective distance. What was at stake in asserting word-for-word equivalences was all too apparent from their postindependence vantage point: the successful imposition of Urdu as the official language in Pakistan could never fully be offset by its failure to maintain parity with Hindi in India.

When examined from the perspective of its material conditions of production, this hybrid work owes its existence both to preexisting forms of courtly patronage and to an emerging market of literate middle-class consumers. Sidney Landau usefully distinguishes between academic and commercial dictionary production, enumerating important recurrent distinctions between the two types.[4] The *Farhang-i Āṣafiyah*, however, cannot be so neatly categorized. As a large, four-volume reference book in quarto format, it could not have been expected to have become a household item, even for highly literate families. When in 1878 Sayyid Aḥmad began publishing in serial form an early version of the dictionary, the *Armaġān-i Dihlī* and later the *Hindūstānī Urdū Luġhat* in octavo, his intention then had been to make that particular work affordable for a greater portion of the public.[5] The massive quarto volumes of the *Farhang-i Āṣafiyah*, despite subventions by the Hyderabad state, remained beyond the means of most individuals, with half of the thousand copies acquired by the niẕām's government for distribution to libraries and schools.[6] The great variety of encomia to patrons in the introductory essays of the *Farhang-i Āṣafiyah* reminds the reader that it was produced in a scholarly environment that only distantly resembles the commercial publishing industry of the postindependence period.

The constellation of genres that constitute the precolonial Persianate tradition of lexicography were intended to relay the personal authority, indeed the charisma, of their compilers and the poets they cited in their entries. The capacity of these two partially overlapping groups—lexicographers and poets—to project their lexical legitimacy depended upon the author's skill in manipulating well-established techniques of authentication (*isnād*) established in the first Islamic centuries. Beyond lexicography, these techniques were applied to a variety of disciplines, from determining the appropriateness of ritual practices and the application of *sharīʿat* (Islamic law) to conveying through biographical dictionaries (*taẕkirah*) the modes of comportment and literary style appropriate within the imperial court and other gatherings of social elites. Lexicographic works could thus relay the charisma and authority not just of individual figures but, potentially, of states and even nations. As containers for culture and authority, they were able to transmit their contents to potential users scattered over great distances, physical or otherwise.

At the turn of the nineteenth century, the task of compiling dictionaries became an increasingly collaborative activity insofar as it was no longer entirely tied, at the production stage, to the individual compiler's personal mining of texts for lexical content and examples of usage or, at the distribution stage, to interpersonal exchanges of orally transmitted information or handwritten manuscripts. New lexicographic techniques incorporated linguistic fieldwork into the lexicographer's toolbox as part of the rise of a linguistic protoanthropology associated with the coalescence of ethnographic methods and theoretical categories. These techniques were, of course, not an entirely indigenous development. By the end of the nineteenth century, Urdu lexicographers had been reinstated with new authority through ties to institutions firmly grounded within a political and legal system wherein European colonial power and cultural influence was paramount.

While the compilation of dictionaries has always been a collaborative effort (despite repeated claims of works being produced "viva voce et ex nihilo" and the concomitant complaints of toiling through long, lonely drudgery), these new techniques lent themselves to the establishment of professional institutions devoted to lexicographic production. Indeed, as will be discussed below, several prominent Urdu lexicographers of the nineteenth century took great pride in, and acquired credibility through, their former positions as assistants to S. W. Fallon, a prominent English lexicographer and inspector of schools. The studies presented in this book demonstrate that South Asian intellectuals have been skillful in adapting new forms of knowledge in the service of personal ends, refashioning these techniques in order to consolidate their position within a changing political order and to ensure their financial advantage in light of emerging economic opportunities. For some, these material forms of knowledge offered a means by which to establish one's position as a representative of a community and, by extension, to articulate both a definition of the group's boundaries and, ultimately, the political demands of that community within the existing (and future aspirational) political discourse.[7]

In short, nineteenth-century lexicographers were becoming increasingly adept at producing texts that abstracted a national language from the messy reality of colloquial speech. An earlier ideal in which individuals would demonstrate their command over a repertoire of multiple complementary and often distinct linguistic registers—conventionalized communicative codes indexed to particular social contexts—gave way to the logic of the single, standardized "mother tongue" capable of felicitously performing all the functions sanctioned by the state. As the concept of the sovereign nation-state grew through the twentieth century to cover nearly the entire globe, so too did the claims of the nation-state to represent and control the lives of (nearly) all the humans beings residing within its boundaries. Language was one of the means of this expansion. In order to establish a single semiotic code as capable of conveying any and all meaning, it needed to be divorced from any single social domain, be it a socioeconomic class or a performative context. Lexicographers, by simultaneously simplifying and abstracting language from its traditional social functions, enabled the nineteenth-century proliferation of languages like Urdu into new social domains, extending their capacity to serve new social functions and mediate the social life of new communities.[8] Dictionaries were a primary and indispensable means of transforming a repertoire of multiple, socially delimited, and often contradictory linguistic registers into a single "national language" ideally accessible to all citizens regardless of their social background. To make Urdu a language of state, it had to be made, to use James C. Scott's useful term, *legible*, that is to say, completely accessible to the state and its constituent members.[9] Unlike Urdu, whose lexicographers were unable to complete the process of abstraction from its original function as a limited social register operating within a Mughal-Persianate socioeconomic and cultural context, it was Modern Standard Hindi that emerged as a more successful planned language, purpose built to serve nationalist political ends.[10] While the vision Urdu lexicographers projected of their language contrasted with that of Hindi, dictionaries did not alone determine the failure of Urdu to remain the official language of India after independence. Those who compile dictionaries must document a constantly evolving underlying linguistic reality—an activity Jonathon Green has characterized as "chasing the sun."[11]

THE EUROPEAN "INVENTION" OF THE URDU DICTIONARY

Sayyid Aḥmad's work occupies an uneasy place, informed as it is by modern (primarily European) methods of dictionary production while clearly demonstrating itself to be heir to a well-developed and no less sophisticated Persianate tradition of lexicography whose origins may be traced to the eleventh century or earlier. This liminal status is suggested by its double title, *Hindūstānī Urdū Luġhat* and *Farhang-i Āṣafiyah*. The Persian-derived *farhang* has come in modern Persian to mean "culture" in the sense of a "civilization" and "education,"[12] its archaic semantic associations with lexicography relegated to the precolonial period. The term, as it applies to lexicography, has been defined by Solomon Baevskii as a "defining dictionary of Persian vocabulary" to distinguish it from other genres like the *niṣāb*, or multilingual vocabularies in rhyming couplets.[13] Though partially synonymous, the Arabic-derived *luġhat* (pl. *luġhāt*) in the nineteenth century largely replaced *farhang* in specifically denoting a comprehensive monolingual dictionary organized alphabetically by the sequence of the letters comprising its headwords—a genre widely reproduced and recognizable across languages and cultures.

Despite his numerous publications on language, history, and education—for which he received both awards and remuneration from the colonial government—Sayyid Aḥmad nevertheless struggled to gain recognition as a poet from the Urdu literary establishment. Sayyid Aḥmad's credibility as a lexicographer had been won in large part through a seven-year assistantship to the British folklorist and pedagogue Dr. S. W. Fallon, himself the chief author of *A New Hindustani-English Dictionary, with Illustrations from Hindustani Literature and Folk-Lore* (1879). In his capacity as an employee of the British government, Sayyid Aḥmad served as superintendent of the Ethnographic Survey in Delhi and head *maulvi* (instructor) of Persian and Urdu at Shimla's M. B. High School.[14] From 1897 to 1918, he also served as examiner of Persian and Urdu for various universities. The British government in 1914 bestowed upon him the title "Ḳhān Ṣāhib" to honor his scholarly and literary service. Toward the end of his life, he would become a pensioner of the niẓām of Hyderabad.[15] As the recipient of state largesse, Sayyid Aḥmad thus perceived himself as representing the prestige and values of the institutions that financed the production of his work. These forms of institutional accreditation point to an increasingly professional cadre of lexicographers in the second half of the nineteenth century. This example of classic Durkheimian professionalization, however, would also lead to the alienation of figures like Sayyid Aḥmad from preexisting Persianate literary networks based on lineages of discipleship (*silsilah*s) drawn through charismatic poetic preceptors.

Sayyid Aḥmad's response to this alienation was to insert a surfeit of subjectivity into the text of his lexicographic projects. The frontmatter and definitions of the *Farhang-i Āṣafiyah* are marked by the presence of a strong authorial voice and projection of a literary persona through numerous verses composed and quoted by the author. The persistence of these seemingly anachronistic elements is evidence not just of Sayyid Aḥmad's anxieties regarding his status as an authority on a language whose role was rapidly changing in society but also of his innovative (if not always successful) efforts to frustrate would-be plagiarists in the increasingly competitive market of dictionaries during this period. The critical reception of the *Farhang-i Āṣafiyah* since its publication has not adequately accounted for the conditions in which Sayyid Aḥmad compiled his work.

Through a failure to recognize its connections with preexisting Persianate models of linguistic authority and his creative responses to market challenges, Sayyid Aḥmad has been unfairly disparaged in much existing scholarship on the Urdu language and its lexicography.

An example of this derisive attitude may be found in Sayyid Ḵhwajah Ḥusainī's essay "*Farhang-i Āṣafiyah Tanqīd ke Āʾīne meṅ*" (The *Farhang-i Āṣafiyah* in the mirror of criticism), published in the first volume of the journal *Urdū Adab*. He begins with an acknowledgment of the role of Sayyid Aḥmad and his dictionary in inaugurating a new era in Urdu lexicography:

> In light of the roots of the modern art of lexicography, the *Farhang-i Āṣafiyah* is the first comprehensive, extensive, and authoritative (*mustanad*) dictionary (*luġhat*). Because of this work, Sayyid Aḥmad Dihlawī should be counted among the great benefactors of the Urdu language. He should be accorded the very same importance and eminence in status as a lexicographer in the history of Urdu as has been accorded to Johnson in the English language.[16]

In 1887, prior even to the dictionary's publication, the Urdu poet and critic Alṭāf Ḥusain Ḥālī celebrated its author's efforts in similarly heroic terms:

> When Johnson proposed in 1755 [*sic*] to write the first dictionary of the English language, then he hoped that a wealthy nobleman would become the patron of his dictionary. . . . Ultimately, having relied on only his own hand and arm, with the hope of gaining the public's approval, he began his work and with great perseverance brought it to completion; the gift of his labors was received by the entire nation. Though after this, Webster and Ogilvie wrote such extremely fine dictionaries that Johnson's dictionary cannot compare, nevertheless, so long as England and the English language remain on the face of this earth, Johnson's name will always be taken with the utmost respect and reverence. It is our hope that the Urdu dictionary will attain this very regard in Hindustan that Johnson's dictionary in England first had attained in England. The compiler of the Urdu dictionary has also, with regard to his bravery, perseverance, labor, and self-help (*salf-halp*), accomplished exactly the same feat as had been done by Johnson.[17]

The archaeologist Ġhulām Yazdānī (1885–1962) even recalled that Sayyid Aḥmad's "countenance and habit resembled Doctor Johnson's face, appearance, and qualities: Both were poor in sight, both were awkward of body (*be-hangam-i jism*) on account of their corpulence."[18] Veiled within Ḥusainī's praise, however, is also a justification for subjecting Sayyid Aḥmad's work to a sort of scrutiny it cannot withstand. For, in comparing Sayyid Aḥmad with Samuel Johnson, he reinforces the notion that the development of Urdu lexicography would necessarily follow *English* lines, and it would follow from this that the *Farhang-i Āṣafiyah* must be judged by the standards of an English tradition of lexicography.

The first broad historical survey of Urdu lexicography was presented in Dr. ʿAbdul Ḥaq's lengthy introductory essay in the *Luġhat-i Kabīr-i Urdū* (Great dictionary of Urdu),[19] a work modeled on the *Oxford English Dictionary*. Ḥaq intended for the *Luġhat-i Kabīr-i Urdū* to displace the *Farhang-i Āṣafiyah* as the primary authoritative dictionary of the Urdu language. He begins his introductory essay with the following remarks about the origins of Urdu lexicography:

> The first to write dictionaries (*luġhat*) in Urdu were Europeans, and in particular, the English. This is not peculiar to Urdu alone, as the first dictionaries of almost every modern Indian language were written by foreigners, although they paid greater attention to Urdu. The reason is that at the beginning the English came to pursue trade. Traders must, having gone abroad, out of necessity learn such languages which are understood generally in the country [in which they wish to conduct trade]. Then, by means of trade, conquest and governance progress, this necessity increases. Out of this necessity, the College of Fort William was established, where modern Urdu prose found glory, and modern Hindi's foundation was set.[20]

Here Ḥaq, the "Grand Old Man of Urdu,"[21] grants European lexicographers full credit not just for having authored the first dictionaries of Urdu but also for having created the impetus for the development of Modern Standard Hindi. According to Ḥaq, the creation of each required the decisive intervention of European scholarship, and, as such, each could and would be liable to charges of not measuring up to the standards of their European counterparts.[22] Literary critics and translators writing in the wake of ʿAbdul Ḥaq have followed him in bemoaning the inadequacies of modern Urdu prose and poetry, arguing that the difficulties advocates of the language face in asserting its political and aesthetic relevance are attributable to the inability of Urdu-language authors to jettison the literary baggage of an earlier age—in particular the metaphorical excesses of the Urdu *ġhazal*.[23] For ʿAbdul Ḥaq, the quality of a particular language's monolingual dictionaries demonstrates a strong correlation with the status of the language as a whole and, ultimately, that of the nation.[24] Just as the nation seems to be the inevitable political unit of the twentieth century,[25] so too does the modern dictionary, as defined by an international standard, appear as the natural lexicographical unit.

While later historians of lexicography would base their own surveys upon the foundational research of Ḥaq, they were more careful to qualify their claims. The most notable historian of lexicography to follow Ḥaq has been Masʿūd Hāshmī, who divides his survey of the historical background of Urdu lexicography on the basis of the languages covered, with chapters devoted to Persian–Urdu *niṣābs* (multilingual vocabularies in verse), Urdu–Persian dictionaries, Urdu–English dictionaries, English–Urdu dictionaries, and, finally, "the origins of Urdu–Urdu lexicography."[26] By organizing his history along these principles he reinforces the narrative offered by Ḥaq, in which English interventions are considered decisive in creating the conditions for the compilation of a "modern" monolingual comprehensive dictionary of Urdu. In another text, *Urdū Luġhat Nawīsī kā Tanqīdī Jāʾizah* (A critical analysis of Urdu lexicography), Hāshmī begins his chapter on "The First Period of Urdu–Urdu Lexicography (*luġhat nawīsī*)" with the following framing statements:

> As has already been mentioned by the middle of the nineteenth century, Persian–Urdu, Urdu–Persian, English–Hindustani, and Hindustani–English lexicography had become quite advanced. In particular, having received a fillip from the Hindustani–English lexicography of Dr. Fallon and T. Platts [*sic*], in this very period, too, Urdu–Urdu lexicography originated.[27]

Again, following the briefest mention of a preexisting Persianate lexicographical tradition, Hāshmī gives pride of place to two British lexicographers, essentially crediting them with fulfilling the ambitions of the new science of lexicography or, in Hāshmī's terms, the writing of *luġhat*s (dictionaries).

LEXICOGRAPHY AND THE SELF

For a figure as important to the history of Urdu lexicography in particular and the Urdu language in general, surprisingly little material is available describing the life of Sayyid Aḥmad. Most of what little we do know actually comes from his own pen, especially his lengthy introductory essays within the *Farhang-i Āṣafiyah.* He concludes the introduction to the revised second edition with a section entitled *Hamāri Paidā'ish* (our birth) that follows another containing a "brief history of Delhi." His "brief history" prominently features the author's ancestors and in particular the author's father, firmly situating the author in a scholarly milieu in proximity to some of Delhi's most prominent literary figures.[28] He presents the following information in the final section, on his birth, as a brief autobiographical notice:

MY BIRTH

> I was born on the 9th of [the month] Muḥarram al-Ḥarām, AH 1262 corresponding to January 8, 1846, in Balātī Begam kā kūćah ['Balātī Begam's alleyway']. It is there that my umbilical cord was buried. Up to this time, my parents had taken residence in the house of Ḥāfiẓ Bahāruddīn Ṣāhib, an honorable minister and servant of the king. Six or seven months later, having bought our own personal residence from Motī Begam, wife of Mīr Ẓuhūr ʿAlī, we resided there, in the garden of Ṣābir Bak̤hsh Ṣāhib. Based on my memory, we only had our pots and pans here. Just as my late father had taken nothing from his kinfolk of his own ancestral share, so too was it my intention. I have resisted greed and personal avarice. God protect the presence of the Niẓām [his patron, the sixth Aṣaf Jāhī Niẓām of the princely state of Hyderabad], who bestowed upon me, for life and for my fortunate son, a pension on February 22nd, 1915, delivering us from worry, generation after generation. Allah is enough, all else is vainglory.
>
> Sayyid Aḥmad Dihlawī (K̤hān Ṣāhib)
> Author of the *Farhang-i Āṣafiyah*, etc., etc.
> February 4, 1916[29]

Perhaps it is this very excess of personal detail, appearing as it did in the introduction to his best-known work, that has obviated the need for the publication of a biographical monograph.[30] The most important recent secondary sources include an unpublished master's thesis[31] and K̤hāliq Anjum's brief biographical sketch in his introduction to another work of Sayyid Aḥmad entitled *Rusūm-i Dihlī.*[32]

The account that Sayyid Aḥmad gives us of his ancestry is based on memory, as the written documentation of his family tree was lost during a fire that swept through his home in 1912. According to him, his ancestors were once *ʿulamā* and *sayyids* of Bukhara, and he was descended through both parents from the prophet Muḥammad through both his

FIGURE 4.1 Seal appearing in *Farhang-i Āṣafiyah*: "M. Saiyid Ahmad, Author of New Large Hindustani Dictionary"

grandchildren Ḥasan and Ḥusain.[33] A certain Ḥajjī Sayyid Sulaimān Shāh, the *raʾis* (headman) of Bārū village in Mulkī district, Bihar province, was the most distant ancestor he could recall; Sayyid Aḥmad was his eighth-generation descendant. Sayyid Aḥmad's father Sayyid ʿAbdul Raḥmān Mūṅgerī was according to Sayyid Aḥmad,

> a Muslim of very firm and steadfast faith. Having heard of the fame of the *ʿulamā* of Delhi, [he,] out of a desire for the advancement of religiousness and to complete the customary books (*kutab-i mutadāwalah*), having left his home at a young age, came to Delhi. Having come here, he married into the tribe of *Faqīhah* [theologians] of the Sayyids of ʿArab Sarai [near Humāyūn's tomb].[34]

His father was a follower of Maulvī Shāh Ismāʿīl (1781–1831) and Maulvī Sayyid Aḥmad of Rae Bareilly (1786–1831), important nineteenth-century Islamic reformers who led a failed *jihād* against the Sikh Kingdom of Ranjit Singh.[35] This first Sayyid Aḥmad (of Rae Bareilly) became infamous as the "freebooter-saint" and "Prophet" in William Wilson Hunter's (1827–1902) popular 1872 anti-Muslim polemic. Hunter identified this Sayyid Aḥmad as the root cause of a menacing "Rebel Camp" of fanatics poised "on the Panjáb Frontier" to overthrow British rule in India.[36] Following the assassination of the movement's leaders in 1831, Sayyid ʿAbdul Raḥmān returned to Delhi, where he served as a tutor for the sons of two Delhi ministers and permanent *īmām* of a small mosque near the shrine of Shāh Ṣābir Baḳhsh.[37]

Despite Sayyid ʿAbdul Raḥmān's commitment, at least in his youth, to ending Sikh and British rule in India, this did not prevent him from being reabsorbed upon his return back into the urban fabric of premutiny (pre-1857) Delhi. Sayyid ʿAbdul Raḥman had two sons, Sayyid Aḥmad, named for the deceased reformer, and Sayyid Ḥusain. Sayyid Ḥusain, the younger of the two, passed away in 1868 at the age of nineteen. Because Sayyid Aḥmad states that his own mother died during childbirth, Sayyid Ḥusain would have had a different mother. When Sayyid Aḥmad was still an infant, his father bought a house in the garden of the tomb of Shāh Ṣābir Baḳhsh near the mosque at which he was the *īmām* in what is currently a very built-up section of the Darya Ganj section of the walled city of Shāhjahānābād. It was here that his father passed away. Sayyid Aḥmad was educated privately and later attended Delhi Normal School.[38] In 1900, he moved into the *ḥavelī* of Muẓaffar Ḳhān at Turkoman Gate, on the southern edge of the walled city. In 1908, he moved to a new home on Kūćah Panḍit in the alleyway of Sawār Ḳhāṅ. Four years after a disastrous house fire on February 8, 1912, Sayyid Aḥmad moved to Galī Shāh Tārā, and it was there that he spent his final years.[39]

Sayyid Aḥmad Dihlawī married twice. His first wife, Muġhlānī Begam, bore him fourteen children, though only two daughters, Sayyid Begam and Maḥmūdī Begam, survived past early childhood. She is described in the sources as having lost her sanity toward the end of her life.[40] Sayyid Aḥmad divorced her and married Ḥātim Zamānī Begam, who bore him a son on December 13, 1911, whom he named Saʿīd Aḥmad, with the nickname 'Darbār Aḥmad'. Here was an opportunity for Sayyid Aḥmad to undo the nominal damage done by his own father: he chose the unusual name Darbār (court, royal audience) to commemorate the fact that the birth of the child coincided with the visit of King George V to the Imperial Delhi Darbār and thus assert his own allegiance to the British crown.[41] Perhaps it was this decisive break from his past to which Sayyid Aḥmad was alluding when he wrote in the introduction to the second edition of his *Farhang* four years later: "Just as my late father had taken nothing from his kinfolk of his own ancestral share, so too was it my intention."[42] At the time of his son's birth, Sayyid Aḥmad was sixty-five years of age. Probably in view of his advanced age, the niẓām of Hyderabad allotted his son Darbār Aḥmad in 1915 a monthly stipend of Rs. 50 (£3 6s. 8d.).[43] In 1916, when Sayyid Aḥmad prepared for his son's circumcision and *bismillāh* ceremonies, the nawāb of Hyderabad gave an additional award of Rs. 500 (£33 6s. 8d.). Darbār Aḥmad emigrated to Karachi after the partition of India and Pakistan. His monthly stipend from the niẓām had been suspended, but despite "extreme poverty" he managed to find employment in the Karachi Public Works Department and reside in "in stable and elegant surroundings." His mother, Sayyid Aḥmad's second wife, Ḥātim Begam, passed away in 1954 in Karachi.[44]

Sayyid Aḥmad, in a section of the introduction to the first edition of his *Farhang-i Āṣafiyah* entitled *sabab-i tālīf* (reason for penning), claimed to have cultivated his love of lexicography from a very young age. He asserts his membership among the ranks of professional lexicographers by deploying the parallel metaphor of a nation discovering itself through a shared language:

> Some have set about investigating different languages and their relationships with one another. They have researched the separate categories and families of languages. Having gathered only the words of their own nation, some have shown off their own jewels.[45]

As he continued, though, he developed a "passion" that at first seemed quite at odds with the staid scientific research of his contextual contemporaries. The passion that developed in him became more like an encounter with a frightful demon, luring the author forward onto a path of lexicographical self-destruction:

> Then: a passion appeared in my heart for the science of language and the compilation of dictionaries. Although at first glance, because it was unconnected with scientific methods, it was considered pointless and unworthy of serious regard, nevertheless that irresponsible beloved spirit of passion made peace with me as one human does with another.[46]

As the author came to understand this demonic possession better, he was able to redirect it toward a more productive form of madness:

> I was made to wander about alleyways. I was made to be seated among all sorts of company. Instead of grasping at straws (*tinke cunna*, i.e., 'acting insane'), I was made to select choice phrases (*fiqrah*) from various places. I was brought to laughter in the gatherings of joy. I was brought to tears in processions of grief. Removed from the ease of the free, I was made the servant of each and every one. Whence spread our investigations in all company and each society. And even this verse has become verified:
>
> *galiyoṅ meṅ ab talak bhī mażkūr hai hamārā*
> *afsānah-i muḥabbat mashhūr hai hamārā*
>
> Even now in the alleyways there is mention of us
> The story of our love is famous[47]

What becomes clear from the verses that conclude this episode is that the author is framing his interest in lexicography by typecasting himself as the infatuated madman, the possessed, or Majnūn, of poetry.

Sayyid Aḥmad demonstrated an interest in composing poetry from his years as a student with the *taḵhalluṣ* (nom de plume) 'Sayyid'. While still in school, he wrote a lengthy Persian poem called the *Ṭiflī nāmah* (Book of childhood), and in 1868, when Sayyid Aḥmad was twenty-two years old, he wrote a didactic work entitled *Inshā-yi Taqwiyatah al-Ṣibyān* (Treatise on the edification of children) in order to teach children the useful skills of neat handwriting and other aspects of professional copying. In the composition of *ġhazal*s he is recorded as having received instruction and corrections from Quṭbuddīn 'Mushīr', a disciple of Shāh 'Naṣīr' (d. 1838), a major nineteenth-century Urdu poet. He showed his *qaṣidah*s (laudatory odes) and *qiṭʿah*s (verse sets) to 'Zakī' Dihlawī (1839–1903). Despite his being able to claim this respectable literary lineage, Sayyid Aḥmad was, in the judgment of Ḳhalīq Anjum, "so engaged in lexicography that he did not even have any judgment of poetry and versification. . . . On the basis of whatever verses of his have come before my eyes, from them it would seem that he did not compose poetry well."[48]

Sayyid Aḥmad projects a poetic persona in ostensibly nonpoetic genres, as when he explains, in the introduction to the *Farhang-i Āṣafiyah*:

> Among native speakers (*ahl-i zabān*) has there been any person knowledgeable in a language who has not focused in this direction [i.e., in pondering language]? Most probably, this game is written in our fate, and God almighty has made us for this reason in particular from the beginning of life his spurned one, a madman for him, a wailing lover.[49]

Spurred on by the madness of an archetypal lover drawn from the cast of Persianate poetic figures, Sayyid Aḥmad began his lexicographical work, claiming it to be a salve for his wounds, and in the process he discovered that it might prove to be of help to others as well. Who, then, did Sayyid Aḥmad Dihlawī believe would benefit from a work like this? First, and foremost:

> A *poet* will obtain help from it. Researchers of language will benefit from it. As regards authors, synonyms—words with the same meanings, same aspects—shown together in this dictionary will save them from having to use a single type of word several times in a passage. That is, this dictionary is a treasury, which is called a Thezaurus [*sic*, written in Roman script in the original text] in English, and a *maḳhzan* in Urdu. Often from historical events, traces of the terminological cause of naming may be discovered. Distinction may be made by means of it between obsolete and nonobsolete terms. Through this [book], it will be decided whether expressions are correct or incorrect, and whether they are masculine or feminine. Different classes of various particular technical terms (*iṣṭilāḥeṅ*) will be known from this. Muslims and Hindus will benefit from this. The life and times of many *faqīrs* and saints of India arranged by year will be arrived at through it. Even the nature of an abundance of discoveries and inventions will be known through it. In short, its having been written is an absolute and entire confirmation of the language and it is thus an extremely important *national* work. In truth, it is out of a love of God that the end was achieved, despite what little I am and what little ability I have.[50]

For the translator of these passages, raised in a culture that has treated lexicography as the epitome of mental drudgery,[51] what is striking is not so much the passion with which Sayyid Aḥmad Dihlawī approaches his work but rather the literary idiom in which he expresses that passion. He intended his work not merely to resemble the modern notion of a "standard-descriptive dictionary"[52] but rather to approach that of the descriptivist lexicographer's equivalent of a cultural salvage mission.

The eminent historian of colonial India, Gail Minault, summarizes Sayyid Aḥmad's oeuvre in this way:

> As one associated with the reformist *ulama*, Sayyid Ahmad could expect his study to contribute to the reform, even extinction, of many of the customs he records. Sayyid Ahmad's dictionaries, glossaries, and patient listing of customs, rituals, and idioms grew out of the Delhi renaissance but were also, in a sense, its final chapter. If the Delhi renaissance sought to preserve *sharif* culture by reforming it, Sayyid Ahmad sensed that something was being lost in the process, and he sought to preserve that elusive quality by freezing it.[53]

Thus, he envisioned his work not merely as a *luġhat* (dictionary) but as a "Thezaurus in English, and a *maḳhzan* in Urdu," literally as a "treasury" of the culture around him and, indeed, a work of *national* importance. Luckily for Sayyid Aḥmad, he was able to find a series of patrons for the expression of this lexicographical intoxication:

> Being stuck in an entanglement, I placed my hands in the power of others. Whatever could be accomplished was accomplished, and sometimes I taught the boys of a *madrasah*. Sometimes I created different books. I found favor. At some point, I was made the "Assistant Dictionary" [*sic*] of lexicographers like Fallon. Sometimes I was engaged in the completion of belles-lettres (*inshā*ʾ) and essay writing. Sometimes, taking upon myself the tutoring of the sons of noblemen, I came into contact with them. From favors and from honors, in whichever way I applied myself to this aim, I caught a glimpse of this unknown heart-ravisher. Hope and attainment were prolonged this far that even my attainment [this dictionary] started to come into view.[54]

He depicts his dictionary, the "unknown heart-ravisher," as the seemingly unattainable beloved of Urdu poetry and the lexicographer as the lover driven to madness and self-destruction in pursuit of union with his beloved.

In the years that followed, Sayyid Aḥmad would become a successful pedagogue, a prizewinning author and historian, and the compiler of a number of major lexicographical works of his own. His *Rusūm-i Dihlī* is an important ethnography detailing the customs of Delhi's varied social groups.[55] His analysis of Hindu rituals and the cultural syncretism of Delhi's culture is so incisive that, in the estimation of one scholar, it would not be inappropriate to "place him in the ranks of professional anthropologists."[56] Today, however, Sayyid Aḥmad is known primarily for his lexicographical works, including the *Muṣṭalaḥāt-i Urdū* (Idioms of Urdu), published in 1871, and the *Armaġhān-i Dihlī* (Souvenir gift of Delhi), which was printed in brief installments beginning in 1878 and ultimately reprinted in collected form in 1888 as the *Luġhāt-i Urdū (Ḳhulāsah-yi Armaġhān-i Dihlī)* (Urdu vocabulary: an abridgment of *Armaġhān-i Dihlī*) in Shimla.[57] He also published in 1918, shortly before his death, the *Luġhāt al-Nisāʾ* (Dictionary of women), a short vocabulary of phrases drawn from the speech of Delhi women. These titles, however, pale in their significance when placed next to the multivolume dictionary for which Sayyid Aḥmad became famous, the *Farhang-i Āṣafiyah*. The first and second volumes of its first edition were published in 1888, the third in 1898, and the fourth and final volume in 1901. It is improbable, however, that this great work would have achieved its current status or have taken the form it did had its author not enjoyed the opportunity to serve for several years as an assistant to S. W. Fallon. It was also this association with Fallon that has left the *Farhang-i Āṣafiyah* most vulnerable to the repeated criticism of having failed to fulfill the promise of serving as the first truly "modern" international dictionary of the Urdu language.[58]

In the introduction to the *Luġhat-i Nisā* Sayyid Aḥmad gives us a glimpse of the new economic realities to which Urdu authors were forced to adapt in the postmutiny period. He describes completing the book in 1874 while employed by Fallon, incorporating many of the women's expressions he collected for it into his *Armaġhān-i Dihlī* (or *Hindustānī Urdū Luġhāt*, which would later become the *Farhang-i Āṣafiyah)*. As discussed above, he was not able, however, to publish the *Luġhat-i Nisā* for another four decades, attributing the delay to the low priority assigned to women's education by society as a whole. From his discussion of Deputy Nażīr Aḥmad's "prize-winning" novels[59] and his own *Kanz al-Fawāʾid* (Treasure of advantages, also known as *Munāẓarah-i Taqdīr* 'Contest of fates'), awarded Rs. 200 (£13 6s. 8d.) in 1869, and *Waqāʿīʾ-i Durāniyah* (The Duranian events), a history of the Afghan royal family for which he received Rs. 150 (£10) in 1871,[60] its unpublished state was more plausibly the result of his inability to win a subvention from the colonial government. Following his period of employment on Fallon's dictionary projects, Sayyid Aḥmad was able to secure a short-term position from the king of Alwar, compiling an account of the latter's travels. He remained for six months in Alwar, after which, according to Ḥamid Ḥasan Qādirī, he went on to become the assistant translator for the Punjab Government Book Depot and a teacher of Persian in Delhi.[61]

In 1888, Sayyid Aḥmad Dihlawī, in his capacity as an official in the Department of Public Instruction, was transferred from Delhi to the summer capital in Shimla. It was here that Sayyid Aḥmad had the good fortune of being able to present his project to Sir Āsmān Jāh Bahādur, the prime minister of the state of Hyderabad. As has been mentioned above, sections of the future *Farhang-i Āṣafiyah* had already been published in serialized form under the name *Armaġhān-i Dihlī*. In addition to this, he had published parts of the work under the name *Muṣṭalaḥāt-i Urdū* and *Sayyid al-Luġhāt*.[62] Sayyid Aḥmad thus presented a draft of the dictionary to Sir Āsmān Jāh Bahādur in Shimla, who brought it with him back to Hyderabad.[63] Sir Āsmān Jāh Bahādur awarded Sayyid Aḥmad Rs. 500 (£33 6s. 8d.) and formed a committee to consider the possibility of the Hyderabad state's purchasing copies of the dictionary. This committee recommended the acquisition of four hundred copies of the work for Rs. 9,000 (£600), with an advance sum of Rs. 4,500 to be paid immediately.[64] In a petition dated February 17, 1895, and addressed to Sir Waqār al-Umarā, who succeeded Āsmān Jāh in 1893 as prime minister of the state of Hyderabad, Sayyid Aḥmad requested that he be granted the remainder recommended on completion of his work. The prime minister gave his assent for an award of Rs. 5,000, and in February 1896 arranged for Sayyid Aḥmad a monthly stipend of Rs. 50. The next prime minister, Mahārājah Kishan Parshād, granted a further award of Rs. 3,000 (£200) in 1906 to enable the dictionary to be published in a single uniform size, the previous edition having been printed with a mix of small and large lithograph plates.[65] The government of Punjab also gave an award of five hundred rupees and purchased one thousand rupees' worth of books.[66]

While it would appear as though Sayyid Aḥmad had access to a virtually unlimited amount of financial support for his project, the veteran lexicographer would suffer a severe setback when, during the night of February 8, 1912, he would lose his "home, household goods, library, and a blessed nine-year-old child" to fire. He also lost an entire run of the first, second, and third volumes of the revised second edition of the *Farhang-i Āṣafiyah*, received from the publisher in Lahore just days before, these volumes having been stored in his home "stuffed in gunny sacks . . . stacked up to the roof in half the hallway."[67] Learning of this, Sayyid Aḥmad's friends and sympathizers wrote many letters to the editors of various Urdu-language journals, including the Hyderabad paper *Mushīr-i Dakan*, which described the fire in its March 18, 1912, edition.

On May 2, 1912, an appeal was published under the title "Government's Attention to the Indigent Condition of the Author of the *Farhang-i Āṣafiyah*," concluding: "Since the language of the administration of the Honorable Government [of Hyderabad] is Urdu, and Urdu has acquired honor and pride as a language of government, for this reason the Honorable Government cannot request any less than giving aid in the work of this incontrovertibly important author according to his necessity and exigency."[68] Various prominent citizens, including the royal imam (*shāhī imām*) of Delhi's Jāmᶜa Masjid and Alt̤āf Ḥusain Ḥālī, joined Sayyid Aḥmad in sending petitions to the niz̤ām's government requesting the transfer of Sayyid Aḥmad's pension to his young son and an additional subvention in support of reprinting the destroyed copies of the revised *Farhang-i Āṣafiyah*.

As a result of these efforts, ᶜUs̤mān ᶜAlī Ḳhāṅ Āṣaf Jāh VII took the unusual step in February 1915 of issuing without first consulting his Tribunal Assembly the following order:

> On the basis of specific causes (which in the future will not become a precedent for others) [Sayyid Aḥmad's] Rs. 50 pension as per his request should be granted to his son in the form of a *manṣab*. In addition to this, with the aim of the publication of his works and writings (which are a great treasure of the Urdu language), in the name of Sayyid Aḥmad Dihlawī Rs. 50 per month will be continued from the date of this order for life.[69]

The chancellor of the niz̤ām's Political Department estimated the expense of printing one thousand copies of the four volumes of the revised second edition of the *Farhang-i Āṣafiyah* to be Rs. 10,000. He suggested that the author be granted Rs. 2,500 on completion of each revised volume in exchange for five hundred copies. He also recommended that the niz̤ām's government purchase five hundred copies of an abridged edition of the *Farhang-i Āṣafiyah* at the price of Rs. 4.5 per copy and 350 copies of the *Luġhāt al-Nissā* at the price of Rs. 3.5 per copy for school libraries. Sayyid Aḥmad's long-delayed project reconstructing and revising a standalone lexicographical project dealing exclusively with the spoken language of women would thus be published in 1918, the same year as the revised second edition of his masterwork, the *Farhang-i Āṣafiyah*. Sayyid Aḥmad passed away that very year, at the age of seventy-two, on April 30, 1918. He was buried in a garden situated on Qut̤b Road.[70]

DICTIONARY DACOITS

One can hardly deny that Sayyid Aḥmad's dictionaries possess a unique quality, in view of their author's predilection for intermixing an abundance of extralinguistic personal information and opinion with more strictly linguistic data. Sayyid Aḥmad complained bitterly of being a victim of gross iniquities, accusing several individuals of having "committed daylight robbery" in the 1918 introduction to the second edition of the *Farhang-i Āṣafiyah*. The first individual he accuses is a "villainous" (if unnamed) Kashmiri who, "appearing as a friend took an advance with the aim of printing our dictionary, committed robbery having gathered 9,000 rupees. An arsonist burnt our heart. Dacoits ['bandits'] of authorship laid their hands upon our dictionary and committed daylight robbery."[71] This character reappears in his explanation of the term *kashmīrī*:

> These people are famous for their qualities—mostly of treachery, deceit, fraud, and plotting—such as the case when the author was cheated out of Rs. 9,000 by a Kashmīrī Panḍit in 1896. As a result of this, the publication of the *Farhang-i Āṣafiyah* was delayed and the soundness of the third volume was spoiled. Someone said it right when
>
> A king said to the Kashmiri
> Would that I be freed of you!
>
> This verse on the scourge of men verifies this matter.[72]

This, for ʿAbdul Ḥaq, is among "a number of very strange things" (*baʿẓ ʿajīb ʿajīb ćīzeṅ*) one comes across in perusing the dictionary's entries.[73]

This entry briefly achieved some notoriety during a parliamentary session in 1975, a year after the entire work was reprinted under the aegis of the Taraqqī-yi Urdū Board in New Delhi. The Indian MP Om Prakash Tyagi asked the minister of Education, Social Welfare, and Culture,

> (a) whether the dictionary entitled "Farhangi Asafi" published by the Urdu Taraqi Board contains insulting language and expressions about Kashmiri brethren;
> (b) if so, the action taken by Government against the writers and publishers of the said dictionary; and
> (c) if not, the reasons therefor?[74]

The deputy minister responded by explaining that the dictionary was "compiled towards the close of 19th Century by the late Maulavi Syed Ahmed Delhvi." Long out of print and "regarded by Urdu scholars as a standard work," the Taraqqī-yi Urdū Board (an administrative division of the Ministry of Education, Social Welfare, and Culture) had decided to reprint the whole work "for the benefit of scholars as well as the Urdu knowing public." Acquiescing to Tyagi's apparent concern for the preservation of communal harmony, the deputy minister announced,

> Government considers it unfortunate that the late compiler and publisher of the Dictionary included certain objectionable remarks under the entry "Kashmiri." In the light of this, the entire stock of unsold copies of the reprint brought out has been frozen with a view to undertaking a review of the contents of the Dictionary.[75]

The National Council for the Promotion of the Urdu Language would remove the passage in question from subsequent editions. It is not clear how this entry came to Tyagi's attention, but ʿAbdul Ḥaq's essay in which he noted these eccentricities had been published quite recently in the posthumous introduction to the 1973 Karachi edition of his unabridged *Luġhat-i Kabīr-i Urdū* (The great dictionary of Urdu), a then-unfinished work that directly competed with the *Farhang-i Āṣafiyah*.[76]

It would be difficult to separate the unique stamp of Sayyid Aḥmad's personality from the other qualities of the *Farhang-i Āṣafiyah* that make it such a useful reference work. Indeed, this may have been part of a strategy by Sayyid Aḥmad to protect this text—his masterwork—from the very real danger posed by legions of potential imitators in the highly competitive late nineteenth-century market for dictionary production.[77] Lexicographers vied for official patronage and institutional approval in an effort to attain inclusion in educational curricula or a subsidized print run. When a work as influential and valuable as the *Farhang-i Āṣafiyah* did appear, it thus was only a matter of time before less scrupulous publishers would present their own black-market reprint versions or absorb significant amounts of the "original" text into a new dictionary, republishing the resulting work under a different title.[78] In the introduction to the second edition of the *Farhang-i Āṣafiyah* Sayyid Aḥmad decries what he perceives to be the rampant plagiarism to which his earlier editions had been subject, going so far as to name specific works, their authors, and individual dictionary entries:

> Several famous poets (*nāmī-girāmī shāʿiroṅ*), Arabic-Persian experts, [and] nonintimates of the art of lexicography, were intent on coining big words (*luġhat-tarāshī par kamar bāndhī*), having lifted tracings from the *Armaġhān-i Dihlī*. . . . [For example there is] the way that the compiler of the *Amīr al-Luġhāt* [by Amīr Mīnāʾī, published in 1891], having taken the term *āṅkh* ['eye'] in the 1878 edition of the *Armaġhān-i Dihlī*, copied its derivation and meaning just as it is in the form in which it was printed. In this very way the author of the *Nūr al-Luġhāt* [by Nūr al-Ḥasan Nez Kākorwī, published 1917] also followed in his footsteps, a full three decades after the year of the publication, [when he] decided to make an exact copy of the printed version of the *Farhang-i Āṣafiyah*'s term *bāt* ['speech', 'affair', 'news', 'thing'] and its derivation.[79]

The implication is that these "nonintimates of the art of lexicography" made use of Sayyid Aḥmad's own labor without proper attribution. In evaluating this claim of plagiarism, Ḥāmid Ḥasan Qādirī, a historian of Urdu, examined this "very serious criticism" and articulates a fairly commonsense standard for determining what one lexicographer may legitimately borrow from the work of another: first, while the terms and expressions that appear in one dictionary are the common property of a community of language users and may be reproduced in other works,[80] the occasion of their first appearance in a lexicographic work, which is to say the *selection* of particular lemmata, may be justifiably considered the work of a single author (and should therefore be acknowledged by subsequent authors).[81] And, second, if the headwords (or lemmata) themselves admit to reproduction in subsequent lexicographic works, the definitions and poetic prooftexts that appear within the associated entries of dictionaries are the personal property of the collector/author and hence may not be reproduced without attribution. Thus, the word-for-word reproduction of definitions and poetic prooftexts constitutes an illegitimate form of plagiarism and is deserving of reproof.[82]

While Sayyid Aḥmad must be credited for his willingness to adopt new methods of dictionary compilation, and one may even sympathize with him for falling victim to plagiarists and the ruthlessness of the commercial publishing industry, it is equally the case that Sayyid Aḥmad was not writing in a lexicographic vacuum. Recently, the Ḳhudā Baḳhsh Oriental Public Library undertook to republish, under the editorship of Muḥammad Żākir Ḥusain, a largely forgotten dictionary, the *Maḵẖzan-i Fawāʾid* (Treasury of benefits), compiled in the middle of the nineteenth century. The author of this work, Niyāz ʿAlī Beg 'Nakhat',[83] was a resident of Shāhjahānābād. Sayyid Aḥmad describes him as one "who set in verse the *Sikandar Nāmah* in Urdu and had written a [book of] *muṣṭalahāt* (terminologies); he passed away c. AH 1266 [AD 1849/50]."[84] The most complete contemporary account was prepared in a *tażkirah* entitled *Gulistān-i Suḵẖan* (Garden of speech, 1854)[85] by the poet and author Qādir Baḵhsh Bahādur 'Ṣābir' (1808–1882), who described Nakhat as coming "from a family of nobility and illustrious high-mindedness," a person disposed toward jesting in his temperament and one who had "acquired the art of poetry (*fann-i suḵẖan*) from the late Shāh [Naṣīruddīn] 'Naṣīr'."[86] obliquely adding that "in that field (*maidān*), he placed a step beyond its limit."[87] He had a reputation for being extremely generous, and it was thanks to his being constantly good countenanced (*farāḵẖ-rū*, i.e., 'merry') and generous (*kushādah-dast*) that he encountered financial difficulties. To make matters worse, according to Ṣābir, "both of his [Nakhat's] legs, from receiving a violent blow, had became useless, so that he [could] not remain running incessantly on the path to servitude and in the period of service." It was then that he decided "to travel limping (*lang langān*) to Lahore" after "having understood that a manuscript" would be a way of demonstrating his worth to a prospective patron.

In Lahore, Nakhat presented a *qaṣīdah* (ode) to the crown prince of the kingdom of Punjab, Rājah Sher Singh, the son of Ranjīt Singh (r. 1801–1839), who had been installed on the throne in January 1841.[88] The poem was favorably received, and Nakhat was appointed to the court with a stipend. Eventually, Ṣābir relates, he became a favorite of the king, so that, in spite of his lameness, even "the assembly of the excursion and the hunt was not absented from his companionship." The poet even dared to hope that "perhaps the heavens would now forgo the hustle-bustle and unkindnesses [of life] on the road for [this] comfortable arrangement." Sadly, however, this happy state of affairs was not destined to last: on September 14, 1843, Nakhat learned that Sher Singh would honor him with "a striking gift." The following day, Nakhat was present when Sher Singh was killed by a disaffected rival while inspecting troops.[89] Ṣābir relates: "Inverted, fate was turned topsy-turvy, [and Nakhat] took the road to Shāhjahānābād where, swallowing the breath of death [i.e., 'bearing patiently'], he passed his time in repose."[90] Following his return to Delhi, "he compiled a *farhang* of terminologies (*muṣṭalaḥāt*) in the Urdu language of approximately fifty or sixty sections."

It was this *farhang* of idioms that has recently drawn the attention of the Urdu scholarly world. Published only once in 1845, it was a seemingly forgotten document of the state of Urdu lexicographic research at the middle of the nineteenth century. More than a hundred years later, the late Urdu critic ʿAndalīb Shādānī in 1954 described a copy of the work in his possession, which copy had apparently once been a part of the vast Fort William Collection (whose contents have long since been scattered among various public institutions and private hands).[91] Since the title page of the work was missing, Shādānī reproduced the following lines from the printer's colophon:

> The book, *Makhzan-i Fawāʾid*, which Mirzā Niyāz ʿAlī Beg with the pen name 'Nakhat' compiled, including *iṣṭilāḥāt* ['terminologies'] and *muḥāwarāt* ['idioms'] and *misl* ['proverbs'] of the Urdu language with verses and poems of famous poets of India of a high nature, through the bidding of that Fount of Titles (*Mambaʿ al-Alqāb*), Principal of the Delhi Madāris—May his prosperity continue!—in the Dār al-Islām Press which is in the house of Munshī Nūruddīn Aḥmad located in the Muḥallah of Pīpal Mahādev in Shāhjahāṅābād, [was] completed with the aid of Ḥusain Bānī, [and] printed in the month of July 1845.[92]

Ḥusain was unable to find any trace of the Shādānī/Fort William copy and instead relied upon two incomplete copies of the work, a print edition from the library of the Anjuman-i Taraqqī-yi Urdū in Karachi, Pakistan, and a handwritten copy kept in the Ḳhudā Baḳhsh Oriental Public Library in Patna, India.

In editing this work, Ḥusain noticed that the *Maḳhzan-i Fawāʾid* reproduces not so much the content but rather the intent and format of earlier texts that focused in part or whole upon Urdu idioms. These include the *Shams al-Bayān* of Ṭapish (see the previous chapter), the fourth and fifth chapters of the *Daryā-i Laṭāfat* by Inshā (on "The idioms of the language of Delhi"[93] and "The language and idioms of Delhi's women (*ḳhawātīn*)"), a glossary of phrases used by women included in the 1828 *Dīwān-i Reḳhtī* by Saʿādat Yār Ḳhān 'Rangīn' (1756–1834/5),[94] and the *Risālah-i Qawāʿid-i Ṣarf o Naḥw-i Urdū* by Imām Baḳhsh 'Ṣahbāʾī' (c. 1802/3–1857), completed the same year as the *Maḳhzan-i Fawāʾid* (1845) and published in 1849.[95] Nevertheless, after examining the three aforementioned works that predate the *Maḳhzan*, Ḥusain ultimately concludes, "it is clear that apart from Rangīn's *Dīwān-i Reḳhtī*, there was no other source under the examination of the author.

In short, the search for terms, the determination of meanings, and the obtaining of prooftexts . . . was also carried out by him [alone]."[96] This conclusion is corroborated by the text of the handwritten Ḳhudā Baḳhsh manuscript, which was not an exact copy of the *Maḳhzan* but rather an abridgment of that work under the name *Luġhat-i Muḥāwarāt-i Urdū*. The person who copied it out did not solely limit himself to entries from the *Maḳhzan-i Fawāʾid* but, as Ḥusain notes,

> also completed the work of gathering words from the *Daryā-i Laṭāfat*, *Muḥāwarah-i Zanān* ['Women's idioms' in Rangīn's *Dīwān-i Reḳhtī*], and, in order to separate these three, after the illustration and explanation of the terms, he made reference [to his sources] by means of [the indication] "*az maḳhzan-i fawāʾid*" ['from the *Maḳhzan-i Fawāʾid*'], "*az daryā-i laṭāfat*" ['from the *Daryā-i Laṭāfat*' of Inshā], and "*dar maḥāwarah-i zanān*" ['in the *Maḥāwarah-i Zanān*'].[97]

These works were seen by the anonymous copyist of the Ḳhudā Baḳhsh manuscript as distinct, if related, works worthy of being collated as an omnibus text.

After establishing that the written sources for Nakhat's dictionary were primarily the *dīwāns* (collections of poetry) of prominent literary figures,[98] Ḥusain takes great pains to show that despite the text's appearance of having gone undetected for more than a century and a half it was still an important source of later dictionaries, including Sayyid Aḥmad's *Farhang-i Āṣafiyah*. As Ḥusain dourly notes, "given the perfidy of those great ones [prominent later lexicographers who did not acknowledge their debt to the *Maḳhzan*], for years the scholarly world was deprived of an important sourcetext."[99] He proceeds to document in meticulous detail some of the numerous occasions on which Sayyid Aḥmad lifted without attribution material from Nakhat's dictionary, dividing his analysis into four distinct parts. The first two deal with "correspondences in definitions and prooftexts" and more serious "word-for-word similarities in prooftexts" (here "prooftexts" refers to examples of the usage of a particular term or phrase extracted from a literary source). The third lists "unattested inclusions for terms similar to the *Maḳhzan-i Fawāʾid*." Despite the assiduity with which Nakhat documented the authors of the verses he cites as prooftexts in his definitions, Ḥusain nevertheless discovered an occasional missing or incorrect attribution. These errors, however, are frequently reproduced in the *Farhang-i Āṣafiyah*, an oversight Ḥusain alleges Sayyid Aḥmad could have avoided with "even the slightest of efforts."[100] Ḥusain here ignores the potential difficulties Sayyid Aḥmad would have faced in locating the sources from which Nakhat drew his prooftexts. Many of them may no longer have been readily available by the last quarter of the nineteenth century as a result of the massive loss of manuscripts and books that accompanied the violence and displacement suffered by Delhi's residents in the years 1857 and 1858. In fairness to Sayyid Aḥmad, the *Makḥzan-i Fawāʾid* may have been one of the only sources from which to discover the verse of a poet whose collected works may have been lost in the intervening years.

It is the seeming invitation from lexicographers like Nakhat and Sayyid Aḥmad to read their dictionaries as though they are poetic anthologies that makes the statement that introduces the fourth and final section of Ḥusain's case against Sayyid Aḥmad's misappropriation of the *Makḥzan-i Fawāʾid*, titled "Incorrect Attributions of Verses to Poets Similar to the *Makḥzan-i Fawāʾid*," so very incomprehensible. As Ḥusain categorically states,

> Dictionaries should not become *tażkirahs* of poets such that a mistaken attribution of verses would pose any great obstacle in [determining] the meaning [of a term]. Should the work of 'Żauq'[101] be associated with 'Ġhālib' or that of any other celebrated poet, then this does not make any difference in the credibility of the chain of transmission. But it is appropriate that a verse be associated with the original poet. From this the credibility of the proof text (*sanad kā ĕʿtibār*) becomes established. This sort of error are to be found in the *Makḥzan-i Fawāʾid*, and this very thing appears in the *Farhang-i Āṣafiyah*, too.[102]

Ḥusain rejects the treatment of dictionaries as "*tażkirah*s of poets" while acknowledging that people *do* in fact treat them as such by reproducing erroneous *asnād* (authoritative sources) in dictionary entries in subsequent lexicographic works. It ignores a long tradition in Persianate lexicography of dictionaries serving as memorial anthologies of poetry and the lives of poets. This is to say nothing of the immense variety of texts and contexts in which dictionaries are consulted (though rarely accurately cited) as integral to the formation and implementation of policies with very real social consequences.

The examples Ḥusain gives of Sayyid Aḥmad's copying of verses misattributed by Nakhat in his *Makḥzan* only make the illogic of his assertion that "dictionaries should not become *tażkirahs* of poets" all the more apparent. In his entry for *ṭopī-wāle* Nakhat copies this quatrain by Mīr Taqī Mīr (1722–1810) by way of a prooftext (*sanad*):

dillī ke kaj kulāh laṛkoṅ ne
kām ʿushāq kā tamām kiyā
ko'ī ʿāshiq naẓar nahīṅ ātā
ṭopī wāloṅ ne qatl-i ʿām kiyā

Delhi's boys, wearing their caps askew,
Have finished off the lovers.
There is not a single a lover in view:
The *ṭopī wāle* have carried out a general massacre.

The idiom in question is defined in the *Makhzan* as "a Qizilbāsh or Durrānī man of *wilāyat* [Persia],"[103] though here it clearly has the primary—that is, nonidiomatic and literal—meaning of any person, but especially a young boy, who wears a cap. Ḥusain wryly notes that "although this appears on page 28 of the first edition of [Mir Taqī Mīr's 1752] *Nikāt al-Shuʿarā* under the name 'Payām' . . . the author of the *Farhang-i Āṣafiyah* has also believed it to belong to Mīr."[104] Thus, he implicates the author of the *Farhang-i Āṣafiyah* in carelessly neglecting to verify the provenance of a verse preserved in one of the earliest and most celebrated *taẕkirah*s of the Urdu literary tradition.[105] Ironically, Sayyid Aḥmad appears here to treat Nakhat's dictionary as a source of poetic prooftexts equal in authority to the *taẕkirah*s.

Whether or not this authority was deserved, it cannot be denied that users of dictionaries—and even fellow lexicographers—read dictionaries not just for their definitions but also for the delight of discovering apposite verses that both defined and deftly applied the term. The abovementioned verse by Payām (d. 1744)[106] has a particular charm in that it self-consciously encapsulates through a single image (the *ṭopī wālā*) two seemingly disparate historical character types that connoisseurs of *rekhtah* poetry would have associated with the reign of Emperor Muḥammad Shāh (1719–1748). The figure of the attractive young boy who rakishly wears a hat askew is a celebrated image central to *amrad-parastī*, literally "the worship of beardless youths," which is particularly identified with the works of Delhi poets active in the first half of the eighteenth century.[107] Inshā devotes an entire chapter of his *Daryā-i Laṭāfat* to *bāṅke* (dandies), a term that literally means "crooked" and refers to the manner in which these youths wore their hats or turbans. Inshā reports, in his own characteristic way, that "the character of these people is crooked [untoward, cranky], even their gait shows a swagger (*aiṇṭh*), they examine their bodies a great deal, and calling every feminine thing masculine is both their habit and their style."[108] Inshā adds, somewhat glibly, "there are *bāṅkās* in every town, be it Delhi or the cities of the Deccan, Bengal, or Punjab—these all have a single nature and a single language. . . . In this way, they say for *hamārī bakri* ['our (female) goat'] *hamārā bakrā* ['our (male) goat'], just the [same] way that in every town the turbans, ringlets, and pellet-bows . . . of Afghans do not change."[109]

The other characters to which this particular verse makes reference is the infamous Qizilbāsh, or "red heads," the core of the army of Tahmāsp Qulī Ḳhān, the great Central Asian conqueror who took the name Nadir Shah upon his coronation in 1736.[110] On March 21, 1739, the first day of the Persian New Year (*nau rūz*) and a day after Nadir Shah made his grand entrance into Delhi at Muḥammad Shāh's invitation (extracted, it must be stressed, under some duress after the Mughals offered only desultory battle at Karnal) to host the Iranian king for two months in the Mughal capital, a rumor spread through the city that Nadir Shah had been assassinated. This gave encouragement to residents of Shāhjahānābād, some of whom attacked the Qizilbāsh billeted in the city, killing some three thousand soldiers.[111] The following day, Nadir Shah, still very much alive, ordered a general massacre (*qatl-i ʿāmm*), which by some accounts caused the death of several tens of thousands of residents.[112] The horrific violence visited upon the city during these two days reminded many contemporary authors of another event, more than three centuries earlier:

> Since the days of Hazrat Sáhib-kirán Amír Tímúr, who captured Delhí and ordered the inhabitants to be massacred [in 1398], up to the present time, AH 1151, a period of 348 years, the capital has been free from such visitations. The ruin in which its beautiful streets and buildings were now involved was such that the labour of years could alone restore the town to its former state of grandeur.[113]

That the first event was deeply embedded in the collective memory of the populace made the latter seem all the more significant, so that it came to represent more than anything else the decline of the Mughal Empire and the lost independence of its rulers. It even entered into the vocabulary of the city's shopkeepers: one historian notes that "to-day in the Delhi bazaar a 'Nadir Shahi' signifies a massacre."[114] Payām, the author of these verses, would have composed them at some point after the massacre took place in 1739 and prior to his own death in 1744. The net effect of equating the destruction wrought by the glances of Delhi's dandies with that done by the swords of Qizilbāsh soldiers is to derive self-conscious, if rather dark, humor from the fresh wounds of a traumatic event.[115] Without attributing any particular motivations to the compiler, one may conclude from the inclusion of these verses in a dictionary compiled a century later that their value was felt to lie not so much in clearly demonstrating the signification of a particular term (in this case, *ṭopī wālā*) but rather in conveying a surplus of meaning for participants of the literary culture of which it was an exemplar.

While Ḥusain has lambasted Sayyid Aḥmad for slavishly copying even the errors of Nakhat, it is in the slight differences between the entries of both books that the changes to the political and linguistic landscape of the intervening years come into sharpest relief. The perfunctory definition that Nakhat offers for the phrase *ṭopī wālā*—"a Qizilbāsh or Durrānī man of *wilāyat*"—forgoes the literal ("one who wears a hat") for a literary and contextually specific technical signification and serves as a justification for the author's inclusion of seven verses by four authors, including the aforementioned verse set by Payām (misattributed, it will be recalled, to Mīr), a couplet by Inshā, and two more verse sets of two verses each, one by Shāh Naṣīr and another that Nakhat himself composed.[116] Sayyid Aḥmad's definition not only offers far greater detail than Nakhat's "a Qizilbāsh or Durrānī man of *wilāyat*" but also supplements this definition with a literal meaning ("one who wears a hat") and an additional idiomatic signification ("A Frank. Englishman. European"):

> *ṭopī wālā*—H[indī]—masculine noun (1) One who wears a hat*:*
> Delhi's boys, wearing their caps askew,
> Have finished off the lovers.
> There is not a single lover in view:
> The *ṭopī wāle* have carried out a general massacre.} a *qiṭʿah* of 'Mīr' Taqī
>
> (2) Qizilbāsh troops, a Durrānī and Wilāyatī [Persian] man who originally wore a red cap, [and who] had come to Hindustan along with Nādir Shāh and Aḥmad Shāh [Durrānī] in AD 1739 and 1759.
>
> That young fop is no less than a *ṭopī wālā*
> Seeing him alone, oh heart!, how we will go?
> We passed through his alleyway, when tears came without an army,
> Having taken us along with them, we will go to the Durrānī camp
> } a *qiṭʿah* of Shāh 'Naṣīr'
>
> (3) A Frank. Englishman. European.[117]

The charm of this verse by Payām is in its jarring conflation of the literal and extended idiomatic significations of the phrase *ṭopī wālā*. One would then expect that it could only be fully appreciated if presented following the second definition: while still meaningful for those unaware of its connection with the soldiers of Nadir Shah's army, the verse set only acquires its bittersweet quality with that knowledge.[118] Sayyid Aḥmad, however, instead places this particular *qiṭʿah* with the first (literal, least marked) meaning. He selects for this the same verse set by Nasīr that appears in Nakhat's dictionary as evidence of the second meaning. For the third, he provides no prooftext at all.

Sayyid Aḥmad's choice of sequencing prooftexts may well be explained away as yet another artifact of his plagiarism: since he did not investigate the origin of the verse he misattributes to Mīr, why would he care whether that particular verse best explains the signification "one who wears a hat"? The logic of the verses dictates that these *ṭopī wāle* cannot be just any ordinary people but are rather the handsome, if foppish, boys of Shāhjahānābād, whose glances are just as cruel for the poet as were the swords of Nadir Shah's Qizilbāsh soldiers. Nowhere in Sayyid Aḥmad's definition (to say nothing of the laconic Nakhat) would someone not acquainted with the tropes of Persianate poetry—particularly the *reḳhtah* poetry of the first half of the eighteenth century—get a sense of *ṭopī wālā* as "a foppish boy who wears his hat askew; a beardless youth sporting a cap who attracts the attention of older men." While Sayyid Aḥmad's entry has clear correspondences with Fallon's dictionary, that work completely ignores Sayyid Aḥmad's second signification and reproduces entirely different prooftexts:

> *ṭopī-vālā*, n. m. 1. One who wears a hat. [song. *Taiṅ to merā man har līnā, ṭopī*—wale saṅvaryā. Wom.
>
> 2. A European.
>
> *Kamdve dhotī-vālā, uṛāve ṭopī-vālā*. Prov. [The naked loins-clad earn, the black hat-wearers spend.[119]

In addition to the unwarranted insertion of the terms "naked" and "black" into his English translation of the proverb, Fallon's prejudices are further revealed in his omission of the extended literary sense of the term. This is in keeping with his stated disdain (with a few notable exceptions) for what he considered the pedantry of *reḳhtah* poetry and the special terminology employed in the poetry of Delhi.[120] And if the entry that precedes it is any indication,[121] he did not hesitate to provide additional significations for the term merely out of deference to a Victorian sense of propriety.[122] For similar terms like *bāṅke*, *kaj-kulā*, and *chailā*, he makes it quite clear that he was aware that a boy of this sort fancied himself a "Don Juan" or "Lothario."[123]

Why did Sayyid Aḥmad choose, in adapting Nakhat's entry into his own dictionary, to reproduce only the verse sets by Mīr (Payām) and Shāh Naṣīr and not those by Inshā and Nakhat? His exclusion of Inshā's verse may have been either accidental or for aesthetic or practical reasons. The verse in question is as follows:

khā liyā jo ćimaṭ ke khāloṅ ko
nām rakhte haiṅ ṭopī wāloṅ ko

Since in embracing, they [even] devoured the skins,
[Yet] they pour abuse on the *ṭopī wālās*?

There are a number of problems with this verse. It does not appear in the collected works of Inshāllāh Ḳhān Inshā,[124] though he does define the *ṭopī wāle* as "of the *wilāyatī* (European, foreign, Persian) force" in his *Daryā-i*

FIGURE 4.2 Topywallas in "Missionary Influence; or, How to Make Converts," from *The Grand Master; or, Adventures of Qui Hi? in Hindostan. A Hudibrastic Poem in Eight Cantos by Quiz* (1816). Courtesy of the Posner Memorial Collection, Carnegie Mellon University Libraries, Pittsburgh, Penn.

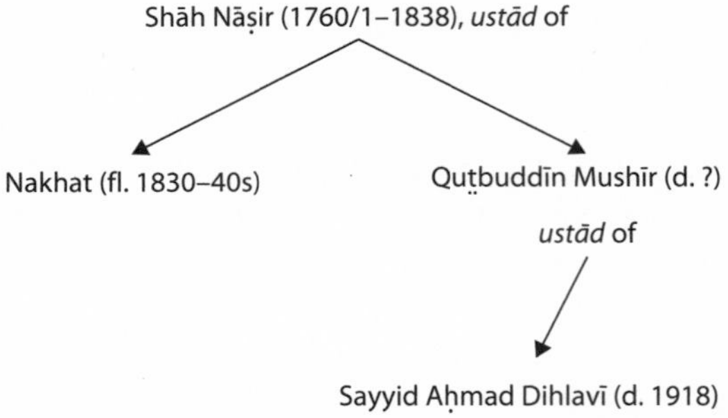

FIGURE 4.3 Sayyid Aḥmad's *silsilah* (chain) of poetic discipleship

Laṭ̤āfat.[125] Its graphic connotations may also have recommended its exclusion from the *Farhang-i Āṣafiyah*, implied in the connection (*rabṭ̤*) between "hat" and "skins," the ambiguity of the signification of the verb *cimaṭnā* (to stick, be glued, take in close embrace, to follow close at the heels), and the absence of a named agent.[126] The poet feigns outrage at the hypocrisy of the beloved whose coquettishness he hyperbolically compares with the cruelty of an invading army: both, it is claimed, make their caps with the "skins" of the slain. The suggestion of cannibalism may have been the cause of its exclusion if indeed it was omitted by virtue of its signification.[127] Other verses by Inshā do appear throughout the *Farhang* as well as a biographical notice under the headword *inshā*ʾ.[128]

The same considerations may be at play in explaining Sayyid Aḥmad's rejection of the verse set Nakhat himself penned for his entry.[129] Unlike Inshā, however, Nakhat's verses do not appear anywhere in the *Farhang-i Āṣafiyah*. If lexicographers treated the dictionaries of their predecessors as *taẕkirah*-like anthologies of poetry, mining them as much for their prooftexts as for their corpus of terms and definitions, this usefulness did mean that the poetry of their lexicographic forebears would be guaranteed entry into later dictionaries. Indeed, if Sayyid Aḥmad were to include the verses of any poet, it would seem that Nakhat would be a natural fit: we are informed by Ṣābir and other *taẕkirah* biographers that Nakhat "acquired the art of speech (*fann-i suḵhan*) from the late Shāh [Naṣīruddīn] 'Naṣīr'."[130] Naṣīr, it should be recalled, was also the *ustād* or teacher of Quṭ̤buddīn Mushīr, the person from whom Sayyid Aḥmad took corrections in his *ġhazals*.[131] Naṣīr, as the *ustād* of Nakhat and a *ṣāḥib-i dīwān* (author of a full collection of verses, especially in multiple genres), possessed greater poetic authority than his student, who would have been familiar to Sayyid Aḥmad more for his dictionary than his poetry.[132] Without a *dīwān* of his own, whatever independent verses Nakhat did produce were confined largely to his dictionary and perhaps a few contemporary *taẕkirahs*. To have cited a poet without a *dīwān* would surely have invited greater scrutiny of Sayyid Aḥmad's sources, leaving him liable, at the very least, to charges of having privileged a minor poet as an authority on language use. This is not to say, however, that lexicographers could not also be considered great poets. Though the verses of Nakhat and Sayyid Aḥmad (whose *taḵhalluṣ* was 'Sayyid') never enjoyed great esteem, this fact is at odds with the great respect accorded to the poetry of such occasional lexicographers as Ṭapish, Inshā, and Rangīn. Verses by each of them appear in the *Maḵhzan-i Fawāʾid* of Nakhat, the *Maḵhzan al-Muḥāwarāt* of Munshī Ćiraṇjī Lāl (discussed below),[133] and Sayyid Aḥmad's own *Farhang-i Āṣafiyah.*

CONCLUSION: NEW FIELDS, NEW WALLS

By the middle of the nineteenth century, however, lexicography, like *reḵhtah* poetry a century earlier, was becoming a lucrative mode of literary production in an emerging Urdu print culture. Under new forms of patronage,[134] with access to vast new markets where unprecedented economies of scale were achieved through advances in print and paper technologies, and buoyed by a regular influx of capital invested by a colonial state increasingly interested in taking an active role in the education of its subjects, lexicography was becoming a profession. As discussed in the second chapter, this represented a shift in lexicography away from what Bourdieu called the field of "restricted production," which he defined as "a system producing cultural goods (and the instruments for appropriating those goods) objectively destined for a public of producers of cultural goods," to a field of "large-scale cultural production" characterized by "the production of cultural goods destined for non-producers of cultural goods, 'the public at large.'"[135] As lexicography moved from being the pursuit of an amateur and ill-defined group of littérateurs—whose primary criteria for membership the sociologist Susanne Janssen has characterized as evaluation in a "reputational" paradigm, "where professional hierarchy is based on reputation"[136]—to an increasingly professional sphere of production, it became essential that the credentials of would-be lexicographers be tested against a uniform set of standards with more general purchase. In a purely market-driven system, credibility would be determined solely by the success of a given publication in the marketplace. Since, however, the compilation of dictionaries was time and work intensive, any comprehensive work required significant prior and subsequent capital investments.

While the nineteenth century brought decisive changes to the economic bases underlying the modes of producing, distributing, and consuming texts, dictionaries that were monumental in scale were indeed produced in South Asia prior to the advent of European colonial rule, especially under the patronage of premodern and early modern states (most notably the Mughal Empire). While lexicographers still had access to various forms of state patronage (Sayyid Aḥmad's prizewinning productions and relationship with niẓāms of Hyderabad being a case in point), what distinguished the monumental dictionaries of nineteenth-century South Asia from those of earlier periods was the potential for investors to recoup very quickly, through sales within a rapidly expanding mass market of potential private purchasers, the preproduction costs associated with the creation of didactic texts. This, in turn, rewarded the pooling of smaller individual capital investments by corporate groups seeking returns in cash, largely replacing an earlier model of finance primarily by donations issued by individuals (or state entities) whose primary motivation was the acquisition of social merit rather than financial benefits. With the rise of corporate financing, competition for financing grew apace: proposals for projects that promised a rapid turnover of investor expenditures were assured of greater access to capital.[137]

Partly as a result of these new commercial possibilities, our romantic image of the lonely lexicographer drudging away in solitude increasingly gives way to corporate, institutional efforts carried out in scriptoria expressly designed for the efficient processing of source texts, including the storage and retrieval of massive collections of notecards. The corporate production of lexicographic works permitted the collection of newer and far more extensive pools of lexical data than would have been possible through the efforts of a single person. There is nothing new about a dictionary purporting to represent the work of multiple lifetimes: lexicographers have always understood themselves to be standing on the shoulders of giants.[138] What was unprecedented in South Asia, however, was the potential to produce the equivalent of several lifetimes' worth of new lexicographic research within a matter of a few years. Fallon notes in the introduction to his dictionary:

> For such words and significations as are met with in the written language, authorities might be quoted. But the lexicographer who ventures beyond the safe boundary of the written literature, in the attempt to fix and give permanence to what yet lives only in individual minds and in the passing utterances of the tongue, treads on dubious ground. Examples from the spoken tongue which might illustrate and justify certain uses of a word, will not have the weight of authorities cited from the written language. Moreover to set them down as they are heard or remembered, and afterwards to compare conflicting idioms and forms of speech in order to determine which are the most current and which are sanctioned by good usage, would be the work of a lifetime, or rather an Academy.[139]

The rise of lexicographic institutions, like the one inaugurated by Fallon in the 1870s, enabled a division and specialization of labor: an individual working as part of a team of lexicographers might be assigned a limited set of tasks (for example, researching etymologies or collating prooftexts from notecards) for a subset of lemmata within the entire lexical corpus. That individual's performance, rather than being determined by his authentic participation within a courtly milieu of politeness and literary competence, was instead evaluated by his efficiency at carrying out the particular task—be it as erudite as researching etymology or as mundane as collating pieces of paper. The three primary aspects of lexicographic production, distribution, and consumption thus developed their corporate, mass character in parallel.

We should not be tempted to locate in the *Shams al-Bayān* of Ṭapish the last vestiges of a "purely" Persianate or Indic mode of lexicographic production.[140] Similarly, the inspiration for Nakhat in producing his *Makḥzan* came from a directive issued by the principal of Delhi College, Felix Boutros (d. 1864). Boutros was appointed to this position in early 1841 from his previous post as deputy collector in Bihar.[141] Being himself comfortable in several South Asian languages, Boutros founded in the early 1840s the Vernacular Translation Society, which, under the aegis of the Delhi College, commissioned translations of textbooks in the fields of medicine, law, science, economics, and history.[142] Unlike textbooks prepared by the society that were published at its own press, the Maṭbaʿ al-ʿUlūm (Press of the Sciences), the *Makḥzan-i Fawāʾid* was, by contrast, printed at a private press, the Maṭbaʿ-i Dār al-Islām.[143] If the *Makhzan* was not itself a project of the society, it was nevertheless part of a larger project pursued by Boutros and the society to prepare what Michael Dodson has characterized as "an appropriate 'feeder language' for the introduction of scientific terminology into Urdu . . . due to its peculiar ability to easily absorb foreign nomenclatures."[144] Like Ṭapish before him, however, Nakhat lost his European interlocutor the same year his dictionary was published: Boutros left his position as Delhi College in 1845 and returned to Europe because of poor health.[145]

Rather than advancing Urdu's capacity to accommodate putatively foreign "concepts" as contained in European textbooks, the *Makhzan-i Fawāʾid* instead prepared the ground for Urdu to serve as a medium capable of defining and explaining itself. Few if any monolingual dictionaries of the Urdu language had been compiled prior to 1845. Another work commissioned by Boutros, the aforementioned *Risālah-i Qawāʿid-i Ṣarf wa Naḥw-i Urdū* by Imām Bakhsh Ṣahbāʾī, was probably completed before Boutros's departure in 1845 (it was only published in 1849).[146] By virtue of its two chapters on Urdu terms (*luġhāt*) and coined phrases (*ẓarb al-miṡāl*), Ḥāshmī's history of Urdu lexicography mistakenly gives Ṣahbāʾī's *Risālah* pride of place as the first dictionary to include "the spoken language of Urdu" with definitions and explanations of etymology and grammar in Urdu.[147] Like Nakhat, the reputation of Sahbāʾī is based on his work primarily as a scholar and only secondarily as poet.[148] Both men's authority was derived more through their connections with British-sponsored institutions of higher learning than through their success as poets. What little success Nakhat achieved through his poetry ended in tragedy; Ṣahbāʾī chose to compose poetry in Persian, a language whose pool of potential patrons willing to support professional poets had, by the middle of the nineteenth century, largely evaporated.[149] Works like the *Makhzan* and *Risālah-i Qawāʿid* were instrumental in establishing Urdu's versatility as a language—that is to say, in establishing that language's capacity to serve the needs of a community in a wide range of contexts, anticipating the monolingual ideal espoused by later nationalist movements. By expanding the range of lexical inquiry to include new domains of linguistic use, the poetic register of classical Urdu, upon which the corpus of early dictionaries had once been primarily based, was becoming increasingly peripheral in the compilation of new, more comprehensive works.

Insofar as the *Farhang-i Āṣafiyah* incorporated the contents of the earlier *Makhzan-i Fawāʾid*—itself a work commissioned by an official of the East

India Company—the extent to which Sayyid Aḥmad owed his method to S. W. Fallon must remain a matter of some debate. ʿAbdul Ḥaq, while recognizing that the "the Urdu language must always acknowledge its debt to him," attributed both the text's innovations and what he perceived to be its shortcomings to the influence of his former employer.[150] In many ways, the methods employed by Sayyid Aḥmad in compiling his dictionary were quite new to Urdu lexicography. He cast a wide net in trolling for new lexical material, innovating by including in his dictionary examples of language that did not derive directly from the poetic corpus of classical Urdu poetry alone:

> Common expressions (*ʿāmm muḥāwarah*) are included in this. All the peculiar and special expressions (*ḳhāṣṣ ḳhāṣṣ muḥāware*) enter into this. Listen to the calls of *faqīrs* in this. See the voices of street vendors (*saude wāloṅ ki awāzeṅ*) in this. There is merriment (*dil lagī*) in this. There is fun (*ẓarāfat*) in this. On many many occasions, the intermixed daily existence of all sorts of different occupations, gamblers (*juwāriyoṅ*), thugs, brokers (*dallāloṅ*), horse trainers (*ćābuk sawāriyoṅ*), rascals (*bad maʿāshoṅ*), by whom the majority of people have been deceived. The arrangement of letters [or 'spellings'] also included in this book is that of the words which are current among this class of men, it is written in their name. I have not excluded the speech of women in this. I have not avoided the concerns of the ignorant (*jāhil*). I have included necessary legal terms; I have shown [them], having corrected the mistaken expressions of the courts of justice.

Sayyid Aḥmad's primary innovation was in the manufacture from his source materials of surplus value—that is to say, the imbrication of elements of "merriment" and "fun" within an otherwise utilitarian generic stock of lexical information.

What Sayyid Aḥmad may have intended as "merriment" and "fun" others may rightfully contend to be an example of the inefficiencies of a captive market composed primarily of state agencies and royal patrons, anachronistic relics of a prenationalist political and economic order. Critics have seized upon the reckless catholicity of Sayyid Aḥmad's dictionary, attributing its self-indulgent inclusion of personal detail and lack of regard for national honor to the harmful moral influence of his English mentor. In the assessment of ʿAbdul Ḥaq, "in several places, recourse is taken to extreme prolixity so that the book is such that the author seems not to dispense justice, but tyranny. There are points while reading this book when anyone would burst out laughing. Other times one gets angry."[151]

Debates continue to this day about the appropriateness of including extralinguistic or otherwise "encyclopedic" information in dictionary entries, and there is a well-established tendency whereby certain dictionaries (those of Webster and Larousse, for example), will typically contain more extensive extralinguistic information (in the form of discussions of usage, pictorial illustrations, etc.) than their counterparts. According to the prominent theorist of lexicography Ladislav Zgusta,

> from the point of view of pure theory, encyclopedic glosses should have no place in a purely linguistic description; indeed, no linguistic dictionary should give too many of them. But on the other hand, a useful dictionary of a dead language or of a contemporary one spoken in an exotic culture will have to give encyclopedic notes on the denotate [*sic*] unknown to us.[152]

A distinction is sometimes drawn between, on the one hand, *prescriptivist* lexicographers who argue that the task of a dictionary is to distill a normative written lexicon from the total stock of lexical units in a language and, on the other hand, *descriptivist* lexicographers attempting to describe part or whole of that lexicon in its entirety regardless of supposed notions of correctness or authenticity.[153] Sayyid Aḥmad was preoccupied not just with the promulgation of the Urdu language and its extension into new social and political domains but also with "freezing" elements of Delhi's culture before they melted away. This cultural salvage mission resembled in many ways what Zgusta calls "a useful dictionary of a dead language or . . . a contemporary one spoken in an exotic culture." If Ḥaq, in his own *Luġhat-i Kabīr-i Urdū*, aimed to compile the most comprehensive dictionary of Urdu to date, it is clear, too, that there were lexical units treated by Sayyid Aḥmad that were not deemed appropriate for inclusion in Ḥaq's own standard-normative work.[154] Fallon had emphasized the value of including terms that were potentially "abusive, indelicate or obscene" on the basis of both professional principles and practicality:

> The integrity of the language; the demands of the philologist, the sociologist, and the philosopher; the perfect knowledge of the language which would be impossible if any part were kept back; the insight into the language and into the mind of the people which is obtained by this very class of words, and especially by the *double-entendres*; and above all, *the absolute importance of this*

> *knowledge to judicial officers*, together call for the insertion of every such word and phrase without reserve or exception.[155]

Maulvī ʿAbdul Ḥaq was quick to blame the inclusion of such "obscene" (*fōḥsh*) materials in Sayyid Aḥmad's dictionary as the "benefit of companionship (*faiẓ-i ṣōḥbat*) with Dr. Fallon," in whose footsteps "the author of the *Farhang-i Āṣafiyah*, too, also follows."[156] Whether Sayyid Aḥmad's work suffers or benefits from a surfeit of subjectivity, it also possesses the distance of an ethnography, that is to say, the expression of the separation, even nostalgia, felt by its author toward an increasingly inaccessible past.

If ʿAbdul Ḥaq faulted Sayyid Aḥmad for his inclusion of "obscene terms and expressions," he could at least credit as "extremely praiseworthy" the efforts of its author to include "certain expressions and Hindi terms which up to now no Urdu lexicographer has recorded." There is much evidence throughout the introductory essays of the *Farhang-i Āṣafiyah* that its author considered his work to be of "national" importance. In one place he sums up: "In short, its having been written is an absolute and entire confirmation of the language, and is an extremely important national (*qaumī-mulkī*) work."[157] The decision to include a particular term in the corpus of any lexicographic work is always a political one, regardless of whether the political aspirations are explicit (as in the case of this *qaumī-mulkī* work). Lexical works always map out a lexical domain: insofar as a dictionary purports to describe the speech of the individual language users, it claims its right to absorb those individuals into the logic that undergirds the production, distribution, and consumption of that text. Descriptivist modes of lexicography subject new domains to this logic, complementing the parallel lexicographic codification of linguistic norms that consolidate already subject domains.[158] Both prescriptive and descriptive projects effect a sort of lexicographic conquest on the objects of their study. Sayyid Aḥmad, in this analysis, may be said to belong quite decidedly to the descriptivist camp, expanding the domains to which Urdu lexicography could stake its national claims. It was on these grounds that ʿAbdul Ḥaq could criticize Sayyid Aḥmad for leaving out "many Persian and Arabic terms that are commonly used in Urdu literary books."[159] In the following sentence, Ḥaq adds: "This, too, was an effect of his association with Dr. Fallon," as if his association with the colonial regime had doomed the work from the very outset. The *Farhang-i Āṣafiyah*, through its inclusion of lexical material largely unknown to the Urdu lexicographic tradition, was part of an effort by the Urdu literary elite to represent constituencies within South Asia that had previously been considered peripheral at best to expressions of political legitimacy.

From one perspective, ʿAbdul Ḥaq seems far too generous in his treatment of Sayyid Aḥmad, blaming many of the *Farhang-i Āṣafiyah*'s apparent shortcomings on his "association with Dr. Fallon."[160] When the venerable "Grand Old Man of Urdu" was composing his own introductory essay in the new nation-state of Pakistan, he must have understood that a great nation required a great dictionary and that his role as a lexicographer demanded as much skill in diplomacy as it did in philology. As we have seen, however, the literary persona cultivated by Sayyid Aḥmad resembled that of a poet more than a professor and was quite unlike that of the scholarly Ḥaq compiling his work in the heady years just before and after the partition of India and Pakistan. It would seem fairer to conclude that neither Ḥaq nor his successors have been willing to acknowledge how vastly different their own expectations of a dictionary's function are from those prevalent in the late nineteenth century. The concerns of a nationalist lexicographer anticipating the creation of a new Islamic state of Pakistan would naturally gravitate more toward the consolidation of an Islamic identity centered around the "many Persian and Arabic terms that are commonly used in Urdu literary books" than the inclusion of politically marginal language users within a colonial government of continental proportions.

[5] 1900: GRASPING AT STRAWS

S. W. FALLON

Samuel William Fallon (1817–1880) is considered, along with John T. Platts (1830–1904), to be one of the two great British[1] lexicographers of the Urdu language in the latter half of the nineteenth century. Unfortunately, little is known about Fallon's life, apart from a few autobiographical items contained in the prefatory material in his works.[2] The preface of his *A New Hindustani-English Dictionary* declares that he "died in England of mental exhaustion, leaving his work incomplete" on October 3, 1880.[3] Like Platts, who had served as inspector of schools in the Central Provinces of India, Fallon pursued a career in the educational administration of India. Fallon's most important work was his *Hindustani-English Dictionary*, published in Benares and London in 1879.[4] While at least fifteen other dictionaries of Hindi or Urdu were compiled by British nationals in the mid-nineteenth century, the projects undertaken by Platts and Fallon have the added distinction of having employed as assistant lexicographers a number of people who would later go on to make their mark in their own right as Urdu lexicographers. One of these was Munshī Ćiraṇjī Lāl, whose 1886 work *Makhzan al-Muḥāwarāt* was heavily influenced by Fallon's emphasis on the collection of idiomatic spoken expressions (*muḥawarāt*). Another was Sayyid Aḥmad Dihlawī, who worked under Fallon for some seven years.[5]

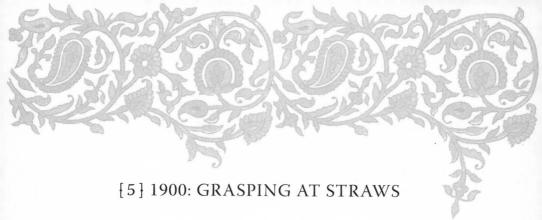

Fallon's work is notable today for having included for the first time a new range of lexicographical material. In illustrations of usage, the work drew from folksongs and proverbs as well as literature. For the first time in a Hindustani-English dictionary, the ordinary conversational terms and the particular speech of women were to be included in a comprehensive work: "He who would find the best idioms of the native stock, with the truly naturalized portion of the foreign element—words which have acquired the most extended and varied meanings and expressiveness by long use—must look for them in the conservatism of the female instinct."[6] Following Fallon's death, another work was published posthumously in 1883, entitled *A New English-Hindustani* dictionary. In this book, the author presented, by the inclusion of supporting usages for English terms and idioms, parallel Urdu passages for those drawn from English literature. His staff completed this work under the supervision of the Reverend J. D. Bate.[7] Gerry Farrell, an ethnomusicologist of nineteenth-century India, discovered a letter written by Fallon in 1873 to the officiating secretary to the Government of Bengal, General Department, in which he proposed a project to collect folksongs to be applied to a number of immediate ends, namely,

1. Selections for the series of Hindi and Hindustani school readers, to be compiled by Rae Sohan Lal, Head-master, Patna Normal school;
2. A body of select Hindustani and Hindi literature for all classes of readers;
3. Materials for a popular nomenclature for treatises in arts and sciences;
4. Materials for a dictionary of spoken Hindustani or Hindi;
5. A collection of good idioms for the spoken tongue, with examples classified and arranged as aids to Hindi composition.[8]

Many of these folksongs, along with proverbs, folktales, and other idioms, found their way into Fallon's *New Hindustani-English Dictionary*. What will be recognized in this prospectus and in all of Fallon's subsequent published work is a marked preference for the spoken idiom over the literary in the selection of literary material: "The wealth of the language is in the spoken tongue; and how rich and expressive that is. . . . The best part of the language cannot be left out, if the language is to be represented in its integrity. The living utterances of the people are almost absent from our Dictionaries."[9] In this regard, the nearly contemporary publication of Platts's dictionary (1884), based on a copious survey of printed texts including newspapers, was fortuitous. Platts was cognizant of these differences and explained them as follows:

> The Hindústání Dictionary of Fallon aims at a special object, distinct from that pursued in the pages of this work: it aims, rather at the collection of a

> particular class of words and phrases. Hundreds of words that occur in Hindí and Urdú literature Dr. Fallon thought proper to give no place to in his Dictionary, because, from his point of view, they were pedantic. This must, necessarily, considerably diminish the usefulness of his book so far as students are concerned. The work is, notwithstanding, one of considerable merit, and will, no doubt, be valued by scholars on account of the numerous proverbs and quotations from the poets which it contains.[10]

Together, these two dictionaries provide an unprecedented range of lexical data drawn from complementary historical, occupational, and literary sources.

What is of more immediate relevance, however, is the relationship, personal and professional, between Fallon and Sayyid Aḥmad. Unfortunately, very little evidence survives to document this intriguing partnership. Indeed, in the preface to his Hindustani–English dictionary Fallon goes so far as to complain:

> The difficulties attending the compilation of this work have been singularly great and uncommon. In most novel undertakings, if the instruments are not available, they can be designed and made by inventive power and skill. But mental gifts are not made, and special acquirements require time. The pure taste for the natural, and true, and simple is especially rare in the native literary class in India who, almost to a man, despise truth to nature as all too tame and common, and the mother tongue as the language of vulgar, illiterate people. Their admiration is for the extravagant and unreal, the foreign and the factitious.[11]

In the paragraphs that follow, Fallon describes the difficulties that he faced in seeking out a staff that shared his vision. The more educated a potential assistant might be, the greater the chances he would prove himself to be a pedant, led astray by his exposure to "native education":

> The lamentable result of all this is that men whose natural taste is yet uncorrupted and who possess some command of the popular language and its Folklore, cannot read and write; and those who can read and write have vitiated tastes, without a due command of the mother tongue, while they commonly conceal what they do not know of it.[12]

In the unlikely event that an assistant would be found who was somehow able to rise above the prejudices that accompany the values of the educational system while cultivating the technical skills required of a modern lexicographer, he would succeed only in making himself vulnerable to attack from both sides, for "the man who professes to be a master of the inexhaustible and growing idioms of the living speech of numerous classes of a numerous people, would have need to be well armed against the criticisms of many thousands who are more or less versed in the true idioms of their mother tongue."[13] In conclusion, Fallon explains that "it will not be difficult to understand why the compiler has not yet succeeded in getting together a competent establishment of native assistants for the work which he has undertaken."[14]

In light of Fallon's apparent disappointment in his staff of Indian assistants, it is difficult to confirm independently Sayyid Aḥmad's claims of having received encouragement from Fallon for his own lexicographic projects. In a passage from the 1918 introduction to the *Luġhāt al-Nisāʾ*, Sayyid Aḥmad provides further information about his relationship to Fallon:

> During the time when I was revising the *Farhang-i Āṣafiyah* [it was not given this name until much later] and was engaged in trying to complete it, on that occasion, Sir (*janāb*) S. W. Dr. Fallon Ṣāḥib Bahādur Inspector of Schools for Bihar Province, on hearing about the publication of my dictionary, came to Delhi and having requested to examine several sections of the *Farhang*, became extremely pleased. And in order to have his own Hindustani–English dictionary prepared, having been granted permission by Mister Cooke Ṣāhib Bahādur, Inspector of the School Circuit of Ambālah, and whose subordinate I was, I was called to the station of Dānāpūr.

It is unclear when their first meeting took place. Ḳhāliq Anjum states without citing any sources that Fallon had called Sayyid Aḥmad to Dānāpūr in 1873 and was engaged in this project for seven years.[15] Sayyid Aḥmad's mention of "revising the *Farhang-i Āṣafiyah*" here is somewhat misleading, for he himself acknowledges that this only became the title of his dictionary once he had secured in 1896 the niẓām's patronage for the publication of the third and fourth volumes of his *Hindūstānī Urdū Luġhāt*. The dictionary, news of whose publication Fallon would have heard, was probably Sayyid Aḥmad's *Muṣṭalaḥāt-i Urdū* (Idioms of Urdu), published in 1871, and not the *Armaġhān-i Dihlī* (Souvenir gift of Delhi), which only began to be printed in installments beginning in 1878 and would later be reedited and published in four volumes as the *Farhang-i Āṣafiyah* in

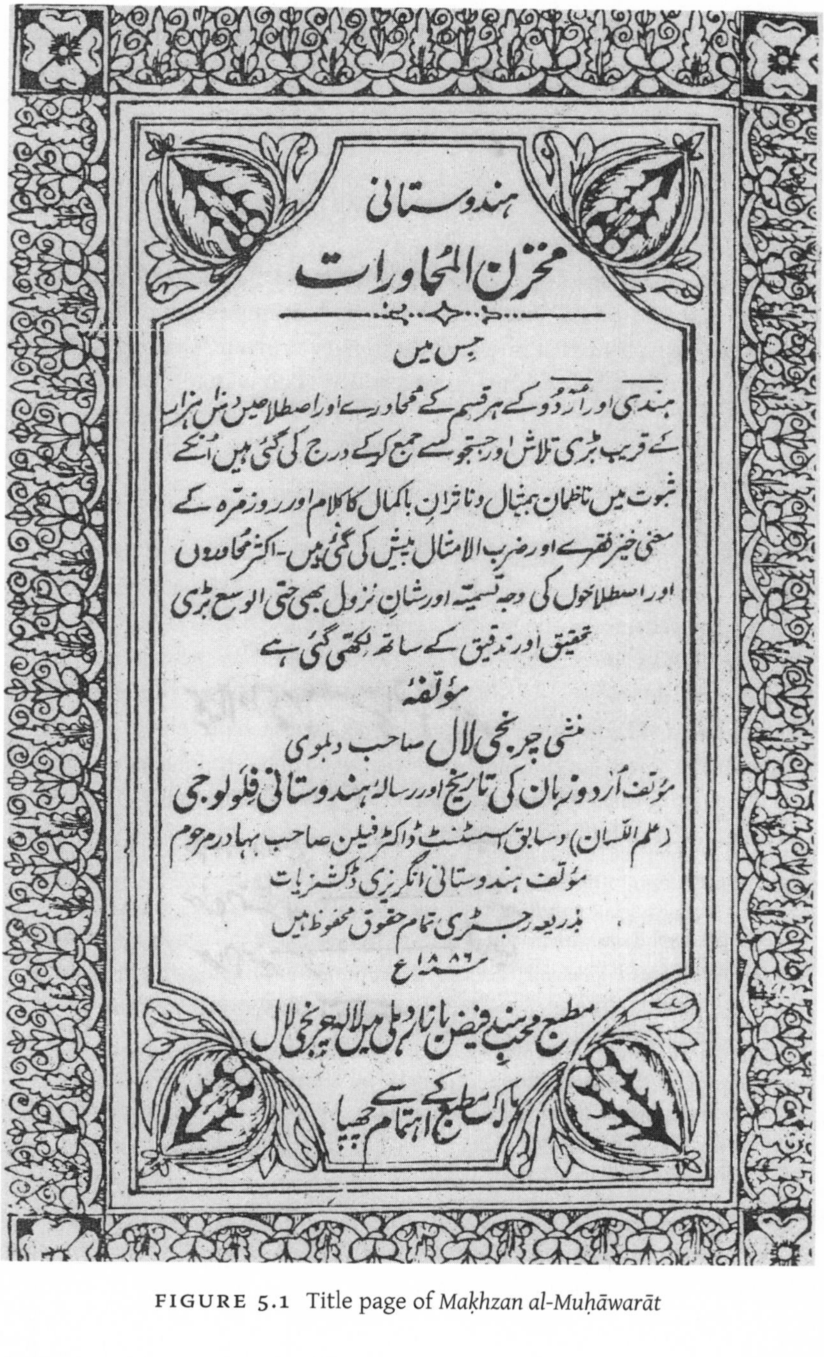
ہندوستانی

مخزن المحاورات

جس میں

ہندی اور اردو کے ہر قسم کے محاورے اور اصطلاحیں دس ہزار
کے قریب بڑی تلاش اور جستجو کے جمع کر کے درج کی گئی ہیں انکے
ثبوت میں ناظمان بےمثال و ناثران باکمال کا کلام اور روزمرہ کے
معنی خیز فقرے اور ضرب الامثال پیش کی گئی ہیں۔ اکثر محاوروں
اور اصطلاحوں کی وجہ تسمیہ اور شان نزول بھی حتی الوسع بڑی
تحقیق اور تدقیق کے ساتھ لکھی گئی ہے

مؤلفہ

منشی چرنجی لال صاحب دہلوی
مؤلف اردو زبان کی تاریخ اور رسالہ ہندوستانی فلولوجی
(علم اللسان) و سابق اسسٹنٹ ڈاکٹر فیلن صاحب بہادر مرحوم
مؤلف ہندوستانی انگریزی ڈکشنریات

بذریعہ رجسٹری تمام حقوق محفوظ ہیں

۱۸۸۶ء

مطبع محب ہند فیض بازار دہلی میں لالہ چرنجی لال
مالک مطبع کے اہتمام سے چھپا

FIGURE 5.1 Title page of *Makhzan al-Muhāwarāt*

the year of its author's death, 1918.[16] This seems all the more plausible if the "Mister Cooke" to which he is referring is the same Theodore Cooke (1836–1910) who had been appointed "to the 2nd grade of the Education Department, 1st November 1872."[17]

ĆIRAṆJĪ LĀL

The "effect" of "association with Dr. Fallon" may be gauged by the similarity of Sayyid Aḥmad's work to that of a contemporary lexicographer and fellow assistant in Fallon's own dictionary projects, the English translation of the title page of which is reproduced below in its entirety:

> *Hindūstānī*
> *Makhzan al-Muḥāwarāt*
> In which
> Having gathered with great effort and research all sorts of Hindi and Urdu idioms (*muḥāwarah*) and terminology (*iṣṭilāḥ*), [of which] approximately 10,000 have been entered; as proof of them the works of incomparable versifiers and accomplished prose writers (*nāẓimān-i be-miṡāl o nāṡirān bā-kamāl*) and meaning-producing phrases of daily speech (*roz-marrah ke maʿnī-khez fiqre*) and proverbs (*ẓarb al-maṡāl*) have been presented. The reason for the coining of most idioms (*muḥāwarah*) and terminologies (*iṣṭilāḥ*) and nature of their derivation, to the extent possible, have also with great research and scrutiny been recorded.
> The author
> Munshī Ćiraṇjī Lāl Ṣāḥib Dihlawī
> Author of *Urdū Zabān kī Tārīkh* ['History of the Urdu language'] and *Risālah-i Hindūstānī Filolojī* ['Treatise on Hindustani philology'] (Linguistics) and formerly Assistant to the late Doctor Fallon Ṣāḥib Bahādur, author of the *Hindūstānī-English Dictionary*
> All rights reserved by means of Registry
> AD 1886
> Muḥibb-i Hind Press, Faiẓ Bāzār Dihlī, Lālah Ćiraṇjī Lāl
> Printed under the supervision of the owner of the press[18]

From the title page alone, the similarity between content and approaches of the two works is readily apparent.

Munshī Lālah Ćiraṇjī Lāl was, like his colleague Sayyid Aḥmad, a native Dihlawī and resident of Daryā Ganj, a wealthy and predominantly Hindu neighborhood located to the south of the Red Fort, and one that had been largely rebuilt in the aftermath of the violent events of 1857 and 1858. In his review of the work, the eminent educator and Urdu author Munshī Muḥammad Żakā Allāh (c. 1832–1910),[19] who was then serving as professor of vernacular literature and science at Muir College, Allahabad, listed Ćiraṇjī Lāl's educational qualifications: "Munshī Ṣāḥib is the holder of a diploma (*sanad yāft*) of the highest honors from the Normal School, Delhi, and has passed the entrance exam in Calcutta University and had taken Sanskrit in this exam [for] Eastern languages (*mashriqī zabān*)."[20] It is remarkable how similar the two figures were in their educational and professional backgrounds, both having attended Delhi's Normal School and been employed by Fallon in his projects. If anything, Ćiraṇjī Lāl could claim more distinguished credentials as a lexicographer. He was senior to Sayyid Aḥmad in age, having been listed as assisting J. S. Reid in his *Urdú-Hindí-English Vocabulary, Compiled for the Use of Beginners*.[21] That work was published in 1854, when Sayyid Aḥmad would have only been about eight years old.[22] And unlike Sayyid Aḥmad, he is actually named in M. D. Fallon's preface as one of the members of Fallon's "efficient staff" who, "under the supervision of Revd. J. D. Bate," helped complete *A New English-Hindustani Dictionary* following Fallon's death in 1880.[23]

Ćiraṇjī Lāl describes his relationship with Fallon in warm terms throughout the acknowledgments that are included in the *dībāćah*, or preface, to his *Maḵhzan al-Muḥāwarāt* (Treasury of idioms). Fallon, then serving as inspector of the Bihar Circuit of Schools, "having come from Patna-ʿAẓīmābād to Delhi, started making his Hindustani-English Dictionary, and having beckoned me from Delhi College's first-year (*air* [for *yīr*?]) class in April 1875, declared me as appointed to be his assistant in his department of dictionaries [*maḥkamah-i luġhāt*, alternatively and perhaps more evocatively, a 'tribunal of words']."[24] This would have been some two years *after* Fallon had requested the services of Sayyid Aḥmad, calling into question the statements of Hāshmī and Ḥusainī concerning Sayyid Aḥmad's supposed seven-year apprenticeship to Fallon. Though Fallon mentions collecting materials for a dictionary in his letter of 1873, R. C. Temple, who edited Fallon's *Dictionary of Hindustani Proverbs* (and to whom Fallon dedicated in 1879 the *New Hindustani-English Dictionary*), states that the author had been collecting materials from 1870 to 1880.[25]

Sayyid Aḥmad claims to have begun work on what would become the *Farhang-i Āṣafiyah* prior to having met Fallon for the first time. If we accept Anjum's assertion that Sayyid Aḥmad went to Dānāpūr in 1873, this seems possible. If, however, like Ćiraṇjī Lāl, Sayyid Aḥmad only began his work at some point following Fallon's arrival in Delhi following his retirement in 1875 but prior to his having left for England at some point after February 1, 1880, he could not have spent more than five years working with him.[26] In this case, these seven years would include the period following Fallon's death until the publication of the *New Hindustani-English Dictionary* in 1883, when he would have been under the supervision of J. D. Bate and Lālah Faqīr Ćand.

Fallon, having retired from his post in 1875, was free to travel through northern India collecting materials for his dictionary:

> He toured in the East to Patna in the Punjab all the way to Lahore, in Rājpūtānah to Ajmer, all well-known cities and large cities, towns and regions and fortified villages (*koh-i manṣūrī*), etc. Having beckoned the greater part of the speakers among noble and ordinary folks in these places, they were caused to say those things.[27]

To this, Fallon adds,

> The compiler has enjoyed the advantage of a residence during many years in Delhi and in Behar, the two poles, so to speak, of the Urdu and Hindi phases of the language which are together represented in the common term Hindustanī. In the Mogal capital we have the polite form of the language impressed upon it by the influence of the Royal Court; while Behar, the most eastern province in which Hindi is spoken, retains traces of the oldest form this vernacular, known as Magadhi or magga, alike removed somewhat from the undue influence exerted in provinces farther west by Mahomedan and Hindu professors of Arabic and Persian, and by Brahman Pundits who have too successfully restored in many instances the Sanskrit forms which the language had already thrown off in the course of development. Other important centers will also be visited; as Mathura, the head-quarters of the Brij dialect; Agra, where the compiler has also resided for some years, and where the language is less Persianized than it is in Delhi and Lucknow; the Ayudhia (Oude) of classic story where traces of the influence of an independent Native court and Native institutions are still to be met with; the sacred Kasi of the Brahmans; with Bikaner and Jodhpore as types of the Marwari form of Hindi.[28]

Though he was no longer serving in an official capacity, Fallon's peregrinations (the term Lāl uses is *daurah*[29]) were not dissimilar to his earlier work as inspector of schools, not to mention that of touring revenue collectors and magistrates dispensing justice on horseback, an image romanticized by figures like John Lawrence and John Nicholson.[30] Unlike earlier nineteenth-century European efforts to collect linguistic data—such as John Leyden's distribution of a wordlist to company officials, similar efforts by Henry Miers Elliot in the 1840s, and questionnaires later dispatched as part of the Linguistic Survey of India under Grierson—Fallon appears to have circulated personally through northern India collecting material for his dictionaries.

Though Fallon was not the only philologist and lexicographer of the Victorian era to make use of "native assistants," he was unusual for featuring them so prominently in the prefatory material to his works. In the acknowledgments of his massive 1,216-page *New Hindustani-English Dictionary*, Fallon "makes his best acknowledgements for the valuable assistance" by naming some fifteen assistants scattered across seven northern Indian cities (Delhi, Dinapore, Ajmer, Meerut, Furrukhabad, Rohtak, and Darbhangah), including "Lālā Faqir Chand, Head Assistant; Munshī Chiranjī Lāl, [and] Munshi Sayad Ahmad" of Delhi.[31] While he does not name any of his assistants in the *Hindustani-English Law and Commercial Dictionary* published before his death,[32] his "Head Assistant," Lālā Faqīr Ćand, is prominently featured on the title pages of two works edited and published posthumously: he is credited as coauthor for Fallon's *New English-Hindustani Dictionary* and assistant editor for the *Dictionary of Hindustani Proverbs*.[33]

By way of contrast, John T. Platts, in the preface to his dictionary, does not mention having been assisted by any individual, "native" or otherwise, in the compilation of his dictionary apart from "having availed [himself] of the labours of [his textual] predecessors" (including Fallon).[34] His work, completed in Oxford in 1884, was very much a "library dictionary": his "claim to originality" is founded first upon having "for many years been engaged in the study of Urdú and Hindí books (in prose and verse) and newspapers with the view of collecting words and phrases for this work" and only secondarily upon "a long residence in India," which permitted Platts to become "acquainted with much of the living colloquial language not found in Dictionaries."[35] Born in Calcutta in 1830, Platts had spent more than two decades in India, serving from 1858–1859 as a teacher of mathematics at Benares College, principal of Saugor School in the Central Provinces from 1859 to 1861, then mathematical professor and headmaster at Benares College. In 1864, Platts rose to become the assistant inspector of schools, second circle, North-Western Provinces, while his final post, before his retirement on March 17, 1872, was as officiating inspector of schools, northern circle, Central Provinces.[36] His earliest known published work,[37] a commentary on a well-known mathematics textbook, demonstrates his other major pedagogical interest. It is tempting to connect these two interests—mathematics and philology—in order to draw a stark contrast between the methods of Fallon and Platts. It would seem, however, that a more useful explanation for their differences in method may be found in the institutional climates in which they conducted their research.

Fallon, working on the ground in India, strikes the imagination as a picturesque figure collecting proverbs and sayings as he toured the countryside, and he was part of the same enthusiastic project of ethnographic enumeration that Shahid Amin has so ingeniously connected with the first all-India census of 1871.[38] This project was carried out at the same time as that other imposition of scientific precision and uniformity on the Indian landscape, William Wilson Hunter's *Imperial Gazetteer of India* (begun in 1869),[39] and it occurred a mere generation after George Everest completed the Great Arc trigonometric surveying project.[40] Platts's *Dictionary* belongs with another great lexicographic work of the period, Francis Steingass's *Comprehensive Persian-English Dictionary*, also completed at Oxford in 1892. Inspiration for these two works are to be located in Blochmann's seminal 1868 article "Contributions to Persian Lexicography," itself written in response to the publication of Lane's incomplete *Arabic-English Lexicon* (1863–1893): "We trust that the standard which Lane's Dictionary [of Arabic] has created will soon be followed by a compiler of a Persian Dictionary." Blochmann explains,

> There exists no reliable Persian Dictionary. Nothing worth the name has been done for Persian lexicography since the days of Castelli and Meninski. This is a matter of surprise, as there are most excellent sources from which a good Persian dictionary could be compiled. The deficiency of all existing dictionaries lies in this, that the compilers, one and all, have used secondary or tertiary sources, instead of having recourse, as Lane did, to original and carefully selected native works.
>
> The sources for compiling a reliable dictionary are the lexicographic works written by *Indians*.[41]

Unlike Fallon, then, Platts compiled his dictionary from the relative comfort of his home in Ealing and, upon being elected teacher of Persian on June 2, 1880, from Oxford.[42]

We learn something of the methods employed by both Fallon and his assistants in the account provided in Ćiraṇjī Lāl's *dībāćah* (preface). Following his introduction to Fallon in April 1875 and assumption of the position of "assistant in his department of dictionaries," Lāl describes how

> the dictionaries, grammars, and treatises on philology (*filolojī*) of various languages were made my responsibility. Having gathered the Hindi terms of the dialects of various parts of northern Hindustan, the lists of terms which the assistant of the aforementioned Ṣāḥib [Fallon] was sending, having selected them [for use] in his dictionary, [I] cited them for inclusion. He appointed me to the additional service of researching the origin of Hindi terms from Sanskrit, adding terms and expressions (*alfāẓ o muḥāwarah*) to the dictionary, and translating them into English. In short, I remained occupied in the work of the dictionary from April 1875 to 1883, in the office of the aforementioned Ṣāḥib. For this reason, I advanced greatly beyond my prior acquaintance and experiences.[43]

Ćiraṇjī Lāl was thus part of the analytical team that turned the raw data collected by Fallon and others into a semifinished lexicographic product. This method approximated the methods employed by James Murray in assigning particular texts to amateur readers and subeditors who would cull distinctive or obscure usages of terms and send the results to his scriptorium in Oxford.[44] That Ćiraṇjī Lāl was assigned the task of researching the Sanskrit etymologies of Hindi terms may have been attributable to his having achieved some scholastic recognition for his abilities in that language. If we believe Ćiraṇjī Lāl and Sayyid Aḥmad, they both worked on Fallon's project for a similar length of time, though Sayyid Aḥmad may have quit the team shortly after Fallon's departure for England early in 1880.

It is clear, too, that by the latter half of the eighteenth century language in northern India was coming to be increasingly associated with the politicization of religious nationalisms. As Vasudha Dalmia has argued (following Brass and others), the development of Hindi as a language of Hindus involved three interlinked processes, namely that of dichotomization ("separation from Urdu, coupled with the claim of absolute autonomy for

Hindi"), standardization (through the production of pedagogical materials like grammars, dictionaries, and school primers), and historicization ("establishing historical links with literary works connected with great ideological movements of the past").[45] Dalmia praises Fallon for his "unconventional approach" and evaluates his work as something that could "be appreciated only by a later age," noting criticism of the project by the prominent author and champion of the Hindi language Harishcandra of Benares (1850–1885), in an essay written in 1884.[46] However, Dalmia's claim that Fallon "did not care to distinguish between Hindi and Urdu" is misleading.[47] Fallon was indeed quite ahead of his time in explicitly enumerating "two main dialects" ("the shifting popular speech of familiar intercourse, which changes every 12 *kos* according to the native proverb, and the comparatively fixed literary language of books and correspondence") plus a "third dialect" ("the vocabulary of women [*reḳhtī* or *zanānī bolī*]"), using ostensibly class- and gender-based criteria.[48] But this division was impractical to maintain beyond the confines of his "Preface and Preliminary Dissertation." While he claimed "the great many Arabic, Persian, and Sanskrit words which are seldom or never used in written or spoken Hindustani" to have been foisted by "Moulvis and Pandits" upon "the vocabulary of the indigenous language of which they are not a part,"[49] this did not prevent him from providing in a separate column to the left of each headword an indication of its etymological origin. He justified the inclusion of this information as vital by pointing out that non-native users of the dictionary would probably be frustrated by the lack of comprehension of certain portions of the lexicon among particular populations of so-called speakers of Hindustani.[50]

If Ćiraṇjī Lāl took great pride in having been assigned the task of researching the Sanskrit derivations of Hindi terms, Fallon took a far more jaundiced view in attributing contemporary Hindi terms to this or other classical languages: "it is inconceivable that the vulgar tongue of the great mass of an unlettered people could have grown out of a difficult literary language which their rude progenitors, it may be presumed, did not know and did not speak."[51] Indeed, Fallon saw in this "vulgar tongue"—and pointedly not in the "artificial . . . strange Arabic sounds" and "dull cold clay of Sanskrit" of "Moulvis and Pandits"[52]—a basis for what he imagined should be a truly "national speech" of Hindustan, even despite its proverbially protean tendency to change every twelve *kos*:

> In the proverbs and songs and familiar speech of each something may be gleaned, well fitted to enrich the common vocabulary and to be incorporated in a general Dictionary of the national speech. This process is necessary moreover to the fusion of many dialects into one common language.[53]

Though the linguistic features might change, the social domains in which they were preserved and operated—what he calls the "proverbs and songs and familiar speech"—provided a model for the more inclusive mode of fashioning the public sphere that he saw as necessary for the formation of a truly common and national language.[54]

Fallon's depiction of Hindustani as a potential "national speech" must be seen, however, as the result of a very carefully constructed self-presentation by a former colonial official of a putatively "scientific" viewpoint. His retirement from official duty only added to the credibility of the lexicographer's claims of having objectified the process of objectification—he was an outside and ostensibly disinterested observer of a messy linguistic reality.[55] Not so for his "native" assistants. The objections leveled against Sayyid Aḥmad for the surfeit of subjectivity in his lexicographic activities have been discussed at length in the previous chapter. Ćiraṇjī Lāl, however, could comfortably occupy neither of the more obvious lexicographic positions—that of the disinterested scientific observer or that of the emotionally entangled poet-participant. As a Hindu lexicographer of what is now considered to be (primarily on the basis of script) the Urdu language, he has not received the recognition of his contemporary and colleague Sayyid Aḥmad because his work is less easily accommodated within the teleological narratives of what became the (most) official languages of the future nation-states of India and Pakistan.

This tension is apparent in Ćiraṇjī Lāl's own depiction of his linguistic subject. Both he and Sayyid Aḥmad give accounts of the rise to prominence of what they call the Hindustani language. For Sayyid Aḥmad, this account stretches back over at least a millennium, to the time of the "earliest period" when "*rājah*s used to rule" and "the residents of Delhi only had Hindi, that is to say the *bhākā* language," and extends to the period—still in the distant past—when the "the Islamic kings of intrepidness and brave work started to advance on this realm" and through "mutual discourse (*ham-kalāmī*) . . . and from exchange (*leṅ-deṅ*)" (the same term used by Mīr Amman; see chapter 3), he explains, "inevitably in their language admixture started to occur." Continuing, he explains that "when in AD 1648 Shāh Jahān founded

Shāhjahānābād and the people of each nation were gathered, then in this period there were many connections between Hindi and Persian and most of *bhākā* and even some Persian words having been altered and substituted occurred little by little." "In short," Sayyid Aḥmad concludes, "from the arrangement of these two languages, in the imperial army a new language was produced, and for this reason, this language's name happened to be *urdū* which gradually came to acquire refinement and regularity so that in 1688 during the reign of Aurangzeb ʿĀlamgīr poetry started to be composed, too."[56] As we would expect from Dalmia's schematic, the nationalization of a linguistic tradition requires historicization, a part of what she calls "a distinctly imperialist stance with regard to the other Indian languages," preferably to a point as distant in the past as is both feasible and credible. If Dalmia describes the convergence of "Hindu" and "Hindi" as increasingly congruent political symbols, Sayyid Aḥmad explicitly links the development of the Urdu language to the establishment of, first, Islamic rule in northern India; second, a new capital in 1648 by Shāh Jahān; and third, the fruits, in 1688, of an expansionist Mughal policy pursued by Aurangzeb.[57]

Ćiraṇjī Lāl, by contrast, is far more modest in his depiction of the historical rise to prominence of his linguistic object of study. As he makes clear from the title page onward, his dictionary is a collection of "all sorts of Hindi *and* Urdu expressions and terminologies" (emphasis added). The result is what he calls "*our* Hindustani language," which, having been "established as the court language (*ʿadālatī zabān*), has spread through nearly the entirety of Hindustan. In government schools, too, it is studied like other languages. Newspapers, too, come out mostly in this language. Laws are also in this very language."[58] The history of *this* language, Hindustani, is confined primarily to the nineteenth century: it is a *new* phenomenon and one clearly emanating from the colonial European political intervention. It was *their* courts, *their* government schools, *their* print technology, and *their* laws that enabled its diffusion throughout the region he calls Hindustan. As a student of a new language, Ćiraṇjī does not see his Hindustani dictionary as beholden to any prior lexicographic traditions.

Not only is the Hindustani language a relatively recent innovation—the most basic lexical units of this dictionary, the *iṣṭilāḥ* ('terminology', 'technical term', or even 'jargon' or 'cant') and *muḥāwarah* (idiom) have, in Ćiraṇjī's understanding, escaped the attention of any lexicographer prior to Fallon. "Those *muḥāwarah* and *iṣṭilāḥ* are also given," Ćiraṇjī proudly notes, "which even until now are not to be found in our books on the study of literature and on the tongues of people."[59] "The source of the term *iṣṭilāḥ*," Ćiraṇjī explains, is the Arabic triliteral root *ṣulḥ*. Continuing in an etymological vein, he adds,

> its literal meaning is "to reconcile with one another." And in its technical meaning (*iṣṭilāḥī maʿnī*) the mutual agreement of some nation [*qaum*, 'tribe' or, more broadly, 'a group of people'] for establishing in addition to the original meaning a new meaning of some term. So, an *iṣṭilāḥ* is that one new meaning which several people mutually use to adorn a term or a few terms for some peculiar expression of intention of theirs, and those very people speak and understand it. This matter is granted that there will necessarily be a relation of some way or other in the literal and technical (*laġhwī aur iṣṭilāḥī*) meaning of some term. Though because that relation may be a distant relation it may not be easily understood, and for this reason often times the two meanings of one term start to seem different, and one becomes inclined towards seeking out their separate sources.[60]

The other key term, *muḥāwarah*, derives from the Arabic *ḥawar*, whose meaning

> is "to return" or "to circle." When some *iṣṭilāḥ*, which a few people establish for some peculiar expression of intention of theirs, becomes more common and spreads among quite a few people, and having mixed to some extent with the first meaning of the term starts to wear the second meaning, then it starts to be called a *muḥāwarah*.[61]

What emerges from Ćiraṇjī's introduction is the notion that British colonial rule has created an entirely new range of possibilities for what may be described in the lexicographic work—spoken expressions, the diverse jargons of illiterate classes of society—and, hence, of what may be considered to be a proper language. Sayyid Aḥmad also deals with these terms under separate headings, and while he describes their etymologies in similar terms, he supports his explanations, as we would expect, through examples from poetry rather than references to speech.[62] The distinction between *lafẓ* or *luġhat* (word or term) and *iṣṭilāḥ* as "a technical term [having] the acceptance and agreement of special groups within the language for their special subjects or disciplines" was not new to Persianate lexicography.[63] Ćiraṇjī, however, seems to have placed special emphasis on the distinction between the terms *iṣṭilāḥ* and *muḥāwarah*: the quality of an *iṣṭilāḥ* as *belonging* to a particular *qaum*—a term with a slippery set of meanings translated variously as "nation," "tribe," or possibly, in its most general sense, "a community of people"[64]—and that of the *muḥāwarah* as becoming "more common" and spreading "among quite a few people" is not clearly drawn in Sayyid Aḥmad's account.

What separates Ćiraṇjī from Sayyid Aḥmad is the former's acute awareness of the discontinuities that differentiate the Hindustani language documented in his dictionary from the existing Persianate traditions. While earlier lexicographers responded to a demand originating in provincial centers for dictionaries as a portable means of conveying the *sharīf* culture of late Mughal Delhi to the farthest reaches of the erstwhile empire, Ćiraṇjī imagined that his work would serve a new class of people interested in operating within a largely distinct sphere of political participation—namely, Indian aspirants to posts in the colonial administration. Under the Mughal-Persianate thematic, state largesse was dispensed through what some have termed "old" or "anthropological" clientelism,[65] whose ideal form was that of the *pīr-murīd* (master-disciple) or *ustād-shāgird* (teacher-student) chain of authority (*silsilah*). Worthiness here was ascertained by the aspirant's ability to perform authentically a set of highly conventionalized social roles, often extrapolated from courtly contexts and formalized in didactic genres of *inshāʾ* (belles-lettres). It privileged the direct interpersonal transfer of knowledge and charisma through individuals rather than corporations or institutions.[66] This clientelistic mode of authentication replicated elements of prevailing political ideologies of inherited kingship on the one hand and methods of establishing religious authority—be they Sufistic, legal, therapeutic, etc.—on the other.[67] Likewise, lexicographic authenticity (*sanad*) operated analogously to other "professional," "political," and "religious" forms of clientelism.

Seeing his dictionary as a pedagogical tool for the acquisition of the Hindustani language, Ćiraṇjī sought to isolate it from the constellation of professional, political, and religious clientelism associated with Mughal-Persianate *sharīf* culture. He instead directed his text at those people for whom "Hindustani" was not a mother tongue. An 1877 order (rescinded in 1896) requiring candidates for government appointments with emoluments greater than Rs. 10 per month to demonstrate proficiency in Urdu contributed to the steady demand for these materials.[68] On at least three occasions in the opening pages of his preface, Ćiraṇjī addresses what he calls the "public." This term appears, at least initially, to have been unfamiliar to Urdu readers: in the first two instances of the term, the lithographic etcher responsible for reproducing Ćiraṇjī's text on limestone plates misspells the term پبلک *pablik* as پیلک *pīlak*, producing the nonsensical signification of "the Indian oriole" or "a large ant."[69] In this regard, Ćiraṇjī's text may be seen as *projecting* a public (or rather, a *pablik*) where none had yet existed. It imagined a population of readers unconcerned with gaining access to an outdated Persianate courtly culture; they would instead apply language as a means to take advantage of the new sites of political discourse—courts, schools, newsprint, and voluntary associations—introduced and regulated by the colonial state.[70] "Hindustani" (and quite pointedly *not* Urdu) was thus both a product of and a vehicle for what Ćiraṇjī perceived as, in essence, modernity. The most efficient way of obtaining entrance into these milieus was, Ćiraṇjī argued, through the twin disciplines of grammar and lexicography:

> So, in such a state, for those residents of Hindustan, for whom this is not a mother tongue (*mādarī zabān*), it is very much necessary that a means for learning this language be present. And what is it? 1) Grammar. 2) Words and expressions (*luġhat o muḥāwarāt*). While some grammar books have indeed been made, nevertheless there has not up to the present been any comprehensive and complete (*jāmĕᶜ aur kāmil*) book, and those that are present which have been made, they are either Hindustani to Farsi or [Hindustani] to English. With this in view, [I] began this work in AD 1884, and in AD 1886, with the aid of several praiseworthy assistants, after great expenditure (*ṣarf*), [we] brought it to a completion.[71]

This passage runs in stark contrast to Fallon's assertion in his preliminary dissertation that a language "is not learnt from Dictionaries." According to Fallon, a language

> is acquired, as all knowledge is acquired, by much exercise in the order and combinations in which words, like things, are presented to the mind in real life. The office of a Dictionary is to make the student "remember," in the Socratic phrase; to give definiteness to what is vague; to throw a bright light on the dim shadows of faded recollections and things imperfectly apprehended; to present to the mind its own image . . . [72]

Of course, the audiences to which these two works were addressed were quite different. Fallon saw his dictionary as offering a vital aid to colonial officials. It may be argued that Ćiraṇjī's work was also addressed to colonial officials, but unlike Fallon, Ćiraṇjī's officials were among the ranks of nongazetteered and aspiring Indian "natives." If Fallon imagined that the "office of a Dictionary is to make the student 'remember,' " for Ćiraṇjī, whose *pablik* would exist only in the future, there was little if anything from the past to recall. By appearing as a "comprehensive and complete" monolingual (that is, Hindustani to Hindustani) text, his work would, in conjunction with a grammar of the language, provide a tool for the acquisition of the language by one whose "mother tongue" differed from the one officially recognized by the state.[73]

Authors like Inshā had long been fascinated by the manner in which non-native speakers fail in their attempts to communicate in a normative linguistic code.[74] Ćiraṇjī also acknowledges the distinction between native and non-native speaker:

> Since they call the *ahl-i zabān* of the language of some place only those individuals who are completely acquainted with the minute differences of meanings of the words, the *iṣṭilāḥs* ['cant', 'jargon', 'terminology'] and *muḥāwarahs* ['idiom'] of that language, and apart from this matter, are [also] born there, and for some time they make it their homeland, and along with this they acquire [abilities in] reading and writing the language of that place [as well as in] the sciences and arts, it cannot be one's good fortune to gain this in any other way. Though every person from that place [in spite of these requirements] considers himself to be an *ahl-i zabān*.[75]

Like Inshā, Ćiraṇjī also places a very high bar on membership in this linguistic club, though unlike Inshā, for whom performance of an elite code of courtly conduct was as important as either linguistic competence or birth and residence in a place, Ćiraṇjī emphasizes abilities in "reading and writing the language of that place [as well as in] the sciences and the arts." Ćiraṇjī also requires that the person be "born there, and for some time they make it their homeland."

What distinguishes Ćiraṇjī's *ahl-i zabān* is the deictic indeterminacy of both the people (*ahl*) and language (*zabān*). *Urdū* had come by the end of the eighteenth century to connote primarily the name of a language, by means of either an abbreviation or a synecdochic transfer of the toponymic phrase *zabān-i urdū-i muʿallā-i shāhjahānābād* (language of the exalted royal encampment of Shāhjahānābād, that is, old Delhi) to the speech of the people residing there. And when Inshā and Ṭapish refer to the *ahl-i zabān* (person/people of the language), their use of the phrase is understood to be an abbreviation of an even longer implied phrase, *ahl-i zabān-i urdū-i muʿallā-ʾi shāhjahānābād* (people of the language of the exalted royal encampment of Shāhjahānābād).[76] For Inshā and Ṭapish, there was no doubt which *zabān* was elevated to a status that required a definition of which *ahl* exactly could claim to belong to it. Unlike Ārzū, for whom *urdū* could mean "the camp of the imperial army" (wherever that might be), for Inshā and Ṭapish, it was obvious that in spite of a mushrooming of self-styled *urdūs* and Shāhjahānābāds all along the length of the Gangetic plain, there was no doubt that the only "true" *urdū* was that of the city of Shāhjahānābād, that is to say, Delhi.[77] By the last quarter of the nineteenth century, however, not only had the *zabān* lost its specificity as *urdū* (or rather, the *urdū-i muʿallā-ʾi shāhjahānābād*); it had also lost its claim as the sole "grand popular language of Hindoostan" capable of conveying the prestige and authority of the colonial government.

At the historical moment when Ćiraṇjī composed the introduction to his dictionary, an increasingly inclusive notion of citizenship accompanied a rapid expansion in the ability of the colonial government to interfere in and shape the lives of its subjects—the development of what Edward Shils has termed a "mass society."[78] While debates were beginning to reach a fevered pitch regarding which "language"—an "Urdu" written in the Arabic script or a "Hindi" written in *devanāgarī*—would serve as *the* "national language," the very notion of a "national language"—a single linguistic code that would serve as a medium between the state and its subjects—was itself a very new development. Ayodhyā Prasād Khattrī (d. 1905), for example, was an early advocate of Khaṛī Bolī Hindi in the *devanāgarī* script as a vehicle of poetry. Through the final decades of the nineteenth century, poetry had been dominated by *nāgarī*-script compositions in other dialects of the language (especially Braj Bhāṣā) and Urdu or *reḵhtah* in the Perso-Arabic script. The British Orientalist Frederick Pincott explained, "he proposes a compromise, one party is asked to abandon a cherished dialect of their language and the other party a customary method of writing it . . . all parties meet on the common ground of Khari Boli, or correct speech, understood by all, and living, growing and changing with the daily requirements of advancing civilization."[79] Ćiraṇjī, by contrast, anticipated that there would be many who, as they came into contact with the state apparatus through its courts, its schools, its laws, and the print media that carried its message to the farthest reaches of its borders, would need to acquire proficiency in a unfamiliar language ("Hindustani") without also needing to master a participatory cultural framework associated with Sanskrit or Persian literary traditions:

> So it is affirmed that a person of one country (*mulk*) cannot be an *ahl-i zabān* of some other country, though there is no reason he cannot be a scholar and erudite expert of that language. In this way in order to make this very difficulty easy it has been decided [by the author] to commit to writing a dictionary (*luġhat*) of *iṣṭilāḥ* and *muḥāwarah*, etc., so that through them the people of one place may acquire the language of another place, since from among the two great means of acquisition of every language, the *luġhat* ['dictionary'] and *muḥāwarāt* ['idioms'] are also a means.[80]

Although Ćiraṇjī clearly prided himself on possessing an intimate knowledge of the language of his hometown, Delhi, he differs from Inshā in his insistence that one should be enabled to participate fully in that communicative code (in its role as official language of state) solely through the consumption of what he terms the "two great means" (*do baṛe żarīʿon*), that is, grammars and dictionaries, and without reference to any interpersonal mode of legitimation. The "comprehensive and complete" dictionary and its pedagogical sibling, the grammar, were to be the means by which an individual, without claiming to be an *ahl-i zabān*, could bypass authentication from within a recognized *silsilah* and instead acquire the means by which to gain access to all the benefits and redress promised by a modern state and the rule of law.

Ćiraṇjī's and Sayyid Aḥmad's dictionaries did not just distill knowledge "downward" toward a new population of potential political agents but also contributed to state surveillance. Margrit Pernau depicts the shift in political legitimacy that took place in the Delhi territory as the replacement of "rule by alliances" with "rule by records," in which "the supporters the British now needed were no longer the commanders of detachments of horses, but those able to wield the pen in their service, no longer nobles, but members of middling groups who hoped to gain social status by serving the British."[81] The *Maḳhzan al-Muḥāwarāt* reflected this changed political reality—the replacement of "paternal rule" with what one scholar has evocatively referred to as "a 'machine rule' of laws, codes, and procedures"[82]—by literally willing into existence a new class of government servants who could efficiently carry out the instructions of the government according to standardized and universal procedures. The effort to bring new social domains under the discipline of dictionaries did not necessarily mean that elite registers would suddenly become legible to nonelites. Instead, information tended to flow in a single direction, exacerbating an already large gulf between a small intermediary class with control of the code and mechanisms through which the rule of law was supposed to function and the vast majority of the population, for whom these operations were entirely opaque. As a result of this gap, a "document Raj"[83] presented immense opportunities for self-advancement to these new intermediaries.[84] Though their intentions may have been innocent, the lexicographic works produced by Fallon and his assistants continued an ongoing colonial project of documenting the forms of language employed by various populations who had resisted previous government efforts to impose the rule of law as well as enumerate and collect taxable property.[85] For the first time since ʿAbdul Wāsĕʿ some two hundred years earlier, the purpose of including information within a dictionary was not emulation—the active reproduction by its users of the lexical content contained within it—but rather a passive comprehension of what ostensibly was someone else's language.

It is for this reason that the distinction between *muḥāwarah* and *iṣṭilāḥ* takes such centrality in Ćiraṇjī's dictionary. As he explains,

> In this [dictionary] I have written those *iṣṭilāḥ* of particular classes (*firqah*: 'party,' 'sect') and occupations which often have become common (*ʿāmm*) or are becoming so, though a separate book could be made for the *iṣṭilāḥ* of every class or occupation.[86]

Being able to identify whether a term *belonged* to a particular ethnic group or whether it had spread throughout the population at large meant, for the intended user of the dictionary (Ćiraṇjī's *pablik*), the difference between the jargon or cant of a governed client population on the one hand and access to the levers of state control on the other. The aspiring civil servant would wish to have a passive comprehension of the former and an active command of the later: among the justifications Fallon provided for the inclusion of "obscene" terms in his dictionary, it will be recalled, was "*the absolute importance of this knowledge to judicial officers*," a clause on which he himself placed primary emphasis.[87] The list of abbreviations Ćiraṇjī offers in the final page of his prefatory frontmatter emphasizes ethnonyms over what might be distinguished as "purely" lexicographic terminology (parts of speech like "noun," "adjective," etc., and other metalinguistic markers like "masculine" and "feminine").

While the familiar "speech of the nobility" and "appears in poetry" are certainly included, the list is dominated by occupational groups (jewelers, butchers, confectioners, palanquin bearers, jockeys) and different "ethnic" groups (Punjabi, Eastern, Hindu, Muslim). Four different symbols are reserved for types of women's speech: "prostitutes' terminology," "women's idiom," "idiom of Muslim women," "idiom of Hindu women."[88] The net effect is of a picturesque catalogue of the diverse populations one encounters across northern India. These groups would also come to represent different constituencies (what are commonly known today in South Asia as "voting blocs") whose political participation exists largely beyond the sphere of a putatively deliberative civil society, occupying instead what Partha Chatterjee has designated as a "political society."[89] To be clear, none of these groups, excepting perhaps the most general categories of *musalmān* and *hindū*, have a place in the *pablik* that Ćiraṇjī imagined. If his work imagined the participation of new linguistic groups in an emerging colonial-print public sphere, he could not imagine at that point in time extending access in the general population to political participation or public education.

Ćiraṇjī Lāl's "Treasury of Idioms" essentially isolated a Hindustani language from a context of courtly *ādāb*. In this sense, he succeeded, where Sayyid Aḥmad could not, in separating Urdu lexicography's six-hundred-year history from a Persianate poetic tradition, and he was better able to emulate the model introduced by S. W. Fallon. He boasted of the range of poets he called upon to support his entries—including Sūr Dās, a poet typically ignored by the Urdu establishment—but lists them without regard "to their period or . . . an opinion of their status (*darjah*)."[90] Though he includes past lexicographers like Inshā, Ṯapish, and Sahbā'ī, other lexicographer-poets like Rangīn and Sayyid (Sayyid Aḥmad Dihlawī) are noticeably absent. Instead, he cites examples of

> proverbs (*maśaleṅ*), phrases from daily speech (*roz-marrah ke fiqre*), *dohe*, riddles (*paheliyāṅ*), *ṭhumriyāṅ*, *holiyāṅ*, *bhajan*, *gharelū-gīt*, *cau-bole* [a verse of four lines], the calls of *faqīrs*, the various sweet calls of Delhi's vegetable sellers (*tarkārī-wāloṅ*), and *chan* [a couplet repeated by a bridegroom at a wedding ceremony].[91]

His definition of the expression *ṭopī wālā* demonstrates this preference for new sources of authentication:

> *ṭopī wālā* - h—masculine noun—(1) youth—a beardless youth—a youth in his prime—a minor: *taiṅ to merā man līnā topī wale suṅwariyā* ['thou hast taken my heart, the bedecked *ṭopī wālā*']—song (2) Englishman—Frank—European: *kamāve dhotī wālā uṭāve ṭopī wālā* ['The one wearing a loincloth saves, the one wearing the cap spends']—proverb.[92]

In selecting the same proverbs as Fallon as prooftexts, the only obvious difference between the entries (apart from their language of presentation) is that Ćiraṇjī considered Fallon's primary definition, "one who wears a hat," too obvious to repeat.[93] He instead offers a list of nearly synonymous terms, though none of them suggesting the sense of foppishness and dandyism that is so apparent in the poetry that Nakhat and Sayyid Aḥmad cite. This seems to be part of a calculated effort by the author to avoid those prooftexts through which "bad effect on the habits and morals of our future descendants would be created."[94]

What he initially describes as the distress (*diqqat*) he felt in selecting supporting verses gives way to indignation when he notes that such erotic Urdu poetry is afforded great prestige in even the homes of the "best families." He suggests that if these terms were to be replaced by their common (that is, nonliterary) equivalents, they would certainly be deemed obscene:

> In Urdu verse, since Perso-Arabic terms like *būsah* ['kiss'], *rukhsār* ['cheek'], *zulf* ['ringlet'], *sāq* ['leg'], *waṣl* ['union', 'intercourse'], *hajr* ['separation'], etc., are . . . not wedded to ordinary conversation . . . the novelty of those terms has saved them from the corruption (*burāʾī*) of their becoming common (*ʿāmm*). If in their place such commonly understood terms as *babbī* ['kiss'], *gāl* ['cheek'], *laṭeṅ* ['ringlets'], *rāneṅ* ['thigh'], *sŏḥbat-dārī* ['union'], *judāʾī* ['separation'], or *bijog* ['separation'] were to be used, then would not this [Hindi] verse immediately start to seem obscene (*fŏḥsh*) and the corrupting nature of their verses be appraised in the eyes of all? Thus, under this pretense, have the most religious of the religious and those of the best families had this erotic Urdu poetry publicly read in their own homes and gatherings.[95]

This indignation represents the author's efforts to strip Urdu of its distinctive literary, historical, and sociopolitical identity. Indeed, neither Fallon nor Ćiraṇjī make any remark of the expression's connection with Qizilbāsh soldiers, let alone their fabled role in the *qatl-i ʿāmm* or general slaughter of the population of Shāhjahānābād in 1739. This demonstrates in miniature the shared aim of Fallon and Ćiraṇjī to present a deracinated and diverse set of linguistic codes as Hindustani, designating a shared, single language understood throughout the greater part of the Gangetic plain. This language, and indeed this dictionary, would afford Delhi, Urdu poetry, and the courtly culture each embodied no specific linguistic privilege above the speech of butchers, village folk, and shopkeepers.

MURDEROUS SCHEMES

Hindustani was thus the term Fallon and Ćiraṇjī Lāl gave to a communicative medium associated both with a geographical region (Hindustan) and also with a particular state that was transitioning, slowly but inexorably, from an elite clientelism to mass politics. It was a language name chosen for its lack of specificity, a language without the ideological and cultural baggage of its grammatical twin, *urdū*. We thus see a completion of the circle: what Amīr Ḳhusrau calls *hindwī* in a famous passage from his narrative poem (*maśnavī*) *Nūh sipihr* was literally an array of languages spoken in the land beyond (that is, to the east of) the Indus:

> . . . In this land
> In every territory, there is
> A language specific, and not so
> By chance either. There are
> Sindhī, Lāhorī, Kashmīrī, Kibar,
> Dhaur Samandarī, Tilangī, Gujar,
> Maʿbarī, Gaurī, and the languages
> Of Bengal, Avadh, Delhi
> And its environs, all within
> Their own frontiers.
> All these are Indic (*hindwī*), and
> Are in common use
> For all purposes since antiquity.[96]

Shamsur Rahman Faruqi, citing Suniti Kumar Chatterjee, argues that *hindwī* is best translated as "Indic," "for Khusrau is identifying the native place, not the appellative, of the languages in question." Thus, "when Ḳhusrau here describes Bengali, Tamil, and other Indian languages as

'Hindvī,' he simply means 'of India.' He does not mean that all these languages have only the common name 'Hindvī.' "[97] Ḳhusrau's use of the term throughout the *Ḳhāliq Bārī*, a multilingual vocabulary in verse sometimes attributed to him, suggest, however, that it was also used to denote the language of the Yamuna-Ganges *doāb* and his adopted home in Delhi.[98] This seems to have been the language, or rather range of speech forms, that ʿAbdul Wāsěʿ considered to be the subject of his *Ġharāʾib al-Luġhāt*. By the time that Ḳhān-i Ārzū compiled his *Nawādir al-Alfāẓ*, however, he criticized Hāṅswī for his inclusion of terms "not of the knowing ones of the imperial camp (*mutaʿarrif-i urdūʾe bādshāhī*) and of the language of Akbarābād and Shāhjahānābād, [but of] the language of the native land of the author of the treatise (*zabān-i waṭan-i ṣāḥib-i risālah*)."[99] The poet Shāh 'Ḥātim' (1699–1783), writing just a few years later, could claim to consider correct only "those few words of the Arabic language and the Persian language that are commonly understood and frequently used in the colloquial discourse (*rozmarrah*) of Delhi which the elite (*mirzāyān*) of Hind and the shrewd eloquent speakers have guarded as their idiom." Furthermore, he had "ceased using the *hinduwī* of all regions, which they call *bhākhā*, except for only the colloquial discourse (*rozmarrah*) which is commonly understood and which the noble have selected as excellent and the smallest quantity of those words which come under attention in the adornment of speech."[100]

A literary register, *reḳhtah*, had risen to prominence in Delhi during the first half of the eighteenth century, and its cultivation would, especially in the latter half of the century, come to offer lucrative opportunities for a professional class that included poets, elegy reciters (*marṡiyah ḳhwāṅ*), storytellers, singers, and instructors (including lexicographers like Ṭapish), not to mention the parade of actors, jesters, dancing boys, courtesans, bakers, greengrocers, and grain parchers Inshā depicts as arriving in Murshidābād from Delhi "seeking profit."[101] As these professional classes fanned out through the vast territories of what had once been the Mughal Empire, new means of authentication came into place to certify the claims of these professional littérateurs as representatives of the literature that was intimately bound with the cultural prestige of the imperial capital. In Ṭapish, an immigrant to Bengal from Delhi, and Inshā, himself born in Bengal as the son of a Delhi émigré, this resulted in a fetishization of their Delhi origins and elaborate rationalizations of their ability to speak authoritatively regarding this literary register. British patronage of the Delhi College and sponsorship of the translation of European textbooks into Urdu through the Vernacular Translation Society had, by the middle of the nineteenth century, created an alternate mode of authentication, in the form of the standardized exam, the diploma, and the printing press, competing with and eventually (in the twentieth century) largely replacing the model of the *ustād-shāgird* (teacher-student) *silsilah* or "chain" of authority. What would come to take its place is a more institutional model of accreditation, one based less upon the transference of individual charisma and more upon the manufacture of a standardized and replicable product. The importance of dictionaries lay in their role both as the catalyst for and the end result of these changes in linguistic authority.

An early if imperfect example of a dictionary reflecting this shift in linguistic authority came in the form of S. W. Fallon's *A New Hindustani-English Dictionary*, published in 1879. The dictionary that Fallon proposed and subsequently completed would give prominence to "the spoken and rustic mother tongue of the Hindi speaking people of India; the exhibition, for the first time, of the pure, unadulterated language of women; and the illustrations given of the use of words by means of examples selected from the every day speech of the people, and from their poetry, songs, and proverbs, and other folklore."[102] Unlike previous lexicographic efforts, however, this would not be a pastiche of "defective" previous works, whose focus had always been on the written and particularly poetic form of the language of urban centers, but would rather be upon the study of new linguistic sources, many of them recorded for the first time from fieldwork carried out among illiterate, rural populations. To create such a work would be beyond the powers of a single individual and would require the efforts of a team. In this it resembled other projects, from the largely unsuccessful attempt a generation earlier by H. H. Wilson to solicit assistance from company officials stationed throughout the Indian subcontinent in the compilation of a massive "Glossary of Words in Current Use in Various Parts of India Relating to the Administration of Public Business in Every Department"[103] to Grierson's more successful linguistic survey that would published a generation later, from 1884 to 1928. While Wilson and Grierson's efforts relied upon dispatches from official and civilian correspondents, Fallon took it upon himself, according to his assistant, to tour "in the East to Patna in the Punjab all the way to Lahore, in Rājpūtānah to Ajmer, all well-known cities and large cities, towns and regions and fortified villages."[104] Those like Ćiraṇjī and Sayyid Aḥmad whom Fallon employed in collating, researching, and compiling these data would later be able to draw upon this experience to assert their own qualifications for producing lexicographic works.

As someone who bore the names of both an unsuccessful anti-British *mujāhid* and a famous Indo-Muslim reformer and British loyalist,[105] and as one who chose to demonstrate his loyalty to the British crown by commemorating the visit of King George V in the name he gave his own son, Sayyid Aḥmad in many ways successfully navigated a potentially treacherous course as a Delhi-born Muslim in the aftermath of 1857.[106] Sayyid Aḥmad's works likewise bear the imprint of a man who struggled to balance his proud links with a *sharīf* Persianate culture against the professional opportunities that arose through the increasingly intensive insertion of the colonial state into the lives of its subjects. His work drew equally upon the rich tradition of Persianate lexicography that preceded him and upon contemporaneous innovations of European lexicographers, ethnographers, and folklorists. His masterpiece, the *Farhang-i Āṣafiyah*, has been attacked by some for adhering too closely to the methods of his mentor, S. W. Fallon, and by others for copying without attribution the contents of less recognized lexicographic forebears. He has been charged, by his contemporaries and later linguistic nationalists alike, with adopting the alien standards of his English patrons in his inclusion of terms and expressions that were deemed obscene and shameful.

At the same time, however, he was accused of failing to maintain adequate distance between himself and the subject of his research, sprinkling his own poetry throughout his dictionary and imposing his own lexicographic persona—an intoxicated, mad lover, a recognizable figure of Persianate poetry. The presence of a strong authorial voice throughout the dictionary struck twentieth-century language reformers as an embarrassing anachronism. Because he is so intensely involved with the object of his study and since it offers him the most compelling idiom for his self-identification, he is unable to isolate completely the object of his study from its own internal logic. Thus, from the monological perspective of national development, potentially useful data remained trapped within a redundant, if internally coherent, tradition. As such, it remained resistant to appropriation by (if not entirely opaque to) political actors like Maulvī ʿAbdul Ḥaq, who were working within the framework of national, scientific, and linguistic development.

Ćiraṇjī, on the other hand, seems on the face of it to have negotiated successfully the new social reality inaugurated by the assumption by the British Crown of formal imperial status throughout its Indian possessions.

His *Maḳhzan al-Muḥāwarāt* maintained a suitable distance between author and subject. Indeed, it hewed so closely to Fallon's bilingual Hindustani–English dictionary that it appeared at times to replicate it word for word. The text of this work did not purport to convey the author's charisma; nor did it offer a complete guide for the outsider seeking to participate in an elite literary culture. Instead, it projected a public of non-native speakers who wished to participate, through state-centered channels of education and employment, in the governance of imperial subjects. This public of internal outsiders were themselves the products of numerous powerful efforts by the colonial government to impose a uniform and standard system of governance upon a diverse population scattered across a vast political, cultural, and topographical landscape.

Why, then, is Sayyid Aḥmad's dictionary today far more celebrated than that of Ćiraṇjī Lāl, a work that has languished till recent years in relative obscurity? Alṭāf Ḥusain Ḥālī argued in his 1887 review that "there are two extremely necessary conditions for writing an Urdu dictionary." The first is that "the writer be a resident of such a city where the language is considered *mustanad*," a term derived from the same Arabic root as *isnād*, the chain of authority familiar from the discussion of *hadīs̤* in chapter 3. From its original signification, "supported," the meaning of *mustanad* had been extended to denote something "authenticated" and, by the end of the nineteenth century, "credentialed" or, more concretely, "having a degree."[107] Ḥālī considered only two cities in Hindustan worthy of consideration in this regard: Delhi and Lucknow. While acknowledging the similarity in the speech of the highest classes in both cities, he gave preference for the language of Delhi over Lucknow, explaining that much of this similarity was attributable to the cultural influence in Lucknow of eminent Delhi émigrés. Moreover, the style of language spoken among Delhi's "ordinary folk" (*ʿawāmm*)—craftspeople and other lower classes—"deserves to be considered more authoritative" than that of Lucknow, which is "contrary to that language which is customary among that very same class in Delhi." He thus proclaimed that "only the language of Delhi is that upon which an Urdu dictionary should have its basis." The second stipulation was that "the writer of the dictionary be a *sharīf* Muslim since proper Urdu is considered even in Delhi to be the language only of Muslims." He cryptically added, using the by-then archaic toponymic, "the social condition of Hindus does not permit *Urdū-i Muʿallā* to be their mother tongue." It was therefore "an altogether happy matter that the first dictionary of our national language upon which all future dictionaries will be based was written by such an individual in which both necessary conditions are present."[108]

In light of the twentieth-century decline of Urdu in India and its new role as an official language of Pakistan, Ḥālī's efforts to limit the population from which Urdu could draw its lexicographers to the Muslim residents of Delhi can only be interpreted as the rearguard action of an increasingly insecure linguistic elite. Efforts by elite Muslims of northern India to engage the colonial government through more representative associational organizations suffered from a combination of what Alok Rai has termed a post-1857 milieu of "competitive loyalism" and David Lelyveld's characterization of *sharīf* anxieties stemming from the British "withdrawal of deference."[109] Sir Sayyid Aḥmad Ḵhān would thus establish in 1886 the Muhammadan Educational Congress to counter the rise of the Indian National Congress, scheduling its meetings to coincide with those of its counterpart. Addressing that body in Lucknow the same year Ḥālī published his review, Sayyid Ahmad Ḵhān asked those assembled to "think for a moment what would be the result if all appointments were given by competitive examination." To resounding cheers, he predicted that government policies, if unchecked, would permit a man "of low caste and insignificant origin, though he be a BA or MA, and have the requisite ability . . . [to be in] a position of authority . . . and have power in making the laws" affecting the lives of the aristocracy. He warned, "over all races, not only over Mohomedans but over Rajas of high positions and the brave Rajputs who have not forgotten the swords of their ancestors, would be placed as ruler a Bengali who at sight of a table knife would crawl under his chair."[110]

As Alok Rai reminds us, despite the temptation "to mock the Avadh landlords and their hangers-on, rallying to the defence of privilege," the *sharīf* elite soon came to understand that "in a democracy numbers matter."[111] As reformers, educators, and administrators called upon the language to lose the contextual specificity that tied it to an elite courtly and literary milieu and instead serve the population as whole, lexicographers became instrumental in turning what functioned as a small set of linguistic registers keyed to particular performative settings into a completely transparent and commensurable medium of communication. Urdu would have to justify its official status not through the charismatic authority of its most celebrated poets but instead by its currency and comprehensibility throughout the territories in which it was being asked to function.[112] Lexicographers and translators, through projects like the Vernacular

Translation Society, sought to populate the Urdu lexicon with the words it needed to function as a so-called modern language capable of expressing as well as any other "national language" any concept in any context or medium. Typically, this entailed the production of technical dictionaries that translated Europe's medical,[113] legal,[114] administrative,[115] and other specialized[116] terminologies into an Urdu idiom.[117] Occasionally, however, it also entailed the translation of another South Asian language or occupational cant into the language of prestige.[118] The title that Sayyid Aḥmad gave the first two volumes of his dictionary, *Hindūstānī Urdū Luġhat* (A Hindustani–Urdu dictionary), suggest in its implied directionality that he considered Urdu, not Hindustani, to be more appropriate as a term for a glossing "feeder language."[119]

Ćiraṇjī saw in *hindūstānī* an umbrella term that could accommodate the wide range of spoken forms throughout northern India, effecting a model of "unity in diversity." "Hindi," he explains, "is that language in which pure Sanskrit words or words directly corrupted from Sanskrit or made from Prakrit are included, and which 4 crore [40,000,000] people speak in large portions of North Hindustan." "Urdu," by contrast,

> is that language in which are included words, mostly from Hindi, at the second level Fārsī, at the third level Arabic, some Turki and now some English, etc., and which, in addition to Delhi, Lucknow, and their environs, wherever the mother tongue (*mādarī zabān*) is Hindustani, the literate folk of every northern [Indian] city and town speak, and these days, taking the form of a language of the courts and newspapers, is spreading through nearly the entirety of Hindustan. In this way, Urdu cannot have any such phrases in which at least one Hindi word will not be found, thus the existence of Urdu is impossible without Hindi, or it may be said in this way that Hindi is the soul (*jān*) of Urdu.[120]

By depicting Hindustani as the mother tongue of the forty million people of northern India and limiting Urdu to urbanized "literature folk," Ćiraṇjī anticipates Amrit Rai's later assertion that Urdu is no more than an elite "class dialect."[121] As evidence of this, Ćiraṇjī computes the number of *muḥāwarah*, or idioms, in his dictionary that are associated with so-called Hindi terms and compares them with the number of idioms associated with terms derived from Farsi and Arabic. The results of his experiment, which he provides for the benefit of the skeptical reader, prove "through means of evidence that can be verified even by someone with a first-grader's knowledge of arithmetic" that

> Hindi *muḥāwarah* are approximately triple the number of Urdu *muḥāwarah*, and this matter is known only from counting those terms which per term have at least five *muḥāwarah*. If one were to compare between those Hindi and Perso-Arabic terms that have two or three *muḥāwarah*, then the ratio of Hindi *muḥāwarah* to Urdu will be four to one.[122]

Not only can Hindi claim to be the source of a greater total number of Hindustani *muḥāwarah* idioms, but it can also claim, according to Ćiraṇjī, to have associated with each term a greater number of significations than those derived from Farsi and Arabic.[123] Ćiraṇjī's characterization is of a Hindustani comprising the sum total of two separate linguistic and literary traditions, a minuscule Urdu overshadowed by an entirely independent Hindi possessing four times as many idioms. This is achieved, however, through a sleight of hand: while Hindi terms are the "soul" (*jān*) of Urdu, he only counts as Urdu those *muḥāwarah*s (idioms) that are based upon "Persian-Arabic" terms.

The result of this semantic wizardry and quantification of headwords was the commodification of a deracinated "common" language that Ćiraṇjī promoted as *hindūstānī*. Shorn of any real literary, historical, and sociopolitical identity, Ćiraṇjī's *hindūstānī* is recognizable for little other than its script, foisted upon a subject people by despotic, alien conquerors, a convenient straw man whose fall would signal the rise of Hindi, the true "soul" not just of Urdu but of forty million North Indians.[124] Adapting for his purposes the seemingly objective rhetoric of the colonial census, he imagines the "homogenous, empty space" of Hindustan filled with a seemingly overwhelming preponderance of both Hindi speakers and Hindi expressions. In doing so, he anticipates the decision to enumerate separately Hindi and Urdu as separate languages in the census of 1901 and the "phenomenal increase in the total number of Hindi language speakers over Urdu language speakers in the subsequent census of 1911."[125]

Arun Agrawal has described a similar process in the field of medical research of what he calls the "scientisation of indigenous knowledge," a means by which to render exotic practices and disciplines legible to the instrumental logic of development. The first demand of that logic, he explains,

> is that useful indigenous knowledge be separated from those other knowledges, practices, milieu, context, and other cultural beliefs in combination with which it exists. Only the forms of indigenous knowledge that are potentially relevant to development, then, need attention and protection. Other forms of such knowledge, precisely because they are irrelevant to the needs of development, can be allowed to pass away.[126]

What he terms *validation* and *abstraction* entails a sifting of "useful" information from the chaff of "irrelevant" contextual baggage in order to ensure that "only those elements of indigenous practices need be retained that can more easily be transplanted into other contexts."[127] A final step involves the generalization of the information, which permits it to be "catalogued, and archived, and then circulated before it can be used more widely."[128] Without a shared mythology, the Hindustani *pablik* imagined by Ćiraṇjī's dictionary failed (to use the terminology of Deutch, Brass, and King) to attach any subjective importance to their objective distinctness and thus could not develop into a coherent *community*, let alone a politically successful *nation*.[129] By contrast, however, the steps that this late nineteenth-century lexicographer took to particularize, validate, and generalize a new "scientific" Hindi language ultimately permitted "the machinery of development [to] crank into action" so that a language could "become the object of further action."[130]

By the turn of the century, it was clear that this experimental form of Urdu was losing its legitimacy as "the language of Hindustan" and that a "new" language—grammatically identical but with Sanskrit-derived *tatsama* loanwords in place of its Perso-Arabic lexical content and written in the *devanāgrī* script—was rising to take its place. Partisans for Urdu could continue to insist that the Arabic script and the Persian lexical content of Urdu "represented" the Indian people as much as a Sanskritized "Modern Standard Hindi." Or, Urdu could retract its claims to represent the people of Hindustani universally and instead accept an identity imposed upon it as the language of Muslims throughout South Asia. In the end, both identities were equal as fictions, if unequal in their plausibility.

The *zabān-i urdū'i muʿallā-i shāhjahānābād* was an anachronism in an age of mother tongues, nationalism, and, subsequently, representational democracy. So, too, was Ćiraṇjī Lāl. Condemned by his Hindu and comprador identity and as the author of dictionaries documenting an all-encompassing, ecumenical Hindustani written in the Arabic script, his contributions to the development of a language were destined for obscurity.

This is not to say, however, that his dictionary was entirely forgotten. Following Munshī Ćiraṇjī Lāl's death in 1898, Lālah Amīr Ćand, then assistant master of St. Stephens Mission High School in Delhi, purchased the plates of the *Maḳhzan al-Muḥāwarāt* and prepared a second edition.[131] In his role as educator, Amīr Ćand recognized the value of and potential profit in republishing this useful dictionary. In the course of his career, however, he would become disillusioned with British rule in India. In 1910 he was placed under police surveillance as a "political suspect"[132] and was observed associating with admirers of the nationalist revolutionaries Lala Hardayal (1884–1939, founder of the Ghadr Party in the United States) and Rash Behari Bose (1886–1945). Largely on the basis of radical pamphlets attributed to him and the discovery of a bomb cap in his home, the forty-year-old Amīr Ćand was in 1914 accused of conspiring to commit bombings in Delhi and Lahore. A failed plot of December 1912 had injured the viceroy of India Lord Hardinge in a procession to commemorate the transfer of the colonial capital from Calcutta to Delhi.[133] During the so-called Delhi Conspiracy Case, Amīr Ćand was characterized by the sessions judge as "not only a murderer on a great scale, but one who has spent his life in furthering murderous schemes which he was too timid to carry out himself."[134] The headmaster was convicted in 1914 and hanged the following year along with three co-conspirators. The *Maḳhzan al-Muḥāwarāt* would not again be published until 1988, this time in Lahore, Pakistan.

CONCLUSION

A poet is not a grammarian or lexicographer. Language is his tool, the material he uses to create. It is thus subservient to him, not he to it.

—attributed to Faiẓ Aḥmad 'Faiẓ' (1911–1984)

IN HIS 1938 review of ᶜAbdul Majīd's Urdu dictionary, the *Jāmiᶜ al-Luġhāt* (1935), the British scholar T. Grahame Bailey (1872–1942) marvels that "one man amid the press of other duties should have been able to carry through so large an undertaking singlehanded." Bailey estimates Majīd's work to be 50 percent larger than the next most comprehensive work compiled to that date. To explain what brought Majīd to assemble so compendious a work, he reproduces the following anecdote:

> Once when he was on prolonged sick leave he was visited by a friend who wished to obtain a good Urdu dictionary. He searched the bookshops, but failed to get one which satisfied him. Khāja ᶜAbdul Majīd confided in him his intention of compiling one, and was strongly urged to do so. A literary editor added his importunities, with the result that the work was begun.

Bailey begins his review by remarking that Urdu readers were fortunate to have had "three large dictionaries . . . entirely in Urdu" published in recent years. He concludes by lauding Majīd for having "produced a work which students of Urdu will not be able to do without."[1] In spite of Bailey's high praise and optimism, it should come as little surprise that Urdu lexicographers continued to be dissatisfied with the state of their field. For, as many a critic has pointed out, what apart from madness and bibliomania could motivate an individual to pursue so many years of painstaking labor?

Six decades after Bailey, another prominent British scholar and translator of South Asian languages, D. J. Matthews, would bemoan the state of Urdu lexicography, writing,

> Urdu must be one of the few major languages of the world that does not possess adequate and up-to-date dictionaries. Even the best of them have glaring omissions and many are hardly legible—a serious shortcoming in a dictionary! . . . Unfortunately modern lexicography is not a forte of the Urdu-speaking world, and it is high time that something was done to address the problem.[2]

The "most useful" work, according to Matthews, is "still" John T. Platts's *Dictionary of Urdū, Classical Hindī, and English* (1884), which, as its title suggests, is neither intended nor suitable for the needs of the present-day Urdu-speaking community. The main problem, according to Maulvī ʿAbdul Ḥaq, a figure known by the sobriquet "Bābā-i Urdū" (Grand Old Man of Urdu), is that "in our dictionaries, typically no description of the meaning of a term is given." "Instead," he explains, one finds,

> several synonyms written across from the term. In addition to these words, there are several senses of the sought meaning. For someone who is unfamiliar [with the term], it proves very difficult to determine to what extent each of them is synonymous with this term, and how, in an ordinary way, to tell which among them is correct. And if someone cannot understand the meaning of a particular synonym, he also will be unable to understand the sense of the word. By merely writing the synonyms of a word, a proper understanding will not be provided.[3]

In his view, for a new nation in which only a small proportion of the population spoke Urdu as a first language (7.6 percent according to the census of 1981),[4] any dictionary that merely provided synonyms would be of little value to the majority of the populace. In an effort to reverse this situation, the government of Pakistan, then barely a decade old, established an Urdu Dictionary Board in 1958 at the urging of Maulvī ʿAbdul Ḥaq. For Ḥaq, the nation's progress had become inseparable from that of its national language:

> To whatever extent a nation is developed it is to that extent that its language is expansive and has the capacity to express subtle thoughts and scholarly

> concerns. And to whatever extent a nation's language is limited, it is to that extent that its place in civilization or rather, amongst humanity (*insāniyat*), is lowered.[5]

This equation of language with nation enabled ʿAbdul Ḥaq to shift the lexicographer's rhetoric of complaint away from personal accounts of dissatisfaction toward a collective obligation to serve both language and nation.

In 1973, the first volume of an new unabridged dictionary of the Urdu language was published in Karachi by the Anjuman-i Taraqqi-yi Urdū (Society for the Advancement of Urdu). Explicitly modeled on the *Oxford English Dictionary*, the first volume was given the title *Luġhat-i Kabīr-i Urdū* (Great dictionary of Urdu).[6] The anjuman had been founded in 1903 as a response to the decision made three years earlier by Sir Anthony MacDonnell, Lieutenant Governor of the North-Western Provinces and Oudh, to permit the use of the *devanāgarī* script in official court documents.[7] Under the leadership of Maulvī ʿAbdul Ḥaq, the anjuman moved its headquarters in 1912 from Aligarh to Hyderabad, where in 1914 it began receiving annual grants from the niẓām.[8] In 1917, the niẓām awarded the anjuman a grant to develop a dictionary of scientific and technical terms.[9] Elements of this work would be incorporated into what would become the unabridged dictionary following the emigration of ʿAbdul Ḥaq to Karachi after the partition of India and Pakistan and, with him, much of the anjuman's staff and materials.

Thirty-seven years after the publication of the first volume of the unabridged dictionary, those who shared ʿAbdul Ḥaq's vision of the twinned destinies of language and nation had been contending with decades of disappointments and setbacks for both. Rauf Parekh begins his May 23, 2010, article in Pakistan's *Dawn* newspaper not where one would expect—by commemorating the completion on Wednesday, April 14, 2010, of the twenty-second and final volume of the dictionary that was now called the *Urdū Luġhāt: Tārīḳhī Uṣūl Par* (Urdu dictionary: on historical principles). Instead, he reproduces Simon Winchester's description of a toast made by the British prime minister Stanley Baldwin in England on a different Wednesday, in this case, June 6, 1928. It was on this earlier date that the twelfth and final volume of the *Oxford English Dictionary* emerged from the printing press. In his article, Rauf constructs a series of parallels between these two dictionaries. Some of these are favorable: "We have been able to do it in only (yes 'only') fifty-two years—fifty-one years and ten months, to be exact—while it took them seventy years," and "We published twenty-two volumes whereas their first edition consisted of twelve." Other comparisons are less complimentary: "No prime minister is here to celebrate the greatest feat of Urdu lexicography, for there are apparently more important tasks to attend to than expressing gratitude and admiration to the compilers of a twenty-two-volume Urdu dictionary." When he laments that the compilation of "the most comprehensive dictionary of a language is one of the most important accomplishments in the history of a nation and should be a source of national pride," his tone betrays great disappointment in the lack of recognition, to say nothing of a lack of financial resources, extended by the state to this project. The reader is not entirely convinced when Parekh claims to be filled with "pride and joy" at the thought that "Urdu is now ranked among the major languages of the world—along with English, German, Arabic and Persian—that have such comprehensive dictionaries." For those involved with compiling the dictionary, he goes so far as to exclaim: "It is an achievement that has made us as proud as winning the 1992 cricket world cup or, perhaps, even prouder."[10]

A persistent sense of shame pervades the history of Urdu lexicography; it extends across borders and languages. Upon presenting to a prominent Urdu literary critic for the third time in as many years the central argument of this book—that an Urdu literary culture developed reflexively in parallel to lexicography—I was met with a response that betrayed exasperation both with me and with these lexicographers, whom the critic considered mediocre poets hardly deserving of the name. After some consideration, however, I realized that I could not myself have penned a better précis of this project than that offered in this criticism. I was reminded that it was the ordinariness of their poetic productions, both in and beyond their lexicographic output, that had originally convinced me that in seeking out their motivations I might stitch together a far richer narrative of a literature's development than that possible in any survey of its most outstanding (which is not to say exemplary) luminaries. These middling poets, far more numerous than might be apparent in the great histories of literature, relied upon lexicographic works both to make sense of and compose the innumerable verses that formed the bulk of the quantity, if not quality, of the literature. The importance of the dictionaries that document the language is not diminished by the quality, or even lack, of their authors' poetic oeuvre.

Historians have both used and abused lexicographic works as sources. Those associated with the so-called Aligarh school have been especially effective in mining lexicographic materials for insights into the material and administrative history of precolonial India, reestablishing the importance of several often overlooked Indo-Persian dictionaries of the seventeenth and eighteenth centuries as essential textual sources.[11] As their concern was with the content of these dictionaries, historians have devoted little attention to the formal features of these works. At the other end of the spectrum, works devoted exclusively to the reconstruction of a history of lexicography, including Baevskii's important monograph,[12] have hesitated to connect the objects of their studies to the social and cultural formations that produced and were themselves documented by these works. In this book I treat lexicographic works, as well as the people who compiled and used them, as vital components and agents of a constant mediation that all humans experience between a lived reality and socially maintained ontological ideologies. In practice, what this means is that lexicographers cultivated neat (and sometimes not-so-neat) lexical gardens, asserting equivalences among terms and contributing descriptive commentaries upon their linguistic application.

In the first chapter of this book, I described a diverse group of people who read, memorized, composed, or compiled lexicographic works. I treat meaning as a socially enacted form of consciousness whose material distillation in lexicographic works, broadly defined, serves as a representation, both as proxy and portrait, of a cosmographical order that united an otherwise factious range of participants hailing from diverse religious, linguistic, and (especially with the advent of European mercantile colonialism) geographic backgrounds. These shared cosmographies were deployed in the compilation of multilingual vocabularies, texts that could not rely on a stable orthography to mediate between lexicons associated both with multiple scripts and with language users that possessed widely divergent oral and literate competencies. Techniques of glossing not only instantiate on a local level denotational equivalences, but also, insofar as every act of reference may be deemed interactionally successful or not (a quality independent of denotational correctness),[13] every act of glossing must carry with it the apparatus of authority through which it is able to enforce what the linguistic anthropologist Asif Agha has called the *mutual coordination* of its participant users.[14] This apparatus of authority—what Pierre Bourdieu calls *symbolic capital*[15]—I argue is keyed to contemporaneous political structures. For the early modern South Asian lexicographic class, this apparatus consisted of a "chain" (*silsilah*) of interpersonal relationships evaluated through the formal technique of *isnād* (authority) that sought to locate in the earliest years of Islam an authentic set of legal, lexical, and ritual precedents. Culturally, this authority was enacted through the performance of a hegemonic cultural code of *ādāb*, inadequately glossed in English as "modes of comportment."

Among the many activities with which *ādāb* is closely associated is the appreciation and composition of Persianate genres of poetry. One of the more obvious purposes to which lexicographic works were employed was the interpretation of literature. This was achieved through a reader's consultation of definitions provided for the words and expressions glossed within the lexicographic work. In their capacity as catalogues of synonymous or near-synonymous terms and in their various arrangements (ranging from hierarchically arranged thematic vocabularies to dictionaries arranged alphabetically by final letter), they also served as aids in the selection of the right word or expression in the composition of poetry. Often, the formal elements of vocabularies composed in verse served as models for what are considered more properly literary genres, introducing readers to such formal elements as prosody, rhyme, ambiguity, and metaphor. Finally, lexicographic works, in following a tradition of citing poetic verses as prooftexts (*asnād*, pl. of *sanad* 'proof', 'certificate', 'testimony'), serve as significant collections of literature, often recording the only extant example of verses that otherwise would not have been preserved. Lexicographic works thus served as a highly portable and efficacious means of transferring a courtly culture of literary *ādāb* not just from one place to another but also from one generation the next.

The burgeoning field of metalexicography attempts both to account for the historical forms of past lexicographic works and to advance contemporary technologies of lexicographical compilation. Important advances in our understanding of cognition have enabled modern lexicographic studies to draw insights in the field of what is known as *Listenwissenschaft*, or "list science."[16] Through experimental psychology, lexicographers have been able to develop methods of arrangement to enhance the cohesion and recall of lexical material, often by assisting the user of a text in discovering the relationship of a particular lexicographic unit to a broader group of terms.[17] In so doing, it has aimed to place lexicography upon a putatively "scientific" basis and has privileged the alphabetical dictionary—a "royal genre" if there ever was one[18]—often to the exclusion of important premodern genres of lexicographic production. As would be clear to any student of premodern lexicography, as indeed has been the case throughout most of human history when writing materials were scarce and literacy confined to a minute proportion of the population, these "new methods" have a much longer history than has generally been appreciated. By reintroducing lexicography to literary studies, and especially by remaining cognizant of early lexicographic techniques analogous (if not always homologous) to oral-formulaic literary production, this book is able to account for the abundance of genres that proliferated throughout southern and central Asia prior to the widespread adoption of print in the nineteenth century. Cognitive approaches can help explain the mechanisms through which certain lexicographic technologies become prevalent under certain material and social conditions. In terms of causality, however, they are limited to demonstrating what some have called the *adjacent possible*—that is, cognitive theories offer the illusion through our subjective observer position of inanimate objects (for example, works belonging to particular genres of lexicography) as autonomous agents possessing a trajectory through evolving conditions of possibility.[19]

The textual reconstruction of the life of an otherwise unknown author has important implications for received notions of lexicographic authority. In the case of ʿAbdul Wāsĕʿ, what little is known about him derives from his name and a few works of a pedagogical nature from the latter half of the seventeenth century. Associated first and foremost with his toponymic *nisbat*, Hāṅswī (of Hāṅsī), his dictionary of Hindvi terms was denigrated by the prominent Indo-Persian philologist Ḳhān-i Ārzū as diverging from the polite speech of Mughal imperial centers. What emerges from Ārzū's criticism is a new valorization of place in the critical evaluation of literary production, supplementing and even replacing individual literary talent and the copiousness of a given lexicon in the determination of lexicographic authority. The authority of the Urdu text could no longer stand on its own independent from the biography of its author. The unattributed lexicon had as little value as the unattributed verse.

The *Shams al-Bayān* of Mirzā Jān Ṭapish is an unusual text: commissioned by a provincial nobleman, it is an Urdu dictionary devoted to the idioms of the Mughal capital that are preserved in poetry. Despite the unusual choice of lexical material, the method employed by its author in compiling the work follows a thousand-year Islamic tradition of asserting veracity through the citation of poetic prooftexts. The author in his introduction to the text suggests that the ability to compile this work was vouchsafed him by birth in the imperial capital, and the authority of its contents was assured through his adherence to a promise to offer a "Hindi verse . . . from the measured language of Delhi so that for each [expression it may be determined] which are according to them correct." His recourse to the technology of *isnād*, or a "chain of transmission," conforms to longstanding Islamic juridical custom and underlines his role in establishing an Urdu literary canon. Moreover, his deployment of a consistent lexicographic method also enabled the wholesale incorporation of his lexical content into early British dictionary projects. The *Shams al-Bayān* reveals the Urdu literary situation at the turn of the nineteenth century to have been in transition: the lack of a widely written prose of ordinary Urdu speech meant that the spoken expressions represented in this work could only gain credibility when connected with an authoritative poetic prooftext.

The career of Sayyid Aḥmad Dihlawī exemplifies the changes in the prevailing modes of authority indexed by nineteenth-century lexicography. As the object of lexicographic inquiry expanded to include new domains of language, including specimens that had never previously been committed to written form, the glossary function of the lexicographic work—that is to say, its relationship as a commentary on or supplement to a defined written corpus—gave way to the function of the modern standard dictionary.[20] What is meant here by a modern standard dictionary is a work that purports to represent the breadth of a linguistic community's social range and domain—communities that by the nineteenth century increasingly correspond with populations of state citizens. Earlier figures like Ḳhān-i Ārzū and Mirzā Jān Ṭapish established their credibility as lexicographers through their status as accomplished authors and critics of poetry. The modern standard dictionary derived its authority through a new metric that esteemed a quantification of linguistic currency over the qualifications of the individual language users represented in verse as prooftexts. This lexicographic method emerged in parallel with cartographic, ethnographic, and historiographic projects that aimed to render legible a subject population and that take textual form as land surveys, censuses, gazetteers, and dictionaries. Sayyid Aḥmad occupies an uneasy space between the earlier charismatic mode of authority and the "corporate" or "scientific model" currently employed in asserting lexicographic authority. His insertion of his own verses as citations—serving, in essence, as *nonce verses*—indicate his attempt to claim an inheritance to a long tradition of poet-lexicographers. Yet, while being content to copy word for word definitions proffered in the work of his predecessors, he is nevertheless unwilling to reproduce verses that had been penned by fellow lexicographers as citations, instead substituting his own or seeking out quotations by nonlexicographers. This reluctance betrays the anxiety of a lexicographer whose trade had not been completely professionalized; stated another way, Sayyid Aḥmad in his specialization as a lexicographer could not completely abandon the desire to project literary charisma through recourse to a poetic persona. Posterity has been unwilling to grant him full membership to what had become, by the twentieth century, two increasingly distinct professional clubs.

In equivalent terms and equivocal verses, through mediating texts and middling figures, the objects studied in this book ultimately reveal the means through which entire systems of meaning come to be articulated. As described by the sixth-century Roman encyclopedist Cassiodorus, "*Definitio* is truly defined as a brief statement propounding the nature of each individual thing distinguished from the commonality according to its own proper significance."[21] The equation of denotations with linguistic forms is not, I argue, an adequate definition of *defining*. In order to be useful to their users, lexicographic works must embed their microstructural glossing of terms and expressions within a coherent (if not always uniformly consistent) macrostructural system of arrangement. This dual process of defining—the assertion of denotational equivalence and the situation of that denotation within a broader form of reference—enabled premodern lexicographers to invoke and reproduce remarkably comprehensive and largely stable ontological ideologies.[22]

Definitio serves functionally to assert an equivalence within difference. In the early stages of Urdu's vernacularization, when orthography was unstable, similarly hierarchical arrangements of terms were often deployed in the macrostructural arrangement of lexicographic texts. The rapid expansion in the number of lexicographic works containing Hindvi vocabulary occurred as the Mughal bureaucracy came to require administrators literate in Persian. During that period, India witnessed significant growth in the number and quality of the *niṣāb* genre of versified vocabularies. As a language comes increasingly to be written down and the orthography becomes increasingly stable, new possibilities emerge in the formal structure and contents of lexicographic works. This occurs for Urdu by approximately the middle of the eighteenth century.[23] The alphabetical arrangement of lexical material privileges the graphic and aural qualities of terms over their denotative content, shifting the organization of material within a text from a system of hierarchically arranged denotations to one of serially arranged visual representations. It also permits new types of literariness, including ambiguities based upon homography. In either situation, the commensurability of terms is assumed, though that commensurability comes to be expressed in thematically structured texts through shared systems of *denotata* and in alphabetically arranged texts through shared systems of signification. Formally, in the latter situation, poetry no longer becomes the most obvious linguistic vehicle for the expression of lexicographic *definitio* and instead becomes relegated to the dictionary entry as mere prooftext. As the value of verse as a didactic medium diminishes, poetry develops its association with an increasingly separate literary sphere of expression. By the latter half of the nineteenth century, the compilation of lexicographic works had became a professional activity increasingly distinct from the composition of Persianate genres of poetry.

Though the political and economic interference brought about by the expansion of East India Company rule in eastern India doubtless effected significant changes in Mughal courtly culture, the contributions of Europeans from the latter half of the eighteenth century was not by itself decisive.[24] The lexicographic evidence suggests that in the Persianate literary culture of northern India the so-called philological revolution attributed to British "Orientalists"[25] had been underway for decades if not an entire century prior to the arrival in Calcutta of William Jones.[26] While the colonial intervention does not represent a decisive shift in lexicography, it did hasten the processes of vernacularization already underway. Thus, lexicography maintained its inclination toward alphabetical arrangement but came to include new linguistic content, including spoken expressions. Political and economic change contributed to a reassessment of the valuation previously afforded to the performance of *ādāb*, central to a wider Indo-Persianate technique of asserting authority and representing charisma. Idiomatic formats and historically specific lexicographic generic forms largely give way to a "royal genre" of the modern standard dictionary as print technologies, mass production and distribution, and education further contribute to the standardization of language. The rise of what Ulrike Stark calls an "associational culture"[27] corresponding with the rapid expansion of the role played by capital creates the conditions for the emergence of *corporate accreditation* in the form of the university diploma, *corporate production* in the form of the bureaus of dictionary compilation, *corporate consumption* in the form of a print-based public sphere, and *corporate financing* in the form of publishing houses.

If, by the end of the nineteenth century, analogous lexical cosmographies gave way to a universal system of graphic representation, so too did the variety of linguistic registers used throughout most of northern India resolve themselves into two "national languages," whose internal coherence and external boundaries were established through their affiliation with either the Perso-Arabic *nastaʿlīq* or *devanāgarī* scripts. When the modern standard dictionary rose to become the most scientific container of lexicographic information, its arrangement deriving from the denotationally arbitrary but quasi-universal visual quality of its corpus, so too do established social hierarchies of subject peoples come to be reduced to the universalizing logic of the modern nation-state, its citizens' allegiance to the center determined by the seemingly arbitrary delineation of political, linguistic, and religious boundaries. As far as a language may be judged by the copiousness of its dictionaries, so too must political determinations obey the vagaries of their own enumerative policies. And, inasmuch as the relationship of script to meaning appears as the arbitrary product of historical accident, so too may the citizen question his or her existential connection to and role within a given state.

Urdu, at the turn of the twenty-first century, has developed a tenuous connection with the script that has defined its modern political existence. The ubiquity of the Roman script and its role in representing the Urdu language owes something to the monopoly it has enjoyed, until recently, in representing Uniform Resource Locator (URL) addresses, the primary means through which Internet domain names are accessed.[28] Regardless of script, every address ultimately makes reference to an irreducible and, in theory, universally accessible numeric value. What perhaps lies ahead is the collapse of the multiple ontologies of the past into a single universal system of virtually instantiated meaning. New technologies that permit dictionary users to gain direct access to lexical content are replacing the serial alphabetical arrangement of the codex format that has dominated dictionary production for more than a millennium. Much touted "Web 2.0" technologies are reintroducing the interactive element previously widespread during the era of pre- and craft-literate lexicography, long suppressed by the division of labor that characterized the era of the print reproduction of texts. Individual users are regaining the ability to amend the lexicon as they please, adding terms, denotations, and other content as they see fit. Most intriguingly, the dictionary of the third millennium, much like its premodern counterparts, need not take fixed form in any physical medium. Modern technologies of lexicography are surely, in

John Leyden's memorable phrase, more than mere "mechanical aids" to memory. Yet, much like the mnemonic techniques embedded deep within the *niṣāb* genre of versified vocabularies, as we spend more of our lives connected to the machines upon which we now so rely, it has once again become increasingly difficult to distinguish a line between an internal mental lexicon and external "mechanical aids."

NOTES

NOTE ON TRANSLITERATION

1. Frances W. Pritchett, *Nets of Awareness: Urdu Poetry and Its Critics* (Berkeley: University of California Press, 1994), xi.
2. John Thompson Platts, *A Dictionary of Urdū, Classical Hindī, and English* (London: 1884), vii.

1. A PLOT DISCOVERED

I first came upon this quotation in Amitava Kumar, *Nobody Does the Right Thing* (Durham, NC: Duke University Press, 2010), 143. An account of the Twain's visit to the school appears in Cyril Clemens, ed. *Mark Twain: Wit and Wisdom* (New York: Frederick A. Stokes Co., 1935), 11.

1. On this work, see Rafique Ahmed, "Ziauddin Ahmed Barni: Critical Analysis of His Scholarly and Literary Contributions" (PhD diss., University of Sindh, 2009), 172–175.
2. Ẓiyāʾ al-Dīn Aḥmad Ḳhān, *Aḳhbārī Luġhāt maʿrūf běh Kalīd-i Aḳhbār Bīnī* (Delhi: Delhi Printing Works, 1915), 64. On the potential challenges involved with tracing "large concepts" like "democracy" across cultures, genres, and temporal periods, see Carol Gluck, "Words in Motion," in *Words in Motion: Toward a Global Lexicon*, ed. Carol Gluck and Anna Lowenhaupt Tsing (Durham, N.C.: Duke University Press, 2009), 4.
3. Ḳhān, *Aḳhbārī Luġhāt*, 1.
4. Ibid., 2.
5. Ziyauddin Ahmad Barni, *Romance of the Oriental Translator's Office (Bombay): A Peep Into the Dim Past, Containing Brief Biographical Sketches, etc.* (Karachi: Ta'alimi Markaz, 1950); Francis Robinson, *Separatism Among Indian Muslims: The Politics of the United Provinces' Muslims, 1860–1923* (Delhi: Oxford University Press, 1993), 368.
6. Ḳhān, *Aḳhbārī Luġhāt*, 13.
7. Ibid., 9.

8. Lydia He Liu, *Translingual Practice: Literature, National Culture, and Translated Modernity—China, 1900–1937* (Stanford, Calif.: Stanford University Press, 1995), 4.
9. See Ernest Gellner, *Nations and Nationalism* (Ithaca, N.Y.: Cornell University Press, 1983), 21–22.
10. Lydia He Liu, "The Question of Meaning-Value in the Political Economy of the Sign," in *Tokens of Exchange: The Problem of Translation in Global Circulations*, ed. Lydia He Liu (Durham, N.C.: Duke University Press, 1999), 14.
11. Ibid., 35.
12. Liu, *Translingual Practice*, 4.
13. See, for example, Sheldon Pollock, *The Language of the Gods in the World of Men: Sanskrit, Culture, and Power in Premodern India* (Berkeley: University of California Press, 2006), 163; Yigal Bronner, "A Question of Priority: Revisiting the Bhāmaha-Daṇḍin Debate," *Journal of Indian Philosophy* 40, no. 1 (2012): 70–71.
14. Pollock, *The Language of the Gods in the World of Men*, 24.
15. Muzaffar Alam, "The Pursuit of Persian: Language in Mughal Politics," *Modern Asian Studies* 32, no. 2 (1998): 317–349; Muzaffar Alam, "The Culture and Politics of Persian in Precolonial Hindustan," in *Literary Cultures in History: Reconstructions from South Asia*, ed. Sheldon Pollock (Berkeley: University of California Press, 2003), 131–197; Muzaffar Alam, *The Languages of Political Islam: India, 1200–1800* (Chicago: University of Chicago Press, 2004); Muhammad Aslan Syed, "How Could Urdu Be the Envy of Persian (*rashk-i Fārsī*)! The Role of Persian in South Asian Culture and Literature," in *Literacy in the Persianate World: Writing and the Social Order*, ed. Brian Spooner and William L. Hanaway (Philadelphia: University of Pennsylvania Museum of Archaeology and Anthropology, 2012). For recent works with a focus on lexicography in particular, see Solomon I. Baevskii, *Early Persian Lexicography: Farhangs of the Eleventh to the Fifteenth Centuries*, trans. N. Killian (Honolulu: University of Hawai'i Press, 2007); Rajeev Kinra, "This Noble Science: Indo-Persian Comparative Philology, c. 1000–1800 CE," in *South Asian Texts in History: Critical Engagements with Sheldon Pollock*, ed. Yigal Bronner et al. (Ann Arbor, Mich.: Association for Asian Studies, 2011).
16. For Persian and Sanskrit, see, e.g., Audrey Truschke, "The Mughal Book of War: A Persian Translation of the Sanskrit Mahabharata," *Comparative Studies of South Asia, Africa, and the Middle East* 31, no. 2 (2011): 506–520; Audrey Truschke, "Defining the Other: An Intellectual History of Sanskrit Lexicons and Grammars of Persian," *Journal of Indian Philosophy* 40, no. 6 (2012): 635–668. For Sanskrit and Chinese, see, e.g., Victor H. Mair and Tsu-Lin Mei, "The Sanskrit Origins of Recent Style Prosody," *Harvard Journal of Asiatic Studies* 51, no. 2 (1991): 375–470; Victor H. Mair, "Buddhism and the Rise of the Written Vernacular in East Asia: The Making of National Languages," *Journal of Asian Studies* 53, no. 3 (1994): 707–751. For Chinese and Arabic, see, e.g., Kristian Petersen, *The Treasure of the Heavenly Scripture: Translating the Qur'an in China* (Oxford: Oxford University Press, forthcoming).
17. Pollock, *The Language of the Gods in the World of Men*, 50.
18. For the original text, compare Yūsuf bin Muḥammad Yūsufī, "Kaside der Luğat-ı Hindi," Nuruosmaniye Kütüphanesı MS 0003495; Ḥāfiẓ Maḥmūd Sherānī, "Baććoṅ ke Taʿlīmī Niṣāb," in *Maqālāt-i Ḥāfiẓ Maḥmūd Sherānī*, ed. Maẓhar Maḥmūd Sherānī (Lahore: Majlis-i Taraqqī-yi Urdū, 1985), 24–26.

19. Lisa Mitchell, *Language, Emotion, and Politics in South India: The Making of a Mother Tongue* (Bloomington: Indiana University Press, 2009), 176.
20. The role of English was analogous, though far from identical, to that played in northern India by Persian. See ibid., 186–187.
21. Major works include Amrit Rai, *A House Divided: The Origin and Development of Hindi/Hindavi* (Delhi: Oxford University Press, 1984); Christopher Rolland King, *One Language, Two Scripts: The Hindi Movement in Nineteenth-Century North India* (Bombay: Oxford University Press, 1994); Vasudha Dalmia, *The Nationalization of Hindu Traditions: Bhāratendu Harishchandra and Nineteenth-Century Banaras* (Delhi: Oxford University Press, 1997); Shamsur Rahman Faruqi, *Early Urdu Literary Culture and History* (New Delhi: Oxford University Press, 2001); Tariq Rahman, *From Hindi to Urdu: A Social and Political History* (Karachi: Oxford University Press, 2009).
22. King, *One Language, Two Scripts*, 15.
23. Fred Barnes, "Meet Mario the Moderate," *New Republic* 192, no. 15 (1985): 19.
24. Iqtidar Alam Khan, "The Middle Classes in the Mughal Empire," *Social Scientist* 5, no. 1 (1976): 28–49; Alam, "Pursuit"; Brian Spooner and William L. Hanaway, "Introduction—Persian as Koine: Written Persian in World-Historical Perspective," in *Literacy in the Persianate World: Writing and the Social Order*, ed. Brian Spooner and William L. Hanaway (Philadelphia: University of Pennsylvania Museum of Archaeology and Anthropology, 2012), 1–68.
25. On this, see the essays collected in Francesca Orsini, ed., *Before the Divide: Hindi and Urdu Literary Culture* (New Delhi: Orient BlackSwan, 2010). See also Rai, *A House Divided*, 84–129; R. S. McGregor, "On the Evolution of Hindi as a Language of Literature," *South Asia Research* 21, no. 2 (2001): 202–217; R. S. McGregor, "The Progress of Hindi, Part 1: The Development of a Transregional Idiom," in *Literary Cultures in History: Reconstructions from South Asia*, ed. Sheldon I. Pollock (Berkeley: University of California Press, 2003), 940–947.
26. Faruqi, *Early Urdu Literary Culture*, 71–77, 109–126.
27. On the role of print in the nineteenth-century rise of vernaculars, see Johannes Fabian, *Language and Colonial Power: The Appropriation of Swahili in the Former Belgian Congo, 1880–1938* (Berkeley: University of California Press, 1986), 77; Benedict Anderson, *Imagined Communities: Reflections on the Origin and Spread of Nationalism* (London: Verso, 2006), 44–45.
28. Gail Minault, "Delhi College and Urdu," *Annual of Urdu Studies* 14 (1999): 119–134; Kavita Saraswathi Datla, "Making a Worldly Vernacular: Urdu, Education, and Osmania University, Hyderabad, 1883–1938" (PhD diss., University of California, 2006), 58–62. Compare with Frances W. Pritchett, *Nets of Awareness: Urdu Poetry and Its Critics* (Berkeley: University of California Press, 1994), 145.
29. Solomon I. Baevskii, "Farhang-e Jahāngīrī," in *Encyclopædia Iranica Online*, ed. Ehsan Yarshater (1999), http://www.iranicaonline.org/articles/farhang-e-jahangiri.
30. Ḳhān, *Aḳhbārī Luġhāt*, 1.
31. Bernard S. Cohn, "The Census, Social Structure, and Objectification in South Asia in Culture and History of India," *Folk* 26 (1984): 31–32, 39; Matthew H. Edney, *Mapping an Empire: The Geographical Construction of British India, 1765–1843* (Chicago: University of Chicago Press, 1997); Anderson, *Imagined Communities*, 163–178.
32. C. M. Naim, "Introduction," in *Zikr-i Mir: The Autobiography of the Eighteenth-Century Mughal Poet, Mir Muhammad Taqi 'Mir', 1723–1810*, ed. C. M. Naim (New Delhi: Oxford

University Press, 1999), 14–15. Naim's observations draw on the research of Qāẓī ʿAbdul Wadūd, *ʿAbdul Ḥaq Bahaisīyat-i Muḥaqqiq* (Patna: Khuda Bakhsh Oriental Public Library, 1995), 34–45.

33. The title literally means "Mīr's Bounty" and refers to Mir's eldest son, Faiẓ ʿAlī. It is "a short book containing five brief narratives about Sufis, *faqirs*, and one *jogi*." Mīr followed up on the *Faiẓ-i Mīr* with his longer autobiographical work, the *Żikr-i Mīr*. Naim, "Introduction," 8.
34. Ibid., 19.
35. For an explanation of the concept of the "Sanskrit cosmopolis," see, e.g., Sheldon Pollock, "The Sanskrit Cosmopolis, 300–1300: Transculturation, Vernacularization, and the Question of Ideology," in *Ideology and Status of Sanskrit: Contributions to the History of the Sanskrit Language*, ed. Jan E. M. Houben (Leiden: Brill, 1996), 197–247. This is developed more fully, with comparisons to Latin in Europe, in Pollock, *The Language of the Gods in the World of Men*. For the place of Persian in South Asia during the second millennium AD, see Alam, "Culture and Politics of Persian." For the emerging "cosmopolitan vernaculars" Braj Bhāṣā and Awadhī, see Shantanu Phukan, "Through a Persian Prism: Hindi and *Padmavat* in the Mughal Imagination" (PhD diss., University of Chicago, 2000); Allison Renee Busch, *Poetry of Kings: The Classical Hindi Literature of Mughal India* (New York: Oxford University Press, 2011).
36. Frances Pritchett's *Nets of Awareness* remains unsurpassed for its vivid and rich historical contextualization of how these social changes affected Urdu literary production in the latter half of the nineteenth century. See esp. chaps. 1–4.
37. A similar argument, applied to examples from early Persian lexicography, appears in Baevskii, *Early Persian Lexicography*, 135–141, 156–157.
38. Fredric Jameson, *The Political Unconscious: Narrative as a Socially Symbolic Act* (Ithaca, N.Y.: Cornell University Press, 1981), 87.
39. Tzvetan Todorov, "The Origin of Genres," in *Modern Genre Theory*, ed. David Duff (Harlow: Longman, 2000), 200.
40. Ireneusz Opacki, "Royal Genres," in *Modern Genre Theory*, ed. David Duff (Harlow: Longman, 2000), 120.
41. Ibid.
42. Benedetto Croce, *Aesthetic as Science of Expression and General Linguistic*, trans. Douglas Ainslie (London: Macmillan, 1922), 32–38.
43. Barbara Fuchs, *Romance* (New York: Routledge, 2004), 58.
44. Fabian, *Language and Colonial Power*, 11.
45. John Frow, *Genre* (London: Routledge, 2006), 10.
46. Jean Matter Mandler, *Stories, Scripts, and Scene: Aspects of Schema Theory* (Hillsdale, N.J.: Lawrence Erlbaum Associates, 1984), 8–14; Walter Kintsch, *Comprehension: A Paradigm for Cognition* (Cambridge: Cambridge University Press, 1998), 83–84.
47. ʿAbdul Ḥaq, "Miṡl-i *Ḳhāliq Bārī*: Ek Qadīmtarīn Kitāb," in *Qadīm Urdū* (Karachi: Kul Pākistān Anjuman-i Taraqqī-yi Urdū, 1961), 198–207; Nażīr Aḥmad, "Ajay Ćand Nāmah," in *Maqālāt-i Nażīr* (New Delhi: Ghalib Institute, 2002), 124.
48. Jonathan D. Spence, *The Memory Palace of Matteo Ricci* (New York: Viking, 1984).
49. Majid Fakhry, *A History of Islamic Philosophy* (New York: Columbia University Press, 2004), 132–166. Compare with John Borelli, "Vijñānabhikṣu: Indian Thought and *the Great Chain of Being*," in *Jacob's Ladder and the Tree of Life: Concepts of Hierarchy and the*

Great Chain of Being, ed. Marion Leathers Kuntz and Paul Grimley Kuntz (New York: P. Lang, 1987), 371–384.

50. Jamal J. Elias, *The Throne Carrier of God: The Life and Thought of ʿAlāʾ ad-Dawla as-Simnanī* (Albany: State University of New York Press, 1995), 72–77.
51. Frances Amelia Yates, *The Art of Memory* (Chicago: University of Chicago Press, 1966).
52. The *Abhidhānacintāmaṇi* by Hemaćandra (c. 1088–1175), an important Jain scholar, modifies the top of the standard hierarchy of cosmological entities to privilege Jain theological figures above Brahmanical ones. See also Claus Vogel, *Indian Lexicography* (Wiesbaden: Harrassowitz, 1979); Madhukar Mangesh Patkar, *History of Sanskrit Lexicography* (New Delhi: Munshiram Manoharlal, 1981), 80–83; Mitchell, *Language, Emotion, and Politics in South India*, 172; Sivaja Nair and Amba Kulkarni, "The Knowledge Structure in Amarakośa," *Lecture Notes in Computer Science* (2010): 173–189.
53. Fabrizio Speziale, "Les traités persans sur les sciences indiennes: médecine, zoologie, alchimie," in *Muslim Cultures in the Indo-Iranian World During the Early-Modern and Modern Periods*, ed. Fabrizio Speziale and Denis Hermann (Paris: Institut Français de Recherche en Iran, 2010), 407; Truschke, "Defining the Other," 637.
54. See, for example, the thirteenth-century Persian–Arabic vocabulary, Abū Naṣar Muḥammad Badruddīn Farāhī, *Niṣāb al-Ṣibyān* (Tehran: Ćāpḳhānah-yi Shirkat-i Kāviyānī, 1923). See also this nineteenth-century manuscript recension of the Hindvi–Persian–Arabic *Ḳhāliq Bārī*: Ḳhusrau, "Muṭ̤būʿ-i Ṣibyān," Maulana Azad Library (Aligarh Muslim University), H.G. Urdu 53/31.
55. Baevskii, *Early Persian Lexicography*, x, 42, 154. On the *qaṣīdah*, see, e.g., M. C. Lyons and P. Cachia, "The Effect of Monorhyme on Arabic Poetic Production," *Journal of Arabic Literature* 1 (1970): 3–13; Stefan Sperl and Christopher Shackle, eds., *Qasida Poetry in Islamic Asia and Africa*, vol. 1, *Classical Traditions and Modern Meanings* (Leiden: Brill, 1995).
56. Baevskii, *Early Persian Lexicography*, 127–128.
57. Ibid., 155–156.
58. Sir Walter Scott, "Biographical Memoir of John Leyden, M.D.," in *Poems and Ballads* (Kelso, 1858), 51.
59. Ibid., 66.
60. Ibid., 60–61.
61. Compare Leyden's phrase with this extract relating to the employment of Indians, attributed by John Gilchrist (1759–1841) to the fourteenth-century Central Asian conqueror Tīmūr: " 'when necessity compels you to have recourse to their assistance, *employ them as the mechanical, and support them as the living, instruments of labour.*' I give this extract rather as a caveat against too much confidence, than as any authority for maltreating the people, whom the conqueror probably paints with a caricaturist's pencil." John Borthwick Gilchrist, *The General East India Guide and Vade Mecum: For the Public Functionary, Government Officer, Private Agent, Trader or Foreign Sojourner, in British India, and the Adjacent Parts of Asia Immediately Connected with the Honourable the East India Company* (London, 1825), 542, emphasis added.
62. According to a note on the title page, the text contains 3,881 words on 216 pages. John Caspar Leyden, "A Vocabulary Persian and Hindoostanee [and Maldivian]," British Library MSS Eur B103 (1808).

63. On the use of similar calques in representing the *ṣifāt allāh* or names of Allah in early Awadhī romances, see Aditya Behl and Wendy Doniger, *Love's Subtle Magic: An Indian Islamic Literary Tradition, 1379–1545* (New York: Oxford University Press, 2012), 36–37.
64. Simon Fuller, "The Lost Dhivehi Gospels," in *Maldives Culture* (2003), http://198.62.75.1/www1/pater/images1/dhivehi-lost-gospels.htm.
65. Tom McArthur summarizes the contemporary lexicographic disdain for thematically organized texts as arising from the dual (incorrect) assumptions "(a) that a thematic layout promotes eccentricity, and (b) that an alphabetic layout inhibits eccentricity." "Thematic Lexicography," in *The History of Lexicography: Papers from the Dictionary Research Centre Seminar at Exeter, March 1986*, ed. R. R. K. Hartmann (Gainesville: University Press of Florida, 1986), 160. McArthur, of course, does not agree with these assumptions. He goes on to describe his surprise at discovering how closely the thematic schema he independently developed for his *Longman Lexicon of Contemporary English* corresponded with that deployed in Aelfric's eleventh-century list of Latin and Anglo-Saxon terms. Ibid., 161–163.
66. "*Lughāt-i Hindī*," Asiatic Society of Bengal Persian Society Collection MS 1446.
67. The Fort William College was a school located in Calcutta that trained young East India Company officials for service in India during the first four decades of the nineteenth century. From the seals on the first folio of the work we are able to ascertain that prior to being transferred to the library at the Asiatic Society this text was originally housed in the Fort William College library collection and belonged to William Butterworth Bayley (1781–1860; from a Arabic-script seal with *sāʾīn-i bailī*, "sign of Bayley," written in Arabic script), who was among the first batch of students to enter the new Fort William College in July 1799. For more on the early years of the college, see Thomas Roebuck, *Annals of the College of Fort William* (Calcutta, 1819); Heinrich Ferdinand Blochmann, *Calcutta During the Last Century: A Lecture* (Calcutta, 1867); T. W. Clark, "The Languages of Calcutta, 1760–1840," *Bulletin of the School of Oriental and African Studies, University of London* 18, no. 3, In Honour of J. R. Firth (1956): 453–474; Sisir Kumar Das, *Sahibs and Munshis: An Account of the College of Fort William* (New Delhi: Orion, 1978).
68. Francis Gladwin, *A Vocabulary English & Persian for the College at Fort William in Bengal* (Calcutta, 1800).
69. Compare Thomas Bowrey, "Thomas Bowrey's Collection of Notes on Oriental Languages," British Library MS EUR E 192 (1700), 74a; Thomas Bowrey, *A Dictionary, English and Malayo, Malayo and English. To which is added some Short Grammar Rules . . . and also Several Miscellanies, Dialogues, and Letters, in English and Malayo, etc.* (London, 1701).
70. See Thomas Bowrey, "Draft Manuscript of *A Dictionary, English and Malayo, Malayo and English*," British Library MS EUR E 192 (1700).
71. David Washbrook, " 'To Each a Language of His Own': Language, Culture, and Society in Colonial India," in *Language, History and Class*, ed. P. J. Corfield (Oxford: Blackwell, 1991), 184.
72. Nicholas Howe, *The Old English Catalogue Poems* (Copenhagen: Rosenkilde and Bagger, 1985), 9, 12, 20. This is not to say that lexicographers in the Arabic and Sanskrit linguistic traditions did not have access to an alphabetical alternative. The first major dictionary of the Arabic language, the *Kitāb al-ʿAin*, was produced by the

great Basran linguist Al-Ḳhalīl in the ninth century. Its idiosyncratic arrangement ignored the two "recognized" alphabetical orders prevalent in Arabic, namely that of *alif-bāʾ-jīm* (based on the Semitic alphabet, used in Hebrew and Syriac) and a modified system that groups letters of the same form together, distinguishing them by diacritical points above and below the letter. Instead, he chose to invent his own order, arranging letters based on their source of enunciation, from the back of the throat "upwards and outwards to the labials." John A. Haywood, *Arabic Lexicography: Its History, and Its Place in the General History of Lexicography* (Leiden: Brill, 1965), 37. Haywood attributes the inspiration for this "invention" to Ḳhalīl's milieu in Ḳhurāsān, a cultural contact zone between West Asia, Central Asia, and South Asia. Ibid., 9. On the history of alphabetization in Europe, see Lloyd William Daly, *Contributions to a History of Alphabetization in Antiquity and the Middle Ages* (Bruxelles: Latomus, 1967).

73. Morton W. Bloomfield, "Understanding Old English Poetry," *Annuale Mediaevale* 9 (1968): 18. Cited in Howe, *The Old English Catalogue Poems*, 20.
74. Though not drawing from cognitive science per se, for an inspired example of contemporary *Listenwissenschaft*, see the fascinating study of Valentina Izmirlieva, *All the Names of the Lord: Lists, Mysticism, and Magic* (Chicago: University of Chicago Press, 2008). See also Jack Goody, *The Domestication of the Savage Mind* (Cambridge: Cambridge University Press, 1977), 81.
75. Howe, *The Old English Catalogue Poems*, 20.
76. Pierre Bourdieu makes a similar point in "Social Space and the Genesis of 'Classes,'" in *Language and Symbolic Power*, ed. John B. Thompson (Cambridge, Mass.: Harvard University Press, 1991), 236.
77. Howe, *The Old English Catalogue Poems*, 12.
78. On the idea of the "absolute Encyclopaedia . . . which accommodate the greatest possible quantity of learning in the arbitrary order provided by letters," see Michel Foucault, *The Order of Things: An Archaeology of the Human Sciences* (London: Routledge, 2002), 86. Eric Havelock was one of the first to explore the theoretical implications of this change. The "invention" of the (Greek) alphabet "effectively brought into being . . . prose recorded and preserved in quantity." *Origins of Western Literacy: Four Lectures Delivered at the Ontario Institute for Studies in Education, Toronto, March 25, 26, 27, 28, 1974* (Toronto: Ontario Institute for Studies in Education, 1976), 49. Citing Goody and Havelock (to which one might also add Ong) is not to diminish the importance of parallel technologies less directly connected to literacy nor to relegate them to a primitive past. For a critical view of the application of traditional theories of orality to South Asian history, see Christian Lee Novetzke, "History, Memory, and Other Matters of Life and Death," in *Shared Idioms, Sacred Symbols, and the Articulation of Identities in South Asia*, ed. Kelly Pemberton, and Michael Nijhawan (New York: Routledge, 2009), 224–225.
79. This emphasis on the letters as the universal organizing principle for knowledge leads, as a seemingly inevitable outcome, to the common practice of assigning denotative value to individual letters: Foucault, *The Order of Things*, 102. On the universalizing logic that connects phonetics with nationalism, see Friedrich A. Kittler, *Discourse Networks 1800/1900* (Stanford, Calif.: Stanford University Press, 1990), 35–36, 42–43.
80. Reproduced in *Court Character and Testimony in the NWP and Oudh* (1897), 50. Compare Rai, *A House Divided*, 276; Shamsur Rahman Faruqi, "Unprivileged Power:

The Strange Case of Persian (and Urdu) in Nineteenth-Century India," *Annual of Urdu Studies* 13 (1999).

81. On this, compare, e.g., Alex Weingrod, "Patrons, Patronage, and Political Parties," *Comparative Studies in Society and History* 10, no. 4 (1968): 377–400; Simon Digby, "The Sufi Shaikh as a Source of Authority in Medieval India," in *India's Islamic Traditions: 711-1750*, ed. Richard Maxwell Eaton (New Delhi: Oxford University Press, 2003); Simon Digby, "Before Timur Came: Provincialization of the Delhi Sultanate Through the Fourteenth Century," *Journal of the Economic and Social History of the Orient* 47, no. 3 (2004): 309–314.
82. Ronald Inden, "Orientalist Constructions of India," *Modern Asian Studies* 20, no. 3 (1986): 402–403, 428–429; Ramya Sreenivasan, "A South Asianist's Response to Lieberman's *Strange Parallels*," *Journal of Asian Studies* 70, no. 4 (2011): 983–993.
83. Alam, "Pursuit," 336, 341; Alam, "Culture and Politics of Persian," 149; Kinra, "This Noble Science"; Truschke, "Defining the Other." On the *sabk-i hindī* or Indian "style" of Persian poetry, see, e.g., Paul E. Losensky, *Welcoming Fighānī: Imitation and Poetic Individuality in the Safavid-Mughal Ghazal* (Costa Mesa, Calif.: Mazda, 1998), 193–249; Shamsur Rahman Faruqi, "A Stranger in the City: The Poetics of *Sabk-e Hindi*," *Annual of Urdu Studies* 19 (2004): 1–93; Rajeev Kinra, "Fresh Words for a Fresh World: *Tāzā-Gū'ī* and the Poetics of Newness in Early Modern Indo-Persian Poetry," *Sikh Formations* 3, no. 2 (2007): 125–149.
84. For interesting parallels in Sanskrit literature, see Yigal Bronner, *Extreme Poetry: The South Asian Movement of Simultaneous Narration* (New York: Columbia University Press, 2010), 16, 129–131. For European analogues, see, e.g., Rita Copeland, *Pedagogy, Intellectuals, and Dissent in the Later Middle Ages: Lollardy and Ideas of Learning* (New York: Cambridge University Press, 2001).
85. This has been more amply documented in scholarship on China. See, e.g., Michael Lackner et al., eds., *New Terms for New Ideas: Western Knowledge and Lexical Change in Late Imperial China* (Leiden: Brill, 2001). For global overviews, see Lydia He Liu, ed., *Tokens of Exchange: The Problem of Translation in Global Circulations* (Durham, N.C.: Duke University Press, 1999); Carol Gluck and Anna Lowenhaupt Tsing, eds., *Words in Motion: Toward a Global Lexicon* (Durham, N.C.: Duke University Press, 2009).
86. Baevskii, *Early Persian Lexicography*, 177–205.
87. James C. Scott, *Seeing Like a State: How Certain Schemes to Improve the Human Condition Have Failed* (New Haven, Conn.: Yale University Press, 1998), 11–22. This was not, however, a purely colonial innovation: Sumit Guha has demonstrated that "the fixing of identities and attributes was an important part of routine administration [under the Mughal state] at the Imperial and local levels, and it was often accompanied by enumeration." Sumit Guha, "The Politics of Identity and Enumeration in India c. 1600–1990," *Comparative Studies in Society and History* 45, no. 1 (2003): 153.
88. Anderson, *Imagined Communities*, 71–76.
89. See, e.g., Ulrike Stark, *An Empire of Books: The Naval Kishore Press and the Diffusion of the Printed Word in Colonial India* (Ranikhet: Permanent Black, Distributed by Orient Longman, 2007), esp. 45–49.
90. King, *One Language, Two Scripts*, 88–125; Alok Rai, *Hindi Nationalism* (Hyderabad: Orient Longman, 2001), 34–36.
91. Washbrook, " 'To Each a Language of His Own,' " 190.

92. Compare Haywood, *Arabic Lexicography*, 42, 68, 73; Baevskii, *Early Persian Lexicography*, 60; Mårten Söderblom Saarela, "Shape and Sound: Organizing Dictionaries in Late Imperial China," *Dictionaries: Journal of the Dictionary Society of North America* 35 (2014): 192.
93. This may have been the impetus for Mirzā 'Ġhālib' to produce his own *niṣāb*. Mirzā Asadullāh Ḳhān Ġhālib, *Fārsī Nāmah-i Kalān maᶜ Qādir Nāmah-i Ġhālib* (Bareily: Lālah Ramćarān Lāl Agarwāl Buk Sellar enḍ Pablishar, n.d.).
94. Javed Majeed, "Modernity's Script and a Tom Thumb Performance," in *Trans-colonial Modernities in South Asia*, ed. Michael S. Dodson and Brian A. Hatcher (London: Routledge, 2012), 103–111.
95. The expression *har das kos bolī badaltī hai* (every twenty miles the dialect/speech changes) or some variant is common throughout northern India. See Washbrook, " 'To Each a Language of His Own,' " 181.
96. On the different formal elements of the prologue in various Islamicate genres, see Behl and Doniger, *Love's Subtle Magic*, 30–58.
97. Joseph W. Reed Jr., "Noah Webster's Debt to Samuel Johnson," *American Speech* 37, no. 2 (1962): 95.
98. For a very general overview of plagiarism in English-language lexicography, see Robert Burchfield, "Dictionaries, New & Old: Who Plagiarizes Whom, Why & When?" *Encounter* 67 (1984): 10–19.
99. Ladislav Zgusta, *Lexicography Then and Now: Selected Essays* (Tübingen: Niemeyer, 2006), 296.
100. Gustave Lanson, "L'histoire littéraire et la sociologie," *Revue de Métaphysique et de Morale* 12 (1904): 621–642; Pierre Bourdieu, *Language and Symbolic Power*, trans. Gino Raymond and Matthew Adamson (Cambridge, Mass.: Harvard University Press, 1991); Pierre Bourdieu, *The Field of Cultural Production: Essays on Art and Literature* (New York: Columbia University Press, 1993); Gustave Lanson et al., "Literary History and Sociology," *PMLA* 110 (1995): 220–235.
101. Kittler, *Discourse Networks*.
102. Mīr Taqī Mīr, *Nikāt al-Shuᶜarā* (Aurangabad: Anjuman-i Taraqqī-yi Urdū, 1935), 1.
103. Imre Bangha, "Rekhta: Poetry in Mixed Language: The Emergence of Khari Boli Literature in North India," in *Before the Divide: Hindi and Urdu Literary Culture*, ed. Francesca Orsini (New Delhi: Orient BlackSwan, 2010), 24–29.
104. On the dominance of poetry over prose in the medieval Persian literary corpus, see Baevskii, *Early Persian Lexicography*, 29–30. On the quotation of poetry in Persian dictionaries, see ibid., 164–171.
105. Alṭāf Ḥusain Ḥālī, "Farhang-i Āṣafiyah," in *Urdū Luġhat: Yādgārī Maẓāmīn*, ed. Abūlḥasanāt (Karachi: Unikarians International, 2010), 59–60.
106. On this term, see Anderson, *Imagined Communities*, 37–46. Recent monographs that add nuance to Anderson's suggestive formulations in the context of northern Indian print culture include Francesca Orsini, *The Hindi Public Sphere 1920–1940: Language and Literature in the Age of Nationalism* (New Delhi: Oxford University Press, 2002); Stark, *Empire of Books*; Farina Mir, *The Social Space of Language: Vernacular Culture in British Colonial Punjab* (Berkeley: University of California Press, 2010).
107. See Manu Goswami, *Producing India: From Colonial Economy to National Space* (Chicago: University of Chicago Press, 2004).
108. Anderson, *Imagined Communities*, 197.

109. This framework is developed in Karl Wolfgang Deutsch, *Nationalism and Social Communication: An Inquiry Into the Foundations of Nationality* (Cambridge, Mass.: MIT Press, 1953). Paul R. Brass applied this model to the postcolonial South Asian context in *Language, Religion, and Politics in North India* (London: Cambridge University Press, 1974), 3–46. For a valuable critique, see Francis Robinson, "Nation Formation: The Brass Thesis and Muslim Separatism," *Journal of Commonwealth & Comparative Politics* 15, no. 3 (1977): 215–230. King's work usefully elaborates and qualifies the conclusions of Brass with new data and discussion of additional literary sources. See King, *One Language, Two Scripts.*

2. 1700: BETWEEN MICROHISTORY AND MACROSTRUCTURES

1. Sayyid ʿAbdullāh, "Muqaddamah," in *Nawādir al-Alfāẕ & Ġharāʾib al-Luġhāt* (Karachi: Anjuman-i Taraqqī-yi Urdū Pākistān, 1951), i.
2. On the limited biographical information that may be gleaned on ʿAbdul Wāsĕʿ's career, see ibid., 3–4.
3. In light of this and other apparently precolonial examples of vernacular lexicography, Washbrook's claim that "there were no dictionaries or lexicographies of the spoken vernaculars prior to colonial times" requires revision. David Washbrook, " 'To Each a Language of His Own': Language, Culture, and Society in Colonial India," in *Language, History, and Class*, ed. P. J. Corfield (Oxford: Blackwell, 1991), 181.
4. Sirājuddīn ʿAlī Ḵhān Ārzū and ʿAbdul Wāsĕʿ Hāṅswī, *Nawādir al-Alfāẕ & Ġharāʾib al-Luġhāt* (Karachi: Anjuman-i Taraqqī-yi Urdū Pākistān, 1951), 248–249.
5. ʿAbdullāh, "Muqaddamah," 3.
6. For a good working definition of the term *dictionary*, see C. C. Berg, *Report on the Need for Publishing Dictionaries Which Do Not To-Date Exist, Prepared by the International Academic Union* (Conseil International de la Philosophie et des Sciences Humaines, 1960), 4. Cited in Ladislav Zgusta, *Manual of Lexicography* (Prague: Academia Mouton, 1971), 197. On the debates regarding the correspondence of the technical terms *farhang* and *luġhat/luġhāt* to this or other normative notions of the signification of the term *dictionary*, see chapters 4 and 5 below.
7. John Borthwick Gilchrist, *A Dictionary, English and Hindoostanee, in Which the Words are Marked with Their Distinguishing Initials; as Hinduwee, Arabic, and Persian, Whence the Hindoostanee, or What is Vulgarly, but Improperly Called the Moor Language, is Evidently Formed* (Calcutta, 1787), 1:vii. This work was published in installments between 1787 and 1790. The dictionary was republished in 1798 as part of a set that included his dictionary, his 1796 grammar, and a new work, entitled *The Oriental Linguist.* Richard Steadman-Jones, *Colonialism and Grammatical Representation: John Gilchrist and the Analysis of the "Hindustani" Language in the Late Eighteenth and Early Nineteenth Centuries* (Oxford: Blackwell, 2007), 74–77.
8. For contrasting views of the importance of the College of Fort William in promulgating new forms of prose literature in Urdu, see Ram Babu Saksena, *A History of Urdu literature* (Allahabad: R. N. Lal, 1940), 239–256; Shaista Akhtar Banu (Begum Ikramullah) Suhrawardy, *A Critical Survey of the Development of the Urdu Novel and Short Story* (London: Longmans, Green, 1945), 13–22; Muhammed Sadiq, *A History of Urdu Literature*, 2nd ed. (Delhi: Oxford, 1984), 290–291. Compare Amrit Rai, *A House*

Divided: The Origin and Development of Hindi/Hindavi (Delhi: Oxford University Press, 1984), 8–13; Alok Rai, *Hindi Nationalism* (Hyderabad: Orient Longman, 2001), 22–23.

9. Gilchrist, *Dictionary*, 1:vii.
10. Ibid.
11. Ibid.
12. Ibid.
13. Barring a few experiments, mostly in producing utilitarian works of a devotional nature, comparatively little Hindi-Urdu prose was being written at that time. Mehr Afshan Farooqi, "Changing Literary Patterns in Eighteenth-Century North India: Quranic Translations and the Development of Urdu Prose," in *Before the Divide: Hindi and Urdu Literary Culture*, ed. Francesca Orsini (New Delhi: Orient BlackSwan, 2010).
14. Gilchrist, *Dictionary*, 1:vii–viii.
15. For an overview, see Ḥāfiẓ Maḥmūd Sherānī, ed. *Ḥifẓ al-Lisān (maʿrūf ba-nām-i Ḳhāliq Bārī)* (Delhi: Anjuman-i Taraqqī-yi Urdū, 1944); Ṣafdar Āh, *Amīr Ḳhusrau baḥaiśiyat-i Hindī Shāʿir: Naẓariyah-yi Maḥmūd Shīrānī ke Tanqīdī Muṭālaʿah ke sāth* (Bombay: ʿUlūmī Buk Ḍipo, 1966); Gyan Chand Jain, "Ameer Khusrau and Khari Boli," in *Life, Times & Works of Amīr Khusrau Dehlavi*, ed. Zoe Ansari (New Delhi: National Amīr Khusrau Society, 1975); Gopī Ćand Nārang, ed. *Amīr Ḳhusrau kā Hinduwī Kalām: maʿ nusḳhahah-yi Barlin, Żaḳhīrah-yi Ishpringar* (Delhi: Ejūkeshanal Pablishing Hāʾūs, 1987), 126–132.
16. See, for example, Pandit Braj Vallabh Mishra, *An English-Hindi Vocabulary in Verse*, 2nd ed. (Calcutta: Gunsindhu Press, 1902); Ahmed-uddin Khan, *The East and West Khaliq Baree* (Moradabad: Afẓal al-Muṭābiʿ Press, 1906).
17. The text is reproduced, albeit without the glossary, in M. Ziauddin, *A Grammar of the Braj Bhākhā by Mirzā Khān (1676)* (Calcutta: Visva-Bharati Book-Shop, 1935). For discussions of this work and its context in the early development of a philology of Hindvi, see R. S. McGregor, *The Formation of Modern Hindi as Demonstrated in Early Hindi Dictionaries* (Amsterdam: Koninklijke Nederlandse Akademie van Wetenschappem, 2000), 7, 26–29; R. S. McGregor, "The Progress of Hindi, Part 1: The Development of a Transregional Idiom," in *Literary Cultures in History: Reconstructions from South Asia*, ed. Sheldon I. Pollock (Berkeley: University of California Press, 2003), 942–944; Arthur Dale Dudney, "A Desire for Meaning: Khan-i Arzu's Philology and the Place of India in the Eighteenth-Century Persianate World" (PhD diss., Columbia University, 2013), 276–277. See also Tej K. Bhatia, *A History of the Hindi Grammatical Tradition: Hindi-Hindustani Grammar, Grammarians, History, and Problems* (Leiden: Brill, 1987), 17–21.
18. McGregor, *The Formation of Modern Hindi*, 27; McGregor, "Progress of Hindi, Part 1," 943–944.
19. See Gilchrist, *Dictionary*, 1:ii, v. For a discussion of the terms *cant* and *jargon* as applied to the South Asian context, see especially Javed Majeed, " 'The Jargon of Indostan': An Exploration of Jargon in Urdu and East India Company English," in *Languages and Jargons: Contributions to a Social History of Language*, ed. Peter Burke and Roy Porter (Cambridge, Mass.: Polity, 1995), 196. For a more general overview of British attitudes toward Indian languages in late eighteenth-century Calcutta, see T. W. Clark, "The Languages of Calcutta, 1760–1840," *Bulletin of the School of Oriental and African Studies, University of London* 18, no. 3, In Honour of J. R. Firth (1956): 453–474; Bernard S. Cohn, "The Command of Language and the Language of Command," *Subaltern Studies* 4 (1985): 276–329.

20. John Borthwick Gilchrist, *The General East India Guide and Vade Mecum: For the Public Functionary, Government Officer, Private Agent, Trader, or Foreign Sojourner, in British India, and the Adjacent Parts of Asia Immediately Connected with the Honourable the East India Company* (London, 1825), 578–579.
21. William Jones, *The Works of Sir William Jones* (London, 1807), 3:34.
22. Rai, *Hindi Nationalism*, 26; Steadman-Jones, *Colonialism and Grammatical Representation*, 47–57.
23. Rita Raley, "A Teleology of Letters; or, From a 'Common Source' to a Common Language," in *Romantic Circles Praxis Series* (2000), http://www.rc.umd.edu/praxis/containment/raley/raley.html.
24. Frances W. Pritchett, personal communication, April 2010.
25. Gilchrist, *Dictionary*, 1:iv.
26. Ibid., 5.
27. On Gilchrist's self-depiction as a "lone traveller" producing works "in isolation, demanding a journey both physical and mental away from the centres of colonial power and into the 'unknown,'" see Richard Steadman-Jones, "Lone Travellers: The Construction of Originality and Plagiarism in Colonial Grammars of the Late Eighteenth and Early Nineteenth Centuries," in *Plagiarism in Early Modern England*, ed. Paulina Kewes (Basingstoke: Palgrave Macmillan, 2003).
28. The conflation of the Persian place name "Hindustan" with a primarily English term for a language is analogous to what occurs with another term, *urdū*, to be discussed at greater length in later sections.
29. John Borthwick Gilchrist, *The Oriental Linguist, an Easy and Familiar Introduction to the Popular Language of Hindoostan* (Calcutta, 1798), i. Cited in Shamsur Rahman Faruqi, *Early Urdu Literary Culture and History* (New Delhi: Oxford University Press, 2001), 32. Gilchrist's statement finds an uncanny echo in the assertion, recorded in the middle of the twentieth century, regarding Scotland in years that followed the 1707 union as a "submergence in the political-economic system of England . . . combined with a flourishing, distinctive life in . . . the social superstructure." George Elder Davie, *The Democratic Intellect: Scotland and Her Universities in the Nineteenth Century* (Edinburgh: Edinburgh University Press, 1961), xv. Cited in John M. Mackenzie, "Essay and Reflection: On Scotland and the Empire," *International History Review* 15, no. 4 (1993): 732.
30. On the official company view of "Hindoostanee" as "the universal colloquial language throughout India, and therefore of the most general utility," see M. Atique Siddiqi, *Origins of Modern Hindustani Literature; Source Material: Gilchrist Letters* (Aligarh: Naya Kitab Ghar, 1963), 97.
31. "Empire and National Identities: The Case of Scotland," *Transactions of the Royal Historical Society (Sixth Series)* 8, no. 1 (1998): 221.
32. Nigel Leask, "Imperial Scots [Review of T. M. Devine, *Scotland's Empire, 1600–1815*]," *History Workshop Journal* 59 (2005): 267.
33. For an overview of the class composition and anxieties of Scottish soldiers and administrators and of the antagonism between them and their English compatriots, see G. J. Bryant, "Scots in India in the Eighteenth Century," *Scottish Historical Review* 64, no. 177 (1985): 22–41.
34. Peter James Marshall, "Review of *A European Experience of the Mughal Orient: The I'jaz-i Arsalani (Persian Letters, 1773–1779) of Antoine-Louis-Henri Polier* (review no. 255),"

Reviews in History (2002), http://www.history.ac.uk/reviews/review/255; Sanjay Subrahmanyam, "The Career of Colonel Polier and Late Eighteenth-Century Orientalism," *Journal of the Royal Asiatic Society (Third Series)* 10, no. 1 (2000): 47.

35. For the fascinating account of the efforts made by another Scottish lexicographer of "Hindustani" to acquire English in his highland homeland, see Duncan Forbes, *Sketch of the Early Life of Duncan Forbes, LL.D. . . . Written by Himself, for the Perusal of His Father in America.* (London, 1859), 1–6.
36. C. A. Bayly, *Empire and Information: Intelligence Gathering and Social Communication in India, 1780–1870* (Cambridge: Cambridge University Press, 1996), 292. On Gilchrist's childhood and early adult life, see Steadman-Jones, *Colonialism and Grammatical Representation*, 64–68.
37. Gilchrist, *Dictionary*, 1:xlii. For other statements in Gilchrist's introduction that are broadly favorable to the Scottish pronunciation of English and Hindustani, see, e.g., ibid., 21, 33, 34, 43.
38. Ibid., vii.
39. Gilchrist, *General East India Guide*, 575, 578, 580.
40. Gilchrist, *Dictionary*, 1:viii.
41. In an effort to expand the range of terms, Gilchrist resorted to explaining words that appeared in Samuel Johnson's *Dictionary of the English Language* "to a number of learned Hindoostanees, who furnished the synonymous vocables in their own speech, and these were of course, successively inserted throughout the whole lexicon." Ibid., 1:xiv.
42. Gilchrist, *General East India Guide*, 581.
43. For a corrective to this mistaken view, see Farooqi, "Changing Literary Patterns."
44. For a brief biography, see Mirzā Asadullāh Ḳhān Ġhālib, *Urdu Letters of Mirzā Asadu'llāh Ḳhān Ġhālib*, trans. Daud Rahbar (Albany: State University of New York Press, 1987), 448.
45. Muṣṭafā Ḳhān Sheftah, *Gulshan-i be Ḳhār: Fārsī*, trans. Ḥamīdah Ḳhātūn (New Delhi: Qaumī Kaunsil barā'e Furoġh-i Urdū, 1998), 252. From an Urdu translation of the original Persian.
46. Garcin de Tassy, *Histoire de la littérature hindouie et hindoustani* (Paris, 1870), 1:93–94.
47. Ibid.
48. Sheftah, *Gulshan-i be Ḳhār*, 252.
49. Pierre Bourdieu, "The Field of Cultural Production; or: The Economic World Reversed," in *The Field of Cultural Production: Essays on Art and Literature*, ed. Randal Johnson (New York: Columbia University Press, 1993), 29.
50. Susanne Janssen, "The Empirical Study of Careers in Literature and the Arts," in *The Psychology and Sociology of Literature: In Honor of Elrud Ibsch*, ed. Dick Schram and Gerard Steen (Philadelphia: J. Benjamins, 2001), 349.
51. Pierre Bourdieu, "The Market of Symbolic Goods," *Poetics* 14, no. 1–2 (1985): 13–44.
52. Pierre Bourdieu, "The Market of Symbolic Goods," in *The Field of Cultural Production: Essays on Art and Literature*, ed. Randal Johnson (New York: Columbia University Press, 1993), 115. An earlier version appears in *Poetics* 14, no. 1–2 (1985): 17.
53. Paul DiMaggio, "Classification in Art," *American Sociological Review* 52, no. 4 (1987): 449–451.
54. Janssen, "Empirical Study of Careers," 326.
55. Muzaffar Alam, *The Crisis of Empire in Mughal North India: Awadh and the Punjab, 1707–48* (Delhi: Oxford University Press, 1986), 141.

56. Mehrdad Shokoohy and Natalie H. Shokoohy, *Ḥiṣār-i Fīrūza: Sultanate and Early Mughal Architecture in the District of Hisar, India*, Monographs on Art, Archaeology, and Architecture, South Asian Series (London, 1988), 81.
57. The sufi *melās* held in or near the town are described in ibid., 88–89, 98–99; P. J. Fagan, *Reprint of Hissar District Gazetteer, 1892* (Chandigarh: Gazetteers Organisation, Revenue Department, Haryana, 1997), 83.
58. Shokoohy and Shokoohy, 10, 97–109.
59. Ibid., 83–84.
60. For a historical account of the construction of the canal, prepared in Persian a century after the fact, see Shokoohy and Shokoohy's English translation of a passage from the *Tārīḵh-i Mubārak Shāhī* in their *Ḥiṣār-i Fīrūza*, 7–8. See also Yaḥiyā ibn Aḥmad ibn ʿAbdullāh Sīrhindī, *The Tārīḵh-i-Mubārakshāhī*, trans. Henry Beveridge (New Delhi: Low Price, 1996), 130. Irfan Habib offers evidence that portions of a canal had been carrying water past Hansi since the eighth century, if not earlier. Irfan Habib, *The Agrarian System of Mughal India, 1556–1707* (New Delhi: Oxford University Press, 1999), 33–34.
61. Stephen P. Blake, *Shahjahanabad: The Sovereign City in Mughal India, 1639–1739* (Cambridge: Cambridge University Press, 1991), 64. Habib (*Agrarian System*, 35) is skeptical of this work actually having been completed, suggesting instead that the plans were not put into action, at least not during the reign of Shah Jahan.
62. Habib, *Agrarian System*, 301.
63. Fagan, *Hissar District Gazetteer*, 57.
64. Ibid., 36. On the life of Shahdād Ḳhān, see Nawwab Ṣamṣām-ud-Daula Shāh Nawāz Khān Awrangābādī Shāhnawāz and ibn Shāhnawāz Abd al-Ḥayy, *The Maāthir-ul-umarā: Being Biographies of the Muhammādan and Hindu Officers of the Timurid Sovereigns of India from 1500 to About 1780 AD*, trans. H Beveridge (Calcutta: Asiatic Society, 1952), 2:747, 750.
65. See Shāhnawāz and Abd al-Ḥayy, *The Maāthir-ul-umarā*, 2:47.
66. C. A. Bayly, *Rulers, Townsmen, and Bazaars: North Indian Society in the Age of British Expansion, 1770–1870* (New Delhi: Oxford University Press, 1993), 88.
67. Fagan, *Hissar District Gazetteer*, 21.
68. Ibid., 22; Bayly, *Rulers, Townsmen, and Bazaars*, 88.
69. Fagan, *Hissar District Gazetteer*, 22.
70. Shokoohy and Shokoohy, *Ḥiṣār-i Fīrūza*, 4.
71. Dara Nusserwanji Marshall, *Mughals in India: A Bibliographical Survey of Manuscripts* (London: Mansell, 1985), 28.
72. As recorded for Rampur MSS 2614J, 2615, and 2616. This text was also printed in the margins of ʿAbdul Wāsĕʿ Hāṅswī, *Risālah-yi Jān Pahcān* (Kanpur, 1851). See also Aloys Sprenger, *A Catalogue of the Bibliotheca Orientalis Sprengeriana* (Giessen, 1857), 85.
73. As recorded for Asiatic Society of Bengal Persian Society Collection MS 1477. See Wladimir Ivanow, *Concise Descriptive Catalogue of the Persian Manuscripts in the Collection of the Asiatic Society of Bengal* (Calcutta: The Asiatic Society, 1924; repr. 1985), 693.
74. See, e.g., Heinrich Ferdinand Blochmann, "Contributions to Persian Lexicography," *Journal of the Royal Asiatic Society of Bengal* 37, no. 1 (1868): 20–24; Hermann Ethé, *Catalogue of Persian Manuscripts in the Library of the India Office* (Oxford: Clarendon, 1937), 2:1349.

75. Blochmann, "Contributions," 24.
76. Copies of these are available in the British Library. Regarding the commentary on the *Būstān*, Ethé informs us that "this copy [I.O. Islamic 530] was finished after a careful collation by Muhammad Nasir, the son of Sayyid Lutf-allah, who was also an inhabitant of Hansi, the 8th of Safar, A.H. 1140 (A.D. 1727, Sept. 25)." *Persian MSS in the India Office*, 2:687. This colophon has played an important part in helping to date ʿAbdul Wāsĕʿ to the seventeenth century.
77. ʿAbdullāh, "Muqaddamah," 6.
78. Numerous manuscript editions of the *Ṣamad Bārī/Jān Pahcān* exist. See, e.g., the late eighteenth-century MS Delhi Persian 925a and the early nineteenth-century MS Delhi Persian 524B described in Salim al-Din Quraishi and Ursula Sims-Williams, *Catalogue of the Urdu Manuscripts in the India Office Library* (London: India Office Library and Records, 1978), 42–43; Bilgrami, "Catalogue of the Persian Delhi MSS," British Library TS (n.d.), 379. An incomplete copy, MS Urdu 57e, is noted under the title *Ṣamad Bārī* by James Fuller Blumhardt, *Catalogue of the Hindustani Manuscripts in the Library of the India Office* (London: Oxford University Press, 1926), 133. It has appeared at least twice in nineteenth-century lithographed editions. See *Fārsī Nāmah, Wāḥid Bārī, Ṣamad Bārī, and Allāh Bārī* (Lahore, 1845); Hāṅswī, *Risālah-yi Jān Pahcān*; James Fuller Blumhardt, *Catalogue of the Library of the India Office: Hindustani Books*, 3 vols., vol. 2, part 2 (London: India Office Library, 1900), 115.
79. See Walter N. Hakala, "The Authorial Problem in the *Ḵẖāliq Bārī* of 'Ḵẖusrau,'" *Indian Economic & Social History Review* 51, no. 4 (2014): 481–496.
80. Each hemistich takes the syntactical form of (1) Arabic term—(2) Persian term—(3) Hindvi term—(4) Imperative verb.
81. Āh, *Amīr Ḳhusrau*, 72.
82. ʿAbdullāh, "Muqaddamah," 6.
83. John Child and Janet Fulk, "Maintenance of Occupational Control: The Case of Professions," *Work and Occupations* 9, no. 2 (1982): 155. Cited in Janssen, "Empirical Study of Careers," 334.
84. Ibid.
85. See, e.g., Qāẓī ʿAbdul Wadūd, *Farhang-i Aṣifiyyah par Tabṣirah* (Patna: Khuda Bakhsh Oriental Public Library, 1981); Gopī Ćand Nārang, ed., *Luġhat Nawīsī ke Masāʾil* (New Delhi: Māhnāmah-i Kitāb Numā, 1985); Shamsur Rahman Faruqi, "Some Problems of Urdu Lexicography," *Annual of Urdu Studies* 7 (1990): 21–30.
86. See the helpful differentiation of *institutional* and *discursive* spaces in Francesca Orsini, *The Hindi Public Sphere 1920–1940: Language and Literature in the Age of Nationalism* (New Delhi: Oxford University Press, 2002), 89–91.
87. The oldest known manuscript of his varied prose and poetry dates from AD 1791/2. Shamsur Rahman Faruqi, "Burning Rage, Icy Scorn: The Poetry of Ja'far Zatalli," lecture under the auspices of the Hindi-Urdu Flagship, University of Texas at Austin, September 24, 2008, http://www.columbia.edu/itc/mealac/pritchett/00fwp/srf/srf_zatalli_2008.pdf.
88. ʿAbdul Wāsĕʿ's grammar, the *Risālah*, was based in part on the introductory essay in the *Farhang-i Rashīdī*. Ivanow, *Concise Descriptive Catalogue of the Persian Manuscripts in the Collection of the Asiatic Society of Bengal*, 693. On the possible sources available to ʿAbdul Wāsĕʿ in compiling the *Ġharāʾib al-Luġhāt*, see Dudney, "Desire for Meaning," 278.

89. "According to Wilensky, an occupation can be counted among the professions if it has the following characteristics: most practitioners have a full-time job; there are special institutes for vocational training as well as professional associations; the occupation is recognized and protected by the state and it has a code of ethics." Janssen, "Empirical Study of Careers," 335. See H. L. Wilensky, "The Professionalization of Everyone?" *American Journal of Sociology* 70 (1964): 137–158. On the professionalization of Persian poets in ninth/fifteenth-century Timurid Iran and Afghanistan, see Paul E. Losensky, *Welcoming Fighānī: Imitation and Poetic Individuality in the Safavid-Mughal Ghazal* (Costa Mesa, Calif.: Mazda, 1998), 140–144.
90. Janssen, "Empirical Study of Careers," 341.
91. The MSS consulted by Sayyid ʿAbdullāh in his edition of the *Nawādir al-Alfāẕ* are listed in ʿAbdullāh, "Muqaddamah," 43–44. See also Bilgrami, "Catalogue of the Persian Delhi MSS," 233. It does not appear that he was able to consult the Rampur MSS 2543 and 2544. ʿAbdullāh, "Muqaddamah," 44. In 2008, I was informed that Rampur MS 2429B was "unavailable." Rampur MS 2544 was completed in 23 Ẕī al-Ḥijjā AH 1281 (May 19, 1865). Additional MSS (J.H. 135 and J.H. 136) are held at the Maulana Azad Library of Aligarh Muslim University.
92. C. A. Bayly, *Empire and Information: Intelligence Gathering and Social Communication in India, 1780–1870* (New Delhi: Cambridge University Press, 1999), 182. Nile Green's recent work adds new insights into the expansion of the Mughal bureaucracy and a preprint community of readers. Nile Green, "The Uses of Books in a Late Mughal *Takiyya:* Persianate Knowledge Between Person and Paper," *Modern Asian Studies* 44, no. 2 (2010): 241–265.
93. This is the same term—and one of the ninety-nine divine epithets—that appears in the author's name.
94. Roland Barthes and Honoré de Balzac, *S/Z*, trans. Richard Miller (New York: Hill and Wang, 1974), 4.
95. There is some controversy about Ārzū's year of birth. Rehanna Khatoon has established on the basis of reliable evidence that it must have been in AH 1099, though more recent sources persist in using the date AH 1101. A discussion of this controversy may be found in *Ahwāl o Āṡar-i Ḵhān-i Ārzū* (Delhi: Indo-Persian Society, 1987), 14; Rehanna Khatoon, "Introduction," in *Muṣmir*, ed. Rehanna Khatoon (Karachi: Institute of Central and West Asian Studies, 1991), 6–7. I direct the reader to the sketch of Ārzū's life that appears in Arthur Dudney's masterful PhD dissertation, "Desire for Meaning," 31–38. For a listing of extant manuscripts of his work, see Marshall, *Mughals in India*, 81–83.
96. See, for example, Abu Lais Siddiqi, "Muthmir: A Linguistic Analysis," in *Muthmir*, ed. Rehanna Khatoon (Karachi: Institute of Central and West Asian Studies, 1991), vii; Nabi Hadi, *Dictionary of Indo-Persian Literature* (New Delhi: Indira Gandhi National Centre for the Arts, 1995), 88.
97. For an overview of the primary source material, see Mohamad Tavakoli-Targhi, *Refashioning Iran: Orientalism, Occidentalism, and Historiography* (Basingstoke: Palgrave, 2001), 23–31. This has been expanded and updated by Arthur Dudney in "Desire for Meaning," 112–131.
98. Charles Pierre Henri Rieu, *Catalogue of the Persian Manuscripts in the British Museum* (London, 1876), 1:1030a; Ḥāfiẓ Maḥmūd Sherānī, "Dībāćah-i Awwal," in *Ḥifẓ al-Lisān*

(maʿrūf ba-nām-i Ḵhāliq Bārī), ed. Ḥāfiẓ Maḥmūd Sherānī (Delhi: Anjuman-i Taraqqī-yi Urdū, 1944), 24; C. M. Naim, "Introduction," in *Zikr-i Mir: The Autobiography of the Eighteenth-Century Mughal Poet, Mir Muhammad Taqi 'Mir', 1723–1810*, ed. C. M. Naim (New Delhi: Oxford University Press, 1999), 7–8.

99. *Zawāʾd al-Fawāʾid*: A list "of Persian verbs and the abstract nouns derived from them." Khatoon, "Introduction," 29.

100. *Sirāj al-Luġhāt*: Ārzū's most important work, covering the Persian poetic corpus lexically to Jāmī (d. 1492). In it, Ārzū comments on and critiques the earlier *Burhān-i Qāṭĕʿ* (completed in 1651 by the Persian émigré Muḥammad Ḥusain b. Ḵhalaf Tabrīzī 'Burhān' and dedicated to ʿAbdullāh Quṭb Shāh of Golconda in the Deccan) and the *Farhang-i Rashīdī* (completed in 1653 by Mullā ʿAbdul Rashīd of Ṭhaṭhah in Sindh). The first "critical dictionary," it was begun under the auspices of Shāh Jahān and completed when the latter was the prisoner of Aurangzeb. Ārzū, in the preface to this work, describes the affinity between ancient Persian and Sanskrit. Blochmann, "Contributions," 18–24; Muḥammad Dabīr Siyāqī, "Borhān-e Qāṭeʿ," in *Encyclopædia Iranica*, ed. Ehsan Yarshater (1989), http://www.iranicaonline.org/articles/borhan-e-qate.

101. Dudney, "Desire for Meaning," 72, 207–208.

102. Faruqi, "Some Problems of Urdu Lexicography," 27; Dudney, "Desire for Meaning," 43–47.

103. The *Mirʾāt al-Iṣṭilāḥ* (1158/1745–46) of Ānand Rām 'Muḵhliṣ', the *Bahār-i ʿAjam* (1162/1748–49) of Tek Chand 'Bahār', and the *Muṣṭalaḥāt al-Shuʿarāʾ* (1767) of Lālah Siyālkoṭī Mal 'Wārastah' were each massive Persian dictionaries produced by prominent Hindu authors. The *Mirʾāt al-Iṣṭilāḥ* compiled by Muḵhliṣ was "an attempt to improve the falling standard of Persian in India," taking the form of "an alphabetically arranged compendium of contemporary Persian usage based on standard works and conversations with newly arrived Iranians." See B. Ahmad, "Ānand Rām Moḵleṣ," in *Encyclopedia Iranica Online*, ed. Ehsan Yarshater (1985), http://www.iranicaonline.org/articles/anand-ram-mokles. For more detail on the life and works of Muḵhliṣ, see George McLeod James, "Anand Ram Mukhlis: His Life and Works, 1695–1758" (PhD diss., University of Delhi, n.d.). James's chapter on the *Mirʾāt* (272–303) is of especial value. For a general discussion of the contributions of Hindus to Persian letters, see Saiyid ʿAbdullāh, *Adabiyāt-i Farsī meṅ Hindūʾoṅ kā Ḥiṣṣah* (Lahore: Majlis Taraqqī-yi Adab, 1967); Muzaffar Alam and Sanjay Subrahmanyam, "The Making of a Munshi," *Comparative Studies of South Asia Africa and the Middle East* 24, no. 2 (2004): 62; Stefano Pello, "Persian as Passe-Partout: The Case of Mīrzā ʿAbd al-Qādir Bīdil and His Hindu Disciples," in *Culture and Circulation: Literature in Motion in Early Modern India*, ed. Thomas de Bruijn and Allison Busch (Leiden: Brill, 2014).

104. Shamsur Rahman Faruqi, "Unprivileged Power: The Strange Case of Persian (and Urdu) in Nineteenth-Century India," *Annual of Urdu Studies* 13 (1999).

105. Khatoon, "Introduction," 14–17.

106. Blochmann, "Contributions," 27; Khatoon, "Introduction," 40–42; Faruqi, "Unprivileged Power," 17, 22; Dudney, "Desire for Meaning," 148–215.

107. Blochmann, "Contributions," 19–20; Khurshidul Islam and Ralph Russell, *Ghalib: Life and Letters* (New Delhi: Oxford University Press, 1994), 257–262; Faruqi, "Unprivileged Power," 29–30.

108. Faruqi, "Unprivileged Power," 26. 'Ġhālib' claimed to have studied for two years under ʿAbdul Ṣamad while a young teenager in Agra. Islam and Russell, *Ghalib: Life and Letters*, 25.
109. Faruqi, "Unprivileged Power," 26.
110. John Thompson Platts, *A Dictionary of Urdū, Classical Hindī, and English* (London, 1884), 209.
111. Francis Joseph Steingass, *A Comprehensive Persian-English Dictionary, Including the Arabic Words and Phrases to Be Met with in Persian Literature* (London, 1892), 924.
112. Ārzū and Hāṅswī, *Nawādir al-Alfāẓ*, 96. The year AH 1196 (AD 1781/2) that appears in one MS of the *Nawādir* must be a mistake since Ārzū's death had occurred decades earlier.
113. Ibid., 4.
114. The word *pānī* (water) is Indic.
115. A work on rhetoric, lithographed in Allahabad in 1830. Blochmann, "Contributions," 27.
116. *aġhāṣī* in Steingass, *Persian-English Dictionary*, 130.
117. Translated from the Persian. Original text in Sirājuddīn ʿAlī Ḳhān-i Ārzū, *Muṯẖmir* (Karachi: Institute of Central and West Asian Studies, 1991), 160–161. See also Stefano Pello, "Persiano e *hindī* nel *Musmir* di Sirāj al-Dīn ʿAlī Xān Ārzū," in *L'Onagro Maestro: Miscellanea di Fuochi Accesi per Gianroberto Scarcia in Occasione del Suo LXX Sadè*, ed. Rudy Favaro et al. (Venezia: Cafoscarina, 2004), 248–249.
118. Farooqi, "Changing Literary Patterns," 228.
119. Frances W. Pritchett, "A Long History of Urdu Literary Culture, Part 2: Histories, Performances, and Masters," in *Literary Cultures in History: Reconstructions from South Asia*, ed. Sheldon Pollock (Berkeley: University of California Press, 2003), 854.
120. For Arabic lexicography, compare John A. Haywood, *Arabic Lexicography: Its History, and Its Place in the General History of Lexicography* (Leiden: Brill, 1965); Kees Versteegh, *The Arabic Linguistic Tradition* (London: Routledge, 1997), 33, 39, 41, 168. For Persian, see Blochmann, "Contributions," 1–3; Solomon I. Baevskii, *Early Persian Lexicography: Farhangs of the Eleventh to the Fifteenth Centuries*, trans. N. Killian (Honolulu: University of Hawai'i Press, 2007), 69–116; Rajeev Kinra, "This Noble Science: Indo-Persian Comparative Philology, c. 1000–1800 CE," in *South Asian Texts in History: Critical Engagements with Sheldon Pollock*, ed. Yigal Bronner et al. (Ann Arbor, Mich.: Association for Asian Studies, 2011).
121. On the eighteenth-century use of Hindi-Urdu for Qurʾānic exegesis, see Farooqi, "Changing Literary Patterns," 231–33.
122. See Sherānī, "Dībāćah-i Awwal," 7–11. Compare with Masʿūd Hāshmī, *Urdū Luġhat Nawīsī kā Pas Manẓar* (Delhi: Maktabah-yi Jāmiʿah, 1997), 106–122.
123. For a brief outline of Urdu–Persian and English–Persian dictionaries, see Hāshmī, *Urdū Luġhat Nawīsī kā Pas Manẓar*, 124–147. For a valuable study of early Hindvi-Dutch works, see McGregor, *The Formation of Modern Hindi*.
124. Ḥāfiẓ Maḥmūd Sherānī, "Fārsī Zabān kī ek Qadīm Farhang meṅ Urdū Zabān kā ʿUnṣur," in *Maqālāt-i Ḥāfiẓ Maḥmūd Shīrānī*, ed. Maẓhar Maḥmūd Shīrānī (Lahore: Majlis-i Taraqqī-yi Urdū, 1987), 203.
125. This is the argument of Professor Nażīr Aḥmad in his "Preface," in *Farhang-i Lisān al-Shuʿarāʾ: bĕh Sāl-i 753–790 Hijrī, ʿAhd-i Fīrūz Shāh Tuġhlaq*, ed. Nażīr Aḥmad (New Delhi: Rāyzanī-yi Farhangī-yi Jumhūrī-yi Islāmī-yi Īrān, 1995), viii.

126. For examples, see Sherānī, "Fārsī Zabān kī ek Qadīm Farhang," 204.
127. Ibid., 203.
128. Ibid., 204. Emphasis added.
129. See, e.g., Ram Babu Saksena, *European & Indo-European Poets of Urdu & Persian* (Lucknow: Newul Kishore Press, 1941); ʿAbdullāh, *Adabiyāt-i Farsī meṅ Hindūʾoṅ kā Ḥiṣṣah*; Alam and Subrahmanyam, "The Making of a Munshi"; Rajeev Kinra, "Master and Munshi: A Brahman Secretary's Guide to Mughal Governance," *Indian Economic & Social History Review* 47, no. 4 (2010): 527–561.
130. Sumit Guha, "Transitions and Translations: Regional Power and Vernacular Identity in the Dakhan, 1500–1800," *Comparative Studies of South Asia, Africa, and the Middle East* 24, no. 2 (2004): 1092–1093. On this text, see also Madhukar Mangesh Patkar, *History of Sanskrit Lexicography* (New Delhi: Munshiram Manoharlal, 1981), 148–150.
131. Valerie Ritter, "Networks, Patrons, and Genres for Late Braj Bhasha Poets: Ratnakar and Hariaudh," in *Before the Divide: Hindi and Urdu Literary Culture*, ed. Francesca Orsini (New Delhi: Orient BlackSwan, 2010), 268.
132. See *Samekita Praśāsana Śabdāvalī, Āngrezī-Hindī Consolidated Glossary of Administrative Terms, English-Hindi* (New Delhi: Standing Commission for Scientific and Technical Terminology, Government of India, 1968), vii–viii.
133. Its terms are arranged according to their final radical in what is known as "rhyme order." See Haywood, *Arabic Lexicography*, 68.
134. Ārzū and Hāṅswī, *Nawādir al-Alfāẓ*, 5.
135. Lloyd William Daly, *Contributions to a History of Alphabetization in Antiquity and the Middle Ages* (Bruxelles: Latomus, 1967), 95.
136. Ibid., 89. On the new possibilities that accompanied the shift from parchment to paper, see ibid., 86.
137. Ārzū was able to acquire, through his friend and student Ānand Rām Muḵhliṣ, the patronage of such important figures as Nawāb Isḥāq Ḵhān, the Ḵhān-sāmān of the emperor Muḥammad Shāh, and his sons, Najm al-Daulah and Sālār Jang.
138. Sherānī, *Ḥifẓ al-Lisān*, 25–26.
139. "*ḍabbā* . . . s.m. A leathern vessel (for holding oil, *ghī*, &c.; syn. *kuppā*); a leather box; a soldier's pouch, cartridge-box;—(fig.) the chest." Platts, *Dictionary of Urdū*, 563.
140. "*shiqshiqat, shiqshiqa*, A substance resembling lights protruding from the mouth of a stallion camel in heat." Steingass, *Persian-English Dictionary*, 750.
141. Ārzū and Hāṅswī, *Nawādir al-Alfāẓ*, 248.
142. For a discussion and image of this behavior, see Mark Liberman, "Somali Words for Camel Spit," *Language Log* (2004), http://itre.cis.upenn.edu/~myl/languagelog/archives/000444.html.
143. Ārzū and Hāṅswī, *Nawādir al-Alfāẓ*, 248–249. Ārzū reproduces two additional meanings for the term: "an illness that occurs in children and elder men (*mardam-i kalān*) which they call 'tightness of breath' and 'shortness of breath'" and "a fragrance holder (*ḵhwushbū dān*), that is to say a perfumers tray (*ṭablahʾi ʿaṭṭār*)." The modern editor of the *Nawādir* notes that "Hāṅswī has the placed these three meanings under three different entries" scattered throughout the chapter devoted to words beginning with the letter ڈ *ḍāl*.
144. Iqtida Hasan, *Later Moghuls and Urdu Literature* (Lahore: Ferozsons, 1995), 98.
145. Faruqi, *Early Urdu Literary Culture*, 25.

146. ʿAbdullāh, "Muqaddamah," 9. For a discussion of this particular use of the term *urdū*, see also ibid., 33.
147. "*ṭulaʿat*, A mind that considers anything attentively; inclined to love; a woman who now peeps out and anon withdraws." Steingass, *Persian-English Dictionary*, 818.
148. "*Tulat* 1 Rejoicing greatly on any prospect. 2 (A woman) now peeping out, and then withdrawing herself." John Richardson, *A Dictionary, Persian, Arabic, and English* (Oxford, 1777), 1186.
149. The introduction of this work served as the basis of ʿAbdul Wāsĕʿ's grammar. The term also does not appear in the same author's *Muntaḳhab al-Luġhāt*, compiled in 1636–1637.
150. Faruqi, *Early Urdu Literary Culture*, 26.
151. Faruqi (ibid.) estimates that he began the dictionary sometime after 1747 and completed it in 1752. Internal evidence suggests that it was completed c. 1743. Since the *Nawādir* is almost entirely based, in terms of lexicon, on ʿAbdul Wāsĕʿ's earlier work and was not compiled, à la Gilchrist, viva voce or ex nihilo, or even from the collation of terms from literary sources (as was the case with the *Sirāj al-Luġhāt* and *Chirāġh-i Hidāyat*), I am of the opinion that it was prepared quite quickly, perhaps in less than a single year.
152. Ibid., 26–27; Blake, *Shahjahanabad*, 31. Shāh Jahān's son and successor, Aurangzeb, maintained his court and camp in Delhi until 1679. Jadunath Sarkar, *History of Aurangzeb* (Calcutta: M. C. Sarkar & Sons, 1912), 3:379.
153. Hameeda Naqvi, "Capital Cities of the Mughul Empire (1556–1803)," *Journal of the Pakistan Historical Society* 13, no. 1 (1965): 212–216.
154. Richardson, *A Dictionary, Persian, Arabic, and English.*
155. Compare, for example, the equivalents Breton provides for the English *Asthma* and *Hooping Cough* with those included under the entry *ḍabbā* from the *Nawādir* reproduced above. Peter Breton, *A Vocabulary of the Names of the Various Parts of the Human Body and of Medical and Technical Terms in English, Arabic, Persian, Hindee, and Sanscrit for the Use of the Members of the Medical Department in India* (Calcutta, 1825), 40–41.
156. The original statement states that it was copied "for me through H. Blochmann." I was unable to decipher the name corresponding with "me" that appears below this statement.
157. Henry Beveridge and Parvin Loloi, "Blochmann, Henry Ferdinand (1838–1878)," in *Oxford Dictionary of National Biography* (2004), http://www.oxforddnb.com/view/article/2659.
158. For a brief biographical sketch, see Henry Beveridge, "Dr. F. J. Steingass," *Journal of the Royal Asiatic Society* (1903): 654–655. Richardson, Johnson, and Steingass incorporated ʿAbdul Wāsĕʿ's definition of *ṭulaʿah* into their own dictionaries.
159. Heinrich Ferdinand Blochmann, "Hánsí," *Proceedings of the Asiatic Society of Bengal* (1877): 121.
160. Sirājuddīn ʿAlī Ḳhān-i Ārzū, "Nawádir-ul-alfáz," National Archives of India Fort William College MS 106 ACC No. 432, 1870.
161. For an overview of Elliot's contributions to the history of South Asia, see Tripta Wahi, "Henry Miers Elliot: A Reappraisal," *Journal of the Royal Asiatic Society of Great Britain and Ireland* 1 (1990): 64–90.
162. Compare this with the *Linguarum Totius Orbis Vocabularia Comparativa*, prepared from wordlists completed at the behest of Catherine the Great, empress of Russia,

by state dignitaries, interpreters, and other interested parties around the world. Discussed in Johannes Fabian, *Language and Colonial Power: The Appropriation of Swahili in the Former Belgian Congo, 1880–1938* (Berkeley: University of California Press, 1986), 1–2.

163. H. H. Wilson, *A Glossary of Judicial and Revenue Terms, and of Useful Words Occurring in Official Documents Relating to the Administration of the Government of British India, from the Arabic, Persian, Hindustání, Sanskrit, Hindí, Bengálí, Uṛiya, Maráṭhi, Guzaráthí, Telugu, Karnáta, Tamil, Malayálam, and Other Languages* (London, 1855), iii.
164. Henry Miers Elliot, *Supplement to the Glossary of Indian Terms* (Agra, 1845), v.
165. E. B. Cowell, "[Review] Memoirs on the History, Folk-Lore, and Distribution of the Races of the North Western Provinces of India," *The Academy* 1, no. 8 (1870): 215.
166. Wilson, *Glossary of Judicial and Revenue Terms*, iii.
167. Ibid., iv.
168. Ibid.
169. Ibid.
170. T. J. Turner and H. S. Boulderson, "Memorandum from the Sudder Board of Revenue, N.W.P., to the Secy. to the Govt., N.W.P.," in *Supplement to the Glossary of Indian Terms* (Agra, 1845), iv.
171. Cowell, "Memoirs on the History," 215. William Crooke, for example, was unable to acquire a copy of the 1845 edition for his 1879 *Glossary of North Indian Peasant Life*. See Shahid Amin, "Editor's Introduction," in *A Glossary of North Indian Peasant Life* (Delhi: Oxford University Press, 1989), xxiv n. 16.
172. Wilson, *Glossary of Judicial and Revenue Terms*; Cowell, "Memoirs on the History," 216.
173. Henry Miers Elliot and John Beames, *Memoirs on the History, Folk-Lore, and Distribution of the Races of the North Western Provinces of India: Being an Amplified Edition of the Original Supplemental Glossary of Indian Terms* (London, 1869), 1:iii. See also the scheme described by Elliot in *Supplement to the Glossary*, v.
174. William Crooke, *A Glossary of North Indian Peasant Life* (Delhi: Oxford University Press, 1989), xx. Compare Bernard S. Cohn, "The Census, Social Structure, and Objectification in South Asia in Culture and History of India," *Folk* 26 (1984): 34; Sudipta Kaviraj, "The Imaginary Institution of India," *Subaltern Studies* 7 (1992): 1–39; Sumit Guha, "The Politics of Identity and Enumeration in India c. 1600–1990," *Comparative Studies in Society and History* 45, no. 1 (2003): 148–151.
175. The details are offered by Wilson in *Glossary of Judicial and Revenue Terms*, iii. Grierson faced similar frustrations in his *Linguistic Survey of India*. See Javed Majeed, "What's in a (Proper) Name? Particulars, Individuals, and Authorship in the Linguistic Survey of India and Colonial Scholarship," in *Knowledge Production, Pedagogy, and Institutions in Colonial India*, ed. Indra Sengupta et al. (New York: Palgrave Macmillan, 2011).
176. Amin, "Editor's Introduction," xx.
177. George Abraham Grierson, *Bihār Peasant Life; Being a Discursive Catalog of the Surroundings of the People of That Province, with Many Illustrations from Photographs Taken by the Author* (Calcutta, 1885), 2.
178. Crooke, *A Glossary of North Indian Peasant Life*, xxvi.
179. Qāẓī ʿAbdul Wadūd, ed., *Ḳhudā Baḳhsh Saminār: Tadwīn-i Matn ke Masāʾil* (Patna: Khuda Bakhsh Oriental Public Library, 1982).
180. This is an error, probably deriving from the copyist who prepared Sayyid ʿAbdullāh's proofs. ʿAbdullāh describes his regrets concerning the preparation of the Persian

text: "In the orthography of Persian expressions I could not follow any rules. The reason for this is that to this day, in the Fārsī of Hindustan, nobody pays heed to these rules upon which today it perseveres. All of the manuscripts of the *Nawādir* follow these principles. Additionally, one will not find any copyist who follows this manner of orthography. . . . In addition to this, my drafts were written so many times and they have seen so many such vicissitudes that for this reason, in spite of the desire to try for the establishment of principles, I was not successful, and for this reason for the time being I will permit it to remain unsystematic, though were it possible that I be granted more time and opportunity to prepare a second edition, God willing, an attempt at placing Persian orthography on a basis of principles would be made." ʿAbdullāh, "Muqaddamah." The "vicissitudes" to which Sayyid ʿAbdullāh is obliquely referring is the violence and destruction that accompanied the displacement of millions of people during the partition of India and Pakistan, still in progress at the time of his writing.

181. Ārzū and Hāṅswī, *Nawādir al-Alfāẓ*, 48.

182. Steingass, *Persian-English Dictionary*, 77.

183. Dudney, "Desire for Meaning," 32–33. For more on Ārzū's connections with the Braj and Gwalior regions, see Khatoon, "Introduction," 6–14. For a similar statement, "the language of Gwalior which is the most eloquent of the languages of Hind" (*zabān-i gwāliyārī kĕh afṣaḥ zabān-hāʾe hind ast*), see Ārzū's entry for *aggal* in *Nawādir al-Alfāẓ*, 26. A discussion of Ārzū's valorization of Braj may be found in Tariq Rahman, "Urdu and the Muslim Identity: Standardization of Urdu in the Eighteenth and Early Nineteenth Centuries," *Annual of Urdu Studies* 25 (2010): 94.

184. The 1845 edition lists the headword using Gilchrist's Roman transcription scheme on the extreme left and a modified version of that introduced by Jones on the extreme right:

AEWARA	ایواره	ऐवारा	Aiwára

Elliot, *Supplement to the Glossary*, 3. Elliot's remarks on transcription are worth quoting in full: "In writing them [i.e., the terms of the *Glossary*] I have endeavored, as far as possible, to conform to the system of Gilchrist—or rather that modification of it in use in our Revenue Surveys—which certainly has the merit of enabling an Englishman to pronounce a word in such a manner as to make it easily comprehended by the natives of Hindoostan. Sir W. Jones' method is better suited to the learned; but since it is becoming of more general use, as our books and translations multiply, I have added a column for its admission; as far, at least, as respects the vowel system" (xvii).

185. Elliot and Beames, *Memoirs on the History*, 2:212.

186. In general, we find the 1884 definitions provided by Platts (*Dictionary of Urdū*, 61, 116, 876) to be more in conformity with those advocated by Ārzū:

P . . . *āgil* (also *agil*), s.m. Enclosure for sheep, sheepcote.
H . . . *aiwārā* (from *ewaṛ* and *wārā* = S. *wāṭakah*), s.m. A shed in a jungle for goats, sheep, or cattle.
H . . . *khaṛak*, or . . . *khiṛak*, s.m. Cow-house, cow-shed; sheep-pen;—pound (for cattle).

187. Elliot, *Supplement to the Glossary*, 40.

188. Tej K. Bhatia and Kazuhiko Machida, *The Oldest Grammar of Hindustānī: Contact, Communication, and Colonial Legacy* (Tokyo: Research Institute for Languages and Cultures of Asia and Africa, Tokyo University of Foreign Studies, 2008), 1:164–166. See also J. Ph. Vogel, "Joan Josua Ketelaar of Elbing, Author of the First Hindūstānī Grammar," *Bulletin of the School of Oriental Studies, University of London* 8, no. 2/3 (1936): 817–822.
189. See Majeed, "What's in a (Proper) Name?" See also Scott's discussion of the "creation of surnames": James C. Scott, *Seeing Like a State: How Certain Schemes to Improve the Human Condition Have Failed* (New Haven, Conn.: Yale University Press, 1998), 64–73.
190. Gilchrist, *General East India Guide*, 538.
191. ʿAbdullāh, "Muqaddamah," 10.
192. Ibid., 11.
193. Faruqi, *Early Urdu Literary Culture*, 24–32.
194. Platts, *Dictionary of Urdū*, 958; Edward William Lane, *An Arabic-English Lexicon, Derived from the Best and the Most Copious Eastern Sources* (London, 1885), 7:2667.
195. On the fundamental difficulties Urdu lexicographers have faced in defining what constitutes a word and, hence, what should and should not be entered in a dictionary, see Faruqi, "Some Problems of Urdu Lexicography," 21.
196. Walter N. Hakala, "A Sultan in the Realm of Passion: Coffee in Eighteenth-Century Delhi," *Eighteenth-Century Studies* 47, no. 4 (2014): 371–388.
197. Carla Rae Petievich, *Assembly of Rivals: Delhi, Lucknow, and the Urdu Ghazal* (Delhi: Manohar, 1992); Ali Jawad Zaidi, *A History of Urdu Literature* (New Delhi: Sahitya Akademi, 1993), 129–134; C. M. Naim and Carla Petievich, "Urdu in Lucknow/ Lucknow in Urdu," in *Lucknow: Memories of a City*, ed. Violette Graff (Delhi: Oxford University Press, 1997).

3. 1800: THROUGH THE VEIL OF POETRY

1. Christopher Rolland King, *One Language, Two Scripts: The Hindi Movement in Nineteenth-Century North India* (Bombay: Oxford University Press, 1994), 88–125; Tariq Rahman, *Language, Ideology, and Power: Language Learning Among the Muslims of Pakistan and North India* (Karachi: Oxford University Press, 2002), 198–233.
2. See, e.g., Nile Green, *Islam and the Army in Colonial India: Sepoy Religion in the Service of Empire* (Cambridge: Cambridge University Press, 2009), 143.
3. Anwar Moazzam, "Urdu Inshā: The Hyderābād Experiment, 1860–1948," in *Literacy in the Persianate World: Writing and the Social Order*, ed. Brian Spooner and William L. Hanaway (Philadelphia: University of Pennsylvania Museum of Archaeology and Anthropology, 2012). See also Nazir Ahmad Chaudhry, ed., *Development of Urdu as Official Language in the Punjab, 1849–1974* (Lahore: Punjab Govt. Record Office, 1977).
4. On this "Diploma Disease," see Ernest Gellner, *Nations and Nationalism* (Ithaca, N.Y.: Cornell University Press, 1983), 26–29.
5. For more on Fendall, see Henry Beveridge, "Old Places in Murshidabad (No. III)," *Calcutta Review* 96, no. 192 (1893): 233–234.
6. K. K. Datta, "Some Unpublished Documents Relating to the Conspiracy of Wazir Ali," *Bengal Past & Present* 55, no. 3–4 (1938): 148.

7. Ibid., 145–146. See also K. K. Datta, ed., *Selections from Unpublished Correspondence of the Judge-Magistrate and the Judge of Patna, 1790–1857* (Patna: Government of Bihar, 1954), 76.
8. Datta, *Selections from Unpublished Correspondence*, 76; Datta, "Some Unpublished Documents," 145–146.
9. See Datta, *Selections from Unpublished Correspondence*, 77. See also C. A. Bayly, *Empire and Information: Intelligence Gathering and Social Communication in India, 1780–1870* (Cambridge: Cambridge University Press, 1996), 95–96.
10. John Shore, "Secret Minutes of the Governor General dated the 13th January, 1798," Cleveland Public Library East India Company Manuscript Collection MS 091.92 Ea77M5.
11. John Shore Teignmouth, *The Private Record of an Indian Governor-Generalship* (Cambridge, Mass.: Harvard University Press, 1933), 166–167.
12. Barun De, "Foreword," in *The Rebel Nawab of Oudh: Revolt of Vizir Ali Khan, 1799*, by Aniruddha Ray (Calcutta: K. P. Bagchi & Co., 1990), ix.
13. Whose fame was such that he even made an appearance as "Cheyte Singh" in the 1844 short story "A Tale of the Ragged Mountains" by Edgar Allan Poe.
14. Aniruddha Ray, *The Rebel Nawab of Oudh: Revolt of Vizir Ali Khan, 1799* (Calcutta: K. P. Bagchi & Co., 1990), 6.
15. Though it does make its appearance. See Hamid Afaq Qureshi, "Had Wazir Ali Hatched an Anti-British All India Conspiracy in 1798?" *Proceedings of the Indian History Congress* 43 (1983): 560 n. 1. For a corrective revision to this approach, see Hamid Afaq Qureshi, *The Flickers of an Independent Nawabi: Nawab Wazir Ali Khan of Avadh*, 2 vols. (Lucknow: New Royal Book Co., 2002).
16. De, "Foreword," xi.
17. This is also the general argument, albeit with some significant ideological and methodological differences, that one finds in C. A. Bayly, *Rulers, Townsmen, and Bazaars: North Indian Society in the Age of British Expansion, 1770–1870* (New Delhi: Oxford University Press, 1993).
18. Qureshi, "All India Conspiracy," 563 n. 48.
19. De, "Foreword," x.
20. Consider, for example, the decisive role played by Gopinath, a Jaipur-based newswriter in the employ of the British. Qureshi, "All India Conspiracy," 555.
21. Datta, *Selections from Unpublished Correspondence*, 77; Datta, "Some Unpublished Documents," 146.
22. There is some debate as to the correct representation of the poet's *taḳhalluṣ* or nom de plume. While several *tażkirahs* have represented it as تپش *tapish*, an examination of the poet's own notebook reveals that he preferred to spell it طپش *ṭapish* (affliction, agitation, palpitation; heat, warmth). Najmul Islām, "Bayāẓ-i Mirzā Jān Ṭapish," *Nuqūsh* 108 (1967): 63. See also James Fuller Blumhardt, *Catalogue of the Hindi, Panjabi, and Hindustani Manuscripts in the Library of the British Museum* (London, 1899), 18. Both are stylistically correct and linguistically cognate. John Thompson Platts, *A Dictionary of Urdū, Classical Hindī, and English* (London, 1884), 309, 751.
23. On colonial efforts to standardize the transliteration of Indian names in Roman script, see Javed Majeed, "What's in a (Proper) Name? Particulars, Individuals, and Authorship in the Linguistic Survey of India and Colonial Scholarship," in *Knowledge*

Production, Pedagogy, and Institutions in Colonial India, ed. Indra Sengupta et al. (New York: Palgrave Macmillan, 2011).

24. ʿĀbid Raẓ Bedār, "Peshguftār," in *Shams al-Bayān fī Muṣṭalaḥāt al-Hindūstān* (Patna: Khuda Bakhsh Oriental Public Library, 1979), 3 n. 1. For synthesis of the *taẕkirah* notices, see Aloys Sprenger, *A Catalogue of the Arabic, Persian, and Hindústány Manuscripts, of the Libraries of the King of Oudh, Compiled Under the Orders of the Government of India* (Calcutta, 1854), 1:297; Garcin de Tassy, *Histoire de la littérature Hindouie et Hindoustani* (Paris, 1870), 3:219–221.
25. See Sprenger, *Oudh Catalogue*, 1:285–86; de Tassy, *Histoire*, 3:86–87.
26. Sprenger, *Oudh Catalogue*, 1:298. Miyān Hidāyat was himself counted among the *shāgirds* of Mīr Dard. Homayra Ziad, "Quest of the Nightingale: The Religious Thought of Khvājah Mīr Dard (1720–1785)" (PhD diss., Yale University, 2008), 117. There are differing accounts of his date of death: de Tassy, *Histoire*, 1:599.
27. Muḥammad Ḥusain Āzād, *Āb-e ḥayāt: Shaping the Canon of Urdu Poetry*, trans. Frances W. Pritchett and Shamsur Rahman Faruqi (New Delhi: Oxford University Press, 2001), 174. See also Ziad, "Quest of the Nightingale."
28. Bedār, "Peshguftār," 3.
29. On the crown prince's love of poetry, see Frances W. Pritchett, *Nets of Awareness: Urdu Poetry and Its Critics* (Berkeley: University of California Press, 1994), 4.
30. Mirzā Jawān Baḳht Jahāndār Shāh, "Appendix: A Narrative, written by the Prince Jehândâr Shàh," in *Memoirs Relative to the State of India* (London, 1786); William Francklin, *The History of the Reign of Shah-Aulum, the present emperor of Hindostaun: containing the transactions of the court of Delhi, and the neighbouring states, during a period of thirty-six years: interspersed with geographical and topographical observations on several of the principal cities of Hindostaun: with an appendix* (London, 1798), 116, 154; Ḥāmid Ḥasan Qādirī, *Dāstān-i Tārīḳh-i Urdū* (Agra, 1966), 135; A. F. M. Abdul Ali, "Prince Jawan Bakht Jahandar Shah," *Bengal Past & Present* 54, no. 1–2 (1937): 10–13.
31. The prince, in his final hours before succumbing to what may have been a severe heart attack, wrote to Jonathan Duncan, then resident at Benares, begging: "For the sake of the Holy Virgin do not send my wife under any circumstance whatever to Shahjahanabad." English translation reproduced from Ali, "Prince Jawan Bakht Jahandar Shah," 17. For more on Duncan, see, e.g., John Duncan, *Selections from the Duncan Records*, 2 vols. (Benares, 1873); Bernard S. Cohn, "The Initial British Impact on India: A Case Study of the Benares Region," *Journal of Asian Studies* 19 (1960): 424, 427; Bernard S. Cohn, "From Indian Status to British Contract," *Journal of Economic History* 21 (1961): 617, 620.
32. Ali gives the date of Mirzā Jawān Baḳht's death as June 1, 1788, basing this on the account given in a Persian letter prepared for the prince's widow on June 12, 1788 to Lord Cornwallis, reproduced in "Prince Jawan Bakht Jahandar Shah," 16. The year of death given by Bedār is AH 1201, which corresponds with AD 1786/1787, a date that, when combined with several other uncorrected errors in chronology appearing elsewhere in that editor's foreword, is less credible. Bedār, "Peshguftār," 3.
33. For a description of an *amīr*'s retinue, see J. F. Richards, "Norms of Comportment Among Imperial Mughal Officers," in *Moral Conduct and Authority: The Place of Adab in South Asian Islam*, ed. Barbara Daly Metcalf (Berkeley: University of California Press, 1984), 259–260.

34. Mirzā Jān Ṯapish Dihlawī, "Shams al-Bayān fī Muṣṭalaḥāt al-Hindūstān," British Library Add. 18,889, 1215, 3b.
35. A copy (VT 901) is preserved in the British Library. See James Fuller Blumhardt, *Catalogue of the Hindustani Manuscripts in the Library of the India Office* (London: Oxford University Press, 1926), vol. 2, part 2, 55. For the original Persian text and details on the sources consulted for the 1979 edition, see Bedār, "Peshguftār," 7.
36. Mirzā Jān Ṯapish Dihlawī, *Shams al-Bayān fī Muṣṭalaḥāt al-Hindūstān* (Patna: Khuda Bakhsh Oriental Public Library, 1979), 9.
37. Muzaffar Alam and Sanjay Subrahmanyam, "Power in Prison: A Mughal Prince in Shahjahanabad, ca. 1800," in *De l'Arabie à l'Himalaya: chemins croisés. En hommage à Marc Gaborieau*, ed. Véronique Bouillier and Catherine Schreiber Servan (Paris: Maisonneuve & Larose, 2004), 311, 328.
38. Ibid., 329–330.
39. Ibid., 329; Muzaffar Alam and Sanjay Subrahmanyam, "Envisioning Power: The Political Thought of a Late Eighteenth-Century Mughal Prince," *Indian Economic & Social History Review* 43, no. 2 (2006): 156.
40. Mirzā ʿAlī Bak̲ht Bahādur Muḥammad Ẓahīruddīn Aẕfarī, *Wāqiʿāt-i Aẕfarī*, Madras Government Oriental Manuscripts 65 (Madras, 1957), 124; Mirzā ʿAlī Bak̲ht Bahādur Muḥammad Ẓahīruddīn Aẕfarī, *Wāqiʿāt-i Aẕfarī* [Urdu Translation], trans. ʿAbdul Sattar (Lahore: Yiktā Kitābeṅ, 2008), 115.
41. Aẕfarī, *Wāqiʿāt-i Aẕfarī*, 124.
42. Emphasis added. Ibid., 124–25; Aẕfarī, *Wāqiʿāt-i Aẕfarī* [Urdu Translation], 115–116.
43. See Ray, *The Rebel Nawab of Oudh*, 197.
44. Qureshi, "Anti-British Plots of Shams-ud-Daullah of Dacca in the Light of Contemporary English Report," *Quarterly Review of Historical Studies* 23, no. 4 (1984): 49. The involvement or distance of Aẕfarī from these intrigues has not to my knowledge been explained, though he himself comments about the disruptions caused by the rebellion in the Benares region. Aẕfarī, *Wāqiʿāt-i Aẕfarī*, 120; Aẕfarī, *Wāqiʿāt-i Aẕfarī* [Urdu Translation], 112.
45. Prior to this, Aẕfarī had arrived in Benares on January 3, 1797 (4 Rajab, AH 1211). He spent the month of Ramaẓān in ʿAẕīmābād (Patna) before taking a boat to Murshidābād. He arrived there on May 1, 1797 (4 Żī-Qaʿdah). Aẕfarī, *Wāqiʿāt-i Aẕfarī*, 120–123; Aẕfarī, *Wāqiʿāt-i Aẕfarī* [Urdu Translation], 111–114.
46. Ray, *The Rebel Nawab of Oudh*, 196–197.
47. Appointed by Warren Hastings in 1772, his opponents claimed that the only way a former dancing girl could have been elevated to such a position was through corruption. See F. P. Lock, *Edmund Burke* (Oxford: Clarendon, 2006), 2:224–225.
48. Ray, *The Rebel Nawab of Oudh*, 197.
49. Qureshi, "Anti-British Plots," 50.
50. For the original text, compare Ṯapish, "Shams al-Bayān," *BL Add. 18,889*, 2b–4a; Ṯapish Dihlawī, *Shams al-Bayān*, 9–10.
51. Ṯapish, "Shams al-Bayān," BL Add. 18,889, 4a.
52. *Hindī* here could refer to either a language (*zabān-i hindī*) or to the region known to Arabs and Persians for more than a millennium as *al-hind*, that is, northern India east of the Indus. See Alok Rai, *Hindi Nationalism* (Hyderabad: Orient Longman, 2001), 12–15.
53. Platts, *Dictionary of Urdū*, 595.
54. Punctuation and spacing were added by the editor. Ṯapish Dihlawī, *Shams al-Bayān*, 34.

55. According to Ḥāmid Ḥasan Qādirī: "This idiom (*rafū cakkar meṅ ānā*) is called [by Ṭapish] an idiom of the ordinary folk of the bāzār for this reason that *rafū cakkar honā* and *cakkar meṅ ānā* are two different idioms. . . . Uneducated people (*jāhil ādmī*) have also introduced the word *rafū* into other idioms, and started saying *rafū cakkar meṅ ānā* for *ḥairān honā* ['being astonished']. Nevertheless, people of the olden times must have said it. Now one does not hear it." *Dāstān-i Tārīḳh-i Urdū*, 137.
56. Ḳhalīl al-Raḥmān Dā'udī, "Pesh Lafẓ [Foreword]," in *Bahār-i Dānish (Urdū Maśnavī)* (Lahore: Majlis-i Taraqqī-yi Adab, 1963), 17–18.
57. For general background, see, e.g., J. Robson, "Ḥadīth," in *Encyclopaedia of Islam*, vol. 3, ed. P. Bearman et al. (Leiden: Brill, 1971), 3:23–28; Marshall G. S. Hodgson, *The Venture of Islam: Conscience and History in a World Civilization* (Chicago: University of Chicago Press, 1974), 1:322–340.
58. Jonathan Brown, "Critical Rigor vs. Juridical Pragmatism: How Legal Theorists and Ḥadīth Scholars Approached the Backgrowth of 'Isnāds' in the Genre of 'Ilal Al-ḥadīth," *Islamic Law and Society* 14 (2007): 1–41.
59. Pritchett, "A Long History of Urdu Literary Culture, Part 2."
60. W. P. Heinrichs et al., "Ta<u>dh</u>kira (a.)," in *Encyclopaedia of Islam*, 2nd ed., ed. P. Bearman et al. (Leiden: Brill, 2000), 10:53.
61. Ibid. It would be misleading, however, to suggest that the science of *ḥadīś* collection always took the form of physical documents. Many *ḥadīś* collectors were admired for their memory. Poets who had memorized thousands of verses could face criticism for misapplying their mental faculties toward vain ends. Implicit in this criticism is the notion that the methods employed by collectors of *ḥadīś* and collectors of verse were analogous if not entirely identical. See Alyssa Gabbay, *Islamic Tolerance: Amīr Khusraw and Pluralism* (Milton Park: Routledge, 2010), 24.
62. Pritchett, *Nets of Awareness*, 64.
63. Islām, "Bayāẓ," 62.
64. Ibid. Islām provides a list of some sixty-three items copied by the hand of Ṭapish himself. See ibid., 64–67.
65. The last date listed in the notebook corresponds with 8 Shaʿbān, AH 1229 (July 26, 1814), commemorating the birth of a son to a certain Piyārī Begam. There are no dates listed in the notebook in the hand of Ṭapish after this date. Ibid., 68–69. Garcin de Tassy (*Histoire*, 3:220–221) estimates his death to have occurred in Patna in approximately 1814.
66. Islām, "Bayāẓ," 63.
67. Ibid.
68. Ibid., 62.
69. Poets, like Amīr Ḳhusrau, were also challenged to demonstrate through *aḥādīś* the licitness of poetry. See Shamsur Rahman Faruqi, "Constructing a Literary History, a Canon, and a Theory of Poetry," in *Āb-e ḥayāt: Shaping the Canon of Urdu Poetry*, ed. Frances Pritchett (New Delhi: Oxford University Press, 2001), 23–27; Gabbay, *Islamic Tolerance*, 27–29.
70. See Tariq Rahman, "Urdu and the Muslim Identity: Standardization of Urdu in the Eighteenth and Early Nineteenth Centuries," *Annual of Urdu Studies* 25 (2010): 95–98.
71. Mīr Inshā'allāh Ḳhāṅ Inshā, *Daryā-i Laṭāfat* [Urdu Translation], trans. Paṇḍit Brajmohan Dittātriyah 'Kaifī' (New Delhi: Anjuman-i Taraqqī-yi Urdū (Hind), 1988), 27–28.
72. Ibid., 64–65.

73. "When King Akbar ascended the throne, then all tribes of people, from all the surrounding countries, hearing of the goodness and liberality of this unequalled family, flocked to his court, but the speech and dialect of each was different. Yet, by being assembled together, they used to traffic and do business, and converse with each other, whence resulted the common Urdu language." Mīr Amman Dihlawī, "Bagh-o-Bahar, or Tales of the Four Darweshes, translated from the Hindustani of Mir Amman of Dihli, by Duncan Forbes, L.L.D.," ed. Frances Pritchett (2005), http://www.columbia.edu/itc/mealac/pritchett/00urdu/baghobahar/index.html. On linguistic interactions among Central Asians, Afghans, and Indians in the early sixteenth century, see Walter N. Hakala, "On Equal Terms: The Equivocal Origins of an Early Mughal Indo-Persian Vocabulary," *Journal of the Royal Asiatic Society (Third Series)* 25, no. 2 (2015): 209–227.
74. Inshā, *Daryā-i Laṭāfat* [Urdu Translation], 27–28. Compare with Amrit Rai's translation in *A House Divided: The Origin and Development of Hindi/Hindavi* (Delhi: Oxford University Press, 1984), 20, 230.
75. Ṭapish most certainly was familiar with the work of Inshā, referring to the latter respectfully as "Inshā'allāh Ḳhāṅ *sallamahuʾl-lāhŏ taʿālā*" (may the most high God save or protect him) in his notebook. Islām, "Bayāẓ," 63. The *Daryā-i Laṭāfat* was coauthored by Inshā and completed after 1807, more than a decade following the publication of the *Shams al-Bayān* in manuscript. A print edition was not published until 1849, and an Urdu translation of the original Persian appeared in 1916. See David Lelyveld, "Zuban-e Urdu-e Mu'alla and the Idol of Linguistic Origins," *Annual of Urdu Studies* 9 (1994): 76.
76. Platts, *Dictionary of Urdū*, 221.
77. Ṭapish Dihlawī, *Shams al-Bayān*, 17.
78. See, e.g., Sprenger, *Oudh Catalogue*, 1:252; Muhammad Umar, *Islam in Northern India During the Eighteenth Century* (New Delhi: Munshiram Manoharlal Publishers for Centre of Advanced Study in History, Aligarh Muslim University, 1993), 202. On the violence associated with poetic rivalries in Lucknow, see Pritchett, *Nets of Awareness*, 51–57; C. M. Naim and Carla Petievich, "Urdu in Lucknow/Lucknow in Urdu," in *Lucknow: Memories of a City*, ed. Violette Graff (Delhi: Oxford University Press, 1997), 167.
79. Garcin de Tassy, *Histoire de la littérature hindouie et hindoustani*, 2nd rev., cor., et considérablement augm. ed. (Paris, 1870), 2:261.
80. Some verses of 'Maḥshar' are preserved in the *Taẕkirah-i Hindī* of Shaiḳh Ġhulām Hamadānī 'Muṣḥafī', completed in 1794–1795, that is, several years after the *Shams al-Bayān* was first "published" in manuscript in 1792. Shaiḳh Ġhulām Hamadānī Muṣḥafī, *Taẕkirah-i Hindī*, trans. ʿAbdul Ḥaq, Sisilah-yi Maṭbūʿāt (Lucknow: Uttar Pradesh Urdū Akādmī, 1985), 236. Ṭapish would have been familiar with the poetry of Maḥshar either by having committed this particular verse to memory or from having heard or read it elsewhere. For more on the *mushāʿarahs* at the home of Mīr 'Dard', see Ziad, "Quest of the Nightingale," 120–122.
81. Inshā, *Daryā-i Laṭāfat* [Urdu Translation], 64.
82. Lelyveld, "Zubān-e Urdū-e Mu'allā'," 75–76.
83. Yūsuf Taqī, *Murshidābād ke Ćār Kilāsīkī Shuʿarāʾ: Qudratullāh Qudrat, Mīr Bāqir Muḳhliṣ, Inshāʾallāh Ḳhāṅ Inshā, Mirzā Jān Ṭapish* (Calcutta: Yūsuf Taqī, 1989), 52. Taqī reports that new research suggests his birth to have occurred in 1753. It had previously been thought to have been in 1756.

84. Em. Ḥabīb Ḳhān, *Inshāʾallāh Ḳhāṅ 'Inshā'* (New Delhi: Sāhityah Akādmī, 1989), 17.
85. Inshā, *Daryā-i Laṭāfat* [Urdu Translation], 41–42. For additional background, see Warren Edward Fusfeld, "The Shaping of Sufi Leadership in Delhi: The Naqshbandiyya Mujaddidiyya, 1750–1920" (PhD diss., University of Pennsylvania, 1981), 116–153.
86. Inshā, *Daryā-i Laṭāfat* [Urdu Translation], 61.
87. Rai, *A House Divided*, 230, 255–259.
88. Lāllū Jī Lāl of Agra, in the introduction to his *Lāl Ćandrikā* (1818), also distinguished among "three dialects in which he had written books, viz. Braj, K[haṛī]B[olī], and Rekhte ki Boli (i.e., Urdu). In his Braj and K[haṛī]B[olī] books he usually endeavoured to avoid Persian and Arabic words, but in the Introduction just mentioned he used them rather freely." Lāl was a contemporary of Ṭapish and Inshāʾ employed in the College of Fort William and the author of the famous *Prem Sāgar* (1803), considered to be one of the earliest prose works of what would become modern Hindi. It is unclear to what kind of writing this particular usage of *reḳhtah* refers. T. Grahame Bailey, "Does Khaṛī Bolī Mean Nothing More Than Rustic Speech?" *Bulletin of the School of Oriental Studies* 8, no. 2/3, Indian and Iranian Studies: Presented to George Abraham Grierson on His Eighty-Fifth Birthday, 7th January, 1936 (1936): 371.
89. Rai, *A House Divided*, 259.
90. Inshā, *Daryā-i Laṭāfat* [Urdu Translation], 61.
91. See, e.g., Francis Robinson, "Technology and Religious Change: Islam and the Impact of Print," *Modern Asian Studies* 27, no. 1 (1993): 229; Nile Green, "The Uses of Books in a Late Mughal *Takiyya:* Persianate Knowledge Between Person and Paper," *Modern Asian Studies* 44, no. 2 (2010).
92. On the *istĕʿmāl-i hind*, see, e.g., Heinrich Ferdinand Blochmann, "Contributions to Persian Lexicography," *Journal of the Royal Asiatic Society of Bengal* 37, no. 1 (1868): 32–38; Muzaffar Alam, "The Pursuit of Persian: Language in Mughal Politics," *Modern Asian Studies* 32, no. 2 (1998): 340–342. On the *sabk-i hindī*, see also Aziz Ahmad, "The Formation of the *Sabk-i Hindī*," in *Iran and Islam: In Memory of the Late Vladimir Minorsky*, ed. C. E. Bosworth (Edinburgh: Edinburgh University Press, 1971); Shamsur Rahman Faruqi, "A Stranger in the City: The Poetics of *Sabk-e Hindi*," *Annual of Urdu Studies* 19 (2004): 1–93; Rajeev Kinra, "Fresh Words for a Fresh World: *Tāzā-Gūʾī* and the Poetics of Newness in Early Modern Indo-Persian Poetry," *Sikh Formations* 3, no. 2 (2007): 125–149.
93. Inshā, *Daryā-i Laṭāfat* [Urdu Translation], 61–62.
94. Inshā remarked upon Ābrū's use of a pronominal expression that is not standard to the Delhi dialect. I have not been able to locate this hemistich in the published *dīwān*. Cf. Najmuddīn Shāh Mubārak Ābrū, *Dīwān-i Ābrū* (New Delhi: Taraqqī-yi Urdū Biyūro, 2000), 230–285.
95. Inshā, *Daryā-i Laṭāfat* [Urdu Translation], 62.
96. Bedār, "Peshguftār," 3.
97. Najmul Islām reproduces several Hindvi verse sets (*kabit*) from the notebook of Ṭapish, penned by a poet with the pen name 'Sadā Ḳhair'. This poetry, which Islām describes as "not without original ideas [*upaj*]" deserves to be "brought to the public's attention." He speculates that "it is possible that 'Sadā Ḳhair' may even be Ṭapish himself," and, even if not, "the presence in the notebook of Hindi works demonstrates Ṭapish's familiarity with and interest in this language." Islām, "Bayāẓ," 77–78.

98. For an alternate view, that is, a defense of poetry as the standard for eloquence, from Amīr Ḳhusrau, see Gabbay, *Islamic Tolerance*, 28–29.
99. See the essays collected in Barbara Daly Metcalf, ed., *Moral Conduct and Authority: The Place of Adab in South Asian Islam* (Berkeley: University of California Press, 1984).
100. Rai concludes his own extended pastiche of quotations from Inshā with a characterization of Urdu as a "class-dialect." Rai, *A House Divided*, 257.
101. Inshā, *Daryā-i Laṭāfat* [Urdu Translation], 66.
102. Ibid.
103. The examples Inshā provides are of unusual names of birds used during the reign Muḥammad Shāh (r. 1719–1748). Ibid.
104. Recent scholarship is increasingly calling this into question, citing the increasing provincialization of the Mughal nobility by the second half of the *seventeenth* century. Muzaffar Alam and Sanjay Subrahmanyam, *Indo-Persian Travels in the Age of Discoveries, 1400–1800* (Cambridge: Cambridge University Press, 2007), 179. See also Gijs Kruijtzer, *Xenophobia in Seventeenth-Century India* (Leiden: Leiden University Press, 2009). For a classic quantitative study of the changing composition of the Mughal elite during the first half of the eighteenth century, see Satish Chandra, *Parties and Politics at the Mughal Court, 1707–1740* (New Delhi: Oxford University Press, 2002).
105. Inshā, *Daryā-i Laṭāfat* [Urdu Translation], 102.
106. Ibid.
107. Alam and Subrahmanyam, "Power in Prison," 328–329.
108. Ibid., 309–310.
109. Aẕfarī, *Wāqiʿāt-i Aẕfarī*, 126; Aẕfarī, *Wāqiʿāt-i Aẕfarī* [Urdu Translation], 116.
110. Aẕfarī, *Wāqiʿāt-i Aẕfarī*, 127; Aẕfarī, *Wāqiʿāt-i Aẕfarī* [Urdu Translation], 117.
111. Inshā, *Daryā-i Laṭāfat* [Urdu Translation], 102–103.
112. Rai, *A House Divided*, 256–257.
113. C. A. Bayly (*Rulers, Townsmen, and Bazaars*, 192) suggests that during the course of the eighteenth century, two divergent socioeconomies began to emerge: an old "Muslim *qasbah* society," formed by "literacy, agrarian dependence and Islam," which went into comparative decline in relation to the emerging bazaar towns dominated by new multi-caste (and predominantly Hindu) 'corporate' groups." On the concept of *qaṣbah* as distinct from British *bāzār* towns more generally, see ibid., 163–196.
114. Inshā, *Daryā-i Laṭāfat* [Urdu Translation], 103.
115. Ibid., 62–63. Muḥammad Ḥusain 'Āzād', however, mistook the presence of Braj elements in early *reḳhtah* poetry as proof of the latter's derivation from the former. For a discussion, see Frances W. Pritchett, " 'Everybody Knows This Much . . .' " in *Āb-e ḥayāt: Shaping the Canon of Urdu Poetry*, ed. Frances W. Pritchett (New Delhi: Oxford University Press, 2001), 1-17.
116. See Charles F. Ferguson, "Diglossia," *Word* 15, no. 2 (1959): 325–340.
117. Joshua Fishman, "Bilingualism with and Without Diglossia; Diglossia with and Without Bilingualism," *Journal of Social Issues* 23, no. 2 (1967): 29–38. For discussions of diglossic models in South Asia, see Harold F. Schiffman and Michael C. Shapiro, *Language and Society in South Asia* (Delhi: Motilal Banarsidass, 1981), 164–173; Harold F. Schiffman, "Diglossia as a Sociolinguistic Situation," in *The Handbook of Sociolinguistics*, ed. Florian Coulmas (London: Basil Blackwell, 1996), 205-216.

118. Harold F. Schiffman, *Linguistic Culture and Language Policy* (London: Routledge, 1996), 42–48.
119. Muzaffar Alam and Sanjay Subrahmanyam, "Empiricism of the Heart: Close Encounters in an Eighteenth-Century Indo-Persian Text," *Studies in History* 15, no. 2 (1999): 267–268.
120. Aẕfarī entitled his work *ʿArūẓ-zādah* (Child of the [handbook on] prosody). T. Chandrasekharan, "Preface," in *Wāqiʿāt-i Aẕfarī*, ed. T. Chandrasekharan (Madras, 1957), ii. Bābur's original *ʿArūẓ Risālası* (Treatise on prosody) was edited and published in Moscow in 1972. Stephen Frederic Dale, "Steppe Humanism: The Autobiographical Writings of Zahir al-Din Muhammad Babur, 1483–1530," *International Journal of Middle East Studies* 22, no. 1 (1990): 72. On MSS of this work, see Dara Nusserwanji Marshall, *Mughals in India: A Bibliographical Survey of Manuscripts* (London: Mansell, 1985), 97–98.
121. Inshā suggests it may be found in Istanbul, "which is the seat of the caliphate of the Sultan of Rūm." Inshā, *Daryā-i Laṭāfat* [Urdu Translation], 27.
122. Ibid., 102.
123. And, as is suggested below, in the record of early Urdu publications by the British.
124. Mīr's tirade against Saudā for his sponsorship of the barber 'Ḥajjām' reflects more the class anxieties of a poet known as much for his occasional misanthropic statements as for his skillful manipulation in poetry of the idiomatic speech of "common folk." Ishrat Haque, *Glimpses of Mughal Society and Culture: A Study Based on Urdu Literature, in the Second Half of the Eighteenth Century* (New Delhi: Concept, 1992), 129–131. See also the English rendition of Mīr's satire "Advice to Bad Poets" appearing in James Noble, *The Orientalist; or, Letters of a Rabbi: With Notes* (Edinburgh, 1831), 285–292. For a useful parallel, see Losensky, *Welcoming Fighānī*, 137–139, 144.
125. Lisa Mitchell, *Language, Emotion, and Politics in South India: The Making of a Mother Tongue* (Bloomington: Indiana University Press, 2009), 187.
126. Alam and Subrahmanyam, "Power in Prison," 329; Alam and Subrahmanyam, "Envisioning Power," 156.
127. McGregor's (loose) translation from the Hindi, appearing in "The Rise of Standard Hindi and Early Hindi Prose Fiction," *Journal of the Royal Asiatic Society of Great Britain and Ireland* 3/4 (1967): 115. Compare with Rai, *Hindi Nationalism*, 21. A slightly different version appears in ʿAbdul Ḥaq's Urdu edition. See Mīr Inshāʾallāh Ḳhāṅ Inshā, *Dāstān-i Rānī Ketkī aur Kunwar Ūde Bhān kī* (Delhi: Educational Book House, n.d.), 11–12.
128. Compare, for example, George Abraham Grierson, "A Bibliography of Western Hindi, Including Hindostani," *Indian Antiquary* 32 (1903): 166; Amy Bard and Valerie Ritter, "A House Overturned: A Classical Urdu Lament in Braj Bhasha," in *Shared Idioms, Sacred Symbols, and the Articulation of Identities in South Asia*, ed. Kelly Pemberton and Michael Nijhawan (New York: Routledge, 2009), 51.
129. Ṭapish Dihlawī, *Shams al-Bayān*, 9.
130. S. C. Banerjee, "Naib Nazims of Dacca During the Company's Administration," *Bengal Past & Present* 59 (1940): 23.
131. Ray, *The Rebel Nawab of Oudh*, 282–283.
132. This appears as "connect" in Banerjee, "Naib Nazims of Dacca," 23.
133. Ray, *The Rebel Nawab of Oudh*, 283.

134. Banerjee, "Naib Nazims of Dacca," 23.
135. Ray, *The Rebel Nawab of Oudh*, 283.
136. Ibid., 283; Badrud-din Ahmad, "Old Judicial Records of the Calcutta High Court," *Indian Historical Records Commission: Proceedings of Meetings* 5 (1923): 75–76; N. K. Sinha, "The Case of Mirza Jan Tuppish: A Treason Trial of 1800," *Bengal Past & Present* 72 (1953): 42.
137. Sinha, "The Case of Mirza Jan Tuppish," 42.
138. According to Ray (*The Rebel Nawab of Oudh*, 284), the jail in which Shams al-Daulah was housed "must have been the jail on the maidan, since demolished, called *Hurreen Bari*." Ṯapish, in the custody of the town guard or major, may have resided inside Fort William itself. Charles Moore, *The Sheriffs of Fort William from 1775 to 1926* (Calcutta: Thacker, Spink, 1926), 105.
139. Sinha, "The Case of Mirza Jan Tuppish," 39.
140. Sinha believes that Ṯapish means Afghanistan instead of Iran. Ibid., 41. The king of Afghanistan, Zamān Shāh (r. 1793–1800, d. 1844), was the grandson of Aḥmad Shāh Abdālī, a commander under Nadir Shah who conquered much of eastern Iran and present-day Pakistan and founded the Afghan Durrānī dynasty.
141. Banerjee, "Naib Nazims of Dacca," 24.
142. Peter James Marshall, "Barlow, Sir George Hilaro, first baronet (1763–1846)," in *Oxford Dictionary of National Biography*, ed. Henry Colin Gray Matthew and Brian Howard Harrison (2004), http://www.oxforddnb.com/view/article/1433.
143. Banerjee reproduces the remarks of the Court of Directors contained in their political dispatch from July 6, 1808, in "Naib Nazims of Dacca," 24. This article also narrates Shams al-Daulah's continuing efforts to secure a pension from the English following the death of his brother and his rise to the status of head of household.
144. Islām, "Bayāẓ," 69.
145. Ibid.
146. Ibid.
147. Thomas Roebuck, *Annals of the College of Fort William* (Calcutta, 1819), 339; Blumhardt, *Hindi, Panjabi, and Hindustani MSS in the British Museum*, 18.
148. Roebuck, *Annals*, 27.
149. From the title page of Joseph Taylor and William Hunter, *A Dictionary, Hindoostanee and English* (Calcutta, 1808). Taylor admitted that he was familiar only with "the Hindoostanee or Rekhta, in the Persian character, which is my particular province and not the Hindee in its own character." Rai, *A House Divided*, 14.
150. Taylor and Hunter, *Dictionary*, 1:321.
151. William Carmichael Smyth, "Preface," in *A Dictionary, Hindoostanee and English*, ed. Joseph Taylor et al. (London, 1820), vi.
152. Moore, *The Sheriffs of Fort William*, 6, 40–41.
153. E. J. Rapson and Michael Fry, "Hunter, William (1755–1812)," in *Oxford Dictionary of National Biography*, ed. Henry Colin Gray Matthew and Brian Howard Harrison (2004), http://www.oxforddnb.com/view/article/14235.
154. Najmul Islām reproduces several verses from the work that he believes are descriptions of the poet's captivity. See Islām, "Bayāẓ," 70–71.
155. See ibid.; Bedār, "Peshguftār," 4–5. See also Dāʾudī, "Pesh Lafẓ [Foreword]."
156. Islām, "Bayāẓ," 68.
157. Ibid.

158. See ʿAbdul Qādir Ḳhānī, *ʿIlm o ʿAmal*, trans. Maulvī Muʿīnuddīn Afẓal Gaḍhī (Karachi: Academy of Educational Research, All-Pakistan Educational Conference, 1960), 1:143.
159. The work was eventually completed and published through the efforts of his friends Thomas Roebuck (1781–1819) and Horace Hayman Wilson (1786–1860) in 1824. See William Hunter et al., *A Collection of Proverbs, and Proverbial Phrases: in the Persian and Hindoostanee Languages* (Calcutta, 1824).
160. See Rapson and Fry, "Hunter, William (1755–1812)." It will be recalled that John Leyden also passed away in Java after visiting an "unventilated native library" in August 1811. For more on Leyden, see chapter 1.
161. Noble, *The Orientalist*, 285, 294–295, 304–305.

4. 1900: LEXICOGRAPHY AND THE SELF

Sayyid Ḳhwājah Ḥusainī, "Farhang-i Āṣafiyah Tanqīd ke Āʾīne meṅ," *Urdū Adab* 1 (1966), 116.

1. Nażīr Aḥmad, "Preface," in *Farhang-i Lisān al-Shuʿarāʾ: bĕh Sāl-i 753–790 Hijrī, ʿAhd-i Fīrūz Shāh Tuġhlaq*, ed. Nażīr Aḥmad (New Delhi: Rāyzanī-yi Farhangī-yi Jumhūrī-yi Islāmī-yi Īrān, 1995), viii.
2. See Anonymous, *A Defence of the Urdu Language and Character: Being a Reply to the Pamphlet Called "Court Character and Primary Education in N.-W.P. & and Oude"* (Allahabad: Liddel's N.-W.P. Printing Works, 1900); Christopher Rolland King, "Images of Virtue and Vice: The Hindi-Urdu Controversy in Two Nineteenth-Century Hindi Plays," in *Religious Controversy in British India: Dialogues in South Asian Languages*, ed. Kenneth W. Jones (Albany: State University of New York Press, 1992); Christopher Rolland King, *One Language, Two Scripts: The Hindi Movement in Nineteenth-Century North India* (Bombay: Oxford University Press, 1994); Vasudha Dalmia, *The Nationalization of Hindu Traditions: Bhāratendu Harishchandra and Nineteenth-Century Banaras* (Delhi: Oxford University Press, 1997); Alok Rai, *Hindi Nationalism* (Hyderabad: Orient Longman, 2001).
3. Jābir ʿAlī Sayyid and Wāriṡ Sarhindī, *Kutub-i Luġhat kā Taḥqīqī wa Lisānī Jāʾizah* (Islamabad: Muqtadirah Quamī Zabān, 1984), 1:109; Masʿūd Hāshmī, *Urdū Luġhat Nawīsī kā Pas Manẓar* (Delhi: Maktabah-yi Jāmiʿah, 1997), 154.
4. Sidney I. Landau, *Dictionaries: The Art and Craft of Lexicography* (New York: Scribner, 1984), 10–13.
5. James Fuller Blumhardt, *A Supplementary Catalogue of Hindustani Books in the Library of the British Museum: Acquired During the Years 1889-1908* (London: British Museum, Longmans & Co., Bernard Quaritch, Asher & Co., Henry Frowde, 1909), 32.
6. Sayyid Aḥmad Dihlawī, *Farhang-i Āṣafiyah* (New Delhi: National Academi [Taraqqī-yi Urdū Board edition], 1974), 1:47; Sayyid Dā'ūd Ashraf, "Farhang-i Āṣafiyah: Ćand Ḥaqāʾiq," in *Guźashtah Ḥaidarābād: Ārkā'īvz ke Ā'ine meṅ* (Hyderabad: Shagūfah Pablīkeshanz, 2003), 139.
7. See Paul R. Brass, *Language, Religion, and Politics in North India* (London: Cambridge University Press, 1974), 3–46.
8. Asif Agha similarly distinguishes between the social *range* and *domain* of linguistic registers. Asif Agha, *Language and Social Relations* (Cambridge: Cambridge University Press, 2007), 125, 142–143, 169–170.

9. James C. Scott, *Seeing Like a State: How Certain Schemes to Improve the Human Condition Have Failed* (New Haven, Conn.: Yale University Press, 1998), 11–22.
10. It would surely be false to assert that the appearance of a heavily Sanskritized diction in Hindi was entirely the result of nineteenth-century machinations. It is rather, as Francesca Orsini has usefully phrased it, "a recurrent feature in the Hindi literary tradition." Sanjay Subrahmanyam et al., "A Review Symposium: Literary Cultures in History," *Indian Economic & Social History Review* 42, no. 3 (2005): 393. See also R. S. McGregor, "On the Evolution of Hindi as a Language of Literature," *South Asia Research* 21, no. 2 (2001): 205–207, 214; R. S. McGregor, "The Progress of Hindi, Part 1: The Development of a Transregional Idiom," in *Literary Cultures in History: Reconstructions from South Asia*, ed. Sheldon I. Pollock (Berkeley: University of California Press, 2003), 928–929; Allison Renee Busch, "Riti and Register: Lexical Variation in Courtly Braj Bhasha Texts," in *Before the Divide: Hindi and Urdu Literary Culture*, ed. Francesca Orsini (New Delhi: Orient BlackSwan, 2010), 100–101.
11. Jonathon Green, *Chasing the Sun: Dictionary Makers and the Dictionaries They Made* (New York: Henry Holt, 1996).
12. Compare Raymond Williams, *Marxism and Literature* (Oxford: Oxford University Press, 1977), 11–20; Wali Ahmadi, *Modern Persian Literature in Afghanistan: Anomalous Visions of History and Form* (London: Routledge, 2008), 45.
13. Solomon I. Baevskii, *Early Persian Lexicography: Farhangs of the Eleventh to the Fifteenth Centuries*, trans. N. Killian (Honolulu: University of Hawai'i Press, 2007), ix, 29.
14. Gail Minault, "Sayyid Ahmad Dehlavi and the 'Delhi Renaissance,'" in *Delhi Through the Ages: Essays in Urban History, Culture, and Society*, ed. Robert Eric Frykenberg (Delhi: Oxford University Press, 1986), 182. He attained this position through the intercession of his mother's brother, Sayyid ʿAbdullāh Shimlavī, Mīr Munshī of the court of a Shimla hill state. Sayyid Yūsuf Buḳhārī Dihlawī, "Maulvī Sayyid Aḥmad Dihlawī," in *Rusūm-i Dihlī* (Rampur: Kitābkār Pablīkeshanz, 1965), 17.
15. Ibid.
16. Ḥusainī, "Farhang-i Āṣafiyah Tanqīd ke Āʾīne meṅ," 105.
17. Alṭāf Ḥusain Ḥālī, "Farhang-i Āṣafiyah," in *Urdū Luġhat: Yādgārī Maẓāmīn*, ed. Abūlḥasanāt (Karachi: Unikarians International, 2010), 62. Johnson was commissioned to compile the dictionary in 1746 and prepared a prospectus, *The Plan of the English Dictionary, Addressed to the Right Honourable Philip Dormer, Earl of Chesterfield; One of His Majesty's Principal Secretaries of State*, in 1747. The *Dictionary* was completed in 1755.
18. Quoted in Dihlawī, "Maulvī Sayyid Aḥmad Dihlawī," 23.
19. He began this work during his residence in Aurangābād, continuing in Hyderābād and following his immigration to Pakistan. He was unable to complete it, and the Anjuman-i Taraqqī-yi Urdū of Karachi published only the first volume, which includes only words beginning with the letter *alif*. Hāshmī, *Urdū Luġhat Nawīsī kā Pas Manẓar*, 155. The project was continued following Ḥaq's death by the Taraqqī-yi Urdū Board in Karachi under the title *Urdū Luġhat Tārīḳhī Uṣūl par*. On the career of Ḥaq, see Kavita Saraswathi Datla, "A Worldly Vernacular: Urdu at Osmania University," *Modern Asian Studies* 43, no. 5 (2009): 1128–1129.
20. ʿAbdul Ḥaq, "Muqaddamah: Urdū Luġhāt aur Luġhat Nawīsī," in *Luġhat-i Kabīr-i Urdū* (Karachi: Anjuman-i Taraqqī-yi Urdū, 1973), 18.

21. Kavita Saraswathi Datla, "Making a Worldly Vernacular: Urdu, Education, and Osmania University, Hyderabad, 1883–1938" (PhD diss., University of California, 2006), 75–80.
22. For a useful overview of historiographical debates on the degree to which European colonial interventions in South Asian society may be characterized as continuous or disruptive, see Ian J. Barrow and Douglas E. Haynes, "The Colonial Transition: South Asia, 1780–1840," *Modern Asian Studies* 38, no. 3 (2004): 471–473.
23. Aḥmad Kalīmuddīn, *Urdū Tanqīd par ek Naẓar* (Lahore: ʿIshrat Pablishing Hāʾūs, 1965); Aḥmad Kalīmuddīn, *Urdū Shāʿirī par ek Naẓar* (Lahore: ʿIshrat Pablishing Hāʾūs, 1965); Muhammad Hasan Askari, "If the Benefit of Translation Is Concealment," *Annual of Urdu Studies* 19 (2004): 195; Muhammad Hasan Askari, "Some Thoughts on Urdu Prose," *Annual of Urdu Studies* 19 (2004): 206. See also Datla, "Making a Worldly Vernacular," 80–85.
24. Datla, "A Worldly Vernacular," 1129–1131.
25. Benedict Anderson's remarks in the preface to the second edition of *Imagined Communities* describes one author's eventual resignation to the ineluctability of this state of affairs.
26. Hāshmī, *Urdū Luġhat Nawīsī kā Pas Manẓar*, 5.
27. Masʿūd Hāshmī, *Urdū Luġhat Nawīsī kā Tanqīdī Jāʾizah* (New Delhi: Taraqqī-yi Urdū Biyūro, 1992), 65.
28. Dihlawī, *Farhang-i Āṣafiyah*, 1:13.
29. Ibid., 1:15.
30. This dearth is bemoaned by Ḳhāliq Anjum in his brief biographical essay in "Muqaddamah," in *Rusūm-i Dihlī*, ed. Ḳhalīq Anjum (New Delhi: Urdū Akādmī, 1986), 9.
31. Shamīm Jahāṅ submitted this work in 1982 under the supervision of Professor Ẓahīr Aḥmad Ṣadīqī, with the title "Sayyid Aḥmad Dihlavī: Life and Literary Service." Unfortunately, I have not been able to consult this work.
32. Anjum, "Muqaddamah," 10. The *Rusūm-i Dihlī* will be discussed in greater detail below.
33. Dihlawī, "Maulvī Sayyid Aḥmad Dihlawī," 13.
34. Cited in Anjum, "Muqaddamah," 12.
35. For a comprehensive and historically balanced study of Sayyid Aḥmad Barelwī's life and its significance, see Marc Gaborieau, *Le mahdi incompris: Sayyid Ahmad Barelwî (1786–1831) et le millénarisme en inde* (Paris: CNRS, 2010).
36. William Wilson Hunter, *The Indian Musalmans* (London, 1876), 12–18. For less biased overviews, see Marc Gaborieau, "The Jihad of Sayyid Ahmad Barelwi on the North West Frontier: The Last Echo of the Middle Ages? Or a Prefiguration of Modern South Asia," in *Sufis, Sultans, and Feudal Orders: Professor Nurul Hasan Commemoration Volume*, ed. Mansura Haidar (New Delhi: Manohar, 2004); Ayesha Jalal, *Partisans of Allah: Jihad in South Asia* (Cambridge, Mass.: Harvard University Press, 2008), 58–113.
37. Dihlawī, "Maulvī Sayyid Aḥmad Dihlawī," 12, 15; Dihlawī, *Farhang-i Āṣafiyah*, 1:13; Anjum, "Muqaddamah," 12. On the shrine, see also Sadia Dehlvi, *The Sufi Courtyard: Dargahs of Delhi* (New Delhi: HarperCollins Publishers India/India Today Group, 2012), 226.
38. Minault, "Sayyid Ahmad Dehlavi," 182.
39. Dihlawī, "Maulvī Sayyid Aḥmad Dihlawī," 12; Anjum, "Muqaddamah," 11–12.

40. Neither Anjum nor Sayyid Aḥmad care to comment whether this may have been attributable, in part at least, to the extreme pressure she must have undergone in trying to bear male issue for her husband's family. Dihlawī, "Maulvī Sayyid Aḥmad Dihlawī," 19–20.
41. For Sayyid Aḥmad's description of the *darbār*, see Dihlawī, *Farhang-i Āṣafiyah*, 1:12.
42. Ibid., 1:15.
43. For a facsimile reproduction of the niẓām's orders and a detailed discussion, see Ashraf, "Farhang-i Āṣafiyah," 138–140.
44. Dihlawī, "Maulvī Sayyid Aḥmad Dihlawī," 20–21.
45. Sayyid Aḥmad Dihlawī, "Muqaddamah-i Ṭabʿ Awwal-i Farhang-i Āṣafiyah," in *Farhang-i Āṣafiyah* (New Delhi: National Academi [Taraqqī-yi Urdū Board edition], 1974), 37.
46. Ibid.
47. Ibid.
48. Dozens of verses by Sayyid Aḥmad are reproduced in Anjum, "Muqaddamah," 23–26.
49. Dihlawī, "Muqaddamah," 1:51.
50. Ibid. Emphasis added.
51. We are accustomed to Johnson's oft-repeated characterization of the lexicographer as a "harmless drudge." Zgusta repeats an earlier opinion of Joseph Justus Scalinger (1540–1609), who declares "in fine Latin verses that the worst criminals should neither be executed nor sentenced to forced labour, but should be condemned to compile dictionaries, because all the tortures are included in this work." Ladislav Zgusta, *Manual of Lexicography* (Prague: Academia Mouton, 1971), 15.
52. Ibid., 210–211.
53. Minault, "Sayyid Ahmad Dehlavi," 184.
54. Dihlawī, "Muqaddamah," 1:37.
55. Sayyid Aḥmad Dihlawī, *Rusūm-i Dihlī* (New Delhi: Urdū Akādmī, 2006). Gail Minault ("Sayyid Ahmad Dehlavi," 183) has characterized Sayyid Aḥmad's useful *Rusūm-i Dihlī*, a description of the customs of Delhi's elite *sharīf* culture, "not [as] a guide for participants [but r]ather, it is a work of cultural preservation." It was a major source for David Lelyveld's valuable discussion of the domestic customs of Delhi's Persianate elite in the section entitled "Growing up *Sharīf*" in *Aligarh's First Generation: Muslim Solidarity in British India* (Princeton, N.J.: Princeton University Press, 1977), 35–55.
56. Minault, "Sayyid Ahmad Dehlavi," 184.
57. Hāshmī, *Urdū Luġhat Nawīsī kā Tanqīdī Jāʾizah*, 69.
58. For Sayyid Aḥmad's thirty-six published works, including several on the subject of women's speech, see the list provided in Anjum, "Muqaddamah," 26–27. Lieutenant Colonel Phillott's own *Ḳhazīnah-i Muḥāwarāt; or, Urdu Idioms* was "Compiled from various sources but chiefly from the Urdu dictionary Farhang-i Aṣafiyya." See his preface to *Ḳhazīnah-e Muḥāwarāt; or, Urdu Idioms* (Calcutta: Baptist Mission Press, 1912).
59. See C. M. Naim, "Prize-Winning Adab: A Study of Five Urdu Books Written in Response to the Allahabad Government Gazette Notification," in *Moral Conduct and Authority: The Place of Adab in South Asian Islam*, ed. Barbara Daly Metcalf (Berkeley: University of California Press, 1984).
60. Sayyid Aḥmad Dihlawī, *Luġhāt al-Nisāʾ* (Lahore: Maqbūl Akademī, 1988), 7–8.

61. Anjum cites a work by Srī Rām, who intimated that his own uncle, Master Piyare Lāl, employed Sayyid Aḥmad at the Department of Public Instruction. Anjum, "Muqaddamah," 14.
62. Ibid., 18.
63. Ibid., 19.
64. Ashraf, "Farhang-i Āṣafiyah," 135.
65. Ibid., 136.
66. Ḥāmid Hasan Qādirī, quoted in Anjum, "Muqaddamah," 19.
67. Cited in ibid., 20.
68. Cited in Ashraf, "Farhang-i Āṣafiyah," 136–137.
69. Reproduced in ibid, 138–139.
70. Dihlawī, "Maulvī Sayyid Aḥmad Dihlawī," 12–13; Anjum, "Muqaddamah," 16.
71. Quoted in Muḥammad Żākir Ḥusain, "Pesh Guftār," in *Maḳhzan-i Fawāʾid: Urdū Muṣṭalaḥāt, Muḥāwarāt aur Amṡāl kā ek Nādir Luġhat*, ed. Muḥammad Żākir Ḥusain (Patna: Khuda Bakhsh Oriental Public Library, 1998), xv.
72. Sayyid Aḥmad Dihlawī, *Farhang-i Āṣafiyah* (New Delhi: National Academi [Taraqqī-yi Urdū Board edition], 1974), 3:528. Refer also to Ḥaq, "Muqaddamah," 41.
73. Ḥaq offers additional examples of this encyclopedic exuberance in ibid., 40–42.
74. Om Prakash Tyagi and D. P. Yadav, "Publication of 'Farhangi Asafi' Dictionary," *Parliamentary Debates: Official Report* 92, no. 7–12 (1975): 105.
75. Ibid. Om Prakash Tyagi is best known for introducing in 1978 the "Freedom of Religion Bill," which aimed to criminalize religious conversion effected through "force or inducement or fraudulent means"—including "threats of divine displeasure" and, potentially, the provision of free education and medical treatment. Lloyd I. Rudolph and Susanne Hoeber Rudolph, "Rethinking Secularism: Genesis and Implications of the Textbook Controversy, 1977–79," *Pacific Affairs* 56 (1983): 24–25.
76. For essays commemorating the completion of this work, see the felicitation volume Abūlḥasanāt, ed., *Urdū Luġhat: Yādgārī Maẓāmīn* (Karachi: Unikarians International, 2010).
77. On the nineteenth-century rise of "legal guidelines about authorial discretion," see Friedrich A. Kittler, *Discourse Networks 1800/1900* (Stanford, Calif.: Stanford University Press, 1990), 286.
78. On the role that technologies, like the codex book and print, have played in both facilitating the appropriation of others' work and in bringing apparent misappropriations to light, see Paulina Kewes, "Historicizing Plagiarism," in *Plagiarism in Early Modern England*, ed. Paulina Kewes (Basingstoke: Palgrave Macmillan, 2003), 7–11. In the same volume, Richard Steadman-Jones ("Lone Travellers," 209–210), examines Gilchrist's denouncement of George Hadley for allegedly plagiarizing his dictionary.
79. Cited in Ḥusain, "Pesh Guftār," xv–xvi.
80. Ibid., xvi.
81. "A dictionary catalogues . . . data to which no claim of property or copyright can be made: in the case of a living language, lexical units, their meanings and their grammar are in current usage of all who speak and write in that language." Ladislav Zgusta, "Copying in Lexicography: Monier-Williams' Sanskrit Dictionary and Other Cases (Dvaikośyam)," *Lexicographica: An International Annual for Lexicography* 4 (1988): 146.

82. Adapted from Ḥusain, "Pesh Guftār," xvi.
83. An alternative version of his name is recorded by Saʿādat Ḳhān 'Nāṣir' in his *tażkirah Ḳhẉush Maʿrakah-i Zebā* as Sayyid Nażir ʿAlī. Ibid., vi, n. 1.
84. Sayyid Aḥmad Dihlawī, *Farhang-i Āṣafiyah* (New Delhi: Qaumī Kaunsil Barāʾe Firoġh-i Urdū Zabān, 1998), 3:2352.
85. C. M. Naim, "Shaikh Imam Bakhsh Sahbaʾi: Teacher, Scholar, Poet, and Puzzle-Master," in *The Delhi College: Traditional Elites, the Colonial State, and Education Before 1857*, ed. Margrit Pernau (New Delhi: Oxford University Press, 2006), 148.
86. On Shāh Naṣīr's role as *ustād* or master-poet preceptor, see Frances W. Pritchett, *Nets of Awareness: Urdu Poetry and Its Critics* (Berkeley: University of California Press, 1994), 9–10, 56–57, 79–80.
87. Qādir Baḳhsh Bahādur Ṣābir, *Gulistān-i Suḳhan* (Lucknow: Uttar Pradesh Urdū Akādmī, 1982), 464.
88. Ibid.; J. S. Grewal, *Sikhs of Punjab* (Cambridge: Cambridge University Press, 2008), 244.
89. Harbans Singh, *The Heritage of the Sikhs* (New Delhi: Manohar, 1983), 191.
90. Ṣābir, *Gulistān-i Suḳhan*, 464–465.
91. On the longstanding problem of theft from the library's collection, see David Kopf, *British Orientalism and the Bengal Renaissance: The Dynamics of Indian Modernization, 1773–1835* (Berkeley: University of California Press, 1969), 119; Kumar Das, *Sahibs and Munshis: An Account of the College of Fort William* (New Delhi: Orion, 1978), 92.
92. Ḥusain, "Pesh Guftār," viii.
93. Mīr Inshāʾallāh Ḳhāṅ Inshā, *Daryā-i Laṭāfat* [Urdu Translation], trans. Panḍit Brajmohan Dittātriyah 'Kaifī' (New Delhi: Anjuman-i Taraqqī-yi Urdū (Hind), 1988), 128–134.
94. Rangīn was, interestingly, the son of 'Miskīn', author of the *Ṭahmās Nāmah*. See chapter 3.
95. This work devotes two chapters to *luġhāt* and coined phrases (*ẓarb al-miṡāl*). Ḥusain, "Pesh Guftār," vi.
96. Ibid., xi.
97. Ibid., ix.
98. Ḥusain lists more than 150 poets from which Nakhat drew his prooftexts, demonstrating both the degree to which poets of earlier generations were already part of an established canon and the importance of lexicographers in bolstering the reputation of living poets in citing them as "authorities" (*asnād*, pl. of *sanad*). Ibid., xiv.
99. Ibid., xv.
100. Ibid., xxv.
101. Shaiḳh Muḥammad Ibrāhīm 'Żauq' (1788–1854) is best known as the poet laureate and *ustād* of the last Mughal emperor, Muḥammad Shāh 'Ẓafar' (1775–1862; r. 1837–1857). Pritchett, *Nets of Awareness*, 78–90.
102. Ḥusain, "Pesh Guftār," xxv–xxvi.
103. "*(muṣṭalaḥat) mardum wilāyatī qizilbāsh aur durrānī.*" Niyāz ʿAlī Beg 'Nakhat' Dihlawī Nakhat, *Maḳhzan-i Fawāʾid: Urdū Muṣṭalaḥāt, Muḥāwarāt aur Amṡāl kā ek Nādir Luġhat* (Patna: Khuda Bakhsh Oriental Public Library, 1998), 140.
104. Ḥusain, "Pesh Guftār," xvi.
105. This *qiṭʿah*, or verse set, contains two of only three total verses by 'Payām' included in Mīr's *tażkirah*. Mīr, *Nikāt al-Shuʿarā*, 26.

106. On the life and poetry of 'Payām', see Mīr Taqī Mīr, *Żikr-i Mīr*, trans. ʿAbdul Ḥaq (Aurangabad: Anjuman-i Taraqqī-yi Urdū, 1928), 74; Ḥasan Aḥmad Niẓāmī, *Shamālī Hind kī Urdū Shāʿirī meṅ Īhām-goʾī* (Aligarh: Educational Book House, 1997), 187.
107. See C. M. Naim, "The Theme of Homosexual (Pederastic) Love in Pre-Modern Urdu Poetry," in *Studies in the Urdu Ġazal and Prose Fiction*, ed. Muhammad Umar Memon (Madison: South Asian Studies, University of Wisconsin, 1979); Tariq Rahman, "Boy-Love in the Urdu Ghazal," *Annual of Urdu Studies* 7 (1990): 1–20.
108. Inshā, *Daryā-i Laṭāfat* [Urdu Translation], 103.
109. Ibid.
110. Laurence Lockhart, *Nadir Shah: A Critical Study Based Mainly Upon Contemporary Sources* (London: Luzac, 1938), 102.
111. 'Ḥazīn' offers a much larger number. *The Life of Sheikh Mohammed Ali Hazin, Written by Himself; Translated from Two Persian Manuscripts, and Illustrated with Notes Explanatory of the History, Poetry, Geography, etc. Which Therein Occur*, trans. Francis Cunningham Belfour (London, 1830), 299. For a listing of various estimates of deaths by authority, see Lockhart, *Nadir Shah*, 147 n. 4.
112. Scholarly consensus has congealed around the number twenty thousand. See Lockhart, *Nadir Shah*, 149; Muzaffar Alam and Sanjay Subrahmanyam, "Empiricism of the Heart: Close Encounters in an Eighteenth-Century Indo-Persian Text," *Studies in History* 15, no. 2 (1999): 272.
113. From the account of Ānand Rām 'Mukhliṣ' in Henry Miers Elliot and John Dowson, *The History of India, as Told by Its Own Historians: The Muhammadan Period* (London, 1877), 8:88.
114. Percy Molesworth Sykes, *A History of Persia* (London: Macmillan, 1921), 2:262.
115. One further valence connects the handsome rakes of Delhi with the cruel yet beautiful and fair-skinned Turk, here depicted as a Qizilbāsh soldier. On the Turk as a motif in Persianate literature, see Annemarie Schimmel, "Hindu and Turk: A Poetical Image and Its Application to Historical Fact," in *Islam and Cultural Change in the Middle Ages, Giorgio Levi Della Vida Biennial Conference, May 11–13, 1973, Near Eastern Center, Univ. of Calif., Los Angeles*, ed. Speros Vryonis (Wiesbaden: Harrassowitz, 1975). On associations of the Qizilbāsh with cannibalism in Safavid Iran, see Shahzad Bashir, "Shah Ismaʾil and the Qizilbash: Cannibalism in the Religious History of Early Safavid Iran," *History of Religions* 45, no. 3 (2006): 234–256.
116. Nakhat, *Makhzan-i Fawāʾid*, 140–141.
117. Sayyid Aḥmad Dihlawī, *Farhang-i Āṣafiyah* (New Delhi: National Academi [Taraqqī-yi Urdū Board edition], 1974), 2:14.
118. On this as a general problem in lexicography, see, e.g., William Frawley, "The Dictionary as Text," *International Journal of Lexicography* 2, no. 3 (1989): 231–248.
119. S. W. Fallon, *A New Hindustani-English Dictionary, with Illustrations from Hindustani Literature and Folk-Lore* (Banaras, 1879), 448.
120. Though examples from Lucknow could also be readily supplied. Frances Pritchett, personal communication, November 2010.
121. The third signification of *ṭopī* offered by Fallon (*New Hindustani-English Dictionary*, 448) is "the nut of the *penis*." Similar definitions are also offered in Dihlawī, *Farhang-i Āṣafiyah*, 2:12.
122. According to a very cursory count, *dandy* or *dandyism* appear ten times in his dictionary, while *fop*, *foppish*, *foppery*, or *foppishness* are used in total some seventeen

times. On the term *fop*, see Susan Staves, "A Few Kind Words for the Fop," *Studies in English Literature, 1500–1900* 22, no. 3 (1982): 413–428.

123. Fallon, *New Hindustani-English Dictionary*, 215, 567, 915.
124. Shyamal Mitra, personal communication, August 2015.
125. Cf. Mīr Inshāʾallāh Ḳhāṅ Inshā and Mirzā Muḥammad Ḥasan Qatīl, *Daryā-i Laṭāfat* (Murshidabad, 1848), 140; Inshā, *Daryā-i Laṭāfat* [Urdu Translation], 120. I thank Tarun Pant (personal communication, August 2015) for bringing this to my attention.
126. John Thompson Platts, *A Dictionary of Urdū, Classical Hindī, and English* (London, 1884), 441. I am grateful to Anjum Altaf, Darakhshan Khan, Samira Junaid, Pasha Muhammad Khan, Robert Phillips, Sajjad Rizvi, Vivek Sharma, and Frances Pritchett for their help interpreting this enigmatic verse. All errors in interpretation, however, are mine alone. Anjum Altaf (personal communication, August 2015) suggests the following translation:

    We are skinned/fleeced/pillaged by those who [seemingly] clasp us closest to their breasts/bosoms
    While [they conveniently] point to [/lay the blame on the heads of] outsiders/foreigners

127. Bashir, "Shah Ismaʾil and the Qizilbash."
128. Dihlawī, *Farhang-i Āṣafiyah*, 1:252.
129. The original, in Nakhat, *Maḳhzan-i Fawāʾid*, 141, appears as follows, with my English translation beneath:

    kahkashāṅ kī teġh rakhtā hai ʿalam
    ʿarṣah-i rūʾe zamīṅ hai qatl gāh
    us ke gardan par hai ḳhūn-i rang-i shafaq
    ṭopī wālā hai yĕh ćarḳh-i kaj-kulāh

    He keeps the Sword of the Milky Way as his standard
    The plain of the face of the earth is a scene of execution
    On his neck is blood the color of twilight,
    A *ṭopī wālā* is this crooked-capped sphere.

130. Ṣābir, *Gulistān-i Suḳhan*, 464.
131. Naṣīr also happened to be the *ustād* of Żauq. See Aloys Sprenger, *A Catalogue of the Arabic, Persian, and Hindústány Manuscripts, of the Libraries of the King of Oudh, Compiled Under the Orders of the Government of India* (Calcutta, 1854), 1:269; Muḥammad Ḥusain Āzād, *Āb-e ḥayāt: Shaping the Canon of Urdu Poetry*, trans. Frances W. Pritchett and Shamsur Rahman Faruqi (New Delhi: Oxford University Press, 2001), 318–329.
132. According to one source, the *dīwān* Naṣīr produced was said to comprise some one hundred thousand verses! Thomas William Beale, *The Oriental Biographical Dictionary* (Calcutta, 1881), 294.
133. Munshī Ćiraṅjī Lāl, *Maḳhzan al-Muḥāwarāt* (Lahore: Maqbū Ikaiḍamī, 1988), 7–8.
134. Naim, "Prize-Winning Adab"; Pritchett, *Nets of Awareness*, 37.
135. Pierre Bourdieu, "The Market of Symbolic Goods," in *The Field of Cultural Production: Essays on Art and Literature*, ed. Randal Johnson (New York: Columbia University Press, 1993), 115. An earlier version appears in *Poetics* 14, no. 1–2 (1985): 17.

136. Susanne Janssen, "The Empirical Study of Careers in Literature and the Arts," in *The Psychology and Sociology of Literature: In Honor of Elrud Ibsch*, ed. Dick Schram and Gerard Steen (Philadelphia: J. Benjamins, 2001), 326.
137. On the growth of corporate printing houses, see Ulrike Stark, *An Empire of Books: The Naval Kishore Press and the Diffusion of the Printed Word in Colonial India* (Ranikhet: Permanent Black, Distributed by Orient Longman, 2007), 64–83.
138. See Zgusta, "Copying in Lexicography," 146–147.
139. Fallon, *New Hindustani-English Dictionary*, vi.
140. A rare example of a work produced seemingly without any European patronage or assistance is the *Nafā'is al-Luġhāt* of Maulvī Auhaduddīn Aḥmad Bilgrāmī, first printed in Lucknow in 1837. Fitzedward Hall, while regretting that "it does not embrace in its plan the whole language, being confined, in great part, to such matters, useful to be understood, as are supposed to be frequently misapprehended," wrote favorably of this dictionary in an 1851 review. Hall is remembered today primarily for his later contributions to the *Oxford English Dictionary*. Fitzedward Hall, "Urdu Lexicography," *Benares Magazine* 3, no. 29 (1851): 880. For a later reprint, see Auḥad al-Din Bilgrāmī, *Nafā'is al-Luġhāt* (Kanpur, 1878).
141. Ikram Chaghatai, "Dr Aloys Sprenger and the Delhi College," in *The Delhi College: Traditional Elites, the Colonial State, and Education Before 1857*, ed. Margrit Pernau (New Delhi: Oxford University Press, 2006), 108. While several sources mention that Boutros was a French scholar of Arabic, Gail Minault has suggested that Boutros was instead an Arab Christian educated in France and with origins in Egypt or the Levant. Gail Minault, "Delhi College and Urdu," *Annual of Urdu Studies* 14 (1999): 124; Gail Minault, "Qiran al-Saʿâdain: The Dialogue Between Eastern and Western Learning at Delhi College," in *Perspectives of Mutual Encounters in South Asian History, 1760–1860*, ed. Jamal Malik (Leiden: Brill, 2000), 266. As M. Ikram Chaghatai has pointed out, "of all three principals of the Delhi College, from its inception to 1857, none was of British extraction and had no experience of educational matters." His predecessor, J. H. Taylor, had an Indian mother; Aloys Sprenger (1813–1893), his successor from 1845 to 1847, was born and largely educated in Austria before becoming an English citizen in 1838. Stephan Procházka, "Sprenger, Aloys Ignatz Christoph (1813–1893)," in *Oxford Dictionary of National Biography*, ed. H. C. G. Matthew and Brian Harrison (2004), http://www.oxforddnb.com/view/article/26176.
142. Minault, "Delhi College and Urdu"; Datla, "Making a Worldly Vernacular," 58–62.
143. Ḥusain, "Pesh Guftār," viii.
144. Michael S. Dodson, "Translating Science, Translating Empire: The Power of Language in Colonial North India," *Comparative Studies in Society and History* 47, no. 4 (2005): 821.
145. When forced to take leave, he arranged to receive a portion of his previous salary from his successor, Aloys Sprenger. Sprenger, it was alleged, did not honor this agreement. The matter was brought before Lord Canning, governor general, who decided in 1856 to strip Sprenger of all his civil appointments, dooming a project long underway to complete a *Catalogue of the Kings of Awadh's Royal Libraries*. Only one volume was published, and following the events in Lucknow during the following two years, the contents of those libraries were largely lost or destroyed. Chaghatai, "Dr Aloys Sprenger and the Delhi College," 124.
146. Naim, "Shaikh Imam Bakhsh Sahba'i," 182, n. 99.

147. Hāshmī, *Urdū Luġhat Nawīsī kā Pas Manẓar*, 150. Ḥāshmī, unfortunately, makes a number of significant errors and transcription in chronology throughout his history.
148. 'Ṣahbā'ī' did not publish any Urdu verse. He did produce a small *dīwān* of poetry in Persian that, while highly regarded by recent scholarship, is ranked by Naim as "meager" and the work of an "amateur." Where 'Ṣahbā'ī' is distinguished from Nakhat and the general tendency of the society as a whole is in his seeking to "make a name" for himself through the composition of verse in Persian alone. Waris Kirmani, *Dreams Forgotten: An Anthology of Indo-Persian Poetry* (Aligarh: Academic Books, 1986); Naim, "Shaikh Imam Bakhsh Sahba'i," 173–174, 183.
149. Naim, "Shaikh Imam Bakhsh Sahba'i," 183.
150. Ḥaq, "Urdū Luġhāt aur Luġhat Nawīsī," 40.
151. Ibid., 41.
152. Zgusta, *Manual of Lexicography*, 272.
153. For a discussion of the positions of the erstwhile Prague school as outlined by a prominent former member, see ibid., 188–190.
154. Later commentators have seen a direct connection between Dihlawī's dictionary and the project initiated by Ḥaq. Sayyid and Sarhindī, *Kutub-i Luġhat kā Taḥqīqī wa Lisānī Jā'izah*, 1:109.
155. Emphasis in the original. Fallon, *New Hindustani-English Dictionary*, vii.
156. Ḥaq's attitude can be understood as the product of post-1857 efforts by Urdu literary critics to reform poetry and respond to charges (real and imaginary) of Muslim immorality. Compare King, "Images of Virtue and Vice"; Pritchett, *Nets of Awareness*, 169–183.
157. Dihlawī, *Farhang-i Āṣafiyah*, 1:51.
158. For more on the descriptivist and norm-oriented lexicographic modes, see Zgusta, *Manual of Lexicography*, 185–196.
159. Ḥaq, "Urdū Luġhāt aur Luġhat Nawīsī," 40–42.
160. Ḳhalīq Anjum is of the opinion that "Sayyid Aḥmad Dihlawī's detractors have publicized that whatever materials Fallon collected for his dictionary, Sayyid Ṣāḥib used in his *Farhang-i Āṣafiyah*. This is a certainly mistaken, negligent, and groundless." Anjum, "Muqaddamah," 14.

5. GRASPING AT STRAWS

1. I use "British" with some trepidation. It is not clear whether Fallon would have considered himself Irish.
2. Gerry Farrell and Neil Sorrell, "Colonialism, Philology, and Musical Ethnography in Nineteenth-Century India: The Case of S. W. Fallon," *Music and Letters* 88, no. 1 (2007): 107. Elsewhere, Fallon's death is erroneously recorded as having occurred in October 1881. Mas'ūd Hāshmī, *Urdū Luġhat Nawīsī kā Pas Manẓar* (Delhi: Maktabah-yi Jāmi'ah, 1997), 60. See, e.g., the biographical notice in the card catalogue preserved at the Oriental and African Studies room in the British Library.
3. From the preface by M. D. Fallon ("Executrix to the Estate of the late Dr. S. W. Fallon") in S. W. Fallon and Lala Faqir Chand, *A New English-Hindustani Dictionary: With Illustrations from English Literature and Colloquial English, Translated Into Hindustani* (Banaras, 1883).

4. Fallon, *New Hindustani-English Dictionary*.
5. Ḥusainī, "Farhang-i Āṣafiyah Tanqīd ke Āʾīne meṅ," *Urdū Adab* 1 (1966): 107; Ḳhāliq Anjum, "Muqaddamah," in *Rusūm-i Dihlī*, ed. Ḳhalīq Anjum (New Delhi: Urdū Akādmī, 1986), 14; Hāshmī, *Urdū Luġhat Nawīsī kā Tanqīdī Jāʾizah*, 80. I am skeptical of the stated length of Sayyid Aḥmad's supposed apprenticeship, though despite some inconsistencies in his own account, there is some supporting external evidence of it having begun in 1873. Also included in Fallon's staff were a Lālah Faqīr Ćand, Lālah Ṭhākur Das, and Lālah Jagan Nāth. Hāshmī, *Urdū Luġhat Nawīsī kā Tanqīdī Jāʾizah*, 59.
6. S. W. Fallon, "Preface and Preliminary Dissertation," in *A New Hindustani-English Dictionary, with Illustrations from Hindustani Literature and Folk-Lore* (Banaras, 1879), iii; Hāshmī, *Urdū Luġhat Nawīsī kā Tanqīdī Jāʾizah*, 59.
7. Preface by M. D. Fallon, "Executrix to the Estate of the late Dr. S. W. Fallon." See also Hāshmī, *Urdū Luġhat Nawīsī kā Tanqīdī Jāʾizah*, 60.
8. Farrell and Sorrell, "Colonialism, Philology, and Musical Ethnography in Nineteenth-Century India," 111.
9. Fallon, "Preface and Preliminary Dissertation," i.
10. John Thompson Platts, *A Dictionary of Urdū, Classical Hindī, and English* (London, 1884), iii.
11. Fallon, "Preface and Preliminary Dissertation," xx.
12. Ibid., xxi. This runs quite against the advice of another seasoned lexicographer: "It can be said that well-educated informants are usually (but not always or automatically) better than less educated ones." Ladislav Zgusta, *Manual of Lexicography* (Prague: Academia Mouton, 1971), 235.
13. Fallon, "Preface and Preliminary Dissertation," xxi.
14. Ibid., xxii. The only South Asian assistant singled out by Fallon for praise is a certain "Raë Soham Lāl, the very able Head Master of Patna Normal School [to whom] the compiler is indebted for the large collection of popular Hindustanī scientific terms which will appear in this Dictionary." Ibid., xviii.
15. Anjum, "Muqaddamah," 14.
16. Hāshmī, *Urdū Luġhat Nawīsī kā Tanqīdī Jāʾizah*, 69.
17. See the (supplementary) "Services" section of *Bombay Civil List Corrected to 1st January 1877, Showing the Names, Designations, and Services of the Civil and Military Servants of Government in the General, Revenue, Judicial, Political, Financial, Ecclesiastical, Educational, Marine, Public Works, and Other Departments; Also a List of H. M.'s Justices of the Peace for Bombay; &c., &c.* (Bombay, 1877), 104. For more on Cooke, see ibid., 92; Anonymous, "Dr. Theodore Cooke," *Nature* 85, no. 2142 (1910): 82.
18. Munshī Ćiraṅjī Lāl, *Maḳhzan al-Muḥāwarāt* (Lahore: Maqbū Ikaiḍamī, 1988), title page.
19. For a useful overview of the author's life, see Mushirul Hasan, "Maulawi Zaka Ullah: Sharif Culture and Colonial Rule," in *The Delhi College: Traditional Elites, the Colonial State, and Education Before 1857*, ed. Margrit Pernau (New Delhi: Oxford University Press, 2006).
20. Reprinted in Lāl, *Maḳhzan al-Muḥāwarāt*, 15.
21. H. S. Reid et al., *Urdú-Hindí-English Vocabulary, Compiled for the Use of Beginners* (Agra, 1854).
22. Sayyid Aḥmad Dihlawī, *Farhang-i Āṣafiyah* (New Delhi: National Academi [Taraqqī-yi Urdū Board edition], 1974), 1:15.

23. "The Proprietors offer the best acknowledgements to his efficient staff Lal Faqir Chand, Head Assistant, Lala Chiranjī Lal, Lala Thakur Das and Lala Jagan Nath of Delhi, and Mr S. H. Wattling, Head Master of Darbhanga School for all aid rendered." M. D. Fallon's preface to Fallon and Chand, *New English-Hindustani Dictionary*. He appears as early as 1847 as assisting Charles C. Fink in translating J. D. D. Todd's *Hints on Self-Improvement*. James Fuller Blumhardt, *Catalogue of Hindustani Printed Books in the Library of the British Museum* (London, 1889), 65.
24. Lāl, *Makhzan al-Muḥāwarāt*, 2.
25. Richard Carnac Temple, "Preface," in *A Dictionary of Hindustani Proverbs, Including Many Marwari, Panjabi, Maggah, Bhojpuri, and Tirhuti Proverbs, Sayings, Emblems, Aphorisms, Maxims, and Similes*, ed. Richard Carnac Temple and Lala Faqir Chand (Banaras, 1886), ii.
26. S. W. Fallon, *A Hindustani-English Law and Commercial Dictionary* (Benares, 1879).
27. Lāl, *Makhzan al-Muḥāwarāt*, 2.
28. Fallon, "Preface and Preliminary Dissertation," vi–vii.
29. "*daura karnā, daure-ko uṭhnā*, v.n. To go on a tour or circuit; to hold sessions." Platts, *Dictionary of Urdū*, 533.
30. For more on the "Punjab School" of administration, under whose jurisdiction Delhi fell, see, e.g., David Gilmour, *The Ruling Caste: Imperial Lives in the Victorian Raj* (London: John Murray, 2005), 159–163.
31. Acknowledgments in Fallon, *New Hindustani-English Dictionary*.
32. Fallon, *A Hindustani-English Law and Commercial Dictionary*.
33. Fallon and Chand, *New English-Hindustani Dictionary*; S. W. Fallon, *A Dictionary of Hindustani Proverbs, Including Many Marwari, Panjabi, Maggah, Bhojpuri, and Tirhuti Proverbs, Sayings, Emblems, Aphorisms, Maxims, and Similes* (Banaras, 1886).
34. Platts, *Dictionary of Urdū*, iii.
35. Ibid., iv.
36. G. S. A. Ranking, "Platts, John Thompson (1830–1904)," in *Oxford Dictionary of National Biography*, ed. H. C. G. Matthew and Brian Harrison (2004), http://www.oxforddnb.com/view/article/35539.
37. John Thompson Platts and Alfred Wrigley, *A Companion to Wrigley's Collection of Examples: Being Illustrations of Mathematical Processes and Methods of Solution* (Cambridge, 1861).
38. William Crooke, *A Glossary of North Indian Peasant Life* (Delhi: Oxford University Press, 1989), xix–xx. See also Arjun Appadurai, "Number in the Colonial Imagination," in *Orientalism and the Postcolonial Predicament: Perspectives on South Asia*, ed. Carol Appadurai Breckenridge and Peter van der Veer (Philadelphia: University of Pennsylvania Press, 1993); Irfan Ahmad, "A Different Jihad: Dalit Muslims' Challenge to Ashraf Hegemony," *Economic and Political Weekly* 38, no. 46 (2003): 4889.
39. Kenneth W. Jones, "Religious Identity and the Indian Census," in *The Census in British India: New Perspectives*, ed. N. Gerald Barrier (New Delhi: Manohar, 1981), 77; J. S. Cotton and S. Gopal, "Hunter, Sir William Wilson (1840–1900)," in *Oxford Dictionary of National Biography*, ed. H. C. G. Matthew and Brian Harrison (2004), http://www.oxforddnb.com/view/article/14237.
40. Alex Tickell, "Negotiating the Landscape: Travel, Transaction, and the Mapping of Colonial India," *Yearbook of English Studies* 34 (2004): 18–30; U. Kalpagam, "Cartography in Colonial India," *Economic and Political Weekly* 30, no. 30 (1995): PE92.

41. Heinrich Ferdinand Blochmann, "Contributions to Persian Lexicography," *Journal of the Royal Asiatic Society of Bengal* 37, no. 1 (1868): 1. Interestingly, this complaint of a lack of a reliable dictionary appears as early as early as the 1770s. Robert Clive, "Proposals for Printing a Persian Dictionary," British Library MS EUR G 37 Box 17, section 66. The result of this work was Richardson's compilation, with the encouragement of William Jones, of massive, if flawed, dictionaries. Richardson, *A Dictionary, Persian, Arabic, and English* (Oxford, 1777); John Richardson, *A Dictionary, English, Persian, and Arabic* (Oxford, 1780).
42. Ranking, "Platts, John Thompson (1830–1904)."
43. Lāl, *Makhzan al-Muḥāwarāt*, 2–3.
44. Simon Winchester, *The Professor and the Madman: A Tale of Murder, Insanity, and the Making of the Oxford English Dictionary* (New York: HarperCollins, 1998), 151–155. Intriguingly, one of the most prominent figures to suggest a new comprehensive Urdu (Hindustānī)–English dictionary, Fitzedward Hall, was himself deeply involved in Murray's dictionary. Ibid., 166–167; W. B. Owen and J. B. Katz, "Hall, Fitzedward (1825–1901)," in *Oxford Dictionary of National Biography*, ed. H. C. G. Matthew and Brian Harrison (2004), http://www.oxforddnb.com/view/article/33652; Fitzedward Hall, "Urdu Lexicography," *Benares Magazine* 3, no. 29 (1851).
45. Vasudha Dalmia, *The Nationalization of Hindu Traditions: Bhāratendu Harishchandra and Nineteenth-Century Banaras* (Delhi: Oxford University Press, 1997), 148.
46. Ibid., 189.
47. Ibid.
48. Fallon, *New Hindustani-English Dictionary*, iii.
49. Fallon, "Preface and Preliminary Dissertation," i–ii.
50. Ibid., vi.
51. Ibid., xiii.
52. See ibid., ii, iii.
53. Ibid., vii.
54. Francesca Orsini, *The Hindi Public Sphere 1920–1940: Language and Literature in the Age of Nationalism* (New Delhi: Oxford University Press, 2002), 19. Lydia Liu describes analogous nationalist efforts by Chinese folklorists to appropriate minority cultures and thereby capture the *Volksgeist*, or spirit of the common people, to produce an "official popular culture." See Lydia Liu, "A Folksong Immortal and Official Popular Culture in Twentieth-Century China," in *Writing and Materiality in China: Essays in Honor of Patrick Hanan*, ed. Judith T. Zeitlin et al. (Cambridge, Mass.: Harvard University Asia Center, 2003), 562.
55. Pierre Bourdieu, "Social Space and the Genesis of 'Classes,'" in *Language and Symbolic Power*, ed. John B. Thompson (Cambridge, Mass.: Harvard University Press, 1991), 243.
56. Dihlawī, *Farhang-i Āṣafiyah*, 1:59–60.
57. Compare this long view of history with that espoused by Mīr Amman in his introduction to the *Bāġh o Bahār.* Mīr Amman Dihlawī, "Bagh-o-Bahar, or Tales of the Four Darweshes, translated from the Hindustani of Mir Amman of Dihli, by Duncan Forbes, L.L.D.," ed. Frances Pritchett (2005), 6–12, http://www.columbia.edu/itc/mealac/pritchett/00urdu/baghobahar/index.html. For a discussion, see Shamsur Rahman Faruqi, *Early Urdu Literary Culture and History* (New Delhi: Oxford University Press, 2001), 36–38.

58. Emphasis added. Lāl, *Maḵhzan al-Muḥāwarāt*, i.
59. Ibid., 2.
60. Ibid., 6. For a discussion of the terms "jargon" and "cant," see Peter Burke, "Introduction," in *Languages and Jargons: Contributions to a Social History of Language*, ed. Peter Burke and Roy Porter (Cambridge, Mass.: Polity, 1995). Burke's characterization (17) of Urdu as a pidgin and "originally the language of the Mughal bureaucracy" may give the reader the incorrect impression that Urdu was an administrative language under the Mughals. It did not officially become so until well into the nineteenth century.
61. Lāl, *Maḵhzan al-Muḥāwarāt*, 6. Gilchrist, as early as 1787, gives *moohavaru* as the "Hindoostanee" equivalent of the English "colloquial." John Borthwick Gilchrist, "Appendix to Part I of the Dictionary," in *A Dictionary, English and Hindoostanee, in Which the Words Are Marked with Their Distinguishing Initials; as Hinduwee, Arabic, and Persian, Whence the Hindoostanee, or What Is Vulgarly, but Improperly Called the Moor Language, Is Evidently Formed* (Calcutta, 1787), 26.
62. These terms are defined in Sayyid Aḥmad's section on the different types of lexical sources included in his work, a surprising list that includes such disparate items *paheliyāṅ* (riddles), *kĕh mukriyāṅ* (spoken misjoinders), *nisbateṅ* (analogues), *tambīh* (correction), *faṣāḥat* (eloquence), and *balāġhat* (rhetoric). Dihlawī, *Farhang-i Āṣafiyah*, 1:60–65. Each, of course, is supported by copious examples in verse. He explains his use of the terms *muḥāwarah* and *iṣṭilāh* in ibid., 1:64–65.
63. Ārzū devotes a section of his *Muśmir* to this. See Abu Lais Siddiqi, "Muthmir: A Linguistic Analysis," in *Muṯẖmir*, ed. Rehanna Khatoon (Karachi: Institute of Central and West Asian Studies, 1991), xx–xxi.
64. Irfan Ahmad discusses the problematic use of the term *qaum* in Pakistan: "The birth certificate issued by municipal offices in Punjab has a distinct compulsory column for caste. It is called 'qaum.'" Ahmad, "A Different Jihad," 4887. See also David Lelyveld, *Aligarh's First Generation: Muslim Solidarity in British India* (Princeton, N.J.: Princeton University Press, 1977), 344–345.
65. Alex Weingrod, "Patrons, Patronage, and Political Parties," *Comparative Studies in Society and History* 10, no. 4 (1968): 380.
66. Lelyveld, *Aligarh's First Generation*, 20–21.
67. On the transmission of *barakat* (blessing, auspiciousness) through Sufi *silsilah*s, see Edward Fusfeld, "The Shaping of Sufi Leadership in Delhi: The Naqshbandiyya Mujaddidiyya, 1750–1920" (PhD diss., University of Pennsylvania, 1981); Simon Digby, "The Sufi Shaikh as a Source of Authority in Medieval India," in *India's Islamic Traditions: 711–1750*, ed. Richard Maxwell Eaton (New Delhi: Oxford University Press, 2003).
68. Alok Rai, *Hindi Nationalism* (Hyderabad: Orient Longman, 2001), 40.
69. The sentence in question reads "If the *pīlak* [for *pablik* = 'public'?], having considered this, were to patronize me, then three or four hundred pages which I have written in a chapter on the quaint phrases of language and in several dictionaries (*kitābin luġhat*) in several drafts of which, having been revised, I will present before the *pīlak* [*sic*, should read *pablik*]." In the following sentence, the lithographer correctly spells the term: "Now I will offer my thanks to those benefactors because of whom today I have gained the opportunity to present my gift (*tŏhfah*) to the *pablik* (public)." Lāl, *Maḵhzan al-Muḥāwarāt*, 2. On early uses of the term in Urdu, see C. Ryan Perkins, "From the Meḥfil to the Printed Word: Public Debate and Discourse in Late Colonial India," *Indian Economic & Social History Review* 50, no. 1 (2013): 47–76.

70. On the rise of an "associational culture" in nineteenth-century northern India, see Lelyveld, *Aligarh's First Generation*, 82; Ulrike Stark, *An Empire of Books: The Naval Kishore Press and the Diffusion of the Printed Word in Colonial India* (Ranikhet: Permanent Black, Distributed by Orient Longman, 2007), 145–146. On the related concepts of *lok*, *jantā*, and *jātī*, see Orsini, *Hindi Public Sphere*, 141–142.
71. Lāl, *Makhzan al-Muḥāwarāt*, 1.
72. Fallon, *New Hindustani-English Dictionary*, v.
73. Compare with Orsini's discussion of the twentieth-century emergence of Hindi hegemony in *Hindi Public Sphere*, 382–383.
74. See, e.g., his discussions on "the language of the Sayyids of Burhā" and "the language of the Afghans" in Mīr Inshāʾallāh Ḳhāṅ Inshā, *Daryā-i Laṭāfat* [Urdu Translation], trans. Paṇḍit Brajmohan Dittātriyah 'Kaifī' (New Delhi: Anjuman-i Taraqqī-yi Urdū (Hind), 1988), 44–46.
75. Lāl, *Makhzan al-Muḥāwarāt*, 7.
76. Compare with Faruqi, *Early Urdu Literary Culture*, 24–27, 32.
77. Inshā, *Daryā-i Laṭāfat* [Urdu Translation], 102–103.
78. Edward Shils, "Mass Society and Its Culture," *Daedalus* 89, no. 2 (1960): 288–314; Edward Shils, "The Theory of Mass Society," *Diogenes* 39 (1962).
79. Quoted from Rai, *Hindi Nationalism*, 84.
80. Lāl, *Makhzan al-Muḥāwarāt*, 7.
81. Margrit Pernau, "Introduction," in *The Delhi College: Traditional Elites, the Colonial State, and Education Before 1857*, ed. Margrit Pernau (New Delhi: Oxford University Press, 2006), 14.
82. J. S. Grewal, *Sikhs of Punjab* (Cambridge: Cambridge University Press, 2008), II.3:128.
83. I owe this evocative phrase to Bhavani Raman. See her *Document Raj: Writing and Scribes in Early Colonial South India* (Chicago: University of Chicago Press, 2012).
84. James C. Scott, *Seeing Like a State: How Certain Schemes to Improve the Human Condition Have Failed* (New Haven, Conn.: Yale University Press, 1998), 48.
85. For a fascinating exploration of the role that written forms of language played as a symbol of colonial power and the role that literacy played in the imposition of people and land to state rule, see Ajay Skaria, "Writing, Orality, and Power in the Dangs, Western India, 1800s–1920s," *Subaltern Studies* 9 (1996): 13–58.
86. Lāl, *Makhzan al-Muḥāwarāt*, 8.
87. Fallon, *New Hindustani-English Dictionary*, vii.
88. Lāl, *Makhzan al-Muḥāwarāt*, 20.
89. Partha Chatterjee, *The Politics of the Governed: Reflections on Popular Politics in Most of the World* (New York: Columbia University Press, 2004), 40.
90. Lāl, *Makhzan al-Muḥāwarāt*, 7–8.
91. Ibid., 8.
92. Ibid., 350.
93. Fallon, *New Hindustani-English Dictionary*, 448.
94. Lāl, *Makhzan al-Muḥāwarāt*, 131.
95. Ibid.
96. Faruqi, *Early Urdu Literary Culture*, 66. This is Faruqi's translation of the original text that appears in Amīr Ḳhusrau Dihlawī Khusrau, *The Nuh Sipihr of Amir Khusraw: Persian Text, with Introduction, Notes, Index, etc.*, Islamic Research Association Series (London: Published for the Islamic Research Association by Oxford University Press, 1950), 12:179–180.

97. Faruqi, *Early Urdu Literary Culture*, 66.
98. On the absence of a distinction between Khaṛī Bolī and Braj by Ḳhusrau, see Amrit Rai, *A House Divided: The Origin and Development of Hindi/Hindavi* (Delhi: Oxford University Press, 1984), 135–137, 184–185, 188.
99. Ārzū and Hāṅswī, *Nawādir al-Alfāẓ*, 248–249.
100. Ẓuhūruddīn Ḥātim, "Dīwān-zādah-i Ḥātim," British Library Delhi MSS Urdu 68, 18th c., 1b. Compare this autograph MS with the printed edition: Ẓuhūruddīn Ḥātim, *Dīwān Zādah* (Lahore: Maktabah-yi Ḳhayābān-i Adab, 1975), 39. For more on this work, see Walter N. Hakala, "A Sultan in the Realm of Passion: Coffee in Eighteenth-Century Delhi," *Eighteenth-Century Studies* 47, no. 4 (2014): 373–375.
101. Inshā, *Daryā-i Laṭāfat* [Urdu Translation], 103.
102. Fallon, *New Hindustani-English Dictionary*, i.
103. H. H. Wilson, *A Glossary of Judicial and Revenue Terms, and of Useful Words Occurring in Official Documents Relating to the Administration of the Government of British India, from the Arabic, Persian, Hindustání, Sanskrit, Hindí, Bengálí, Uṛiya, Maráṭhi, Guzaráthí, Telugu, Karnáta, Tamil, Malayálam, and Other Languages* (London, 1855), iii.
104. Compare Fallon, "Preface and Preliminary Dissertation," vi–vii; Lāl, *Maḳhzan al-Muḥāwarāt*, 2.
105. This latter figure is of course Sayyid Aḥmad Ḳhān (1817–1898), the founder of the Muhammadan Anglo-Oriental College (Aligarh Muslim University). On his life, see Lelyveld, *Aligarh's First Generation*.
106. For useful analogues, see Frances W. Pritchett's discussion of the scholar-critics Muḥammad Ḥusain Āzād (1830–1910) and especially Alṭāf Ḥusain Ḥālī (1837–1914) in *Nets of Awareness: Urdu Poetry and Its Critics* (Berkeley: University of California Press, 1994), 13–15, 26–28, 42–44.
107. Platts, *Dictionary of Urdū*, 1033.
108. Ḥālī, "Farhang-i Āṣafiyah," 59–60. Compare with Rai, *A House Divided*, 259–260, 263–264.
109. Lelyveld, *Aligarh's First Generation*, 309; Rai, *Hindi Nationalism*, 37.
110. Lelyveld, *Aligarh's First Generation*, 307–308.
111. Rai, *Hindi Nationalism*, 59.
112. Ibid., 19.
113. Peter Breton, *A Vocabulary of the Names of the Various Parts of the Human Body and of Medical and Technical Terms in English, Arabic, Persian, Hindee, and Sanscrit for the Use of the Members of the Medical Department in India* (Calcutta, 1825).
114. Fallon, *A Hindustani-English Law and Commercial Dictionary*; Muḥammad Jalīl al-Raḥman Ḳhān Jalandharī Ḳhān, *Qānūn Ḍikshanarī* (Sadhaura, 1893). More recent works include Henry Campbell Black, *Qānūnī, Angrezī-Urdū Luġhat: Blaiks Lā Dikshanarī se Māḳhūz (Based on Black's Law Dictionary)* (Islamabad: Muqtadirah-i Qaumī Zabān, 2002); M. Mohammad Taimur Khan, *Dictionary of Law: English to Urdu* (Lahore: Kashmir Law Times, 2004).
115. Shoukut Ali, *A Hindustani and Persian Guide for the Civilians, Military Officers, Doctors, and Royal Engineers of Her Majesty's Services in India* (Calcutta, 1895).
116. For an early vocabulary of the natural sciences, see Wakīl Dargāhī Lāl, *Jagat-Prakāsh* (Cawnpore, 1892). Muḥammad Maẓhar Karīm's translation of an Arabic dictionary of geography may have been carried out while in confinement following the Mutiny: ʿAbdul Mūmin, *Marāṣid al-Iṭṭilāʿ* [A geographical dictionary], trans. Muḥammad Maẓhar Karīm (Port Blair, 1861). For another Urdu translation of an

original Arabic work, in this case on zoology, see Muḥammad ibn Mūsā Damīrī, *Ḥayāt al-Ḥaiwān*, trans. Maulavī ʿAbd al-Qādir Deobandī (Lucknow, 1905).

117. For general comments, especially on ʿAbdul Ḥaq's role in promoting an official list of technical terms in Urdu, see Kavita Saraswathi Datla, "Making a Worldly Vernacular: Urdu, Education, and Osmania University, Hyderabad, 1883–1938" (PhD diss., University of California, 2006), 85–95.
118. An example would be this work that explains Arabic, Persian, Turkish and other foreign words in use in Hindustani: Muftī Ġhulām Sarwar, *Zubdat al-Luġhāt* [also called *Luġhāt-i Sarwarī*] (Lucknow, 1877). For a Telegu–Urdu dictionary, see Timmā Reḍḍi Tāṭikoṇḍa Reḍḍi, *Shabdārtha-Chintāmaṇi* (Madras, 1906). For terms and expressions used by *Thugs*, a "criminal tribe," see Muḥammad ʿAlī Akbar Allāhabādī Akbar, *Muṣṭalaḥāt-i Ṭhagī* (Calcutta, 1839).
119. "Directionality" is a technical term denoting the "user orientation of the bilingual dictionary according to the direction of the look-up operation." Reinhard Rudolf Karl Hartmann and Gregory James, *Dictionary of Lexicography* (New York: Routledge, 1998), 44.
120. Lāl, *Makhzan al-Muḥāwarāt*, 11.
121. Rai, *A House Divided*, 257.
122. Lāl, *Makhzan al-Muḥāwarāt*, 12.
123. "For example," he notes, "there is one Hindi term *bāt* for which I have given 73 meanings in the *Makhzan*. In Urdu there is not even a single Persian-Arabic word that has fifty meanings." Ibid.
124. I have generally steered clear of broader debates regarding the "court character" at the turn of the century. The reader is directed toward a number of excellent studies on the topic. See, especially, Anonymous, *A Defence of the Urdu Language and Character: Being a Reply to the Pamphlet Called "Court Character and Primary Education in N.-W.P. & and Oude"* (Allahabad: Liddel's N.-W.P. Printing Works, 1900); Christopher Rolland King, "Images of Virtue and Vice: The Hindi-Urdu Controversy in Two Nineteenth-Century Hindi Plays," in *Religious Controversy in British India: Dialogues in South Asian Languages*, ed. Kenneth W. Jones (Albany: State University of New York Press, 1992); Christopher Rolland King, *One Language, Two Scripts: The Hindi Movement in Nineteenth-Century North India* (Bombay: Oxford University Press, 1994); Dalmia, *Nationalization of Hindu Traditions*; Rai, *Hindi Nationalism*; Orsini, *Hindi Public Sphere*.
125. Asha Sarangi, "Enumeration and the Linguistic Identity Formation in Colonial North India," *Studies in History* 25, no. 2 (2010): 201.
126. Arun Agrawal, "Indigenous Knowledge and the Politics of Classification," *International Social Science Journal* 54 (2002): 290.
127. Ibid., 291.
128. Ibid.
129. Brass, *Language, Religion, and Politics in North India*, 28–36; King, *One Language, Two Scripts*, 2–3.
130. Agrawal, "Indigenous Knowledge," 291–292.
131. Title page of Munshī Ćirañjī Lāl, *Makhzan al-Muḥāwarāt*, 2nd rev. ed. (Delhi, 1898).
132. C. H. Oertel, *The Punjab Record; or, Reference Book for Civil Officers*, vol. 50, part 1 (Lahore: Samuel T. Weston, 1915), 109.
133. Amit Kumar Gupta, "Defying Death: Nationalist Revolutionism in India, 1897–1938," *Social Scientist* 25 (1997): 9.
134. Oertel, *The Punjab Record*, 62.

CONCLUSION

Faiẓ Aḥmad Faiẓ, *Selected poems of Faiz Ahmad Faiz*, trans. Shiv Kumar Kumar (New Delhi: Viking, 1995), vii.

1. T. Grahame Bailey, "Review: *Jamiʿ ul-Lug̱āt*. A New Urdu Dictionary by ʿAbdul Majīd," *Bulletin of the School of Oriental Studies* 9 (1938): 440–441.
2. David J. Matthews, "Urdu Language and Education in India," *Social Scientist* 31, no. 5/6 (2003): 68–69.
3. ʿAbdul Ḥaq, "Muqaddamah: Urdū Luġhāt aur Luġhat Nawīsī," in *Luġhat-i Kabīr-i Urdū* (Karachi: Anjuman-i Taraqqī-yi Urdū, 1973), 47.
4. Tariq Rahman, *Language and Politics in Pakistan* (Karachi: Oxford University Press, 1996), 1. This figure would have been substantially lower prior to 1971, when Bengali-speaking East Pakistan declared independence and became Bangladesh.
5. This English translation appears in Kavita Saraswathi Datla, "A Worldly Vernacular: Urdu at Osmania University," *Modern Asian Studies* 43, no. 5 (2009): 1131. The original Urdu appears in ʿAbdul Ḥaq, "Muqadamah," in *Maʿishiyat al-Hind* (Hyderabad: Jāmiʿah ʿUs̱māniyah, 1929), 4.
6. ʿAbdul Ḥaq, ed., *Luġhat-i Kabīr-i Urdū* (Karachi: Anjuman-i Taraqqī-yi Urdū, 1973), vol. 1.
7. Thereby encouraging the recruitment of court scribes who were proficient in both scripts. Christopher Rolland King, *One Language, Two Scripts: The Hindi Movement in Nineteenth-Century North India* (Bombay: Oxford University Press, 1994), 156, 158; Alok Rai, *Hindi Nationalism* (Hyderabad: Orient Longman, 2001), 17–20, 36–49.
8. King, *One Language, Two Scripts*, 163.
9. Ibid.; Kavita Saraswathi Datla, *The Language of Secular Islam: Urdu Nationalism and Colonial India* (2013), 73–74.
10. The original English-language *Dawn* article is reprinted as Rauf Parekh, "A Great Dream Comes True," in *Urdū Luġhat: Yādgārī Maẓāmīn*, ed. Abūlḥasanāt (Karachi: Unikarians International, 2010).
11. A key work in this regard is Irfan Habib, *The Agrarian System of Mughal India, 1556–1707* (New Delhi: Oxford University Press, 1999), 487, 501–502.
12. Baevskii does devote an important chapter to "Persian *Farhang*s as Sources for Cultural History" but largely avoids drawing overarching conclusions regarding the cultural changes that these sources document. Solomon I. Baevskii, *Early Persian Lexicography: Farhangs of the Eleventh to the Fifteenth Centuries*, trans. N. Killian (Honolulu: University of Hawai'i Press, 2007), 177–205.
13. "Normally a person tries to describe correctly what he wants to refer to because normally this is the best way to get his audience to recognize what he is referring to." Keith S. Donnellan, "Reference and Definite Descriptions," *The Philosophical Review* 75 (1966), 292.
14. Asif Agha, *Language and Social Relations* (Cambridge: Cambridge University Press, 2007), 89.
15. Pierre Bourdieu, *Language and Symbolic Power*, ed. John B. Thompson (Cambridge, Mass.: Harvard University Press, 1991), 192.
16. See Valentina Izmirlieva, *All the Names of the Lord: Lists, Mysticism, and Magic* (Chicago: University of Chicago Press, 2008); Jack Goody, *The Domestication of the Savage Mind* (Cambridge: Cambridge University Press, 1977), 81.

17. See, for example, SIL, "The Rapid Word Collection Methodology," *SIL International*, http://www.sil.org/dictionaries-lexicography/rapid-word-collection-methodology; Ellen F. Prince, "Toward a Taxonomy of Given-New Information," in *Radical Pragmatics*, ed. Peter Cole (New York: Academic Press, 1981); William Frawley, "The Dictionary as Text," *International Journal of Lexicography* 2, no. 3 (1989): 231–248.
18. Ireneusz Opacki, "Royal Genres," in *Modern Genre Theory*, ed. David Duff (Harlow: Longman, 2000).
19. On autonomous agents and the adjacent possible, see Stuart Kauffman, "Autonomous Objects," in *Science and Ultimate Reality: Quantum Theory, Cosmology, and Complexity*, ed. John D. Barrow et al. (Cambridge: Cambridge University Press, 2004).
20. Early nineteenth-century glossaries of Anglo-English "jargon" would similarly give way to more comprehensive dictionaries. Javed Majeed, " 'The Bad Habit': *Hobson-Jobson*, British Indian Glossaries, and Intimations of Mortality," *Bulletin of the Henry Sweet Society for the History of Linguistic Ideas* 46–47 (2006): 9.
21. Cassiodorus, *Cassiodori Senatoris Institutiones* (Oxford: Clarendon, 1937), 120. Translated in Nicholas Howe, *The Old English Catalogue Poems* (Copenhagen: Rosenkilde and Bagger, 1985), 34.
22. Prince, "Toward a Taxonomy of Given-New Information," 233–237.
23. See, for example, the poet Shāh Ḥātim's statements regarding the reform of Urdu orthography in Z̤uhūruddīn Ḥātim, *Dīwān Zādah*, ed. Ġhulām Ḥusain Żūʾal-faqār (Lahore: Maktabah-yi Ḳhayābān-i Adab, 1975), 40.
24. As is argued by Aamir R. Mufti in "Orientalism and the Institution of World Literatures," *Critical Inquiry* 36, no. 3 (2010): 458–493. Compare with Amrit Rai, *A House Divided: The Origin and Development of Hindi/Hindavi* (Delhi: Oxford University Press, 1984), 11, 17.
25. Mufti, "Orientalism and the Institution of World Literatures," 459, 461, 473.
26. Compare with Mohamad Tavakoli-Targhi, "Orientalism's Genesis Amnesia," *Comparative Studies of South Asia, Africa, and the Middle East* 16, no. 1 (1996): 1–14; Mohamad Tavakoli-Targhi, *Refashioning Iran: Orientalism, Occidentalism, and Historiography* (Basingstoke: Palgrave, 2001); Arthur Dudney, "A Desire for Meaning: Khan-i Arzu's Philology and the Place of India in the Eighteenth-Century Persianate World" (PhD diss., Columbia University, 2013), 123–131.
27. Ulrike Stark, *An Empire of Books: The Naval Kishore Press and the Diffusion of the Printed Word in Colonial India* (Ranikhet: Permanent Black, Distributed by Orient Longman, 2007), 145.
28. Even in a recent draft proposal for the internationalization of domain names, it remains uncertain how, if at all, multiscript URLs will be implemented. "Guidelines for the Implementation of Internationalized Domain Names" (2007), 3, https://www.icann.org/en/system/files/files/idn-guidelines-26apr07-en.pdf.

BIBLIOGRAPHY

UNPUBLISHED SOURCES

Ārzū, Sirājuddīn ʿAlī Ḳhān. "Nawádir-ul-alfáz." National Archives of India Fort William College MS 106 ACC no. 432. 1870.

Bilgrami. "Catalogue of the Persian Delhi MSS." British Library TS, n.d.

Bowrey, Thomas. "Thomas Bowrey's Collection of Notes on Oriental Languages." British Library MS EUR E 192. 1680.

Clive, Robert. "Proposals for Printing a Persian Dictionary." British Library MS EUR G 37, box 17, section 66.

Ḥātim, Ẓuhūruddīn. "Dīwān-zādah-i Ḥātim." British Library Delhi MSS Urdu 68. 18th century.

Ḳhusrau. "Muṭbūʿ-i Ṣibyān." Maulana Azad Library (Aligarh Muslim University) H.G. Urdu 53/31. 19th century.

Leyden, John Caspar. "A Vocabulary Persian and Hindoostanee [and Maldivian]." British Library MSS Eur B103. 1808.

"Lughāt-i Hindī." Asiatic Society of Bengal Persian Society Collection MS 1446. 13th c. AH.

Shore, John. "Secret Minutes of the Governor General dated the 13th January, 1798." Cleveland Public Library East India Company Manuscript Collection MS 091.92 Ea77M5.

Ṭapish Dihlawī, Mirzā Jān. "Shams al-Bayān fī Muṣṭalaḥāt al-Hindūstān." British Library Add. 18,889. AH 1215.

Yūsufī, Yūsuf bin Muḥammad. "Kaside der Luğat-ı Hindi." Nuruosmaniye Kütüphanesı MS 0003495.

LEXICOGRAPHICAL WORKS

Aḥmad, Nażīr. "Ajay Ćand Nāmah." In *Maqālāt-i Nażīr*, 121–157. New Delhi: Ghalib Institute, 2002.

Ali, Shoukut. *A Hindustani and Persian Guide for the Civilians, Military Officers, Doctors and Royal Engineers of Her Majesty's Services in India.* Calcutta, 1895.

Ārzū, Sirājuddīn ʿAlī Ḳhān, and ʿAbdul Wāsěʿ Hāṅswī. *Nawādir al-Alfāẓ & Ġharāʾib al-Luġhāt.* Edited by Sayyid ʿAbdullāh. Karachi: Anjuman-i Taraqqī-yi Urdū Pākistān, 1951.

Bilgrāmī, Auḥad al-Din. *Nafā'is al-Luġhāt*. Kanpur, 1878.

Black, Henry Campbell. *Qānūnī, Angrezī-Urdū Luġhat: Blaiks Lā Dikshanarī se Māķhūz* [Based on *Black's Law Dictionary*]. Islamabad: Muqtadirah-i Qaumī Zabān, 2002.

Bowrey, Thomas. *A Dictionary, English and Malayo, Malayo and English. To which is added some Short Grammar Rules . . . and also Several Miscellanies, Dialogues, and Letters, in English and Malayo, etc.* London: 1701.

Breton, Peter. *A Vocabulary of the Names of the Various Parts of the Human Body and of Medical and Technical Terms in English, Arabic, Persian, Hindee, and Sanscrit for the Use of the Members of the Medical Department in India*. Calcutta, 1825.

Dihlawī, Sayyid Aḥmad. *Farhang-i Āṣafiyah*. 4 vols. New Delhi: National Academi [Taraqqī-yi Urdū Board edition], 1974.

——. *Farhang-i Āṣafiyah*. 3 vols. New Delhi: Qaumī Kaunsil Barā'e Firoġh-i Urdū Zabān, 1998.

——. *Luġhāt al-Nisā'*. Lahore: Maqbūl Akademī, 1988.

Elliot, Henry Miers. *Supplement to the Glossary of Indian Terms*. Agra, 1845.

Elliot, Henry Miers, and John Beames. *Memoirs on the History, Folk-Lore, and Distribution of the Races of the North Western Provinces of India: Being an Amplified Edition of the Original Supplemental Glossary of Indian Terms*. 2 vols. London, 1869.

Fallon, S. W. *A Dictionary of Hindustani Proverbs, Including Many Marwari, Panjabi, Maggah, Bhojpuri, and Tirhuti Proverbs, Sayings, Emblems, Aphorisms, Maxims, and Similes*. Edited by Richard Carnac Temple and Lala Faqir Chand. Banaras, 1886.

——. *A Hindustani-English Law and Commercial Dictionary*. Banaras, 1879.

——. *A New Hindustani-English Dictionary, with Illustrations from Hindustani Literature and Folk-Lore*. Banaras, 1879.

Fallon, S. W., and Lala Faqir Chand. *A New English-Hindustani Dictionary: With Illustrations from English Literature and Colloquial English, Translated Into Hindustani*. Edited by J. D. Bate. Banaras, 1883.

Farāhī, Abū Naṣar Muḥammad Badruddīn. *Niṣāb al-Ṣibyān*. Tehran: Ćāpķhānah-yi Shirkat-i Kāviyānī, 1923.

Fārsī Nāmah, Wāḥid Bārī, Ṣamad Bārī, and Allāh Bārī. Lahore, 1845.

Ġhālib, Mirzā Asadullāh Ķhān. *Fārsī Nāmah-i Kalān ma' Qādir Nāmah-i Ġhālib*. Bareily: Lālah Ramcarān Lāl Agarwāl Buk Sellar enḍ Pablishar, n.d.

Gilchrist, John Borthwick. *A Dictionary, English and Hindoostanee, in Which the Words are Marked with Their Distinguishing Initials; as Hinduwee, Arabic, and Persian, Whence the Hindoostanee, or What is Vulgarly, but Improperly Called the Moor Language, is Evidently Formed*. 2 vols. Calcutta, 1787.

Gladwin, Francis. *A Vocabulary English & Persian for the College at Fort William in Bengal*. Calcutta, 1800.

Hāṅswī, 'Abdul Wāsě'. *Risālah-yi Jān Pahcān*. Kanpur, 1851.

Ḥaq, 'Abdul. "Miśl-i *Ķhāliq Bārī*: Ek Qadīmtarīn Kitāb." In *Qadīm Urdū*, 198–207. Karachi: Kul Pākistān Anjuman-i Taraqqī-yi Urdū, 1961.

——, ed. *Luġhat-i Kabīr-i Urdū*. 2 vols. Karachi: Anjuman-i Taraqqī-yi Urdū, 1973.

Hartmann, Reinhard Rudolf Karl, and Gregory James. *Dictionary of Lexicography*. London: Routledge, 1998.

Hunter, William, Thomas Roebuck, and Horace Hayman Wilson. *A Collection of Proverbs, and Proverbial Phrases: in the Persian and Hindoostanee Languages*. Calcutta, 1824.

Inshā, Mīr Inshā'allāh Ķhāṅ, and Mirzā Muḥammad Ḥasan Qatīl. *Daryā-i Laṭāfat*. Murshidabad, 1848. Translated into Urdu by Panḍit Brajmohan Dittātriyah 'Kaifī' as *Daryā-i*

Laṯāfat, edited by Maulvī ʿAbdul Ḥaq. New Delhi: Anjuman-i Taraqqī-yi Urdū (Hind), 1988.

Khan, Ahmed-uddin. *The East and West Khaliq Baree*. Moradabad: Afẓal al-Muṯābiʿ Press, 1906.

Khan, M. Mohammad Taimur. *Dictionary of Law: English to Urdu*. Lahore: Kashmir Law Times, 2004.

Ḳhān, Muḥammad Jalīl al-Raḥman Ḳhān Jalandharī. *Qānūn Ḍikshanarī*. Sadhaura, 1893.

Ḳhān, Ẓiyāʾ al-Dīn Aḥmad. *Aḳhbārī Luġhāt maʿrūf bĕh Kalīd-i Aḳhbār Bīnī*. Delhi: Delhi Printing Works, 1915.

Lāl, Munshī Ćiraṇjī. *Maḳhzan al-Muḥāwarāt*. Lahore: Maqbū Ikaiḍamī, 1988.

——. *Maḳhzan al-Muḥāwarāt*. 2nd rev. ed. Delhi: Imperial Book Depot, 1898.

Lāl, Wakīl Dargāhī. *Jagat-Prakāsh*. Cawnpore, 1892.

Lane, Edward William. *An Arabic-English Lexicon, Derived from the Best and the Most Copious Eastern Sources*. Edited by Stanley Lane-Poole. 8 vols. London, 1885.

Mishra, Pandit Braj Vallabh. *An English-Hindi Vocabulary in Verse*. Second ed. Calcutta: Gunsindhu Press, 1902.

Mūmin, ʿAbdul. *Marāṣid al-Iṯṯilāʿ* [*A Geographical Dictionary*]. Translated by Muḥammad Maẕhar Karīm. Port Blair, 1861.

Nakhat, Niyāz ʿAlī Beg 'Nakhat' Dihlawī. *Maḳhzan-i Fawāʾid: Urdū Muṣṯalaḥāt, Muḥāwarāt aur Amṡāl kā ek Nādir Luġhat*. Edited by Muḥammad Żākir Ḥusain. Patna: Khuda Bakhsh Oriental Public Library, 1998.

Phillott, Douglas Craven. *Ḳhazīnah-e Muḥāwarāt; or, Urdu Idioms*. Calcutta: Baptist Mission Press, 1912.

Platts, John Thompson. *A Dictionary of Urdū, Classical Hindī, and English*. London, 1884.

Reḍḍi, Timmā Reḍḍi Tāṭikoṇḍa. *Shabdārtha-Chintāmaṇi*. Madras, 1906.

Reid, H. S., Munshi Chiranji Lal, and Pandit Bunsi Dhar. *Urdú-Hindí-English Vocabulary, Compiled for the Use of Beginners*. Agra, 1854.

Richardson, John. *A Dictionary, English, Persian and Arabic*. Oxford, 1780.

——. *A Dictionary, Persian, Arabic, and English*. Oxford, 1777.

Samekita Praśāsana Śabdāvalī, Āngrezī-Hindī Consolidated Glossary of Administrative Terms, English-Hindi. New Delhi: Standing Commission for Scientific and Technical Terminology, Government of India, 1968.

Sarwar, Muftī Ġhulām. *Zubdat al-Luġhāt* [also called *Luġhāt-i Sarwarī*]. Lucknow, 1877.

Sherānī, Ḥāfiẓ Maḥmūd, ed. "Baććoṅ ke Taʿlīmī Niṣāb." In *Maqālāt-i Ḥāfiẓ Maḥmūd Sherānī*, edited by Maẕhar Maḥmūd Sherānī, 13–99. Lahore: Majlis-i Taraqqī-yi Urdū, 1985.

——. *Ḥifẓ al-Lisān (maʿrūf ba-nām-i Ḳhāliq Bārī)*. Delhi: Anjuman-i Taraqqī-yi Urdū, 1944.

Steingass, Francis Joseph. *A Comprehensive Persian-English Dictionary, Including the Arabic Words and Phrases to Be Met with in Persian Literature*. London, 1892.

Ṯapish Dihlawī, Mirzā Jān. *Shams al-Bayān fī Muṣṯalaḥāt al-Hindūstān*. Edited by ʿĀbid Raẓā Bedār. Patna: Khuda Bakhsh Oriental Public Library, 1979.

Taylor, Joseph, and William Hunter. *A Dictionary, Hindoostanee and English*. 2 Vols. Calcutta, 1808.

Williams, Raymond. *Keywords: A Vocabulary of Culture and Society*. New York: Oxford University Press, 1976.

Wilson, H. H. *A Glossary of Judicial and Revenue Terms, and of Useful Words Occurring in Official Documents Relating to the Administration of the Government of British India, from the Arabic, Persian, Hindustání, Sanskrit, Hindí, Bengálí, Uṛiya, Maráṭhi, Guzaráthí, Telugu, Karnáta, Tamiḻ, Malayálam, and Other Languages*. London, 1855.

OTHER SOURCES

ʿAbdullāh, Sayyid. *Adabiyāt-i Farsī meṅ Hindūʾoṅ kā Ḥiṣṣah*. Lahore: Majlis Taraqqī-yi Adab, 1967.

——. "Muqaddamah." In *Nawādir al-Alfāẓ & Ġharāʾib al-Luġhāt*, i–xlviii. Karachi: Anjuman-i Taraqqī-yi Urdū Pākistān, 1951.

Ābrū, Najmuddīn Shāh Mubārak. *Dīwān-i Ābrū*. Edited by Muḥammad Ḥasan. New Delhi: Taraqqī-yi Urdū Biyūro, 2000.

Abūlḥasanāt, ed. *Urdū Luġhat: Yādgārī Maẓāmīn*. Karachi: Unikarians International, 2010.

Agha, Asif. *Language and Social Relations*. Cambridge: Cambridge University Press, 2007.

Agrawal, Arun. "Indigenous Knowledge and the Politics of Classification." *International Social Science Journal* 54 (2002): 287–297.

Āh, Ṣafdar. *Amīr Ḳhusrau baḥaiśiyat-i Hindī Shāʿir*. Bombay: ʿUlūmī Buk Ḍipo, 1966.

Ahmad, Aziz. "The Formation of the *Sabk-i Hindī*." In *Iran and Islam: In Memory of the Late Vladimir Minorsky*, edited by C. E. Bosworth, 1–9. Edinburgh: Edinburgh University Press, 1971.

Ahmad, B. "Ānand Rām Moḳleṣ." In *Encyclopedia Iranica Online*, edited by Ehsan Yarshater, 1985. http://www.iranicaonline.org/articles/anand-ram-mokles.

Ahmad, Badrud-din. "Old Judicial Records of the Calcutta High Court." *Indian Historical Records Commission: Proceedings of Meetings* 5 (1923): 70–76.

Ahmad, Irfan. "A Different Jihad: Dalit Muslims' Challenge to Ashraf Hegemony." *Economic and Political Weekly* 38, no. 46 (2003): 4886–4891.

Aḥmad, Nażīr. "Ajay Ćand Nāmah." In *Maqālāt-i Nażīr*, 121–157. New Delhi: Ghalib Institute, 2002.

——. "Preface." In *Farhang-i Lisān al-Shuʿarāʾ: bĕh Sāl-i 753–790 Hijrī, ʿAhd-i Fīrūz Shāh Tuġhlaq*, edited by Nażīr Aḥmad, i–xiv. New Delhi: Rāyzanī-yi Farhangī-yi Jumhūrī-yi Islāmī-yi Īrān, 1995.

Ahmadi, Wali. *Modern Persian Literature in Afghanistan: Anomalous Visions of History and Form*. London: Routledge, 2008.

Ahmed, Rafique. "Ziauddin Ahmed Barni: Critical Analysis of His Scholarly and Literary Contributions." Unpublished dissertation, University of Sindh, 2009.

Akbar, Muḥammad ʿAlī Akbar Allāhabādī. *Muṣṭalaḥāt-i Ṭhagī*. Edited by Mīr Karāmath ʿAli. Calcutta, 1839.

Alam, Muzaffar. *The Crisis of Empire in Mughal North India: Awadh and the Punjab, 1707–48*. Delhi: Oxford University Press, 1986.

——. "The Culture and Politics of Persian in Precolonial Hindustan." In *Literary Cultures in History: Reconstructions from South Asia*, edited by Sheldon Pollock, 131–197. Berkeley: University of California Press, 2003.

——. *The Languages of Political Islam: India, 1200–1800*. Chicago: University of Chicago Press, 2004.

——. "The Pursuit of Persian: Language in Mughal Politics." *Modern Asian Studies* 32, no. 2 (1998): 317–349.

Alam, Muzaffar, and Subrahmanyam, Sanjay. "Empiricism of the Heart: Close Encounters in an Eighteenth-Century Indo-Persian Text." *Studies in History* 15, no. 2 (1999): 261–291.

——. "Envisioning Power: The Political Thought of a Late Eighteenth-Century Mughal Prince." *Indian Economic & Social History Review* 43, no. 2 (2006): 131–161.

——. *Indo-Persian Travels in the Age of Discoveries, 1400–1800*. Cambridge: Cambridge University Press, 2007.

——. "The Making of a Munshi." *Comparative Studies of South Asia Africa and the Middle East* 24, no. 2 (2004): 61–72.

——. "Power in Prison: A Mughal Prince in Shahjahanabad, ca. 1800." In *De l'Arabie à l'Himalaya: Chemins Croisés. En Hommage à Marc Gaborieau*, edited by Véronique Bouillier and Catherine Schreiber Servan, 303–334. Paris: Maisonneuve & Larose, 2004.

Ali, A. F. M. Abdul. "Prince Jawan Bakht Jahandar Shah." *Bengal Past & Present* 54, no. 1–2 (1937): 9–17.

Amin, Shahid. "Editor's Introduction." In *A Glossary of North Indian Peasant Life*, xiv–xlii. Delhi: Oxford University Press, 1989.

Amman Dihlawī, Mīr. "Bagh-o-Bahar, or Tales of the Four Darweshes, translated from the Hindustani of Mir Amman of Dihli, by Duncan Forbes, L.L.D." Edited by Frances Pritchett, 2005. http://www.columbia.edu/itc/mealac/pritchett/00urdu/baghobahar/index.

Anderson, Benedict. *Imagined Communities: Reflections on the Origin and Spread of Nationalism*. London: Verso, 2006.

Anjum, Ḳhalīq. "Muqaddamah." In *Rusūm-i Dihlī*, edited by Ḳhalīq Anjum. New Delhi: Urdū Akādmī, 1986.

Anonymous. *A Defence of the Urdu Language and Character: Being a Reply to the Pamphlet called "Court Character and Primary Education in N.-W.P. & and Oude."* Allahabad: Liddel's N.-W.P. Printing Works, 1900.

Anonymous. "Dr. Theodore Cooke." *Nature* 85, no. 2142 (1910): 82.

Appadurai, Arjun. "Number in the Colonial Imagination." In *Orientalism and the Postcolonial Predicament: Perspectives on South Asia*, edited by Carol Appadurai Breckenridge and Peter van der Veer, 314–340. Philadelphia: University of Pennsylvania Press, 1993.

Ārzū, Sirājuddīn ʿAlī Ḳhān-i. *Muṯẖmir*. Edited by Rehanna Khatoon. Karachi: Institute of Central and West Asian Studies, 1991.

Ashraf, Sayyid Dā'ūd. "Farhang-i Āṣafiyah: Ćand Ḥaqāʾiq." In *Guźashtah Ḥaidarābād: Ārkāʾīvz ke Āʾine meṅ*, 134–143. Hyderabad: Shagūfah Pablīkeshanz, 2003.

Askari, Muhammad Hasan. "If the Benefit of Translation Is Concealment." *Annual of Urdu Studies* 19 (2004): 191–199.

——. "Some Thoughts on Urdu Prose." *Annual of Urdu Studies* 19 (2004): 200–207.

Āzād, Muḥammad Ḥusain. *Āb-e ḥayāt: Shaping the Canon of Urdu Poetry*. Translated by Frances W. Pritchett and Shamsur Rahman Faruqi. New Delhi: Oxford University Press, 2001.

Aẕfarī, Mirzā ʿAlī Baḳht Bahādur Muḥammad Ẕahīruddīn. *Wāqiʿāt-i Aẕfarī*. Edited by T. Chandrasekharan. Madras Government Oriental Manuscripts 65. Madras, 1957. Translated into Urdu by ʿAbdul Sattar as *Wāqiʿāt-i Aẕfarī*. Lahore: Yiktā Kitābeṅ, 2008.

Baevskii, Solomon I. *Early Persian Lexicography: Farhangs of the Eleventh to the Fifteenth Centuries*. Translated by N. Killian. Edited by John R. Perry. Honolulu: University of Hawai'i Press, 2007.

——. "Farhang-e Jahāngīrī." In *Encyclopædia Iranica Online*, edited by Ehsan Yarshater, 1999. http://www.iranicaonline.org/articles/farhang-e-jahangiri.

Bailey, T. Grahame. "Does Khaṛī Bolī Mean Nothing More Than Rustic Speech?" *Bulletin of the School of Oriental Studies* 8, no. 2/3, Indian and Iranian Studies: Presented to George Abraham Grierson on His Eighty-Fifth Birthday, 7th January, 1936 (1936): 363–371.

——. "Review: *Jamiᶜ ul-Lugāt*. A New Urdu Dictionary by ᶜAbdul Majīd." *Bulletin of the School of Oriental Studies* 9 (1938): 440–441.

Banerjee, S. C. "Naib Nazims of Dacca During the Company's Administration." *Bengal Past & Present* 59 (1940): 17–29.

Bangha, Imre. "Rekhta: Poetry in Mixed Language: The Emergence of Khari Boli Literature in North India." In *Before the Divide: Hindi and Urdu Literary Culture*, edited by Francesca Orsini, 21–83. New Delhi: Orient BlackSwan, 2010.

Bard, Amy, and Valerie Ritter. "A House Overturned: A Classical Urdu Lament in Braj Bhasha." In *Shared Idioms, Sacred Symbols, and the Articulation of Identities in South Asia*, edited by Kelly Pemberton and Michael Nijhawan, 21–53. New York: Routledge, 2009.

Barnes, Fred. "Meet Mario the Moderate." *New Republic* 192, no. 15 (1985): 16–19.

Barni, Ziyauddin Ahmad. *Romance of the Oriental Translator's Office (Bombay): A Peep Into the Dim Past, Containing Brief Biographical Sketches, etc.* Karachi: Ta'alimi Markaz, 1950.

Barrow, Ian J., and Douglas E. Haynes. "The Colonial Transition: South Asia, 1780–1840." *Modern Asian Studies* 38, no. 3 (2004): 469–478.

Barthes, Roland, and Honoré de Balzac. *S/Z*. Translated by Richard Miller. New York: Hill and Wang, 1974.

Bashir, Shahzad. "Shah Isma'il and the Qizilbash: Cannibalism in the Religious History of Early Safavid Iran." *History of Religions* 45, no. 3 (2006): 234–256.

Bayly, C. A. *Empire and Information: Intelligence Gathering and Social Communication in India, 1780–1870*. Cambridge: Cambridge University Press, 1996.

——. *Rulers, Townsmen, and Bazaars: North Indian Society in the Age of British Expansion, 1770–1870*. New Delhi: Oxford University Press, 1993.

Beale, Thomas William. *The Oriental Biographical Dictionary*. Calcutta, 1881.

Bedār, ᶜĀbid Raẓ. "Peshguftār." In *Shams al-Bayān fī Muṣṭalaḥāt al-Hindūstān*, 3–7. Patna: Khuda Bakhsh Oriental Public Library, 1979.

Behl, Aditya, and Wendy Doniger. *Love's Subtle Magic: An Indian Islamic Literary Tradition, 1379–1545*. New York: Oxford University Press, 2012.

Berg, C. C. *Report on the Need for Publishing Dictionaries Which Do Not To-Date Exist, Prepared by the International Academic Union*. Conseil International de la Philosophie et des Sciences Humaines, 1960.

Beveridge, Henry. "Dr. F. J. Steingass." *Journal of the Royal Asiatic Society* (1903): 654–655.

——. "Old Places in Murshidabad (No. III)." *Calcutta Review* 96, no. 192 (1893): 233–249.

Beveridge, Henry, and Parvin Loloi. "Blochmann, Henry Ferdinand (1838–1878)." In *Oxford Dictionary of National Biography*. Oxford: Oxford University Press, 2004. http://www.oxforddnb.com/view/article/2659.

Bhatia, Tej K. *A History of the Hindi Grammatical Tradition: Hindi-Hindustani Grammar, Grammarians, History and Problems*. Leiden: Brill, 1987.

Bhatia, Tej K., and Kazuhiko Machida. *The Oldest Grammar of Hindustānī: Contact, Communication and Colonial Legacy*. 2 vols. Tokyo: Research Institute for Languages and Cultures of Asia and Africa, Tokyo University of Foreign Studies, 2008.

Blake, Stephen P. *Shahjahanabad: The Sovereign City in Mughal India, 1639–1739*. Cambridge: Cambridge University Press, 1991.

Blochmann, Heinrich Ferdinand. *Calcutta During the Last Century: A Lecture*. Calcutta, 1867.

——. "Contributions to Persian Lexicography." *Journal of the Royal Asiatic Society of Bengal* 37, no. 1 (1868): 1–72.

——. "Hánsí." *Proceedings of the Asiatic Society of Bengal* (1877): 117–124.

Bloomfield, Morton W. "Understanding Old English Poetry." *Annuale Mediaevale* 9 (1968): 5–25.

Blumhardt, James Fuller. *Catalogue of the Hindi, Panjabi, and Hindustani Manuscripts in the Library of the British Museum*. London: 1899.

——. *Catalogue of the Hindustani Manuscripts in the Library of the India Office*. London: Oxford University Press, 1926.

——. *Catalogue of the Library of the India Office: Hindustani Books*. Vol. 2, part 2. London: India Office Library, 1900.

——. *A Supplementary Catalogue of Hindustani Books in the Library of the British Museum: Acquired During the Years 1889–1908*. London: British Museum, Longmans & Co., Bernard Quaritch, Asher & Co., Henry Frowde, 1909.

Bombay Civil List Corrected to 1st January 1877, showing the Names, Designations, and Services of the Civil and Military Servants of Government in the General, Revenue, Judicial, Political, Financial, Ecclesiastical, Educational, Marine, Public Works, and other Departments; also a list of H. M.'s Justices of the Peace for Bombay; &c., &c. Bombay, 1877.

Borelli, John. "Vijñānabhikṣu: Indian Thought and *The Great Chain of Being*." In *Jacob's Ladder and the Tree of Life: Concepts of Hierarchy and the Great Chain of Being*, edited by Marion Leathers Kuntz and Paul Grimley Kuntz, 371–384. New York: P. Lang, 1987.

Bourdieu, Pierre. *The Field of Cultural Production: Essays on Art and Literature*. Edited by Randal Johnson. New York: Columbia University Press, 1993.

——. "The Field of Cultural Production, or: The Economic World Reversed." In *The Field of Cultural Production: Essays on Art and Literature*, edited by Randal Johnson, 29–73. New York: Columbia University Press, 1993.

——. *Language and Symbolic Power*. Translated by Gino Raymond and Matthew Adamson. Edited by John B. Thompson. Cambridge, Mass.: Harvard University Press, 1991.

——. "The Market of Symbolic Goods." *Poetics* 14, no. 1–2 (1985): 13–44.

——. "The Market of Symbolic Goods." In *The Field of Cultural Production: Essays on Art and Literature*, edited by Randal Johnson, 1–34. New York: Columbia University Press, 1993.

——. "Social Space and the Genesis of 'Classes'." In *Language and Symbolic Power*, edited by John B. Thompson, 229–251. Cambridge, Mass.: Harvard University Press, 1991.

Brass, Paul R. *Language, Religion, and Politics in North India*. London: Cambridge University Press, 1974.

Bronner, Yigal. *Extreme Poetry: The South Asian Movement of Simultaneous Narration*. New York: Columbia University Press, 2010.

——. "A Question of Priority: Revisiting the Bhāmaha-Daṇḍin Debate." *Journal of Indian Philosophy* 40, no. 1 (2012): 67–118.

Brown, Jonathan. "Critical Rigor vs. Juridical Pragmatism: How Legal Theorists and Ḥadīth Scholars Approached the Backgrowth of 'Isnāds' in the Genre of 'Ilal Al-ḥadīth." *Islamic Law and Society* 14 (2007): 1–41.

Bryant, G. J. "Scots in India in the Eighteenth Century." *Scottish Historical Review* 64, no. 177 (1985): 22–41.

Buckland, Charles Edward. *Dictionary of Indian Biography*. London: S. Sonnenschein & Co., 1906.

Burchfield, Robert. "Dictionaries, New & Old: Who Plagiarizes Whom, Why & When?" *Encounter* 67 (1984): 10–19.

Burke, Peter. "Introduction." In *Languages and Jargons: Contributions to a Social History of Language*, edited by Peter Burke and Roy Porter. Cambridge: Polity, 1995.

Busch, Allison. *Poetry of Kings: The Classical Hindi Literature of Mughal India*. New York: Oxford University Press, 2011.

——. "Riti and Register: Lexical Variation in Courtly Braj Bhasha Texts." In *Before the Divide: Hindi and Urdu Literary Culture*, edited by Francesca Orsini, 84–120. New Delhi: Orient BlackSwan, 2010.

Cassiodorus. *Cassiodori Senatoris Institutiones*. Edited by R. A. B Mynors. Oxford: Clarendon, 1937.

Chaghatai, Ikram. "Dr Aloys Sprenger and the Delhi College." In *The Delhi College: Traditional Elites, the Colonial State, and Education Before 1857*, edited by Margrit Pernau, 105–124. New Delhi: Oxford University Press, 2006.

Chandra, Satish. *Parties and Politics at the Mughal Court, 1707–1740*. New Delhi: Oxford University Press, 2002.

Chandrasekharan, T. "Preface." In *Wāqiʿāt-i Aẕfarī*, by Mirzā ʿAlī Bak̤ht Bahādur Muḥammad Ẕahīruddīn Aẕfarī, edited by T. Chandrasekharan, i–vii. Madras, 1957.

Chatterjee, Partha. *The Politics of the Governed: Reflections on Popular Politics in Most of the World*. New York: Columbia University Press, 2004.

Chaudhry, Nazir Ahmad, ed. *Development of Urdu as Official Language in the Punjab, 1849–1974*. Lahore: Punjab Govt. Record Office, 1977.

Child, John, and Fulk, Janet. "Maintenance of Occupational Control: The Case of Professions." *Work and Occupations* 9, no. 2 (1982): 155.

Clark, T. W. "The Languages of Calcutta, 1760–1840." *Bulletin of the School of Oriental and African Studies, University of London* 18, no. 3, In Honour of J. R. Firth (1956): 453–474.

Clemens, Cyril, ed. *Mark Twain: Wit and Wisdom*. New York: Frederick A. Stokes Co., 1935.

Cohn, Bernard S. "The Census, Social Structure, and Objectification in South Asia in Culture and History of India." *Folk* 26 (1984): 25–49.

——. "The Command of Language and the Language of Command." *Subaltern Studies* 4 (1985): 276–329.

——. "From Indian Status to British Contract." *Journal of Economic History* 21 (1961): 613–628.

——. "The Initial British Impact on India: A Case Study of the Benares Region." *Journal of Asian Studies* 19 (1960): 418–431.

Cotton, J. S., and Gopal, S. "Hunter, Sir William Wilson (1840–1900)." In *Oxford Dictionary of National Biography*, edited by H. C. G. Matthew and Brian Harrison. Oxford: Oxford University Press, 2004. http://www.oxforddnb.com/view/article/14237.

Court Character and Testimony in the NWP and Oudh. 1897.

Cowell, E. B. "[Review] Memoirs on the History, Folk-Lore, and Distribution of the Races of the North Western Provinces of India." *The Academy* 1, no. 8 (1870): 215–216.

Croce, Benedetto. *Aesthetic as Science of Expression and General Linguistic*. Translated by Douglas Ainslie. London: Macmillan & Co., 1922.

Crooke, William. *A Glossary of North Indian Peasant Life*. Edited by Shahid Amin. Delhi: Oxford University Press, 1989.

Dale, Stephen Frederic. "Steppe Humanism: The Autobiographical Writings of Zahir al-Din Muhammad Babur, 1483–1530." *International Journal of Middle East Studies* 22, no. 1 (1990): 37–58.

Dalmia, Vasudha. *The Nationalization of Hindu Traditions: Bhāratendu Harishchandra and Nineteenth-Century Banaras*. Delhi: Oxford University Press, 1997.

Daly, Lloyd William. *Contributions to a History of Alphabetization in Antiquity and the Middle Ages*. Bruxelles: Latomus, 1967.

Damīrī, Muḥammad ibn Mūsā. *Ḥayāt al-Ḥaiwān*. Translated by Maulavī ʿAbd al-Qādir Deobandī. Lucknow, 1905.

Das, Sisir Kumar. *Sahibs and Munshis: An Account of the College of Fort William*. New Delhi: Orion, 1978.

Datla, Kavita Saraswathi. *The Language of Secular Islam: Urdu Nationalism and Colonial India*. 2013.

——. "Making a Worldly Vernacular: Urdu, Education, and Osmania University, Hyderabad, 1883–1938." PhD diss., University of California, 2006.

——. "A Worldly Vernacular: Urdu at Osmania University." *Modern Asian Studies* 43, no. 5 (2009): 1117–1148.

Datta, K. K. "Some Unpublished Documents Relating to the Conspiracy of Wazir Ali." *Bengal Past & Present* 55, no. 3–4 (1938): 137–150.

——, ed. *Selections from Unpublished Correspondence of the Judge-Magistrate and the Judge of Patna, 1790–1857*. Patna: Government of Bihar, 1954.

Davie, George Elder. *The Democratic Intellect: Scotland and Her Universities in the Nineteenth Century*. Edinburgh: Edinburgh University Press, 1961.

Dāʾudī, Ḳhalīl al-Raḥmān. "Pesh Lafẕ [Foreword]." In *Bahār-i Dānish (Urdū Maśnavī)*. Lahore: Majlis-i Taraqqī-yi Adab, 1963.

de Tassy, Garcin. *Histoire de la Littérature Hindouie et Hindoustani*. 2nd rev., cor., et considérablement augm. ed. 3 vols. Paris: 1870.

De, Barun. "Foreword." In *The Rebel Nawab of Oudh: Revolt of Vizir Ali Khan, 1799*, vii–xiii. Calcutta: K. P. Bagchi & Co., 1990.

Dehlvi, Sadia. *The Sufi Courtyard: Dargahs of Delhi*. New Delhi: HarperCollins India/India Today Group, 2012.

Deutsch, Karl Wolfgang. *Nationalism and Social Communication: An Inquiry Into the Foundations of Nationality*. Cambridge, Mass.: MIT Press, 1953.

Digby, Simon. "Before Timur Came: Provincialization of the Delhi Sultanate Through the Fourteenth Century." *Journal of the Economic and Social History of the Orient* 47, no. 3 (2004): 298–356.

——. "The Sufi Shaikh as a Source of Authority in Medieval India." In *India's Islamic Traditions: 711–1750*, edited by Richard Maxwell Eaton, 234–262. New Delhi: Oxford University Press, 2003.

Dihlawī, Sayyid Aḥmad. "Muqaddamah-i Ṯabʿ Awwal-i Farhang-i Āṣafiyah." In *Farhang-i Āṣafiyah*, 16–71. New Delhi: National Academi [Taraqqī-yi Urdū Board edition], 1974.

——. *Rusūm-i Dihlī*. Edited by Ḳhalīq Anjum. New Delhi: Urdū Akādmī, 2006.

Dihlawī, Sayyid Yūsuf Buḳhārī. "Maulvī Sayyid Aḥmad Dihlawī." In *Rusūm-i Dihlī*, 12–35. Rampur: Kitābkār pablīkeshanz, 1965.

DiMaggio, Paul. "Classification in Art." *American Sociological Review* 52, no. 4 (1987): 440–455.

Dodson, Michael S. "Translating Science, Translating Empire: The Power of Language in Colonial North India." *Comparative Studies in Society and History* 47, no. 4 (2005): 809–835.

Donnellan, Keith S. "Reference and Definite Descriptions." *The Philosophical Review* 75 (1966): 281-304.

Dudney, Arthur. "A Desire for Meaning: Khan-i Arzu's Philology and the Place of India in the Eighteenth-Century Persianate World." PhD diss., Columbia University, 2013.

——. "Why Did Shāh Ḥātim's Collected Works Spawn a Child?" 2010. http://academiccommons.columbia.edu/download/fedora_content/download/ac:125847/CONTENT/Shah_Hatim_essay__final_draft_.pdf.

Duncan, John. *Selections from the Duncan Records*. Edited by A. Shakespear. 2 vols. Benares, 1873.

Edney, Matthew H. *Mapping an Empire: The Geographical Construction of British India, 1765–1843*. Chicago: University of Chicago Press, 1997.

Elias, Jamal J. *The Throne Carrier of God: The Life and Thought of ʿAlāʾ ad-Dawla as-Simnanī*. Albany: State University of New York Press, 1995.

Elliot, Henry Miers, and John Dowson. *The History of India, as Told by Its Own Historians: The Muhammadan Period*. Edited by John Dowson. 8 vols. London, 1877.

Ethé, Hermann. *Catalogue of Persian Manuscripts in the Library of the India Office*. 2 vols. Oxford: Clarendon, 1937.

Fabian, Johannes. *Language and Colonial Power: The Appropriation of Swahili in the Former Belgian Congo, 1880–1938*. Berkeley: University of California Press, 1986.

Fagan, P. J. *Reprint of Hissar District Gazetteer, 1892*. Vol. 10, *Haryana District Gazetteers*. Chandigarh: Gazetteers Organisation, Revenue Department, Haryana, 1997.

Faiẓ, Faiẓ Aḥmad. *Selected Poems of Faiz Ahmad Faiz*. Translated by Shiv Kumar Kumar. Edited by Shiv Kumar Kumar. New Delhi: Viking, 1995.

Fakhry, Majid. *A History of Islamic Philosophy*. New York: Columbia University Press, 2004.

Fallon, S. W. "Preface and Preliminary Dissertation." In *A New Hindustani-English Dictionary, with Illustrations from Hindustani Literature and Folk-Lore*, i–xxiv. Banaras, 1879.

Farooqi, Mehr Afshan. "Changing Literary Patterns in Eighteenth Century North India: Quranic Translations and the Development of Urdu Prose." In *Before the Divide: Hindi and Urdu Literary Culture*, edited by Francesca Orsini, 222–248. New Delhi: Orient BlackSwan, 2010.

Farrell, Gerry, and Sorrell, Neil. "Colonialism, Philology, and Musical Ethnography in Nineteenth-Century India: The Case of S. W. Fallon." *Music and Letters* 88, no. 1 (2007): 107–120.

Faruqi, Shamsur Rahman. "Burning Rage, Icy Scorn: The Poetry of Ja'far Zatalli (Lecture under the auspices of the Hindi-Urdu Flagship, University of Texas at Austin, September 24, 2008)." 2008. http://www.columbia.edu/itc/mealac/pritchett/00fwp/srf/srf_zatalli_2008.pdf.

——. "Constructing a Literary History, a Canon, and a Theory of Poetry." In *Āb-e ḥayāt: Shaping the Canon of Urdu Poetry*, edited by Frances Pritchett, 19–51. New Delhi: Oxford University Press, 2001.

——. *Early Urdu Literary Culture and History*. New Delhi: Oxford University Press, 2001.

——. "Some Problems of Urdu Lexicography." *Annual of Urdu Studies* 7 (1990): 21–30.

——. "A Stranger in the City: The Poetics of *Sabk-e Hindi*." *Annual of Urdu Studies* 19 (2004): 1–93.

——. "Unprivileged Power: The Strange Case of Persian (and Urdu) in Nineteenth-Century India." *Annual of Urdu Studies* 13 (1999).

Ferguson, Charles F. "Diglossia." *Word* 15, no. 2 (1959): 325–340.

Fishman, Joshua. "Bilingualism with and Without Diglossia; Diglossia with and Without Bilingualism." *Journal of Social Issues* 23, no. 2 (1967): 29–38.

Forbes, Duncan. *Sketch of the Early Life of Duncan Forbes, LL.D. . . . Written by Himself, for the Perusal of His Father in America*. London, 1859.

Foucault, Michel. *The Order of Things: An Archaeology of the Human Sciences*. London: Routledge, 2002.

Francklin, William. *The History of the Reign of Shah-Aulum, the present emperor of Hindostaun: containing the transactions of the court of Delhi, and the neighbouring states, during a period of thirty-six years: interspersed with geographical and topographical observations on several of the principal cities of Hindostaun: with an appendix*. London: 1798.

Frawley, William. "The Dictionary as Text." *International Journal of Lexicography* 2, no. 3 (1989): 231–248.

Frow, John. *Genre*. London: Routledge, 2006.

Fuchs, Barbara. *Romance*. New York: Routledge, 2004.

Fuller, Simon. "The Lost Dhivehi Gospels." In *Maldives Culture*, 2003. http://198.62.75.1/www1/pater/images1/dhivehi-lost-gospels.htm.

Fusfeld, Warren Edward. "The Shaping of Sufi Leadership in Delhi: The Naqshbandiyya Mujaddidiyya, 1750–1920." PhD diss., University of Pennsylvania, 1981.

Gabbay, Alyssa. *Islamic Tolerance: Amīr Khusraw and Pluralism*. Milton Park: Routledge, 2010.

Gaborieau, Marc. "The Jihad of Sayyid Ahmad Barelwi on the North West Frontier: The Last Echo of the Middle Ages? Or a Prefiguration of Modern South Asia." In *Sufis, Sultans, and Feudal Orders: Professor Nurul Hasan Commemoration Volume*, edited by Mansura Haidar, 23–44. New Delhi: Manohar, 2004.

——. *Le Mahdi Incompris: Sayyid Ahmad Barelwî (1786–1831) et le Millénarisme en Inde*. Paris: CNRS, 2010.

Gellner, Ernest. *Nations and Nationalism*. New Perspectives on the Past. Ithaca, N.Y.: Cornell University Press, 1983.

Ġhālib, Mirzā Asadullāh Ḳhān. *Urdu Letters of Mirzā Asadu'llāh Ḳhān Ġhālib*. Translated by Daud Rahbar. Edited by Daud Rahbar. Albany: State University of New York Press, 1987.

Gilchrist, John Borthwick. "Appendix to Part I of the Dictionary." In *A Dictionary, English and Hindoostanee, in Which the Words are Marked with Their Distinguishing Initials; as Hinduwee, Arabic, and Persian, Whence the Hindoostanee, or What is Vulgarly, but Improperly Called the Moor Language, is Evidently Formed*, 1–94. Calcutta, 1787.

——. *The General East India Guide and Vade Mecum: For the Public Functionary, Government Officer, Private Agent, Trader or Foreign Sojourner, in British India, and the Adjacent Parts of Asia Immediately Connected with the Honourable the East India Company*. London, 1825.

——. *The Oriental Linguist, an Easy and Familiar Introduction to the Popular Language of Hindoostan*. Calcutta, 1798.

Gilmour, David. *The Ruling Caste: Imperial Lives in the Victorian Raj*. London: John Murray, 2005.

Gluck, Carol. "Words in Motion." In *Words in Motion: Toward a Global Lexicon*, edited by Carol Gluck and Anna Lowenhaupt Tsing, 3–10. Durham, N.C.: Duke University Press, 2009.

Gluck, Carol, and Anna Lowenhaupt Tsing, eds. *Words in Motion: Toward a Global Lexicon*. Durham, N.C.: Duke University Press, 2009.

Goody, Jack. *The Domestication of the Savage Mind*. Cambridge: Cambridge University Press, 1977.

Goswami, Manu. *Producing India: From Colonial Economy to National Space*. Chicago: University of Chicago Press, 2004.

Green, Jonathon. *Chasing the Sun: Dictionary Makers and the Dictionaries They Made*. New York: Henry Holt, 1996.

Green, Nile. *Islam and the Army in Colonial India: Sepoy Religion in the Service of Empire*. Cambridge: Cambridge University Press, 2009.

——. "The Uses of Books in a Late Mughal *Takiyya:* Persianate Knowledge Between Person and Paper." *Modern Asian Studies* 44, no. 2 (2010): 241–265.

Grewal, J. S. *Sikhs of Punjab*. Cambridge: Cambridge University Press, 2008.

Grierson, George Abraham. "A Bibliography of Western Hindi, Including Hindostani." *Indian Antiquary* 32 (1903): 160–179.

——. *Bihār Peasant Life; Being a Discursive Catalog of the Surroundings of the People of that Province, with Many Illustrations from Photographs Taken by the Author*. Calcutta, 1885.

Guha, Sumit. "The Politics of Identity and Enumeration in India c. 1600–1990." *Comparative Studies in Society and History* 45, no. 1 (2003): 148–167.

——. "Transitions and Translations: Regional Power and Vernacular Identity in the Dakhan, 1500–1800." *Comparative Studies of South Asia, Africa, and the Middle East* 24, no. 2 (2004): 23–31.

Gupta, Amit Kumar. "Defying Death: Nationalist Revolutionism in India, 1897–1938." *Social Scientist* 25 (1997): 3–27.

"Guidelines for the Implementation of Internationalized Domain Names." ICANN, 2007. https://www.icann.org/en/system/files/files/idn-guidelines-26apr07-en.pdf.

Habib, Irfan. *The Agrarian System of Mughal India, 1556–1707*. New Delhi: Oxford University Press, 1999.

Hadi, Nabi. *Dictionary of Indo-Persian Literature*. New Delhi: Indira Gandhi National Centre for the Arts, 1995.

Hakala, Walter N. "The Authorial Problem in the *K͟hāliq Bārī* of 'K͟husrau.'" *Indian Economic & Social History Review* 51, no. 4 (2014): 481–496.

——. "On Equal Terms: The Equivocal Origins of an Early Mughal Indo-Persian Vocabulary." *Journal of the Royal Asiatic Society (Third Series)* 25, no. 2 (2015): 209–227.

——. "A Sultan in the Realm of Passion: Coffee in Eighteenth-Century Delhi." *Eighteenth-Century Studies* 47, no. 4 (2014): 371–388.

Ḥālī, Alṭāf Ḥusain. "Farhang-i Āṣafiyah." In *Urdū Luġhat: Yādgārī Maẓāmīn*, edited by Abūlḥasanāt, 59–64. Karachi: Unikarians International, 2010.

Hall, Fitzedward. "Urdu Lexicography." *Benares Magazine* 3, no. 29 (1851): 875–885.

Ḥaq, ʿAbdul. "Muqadamah." In *Maʿishiyat al-Hind*, Hyderabad: Jāmiʿah ʿUs̤māniyah, 1929.

——. "Muqaddamah: Urdū Luġhāt aur Luġhat Nawīsī." In *Luġhat-i Kabīr-i Urdū*, 18–56. Karachi: Anjuman-i Taraqqī-yi Urdū, 1973.

Haque, Ishrat. *Glimpses of Mughal Society and Culture: A Study Based on Urdu Literature, in the Second Half of the Eighteenth Century*. New Delhi: Concept, 1992.

Harbans, Singh. *The Heritage of the Sikhs*. New Delhi: Manohar, 1983.

Hardy, Peter. *The Muslims of British India*. London: Cambridge University Press, 1972.

Hasan, Iqtida. *Later Moghuls and Urdu Literature*. Lahore: Ferozsons, 1995.

Hasan, Mushirul. "Maulawi Zaka Ullah: Sharif Culture and Colonial Rule." In *The Delhi College: Traditional Elites, the Colonial State, and Education Before 1857*, edited by Margrit Pernau, 261–298. New Delhi: Oxford University Press, 2006.

Hāshmī, Masʿūd. *Urdū Luġhat Nawīsī kā Pas Manẓar*. Delhi: Maktabah-yi Jāmiʿah, 1997.

——. *Urdū Luġhat Nawīsī kā Tanqīdī Jāʾizah*. New Delhi: Taraqqī-yi Urdū Biyūro, 1992.

Ḥātim, Ẓuhūruddīn. *Dīwān Zādah*. Edited by Ġhulām Ḥusain Żūʾal-faqār. Lahore: Maktabah-yi K͟hayābān-i Adab, 1975.

Havelock, Eric Alfred. *Origins of Western Literacy: Four Lectures Delivered at the Ontario Institute for Studies in Education, Toronto, March 25, 26, 27, 28, 1974*. Toronto: Ontario Institute for Studies in Education, 1976.

Haywood, John A. *Arabic Lexicography: Its History, and Its Place in the General History of Lexicography*. Leiden: E. J. Brill, 1965.

Heinrichs, W. P., J. T. P. de Bruijn, and J. Stewart-Robinson. "Tadhkira (a.)." In *Encyclopaedia of Islam*, 2nd ed., edited by P. Bearman, Th. Bianquis, C. E. Bosworth, E. van Donzel, and W. P. Heinrichs, 10:53–55. Leiden: Brill, 2000.

Hodgson, Marshall G. S. *The Venture of Islam: Conscience and History in a World Civilization*. Chicago: University of Chicago Press, 1974.

Howe, Nicholas. *The Old English Catalogue Poems*. Copenhagen: Rosenkilde and Bagger, 1985.

Hunter, William Wilson. *The Indian Musalmans*. 3rd ed. London: 1876.

Ḥusain, Muḥammad Żākir. "Pesh Guftār." In *Maḳhzan-i Fawāʾid: Urdū Muṣṭalaḥāt, Muḥāwarāt aur Amṡāl kā ek Nādir Luġhat*, edited by Muḥammad Żākir Ḥusain, 5–30. Patna: Khuda Bakhsh Oriental Public Library, 1998.

Ḥusainī, Sayyid Ḳhwajah. "Farhang-i Āṣafiyah Tanqīd ke Āʾīne meṅ." *Urdū Adab* 1 (1966): 105–116.

Inshā, Mīr Inshāʾallāh Ḳhāṅ. *Dāstān-i Rānī Ketkī aur Kunwar Ūde Bhān kī*. Edited by ʿAbdul Ḥaq. Delhi: Educational Book House, n.d.

Islam, Khurshidul, and Ralph Russell. *Ghalib: Life and Letters*. New Delhi: Oxford University Press, 1994.

Islām, Najmul. "Bayāẓ-i Mirzā Jān Ṭapish." *Nuqūsh* 108 (1967): 62–81.

Ivanow, Wladimir. *Concise Descriptive Catalogue of the Persian Manuscripts in the Collection of the Asiatic Society of Bengal*. Calcutta: The Asiatic Society, 1924.

Izmirlieva, Valentina. *All the Names of the Lord: Lists, Mysticism, and Magic*. Chicago: University of Chicago Press, 2008.

Jain, Gyan Chand. "Ameer Khusrau and Khari Boli." In *Life, Times & Works of Amīr Khusrau Dehlavi*, edited by Zoe Ansari, 307–321. New Delhi: National Amīr Khusrau Society, 1975.

Jalal, Ayesha. *Partisans of Allah: Jihad in South Asia*. Cambridge, Mass.: Harvard University Press, 2008.

James, George McLeod. "Anand Ram Mukhlis: His Life and Works, 1695–1758." PhD thesis, University of Delhi, n.d.

Jameson, Fredric. *The Political Unconscious: Narrative as a Socially Symbolic Act*. Ithaca, N.Y.: Cornell University Press, 1981.

Janssen, Susanne. "The Empirical Study of Careers in Literature and the Arts." In *The Psychology and Sociology of Literature: In Honor of Elrud Ibsch*, edited by Dick Schram and Gerard Steen, 323–357. Amsterdam: J. Benjamins, 2001.

Jones, Kenneth W. "Religious Identity and the Indian Census." In *The Census in British India: New Perspectives*, edited by N. Gerald Barrier, 72–101. New Delhi: Manohar, 1981.

Jones, William. *The Works of Sir William Jones*. 13 vols. London, 1807.

Kalīmuddīn, Aḥmad. *Urdū Shāʿirī par ek Naẓar*. Lahore: ʿIshrat Pablishing Hāʾūs, 1965.

——. *Urdū Tanqīd par ek Naẓar*. Lahore: ʿIshrat Pablishing Hāʾūs, 1965.

Kalpagam, U. "Cartography in Colonial India." *Economic and Political Weekly* 30, no. 30 (1995): PE87–98.

Kaviraj, Sudipta. "The Imaginary Institution of India." *Subaltern Studies* 7 (1992): 1–39.

Kauffman, Stuart. "Autonomous Objects." In *Science and Ultimate Reality: Quantum Theory, Cosmology, and Complexity*, edited by John D. Barrow, P. C. W. Davies, and Charles L. Harper, 654–666. Cambridge: Cambridge University Press, 2004.

Kewes, Paulina. "Historicizing Plagiarism." In *Plagiarism in Early Modern England*, edited by Paulina Kewes, 1–18. Basingstoke: Palgrave Macmillan, 2003.

Ḳhān, Em. Ḥabīb. *Inshāʾallāh Ḳhān 'Inshā'. Hindustānī Adab ke Miʿmār*. New Delhi: Sāhityah Akādmī, 1989.

Khan, Iqtidar Alam. "The Middle Classes in the Mughal Empire." *Social Scientist* 5, no. 1 (1976): 28–49.

Ḳhānī, ʿAbdul Qādir. *ʿIlm o ʿAmal*. Translated by Maulvī Muʿīnuddīn Afẓal Gaḍhī. Edited by Muḥammad Ayyūb Qādrī. Karachi: Academy of Educational Research, All-Pakistan Educational Conference, 1960.

Khatoon, Rehanna. *Ahwāl o Āśar-i Ḳhān-i Ārzū*. Delhi: Indo-Persian Society, 1987.

——. "Introduction." In *Muṣmir*, edited by Rehanna Khatoon. Karachi: Institute of Central and West Asian Studies, 1991.

Khusrau, Amīr Ḳhusrau Dihlawī. *Amīr Ḳhusrau kā Hindvī Kalām: maʿ nusḳhahah-yi Barlin, Żaḳhīrah-yi Ishpringar*. Edited by Gopī Ćand Nārang. Delhi: Ejūkeshanal Pablishing Hāʾūs, 1987.

——. *The Nuh Sipihr of Amir Khusraw: Persian Text, with Introduction, Notes, Index, etc.* Edited by M. Wahid Mirza. London: Published for the Islamic Research Association by Oxford University Press, 1950.

Kia, Mana. "Accounting for Difference: A Comparative Look at the Autobiographical Travel Narratives of Hazin Lāhiji and 'Abd-al-Karim Kashmiri." *Journal of Persianate Studies* 2, no. 2 (2009): 210–236.

King, Christopher Rolland. "Images of Virtue and Vice: The Hindi-Urdu Controversy in Two Nineteenth-Century Hindi Plays." In *Religious Controversy in British India: Dialogues in South Asian Languages*, edited by Kenneth W. Jones, 123–148. Albany: State University of New York Press, 1992.

——. *One Language, Two Scripts: The Hindi Movement in Nineteenth-Century North India*. Bombay: Oxford University Press, 1994.

Kinra, Rajeev. "Fresh Words for a Fresh World: *Tāzā-Gūʾī* and the Poetics of Newness in Early Modern Indo-Persian Poetry." *Sikh Formations* 3, no. 2 (2007): 125–149.

——. "Master and Munshi: A Brahman Secretary's Guide to Mughal Governance." *Indian Economic & Social History Review* 47, no. 4 (2010): 527–561.

——. "This Noble Science: Indo-Persian Comparative Philology, c. 1000–1800 CE." In *South Asian Texts in History: Critical Engagements with Sheldon Pollock*, edited by Yigal Bronner, Whitney Cox, and Lawrence J. McCrea, 359–385. Ann Arbor, Mich.: Association for Asian Studies, 2011.

Kintsch, Walter. *Comprehension: A Paradigm for Cognition*. Cambridge: Cambridge University Press, 1998.

Kirmani, Waris. *Dreams Forgotten: An Anthology of Indo-Persian Poetry*. Aligarh: Academic Books, 1986.

Kittler, Friedrich A. *Discourse Networks 1800/1900*. Stanford, Calif.: Stanford University Press, 1990.

Kopf, David. *British Orientalism and the Bengal Renaissance: The Dynamics of Indian Modernization, 1773–1835*. Berkeley: University of California Press, 1969.

Kruijtzer, Gijs. *Xenophobia in Seventeenth-Century India.* Leiden: Leiden University Press, 2009.

Kumar, Amitava. *Nobody Does the Right Thing.* Durham, N.C.: Duke University Press, 2010.

Lackner, Michael, Iwo Amelung, and Joachim Kurtz, eds. *New Terms for New Ideas: Western Knowledge and Lexical Change in Late Imperial China.* Leiden: Brill, 2001.

Landau, Sidney I. *Dictionaries: The Art and Craft of Lexicography.* New York: Scribner, 1984.

Lanson, Gustave. "L'histoire littéraire et la sociologie." *Revue de Métaphysique et de Morale* 12 (1904): 621–642.

Lanson, Gustave, Nicholas T. Rand, and Roberta Hatcher. "Literary History and Sociology." *PMLA* 110 (1995): 220–235.

Leask, Nigel. "Imperial Scots [Review of T. M. Devine, *Scotland's Empire, 1600–1815*]." *History Workshop Journal* 59 (2005): 262–270.

Lelyveld, David. *Aligarh's First Generation: Muslim Solidarity in British India.* Princeton, N.J.: Princeton University Press, 1977.

——. "Zuban-e Urdu-e Mu'alla and the Idol of Linguistic Origins." *Annual of Urdu Studies* 9 (1994).

Liberman, Mark. "Somali Words for Camel Spit." In *Language Log.* Philadelphia, 2004. http://itre.cis.upenn.edu/~myl/languagelog/archives/000444.html.

Liu, Lydia He. "A Folksong Immortal and Official Popular Culture in Twentieth-Century China." In *Writing and Materiality in China: Essays in Honor of Patrick Hanan*, edited by Judith T. Zeitlin, Lydia Liu, and Ellen Widmer, 553–609. Cambridge, Mass.: Harvard University Asia Center, 2003.

——. "The Question of Meaning-Value in the Political Economy of the Sign." In *Tokens of Exchange: The Problem of Translation in Global Circulations*, edited by Lydia He Liu, 13–41. Durham, N.C.: Duke University Press, 1999.

——. *Translingual Practice: Literature, National Culture, and Translated Modernity—China, 1900–1937.* Stanford, Calif.: Stanford University Press, 1995.

Lock, F. P. *Edmund Burke.* Vol. 2, *1784–1797.* Oxford: Clarendon, 2006.

Lockhart, Laurence. *Nadir Shah: A Critical Study Based Mainly Upon Contemporary Sources.* London: Luzac, 1938.

Losensky, Paul E. *Welcoming Fighānī: Imitation and Poetic Individuality in the Safavid-Mughal Ghazal.* Costa Mesa, Calif.: Mazda, 1998.

Lyons, M. C., and P. Cachia. "The Effect of Monorhyme on Arabic Poetic Production." *Journal of Arabic Literature* 1 (1970): 3–13.

MacKenzie, John M. "Empire and National Identities: The Case of Scotland." *Transactions of the Royal Historical Society (Sixth Series)* 8, no. 1 (1998): 215–231.

——. "Essay and Reflection: On Scotland and the Empire." *International History Review* 15, no. 4 (1993): 714–739.

Mair, Victor H. "Buddhism and the Rise of the Written Vernacular in East Asia: The Making of National Languages." *Journal of Asian Studies* 53, no. 3 (1994): 707–751.

Mair, Victor H., and Mei, Tsu-Lin. "The Sanskrit Origins of Recent Style Prosody." *Harvard Journal of Asiatic Studies* 51, no. 2 (1991): 375–470.

Majeed, Javed. " 'The Bad Habit': *Hobson-Jobson*, British Indian Glossaries, and Intimations of Mortality." *Bulletin of the Henry Sweet Society for the History of Linguistic Ideas* 46–47 (2006): 7–22.

———. "'The Jargon of Indostan': An Exploration of Jargon in Urdu and East India Company English." In *Languages and Jargons: Contributions to a Social History of Language*, edited by Peter Burke and Roy Porter, 182–205. Cambridge: Polity, 1995.

———. "Modernity's Script and a Tom Thumb Performance." In *Trans-colonial Modernities in South Asia*, edited by Michael S. Dodson and Brian A. Hatcher, 95–115. London: Routledge, 2012.

———. "What's in a (Proper) Name? Particulars, Individuals, and Authorship in the Linguistic Survey of India and Colonial Scholarship." In *Knowledge Production, Pedagogy, and Institutions in Colonial India*, edited by Indra Sengupta, Daud Ali, and Javed Majeed, 1–15. New York: Palgrave Macmillan, 2011.

Mandler, Jean Matter. *Stories, Scripts, and Scene: Aspects of Schema Theory*. Hillsdale, N.J.: Lawrence Erlbaum Associates, 1984.

Marshall, Dara Nusserwanji. *Mughals in India: A Bibliographical Survey of Manuscripts*. London: Mansell, 1985.

Marshall, Peter James. "Barlow, Sir George Hilaro, first baronet (1763–1846)." In *Oxford Dictionary of National Biography*, edited by Henry Colin Gray Matthew and Brian Howard Harrison, 2004. http://www.oxforddnb.com/view/article/1433.

———. "Review of *A European Experience of the Mughal Orient: The I'jaz-i Arsalani (Persian Letters, 1773–1779) of Antoine-Louis-Henri Polier* (review no. 255)." In *Reviews in History*, 2002. http://www.history.ac.uk/reviews/review/255.

Matthews, David J. "Urdu Language and Education in India." *Social Scientist* 31, no. 5/6 (2003): 57–72.

McArthur, Tom. "Thematic Lexicography." In *The History of Lexicography: Papers from the Dictionary Research Centre Seminar at Exeter, March 1986*, edited by R. R. K. Hartmann, 157–166. Gainesville: University Press of Florida, 1986.

McGregor, R. S. *The Formation of Modern Hindi as Demonstrated in Early Hindi Dictionaries*. Amsterdam: Koninklijke Nederlandse Akademie van Wetenschappem, 2000.

———. "On the Evolution of Hindi as a Language of Literature." *South Asia Research* 21, no. 2 (2001): 202–217.

———. "The Progress of Hindi, Part 1: The Development of a Transregional Idiom." In *Literary Cultures in History: Reconstructions from South Asia*, edited by Sheldon I. Pollock, 912–957. Berkeley: University of California Press, 2003.

———. "The Rise of Standard Hindi and Early Hindi Prose Fiction." *Journal of the Royal Asiatic Society of Great Britain and Ireland* 3/4 (1967): 114–132.

Metcalf, Barbara Daly, ed. *Moral Conduct and Authority: The Place of Adab in South Asian Islam*. Berkeley: University of California Press, 1984.

Minault, Gail. "Delhi College and Urdu." *Annual of Urdu Studies* 14 (1999): 119–134.

———. "Qiran al-Saᶜâdain: The Dialogue Between Eastern and Western Learning at Delhi College." In *Perspectives of Mutual Encounters in South Asian History, 1760–1860*, edited by Jamal Malik, 260–277. Leiden: Brill, 2000.

———. "Sayyid Ahmad Dehlavi and the 'Delhi Renaissance.'" In *Delhi Through the Ages: Essays in Urban History, Culture, and Society*, edited by Robert Eric Frykenberg, 174–185. Delhi: Oxford University Press, 1986.

Mir, Farina. *The Social Space of Language: Vernacular Culture in British Colonial Punjab*. Berkeley: University of California Press, 2010.

Mīr, Mīr Taqī. *Nikāt al-Shuᶜarā*. Edited by ᶜAbdul Ḥaq. Aurangabad: Anjuman-i Taraqqī-yi Urdū, 1935.

——. *Żikr-i Mīr*. Translated and edited by ʿAbdul Ḥaq. Aurangabad: Anjuman-i Taraqqī-yi Urdū, 1928.

Mitchell, Lisa. *Language, Emotion, and Politics in South India: The Making of a Mother Tongue*. Bloomington: Indiana University Press, 2009.

Moazzam, Anwar. "Urdu Inshā: The Hyderābād Experiment, 1860–1948." In *Literacy in the Persianate World: Writing and the Social Order*, edited by Brian Spooner and William L. Hanaway, 311–327. Philadelphia: University of Pennsylvania Museum of Archaeology and Anthropology, 2012.

Moore, Charles. *The Sheriffs of Fort William from 1775 to 1926*. Calcutta: Thacker, Spink, 1926.

Mufti, Aamir R. "Orientalism and the Institution of World Literatures." *Critical Inquiry* 36, no. 3 (2010): 458–493.

Muṣḥafī, Shaikh Ġhulām Hamadānī. *Tażkirah-i Hindī*. Translated by ʿAbdul Ḥaq. *Sisilah-yi Maṭbūʿāt*. Lucknow: Uttar Pradesh Urdū Akādmī, 1985.

Naim, C. M. "Introduction." In *Zikr-i Mir: The Autobiography of the Eighteenth-Century Mughal Poet, Mir Muhammad Taqi 'Mir', 1723–1810*, edited by C. M. Naim, 1-21. New Delhi: Oxford University Press, 1999.

——. "Prize-Winning Adab: A Study of Five Urdu Books Written in Response to the Allahabad Government Gazette Notification." In *Moral Conduct and Authority: The Place of Adab in South Asian Islam*, edited by Barbara Daly Metcalf, 289–314. Berkeley: University of California Press, 1984.

——. "Shaikh Imam Bakhsh Sahbaʾi: Teacher, Scholar, Poet, and Puzzle-Master." In *The Delhi College: Traditional Elites, the Colonial State, and Education Before 1857*, edited by Margrit Pernau, 145–185. New Delhi: Oxford University Press, 2006.

——. "The Theme of Homosexual (Pederastic) Love in Pre-Modern Urdu Poetry." In *Studies in the Urdu Ġazal and Prose Fiction*, edited by Muhammad Umar Memon, 120–142. Madison: South Asian Studies, University of Wisconsin, 1979.

Naim, C. M., and Carla Petievich. "Urdu in Lucknow/Lucknow in Urdu." In *Lucknow: Memories of a City*, edited by Violette Graff, 165–180. Delhi: Oxford University Press, 1997.

Nair, Sivaja, and Amba Kulkarni. "The Knowledge Structure in Amarakośa." *Lecture Notes in Computer Science* (2010): 173–189.

Naqvi, Hameeda. "Capital Cities of the Mughul Empire (1556–1803)." *Journal of the Pakistan Historical Society* 13, no. 1 (1965): 211–243.

Nārang, Gopī Ćand, ed. *Luġhat Nawīsī ke Masāʾil*. New Delhi: Māhnāmah-i Kitāb Numā, 1985.

Niẓāmī, Ḥasan Aḥmad. *Shamālī Hind kī Urdū Shāʿirī meṅ Īhām-goʾī*. Aligarh: Educational Book House, 1997.

Noble, James. *The Orientalist; or, Letters of a Rabbi: With Notes*. Edinburgh, 1831.

Novetzke, Christian Lee. "History, Memory, and Other Matters of Life and Death." In *Shared Idioms, Sacred Symbols, and the Articulation of Identities in South Asia*, edited by Kelly Pemberton and Michael Nijhawan, 212–232. New York: Routledge, 2009.

Oertel, C. H. *The Punjab Record; or, Reference Book for Civil Officers*. Vol. 50, part 1. Lahore: Samuel T. Weston, 1915.

Opacki, Ireneusz. "Royal Genres." In *Modern Genre Theory*, edited by David Duff, 118–126. Harlow: Longman, 2000.

Orsini, Francesca. *The Hindi Public Sphere, 1920–1940: Language and Literature in the Age of Nationalism*. New Delhi: Oxford University Press, 2002.

——, ed. *Before the Divide: Hindi and Urdu Literary Culture*. New Delhi: Orient BlackSwan, 2010.

Owen, W. B., and Katz, J. B. "Hall, Fitzedward (1825–1901)." In *Oxford Dictionary of National Biography*, edited by H. C. G. Matthew and Brian Harrison. Oxford: Oxford University Press, 2004. http://www.oxforddnb.com/view/article/33652.

Parekh, Rauf. "A Great Dream Comes True." In *Urdū Luġhat: Yādgārī Maẓāmīn*, edited by Abūlḥasanāt, 1–4. Karachi: Unikarians International, 2010.

Patkar, Madhukar Mangesh. *History of Sanskrit Lexicography*. New Delhi: Munshiram Manoharlal, 1981.

Pello, Stefano. "Persian as Passe-Partout: The Case of Mīrzā ʿAbd al-Qādir Bīdil and His Hindu Disciples." In *Culture and Circulation: Literature in Motion in Early Modern India*, edited by Thomas de Bruijn and Allison Busch, 21–46. Leiden: Brill, 2014.

——. "Persiano e *hindī* nel *Musmir* di Sirāj al-Dīn ʿAlī Xān Ārzū." In *L'Onagro Maestro: Miscellanea di Fuochi Accesi per Gianroberto Scarcia in Occasione del Suo LXX Sadè*, edited by Rudy Favaro, Simone Cristoforetti, and Matteo Compareti, 243–272. Venezia: Cafoscarina, 2004.

Perkins, C. Ryan. "From the Meḥfil to the Printed Word: Public Debate and Discourse in Late Colonial India." *Indian Economic & Social History Review* 50, no. 1 (2013): 47–76.

Pernau, Margrit. "Introduction." In *The Delhi College: Traditional Elites, the Colonial State, and Education Before 1857*, edited by Margrit Pernau, 1–32. New Delhi: Oxford University Press, 2006.

Petersen, Kristian. *The Treasure of the Heavenly Scripture: Translating the Qur'an in China*. Oxford: Oxford University Press, forthcoming.

Petievich, Carla Rae. *Assembly of Rivals: Delhi, Lucknow, and the Urdu Ghazal*. Delhi: Manohar, 1992.

Phukan, Shantanu. "Through a Persian Prism: Hindi and Padmavat in the Mughal Imagination." PhD diss., University of Chicago, 2000.

Platts, John Thompson, and Alfred Wrigley. *A Companion to Wrigley's Collection of Examples: Being Illustrations of Mathematical Processes and Methods of Solution*. Cambridge, 1861.

Pollock, Sheldon. *The Language of the Gods in the World of Men: Sanskrit, Culture, and Power in Premodern India*. Berkeley: University of California Press, 2006.

——. "The Sanskrit Cosmopolis, 300–1300: Transculturation, Vernacularization, and the Question of Ideology." In *Ideology and Status of Sanskrit: Contributions to the History of the Sanskrit Language*, edited by Jan E. M. Houben, 197–247. Leiden: Brill, 1996.

Prince, Ellen F. "Toward a Taxonomy of Given-New Information." In *Radical Pragmatics*, edited by Peter Cole, 223–255. New York: Academic Press, 1981.

Pritchett, Frances W. " 'Everybody Knows This Much . . . ' " In *Āb-e ḥayāt: Shaping the Canon of Urdu Poetry*, edited by Frances W. Pritchett, 1-17. New Delhi: Oxford University Press, 2001.

——. "A Long History of Urdu Literary Culture, Part 2: Histories, Performances, and Masters." In *Literary Cultures in History: Reconstructions from South Asia*, edited by Sheldon Pollock, 864–911. Berkeley: University of California Press, 2003.

——. *Nets of Awareness: Urdu Poetry and Its Critics*. Berkeley: University of California Press, 1994.

Procházka, Stephan. "Sprenger, Aloys Ignatz Christoph (1813–1893)." In *Oxford Dictionary of National Biography*, edited by H. C. G. Matthew and Brian Harrison. Oxford: Oxford University Press, 2004. http://www.oxforddnb.com/view/article/26176.

Qādirī, Ḥāmid Ḥasan. *Dāstān-i Tārīḵh-i Urdū*. Agra: 1966.

Quraishi, Salim al-Din, and Ursula Sims-Williams. *Catalogue of the Urdu Manuscripts in the India Office Library*. London: India Office Library and Records, 1978.

Qureshi, Hamid Afaq. "Anti-British Plots of Shams-ud-Daullah of Dacca in the Light of Contemporary English Report." *Quarterly Review of Historical Studies* 23, no. 4 (1984): 48–53.

——. *The Flickers of an Independent Nawabi: Nawab Wazir Ali Khan of Avadh*. 2 vols. Lucknow: New Royal Book Co., 2002.

——. "Had Wazir Ali Hatched an Anti-British All India Conspiracy in 1798?" *Proceedings of the Indian History Congress* 43 (1983): 555–563.

Rahman, Tariq. "Boy-Love in the Urdu Ghazal." *Annual of Urdu Studies* 7 (1990): 1–20.

——. *From Hindi to Urdu: A Social and Political History*. Karachi: Oxford University Press, 2009.

——. *Language and Politics in Pakistan*. Karachi: Oxford University Press, 1996.

——. *Language, Ideology, and Power: Language Learning Among the Muslims of Pakistan and North India*. Karachi: Oxford University Press, 2002.

——. "Urdu and the Muslim Identity: Standardization of Urdu in the Eighteenth and Early Nineteenth Centuries." *Annual of Urdu Studies* 25 (2010): 83–107.

Rai, Alok. *Hindi Nationalism*. Hyderabad: Orient Longman, 2001.

Rai, Amrit. *A House Divided: The Origin and Development of Hindi/Hindavi*. Delhi: Oxford University Press, 1984.

Raley, Rita. "A Teleology of Letters; or, From a 'Common Source' to a Common Language." *Romantic Circles Praxis Series*, University of Maryland, 2000. http://www.rc.umd.edu/praxis/containment/raley/raley.html.

Raman, Bhavani. *Document Raj: Writing and Scribes in Early Colonial South India*. Chicago: University of Chicago Press, 2012.

Ranking, G. S. A. "Platts, John Thompson (1830–1904)." In *Oxford Dictionary of National Biography*, edited by H. C. G. Matthew and Brian Harrison. Oxford: Oxford University Press, 2004. http://www.oxforddnb.com/view/article/35539.

Rapson, E. J., and Michael Fry. "Hunter, William (1755–1812)." In *Oxford Dictionary of National Biography*, edited by H. C. G. Matthew and Brian Harrison. Oxford: Oxford University Press, 2004.

Ray, Aniruddha. *The Rebel Nawab of Oudh: Revolt of Vizir Ali Khan, 1799*. Calcutta: K. P. Bagchi & Co., 1990.

Reed, Joseph W., Jr. "Noah Webster's Debt to Samuel Johnson." *American Speech* 37, no. 2 (1962): 95–105.

Richards, J. F. "Norms of Comportment Among Imperial Mughal Officers." In *Moral Conduct and Authority: The Place of Adab in South Asian Islam*, edited by Barbara Daly Metcalf, 255–289. Berkeley: University of California Press, 1984.

Rieu, Charles Pierre Henri. *Catalogue of the Persian Manuscripts in the British Museum*. 3 vols. London, 1876.

Ritter, Valerie. "Networks, Patrons, and Genres for Late Braj Bhasha Poets: Ratnakar and Hariaudh." In *Before the Divide: Hindi and Urdu Literary Culture*, edited by Francesca Orsini, 249–276. New Delhi: Orient BlackSwan, 2010.

Robinson, Francis. "Nation Formation: The Brass Thesis and Muslim Separatism." *Journal of Commonwealth & Comparative Politics* 15, no. 3 (1977): 215–230.

——. *Separatism Among Indian Muslims: The Politics of the United Provinces' Muslims, 1860–1923*. Delhi: Oxford University Press, 1993.

——. "Technology and Religious Change: Islam and the Impact of Print." *Modern Asian Studies* 27, no. 1 (1993): 229.

Robson, J. "Ḥadīth." In *Encyclopaedia of Islam*, edited by P. Bearman, Th. Bianquis, C. E. Bosworth, E. van Donzel, and W. P. Heinrichs, 3:23–28. Leiden: Brill, 1971.

Roebuck, Thomas. *Annals of the College of Fort William*. Calcutta, 1819.

Rudolph, Lloyd I., and Susanne Hoeber Rudolph. "Rethinking Secularism: Genesis and Implications of the Textbook Controversy, 1977–79." *Pacific Affairs* 56 (1983): 15–37.

Saarela, Mårten Söderblom. "Shape and Sound: Organizing Dictionaries in Late Imperial China," *Dictionaries: Journal of the Dictionary Society of North America* 35 (2014): 187–208.

Ṣābir, Qādir Bak͟hsh Bahādur. *Gulistān-i Suk͟han*. Lucknow: Uttar Pradesh Urdū Akādmī, 1982.

Sadiq, Muhammed. *A History of Urdu Literature*. Delhi: Oxford, 1984.

Saksena, Ram Babu. *European & Indo-European Poets of Urdu & Persian*. Lucknow: Newul Kishore, 1941.

——. *A History of Urdu literature*. Allahabad: R. N. Lal, 1940.

Sarangi, Asha. "Enumeration and the Linguistic Identity Formation in Colonial North India." *Studies in History* 25, no. 2 (2010): 197–227.

Sarkar, Jadunath. *History of Aurangzeb*. Calcutta: M. C. Sarkar & Sons, 1912.

Sayyid, Jābir ʿAlī, and Wāris̤ Sarhindī. *Kutub-i Luġhat kā Taḥqīqī wa Lisānī Jāʾizah*. Islāmābād: Muqtadirah Quamī Zabān, 1984.

Schiffman, Harold F. "Diglossia as a Sociolinguistic Situation." In *The Handbook of Sociolinguistics*, edited by Florian Coulmas, 205-216. London: Basil Blackwell, 1996.

——. *Linguistic Culture and Language Policy*. London: Routledge, 1996.

Schiffman, Harold F., and Michael C. Shapiro. *Language and Society in South Asia*. Delhi: Motilal Banarsidass, 1981.

Schimmel, Annemarie. "Hindu and Turk: A Poetical Image and Its Application to Historical Fact." In *Islam and Cultural Change in the Middle Ages, Giorgio Levi Della Vida Biennial Conference, May 11–13, 1973, Near Eastern Center, Univ. of Calif., Los Angeles*, edited by Speros Vryonis, 107–126. Wiesbaden: Harrassowitz, 1975.

Scott, James C. *Seeing Like a State: How Certain Schemes to Improve the Human Condition Have Failed*. New Haven, Conn.: Yale University Press, 1998.

Scott, Walter. "Biographical Memoir of John Leyden, M.D." In *Poems and Ballads*. Kelso, 1858.

Shāh, Mirzā Jawān Bak͟ht Jahāndār. "Appendix: A Narrative, Written by the Prince Jehândâr Shàh." In *Memoirs Relative to the State of India*, 163–196. London, 1786.

Shāhnawāz, Nawwab Ṣamṣām-ud-Daula Shāh Nawāz Khān Awrangābādī, and ibn Shāhnawāz Abd al-Ḥayy. *The Maāthir-ul-umarā: Being Biographies of the Muhammādan and Hindu Officers of the Timurid Sovereigns of India from 1500 to about 1780 AD*. Translated by H. Beveridge. Edited by Baini Prashad. 2 vols. Calcutta: Asiatic Society, 1952.

Sheftah, Muṣṭafā K͟hān. *Gulshan-i be K͟hār: Fārsī*. Translated by Ḥamīdah K͟hātūn. New Delhi: Qaumī Kaunsil barāʾe Furoġh-i Urdū, 1998.

Shils, Edward. "Mass Society and Its Culture." *Daedalus* 89, no. 2 (1960): 288–314.

——. "The Theory of Mass Society." *Diogenes* 39 (1962).

Sherānī, Ḥāfiẓ Maḥmūd. "Dībāćah-i Awwal." In *Ḥifẓ al-Lisān (maʿrūf ba-nām-i K͟hāliq Bārī)*, edited by Ḥāfiẓ Maḥmūd Sherānī. Delhi: Anjuman-i Taraqqī-yi Urdū, 1944.

——. "Fārsī Zabān kī ek Qadīm Farhang meṅ Urdū Zabān kā ʿUnṣur." In *Maqālāt-i Ḥāfiẓ Maḥmūd Sherānī*, edited by Maẓhar Maḥmūd Sherānī, 202–231. Lahore: Majlis-i Taraqqī-yi Urdū, 1987.

Shokoohy, Mehrdad, and Natalie H. Shokoohy. *Ḥiṣār-i Fīrūza: Sultanate and Early Mughal Architecture in the District of Hisar, India.* Monographs on Art, Archaeology, and Architecture, South Asian Series. London, 1988.

Siddiqi, Abu Lais. "Muthmir: A Linguistic Analysis." In *Muṯẖmir*, edited by Rehanna Khatoon, vii–xlii. Karachi: Institute of Central and West Asian Studies, 1991.

Siddiqi, M. Atique. *Origins of Modern Hindustani Literature; Source Material: Gilchrist Letters.* Aligarh: Naya Kitab Ghar, 1963.

SIL. "The Rapid Word Collection Methodology." *SIL International.* http://www.sil.org/dictionaries-lexicography/rapid-word-collection-methodology.

Sinha, N. K. "The Case of Mirza Jan Tuppish: A Treason Trial of 1800." *Bengal Past & Present* 72 (1953): 39–42.

Sīrhindī, Yaḥiyā ibn Aḥmad ibn ʿAbdullāh. *The Tārīḵh-i-Mubārakshāhī.* Translated by Henry Beveridge. New Delhi: Low Price, 1996.

Siyāqī, Muḥammad Dabīr. "Borhān-e Qāṭeʾ." In *Encyclopædia Iranica*, edited by Ehsan Yarshater, 1989. http://www.iranicaonline.org/articles/borhan-e-qate.

Skaria, Ajay. "Writing, Orality, and Power in the Dangs, Western India, 1800s-1920s." *Subaltern Studies* 9 (1996): 13–58.

Smyth, William Carmichael. "Preface." In *A Dictionary, Hindoostanee and English*, edited by Joseph Taylor, William Hunter, and William Carmichael Smyth, i–viii. London: Printed for the editor by W. Bulmer and W. Nicol, 1820.

Spence, Jonathan D. *The Memory Palace of Matteo Ricci.* New York: Viking, 1984.

Sperl, Stefan, and Christopher Shackle, eds. *Qasida Poetry in Islamic Asia and Africa.* Vol. 1, *Classical Traditions and Modern Meanings.* Leiden: Brill, 1995.

Spooner, Brian, and William L. Hanaway. "Introduction—Persian as Koine: Written Persian in World-Historical Perspective." In *Literacy in the Persianate World: Writing and the Social Order*, edited by Brian Spooner and William L. Hanaway, 1–68. Philadelphia: University of Pennsylvania Museum of Archaeology and Anthropology, 2012.

Sprenger, Aloys. *A Catalogue of the Arabic, Persian, and Hindústány Manuscripts, of the Libraries of the King of Oudh, Compiled Under the Orders of the Government of India.* Vol. 1. Calcutta, 1854.

—. *A Catalogue of the Bibliotheca Orientalis Sprengeriana.* Giessen, 1857.

Sreenivasan, Ramya. "A South Asianist's Response to Lieberman's *Strange Parallels.*" *Journal of Asian Studies* 70, no. 4 (2011): 983–993.

Speziale, Fabrizio. "Les traités persans sur les sciences indiennes: médecine, zoologie, alchimie." In *Muslim Cultures in the Indo-Iranian World During the Early-Modern and Modern Periods*, edited by Fabrizio Speziale and Denis Hermann, 403–447. Paris: Institut Français de Recherche en Iran, 2010.

Stark, Ulrike. *An Empire of Books: The Naval Kishore Press and the Diffusion of the Printed Word in Colonial India.* Ranikhet: Permanent Black, Distributed by Orient Longman, 2007.

Staves, Susan. "A Few Kind Words for the Fop." *Studies in English Literature, 1500–1900* 22, no. 3 (1982): 413–428.

Steadman-Jones, Richard. *Colonialism and Grammatical Representation: John Gilchrist and the Analysis of the 'Hindustani' Language in the Late Eighteenth and Early Nineteenth Centuries.* Oxford: Blackwell, 2007.

—. "Lone Travellers: The Construction of Originality and Plagiarism in Colonial Grammars of the Late Eighteenth and Early Nineteenth Centuries." In *Plagiarism in Early Modern England*, edited by Paulina Kewes, 201–214. Basingstoke: Palgrave Macmillan, 2003.

Subrahmanyam, Sanjay. "The Career of Colonel Polier and Late Eighteenth-Century Orientalism." *Journal of the Royal Asiatic Society (Third Series)* 10, no. 1 (2000): 43–60.

Subrahmanyam, Sanjay, David Shulman, A. R. Venkatachalapathy, F. Orsini, A. R. Mufti, and G. P. Deshpande. "A Review Symposium: Literary Cultures in History." *Indian Economic & Social History Review* 42, no. 3 (2005): 377–408.

Suhrawardy, Shaista Akhtar Banu (Begum Ikramullah). *A Critical Survey of the Development of the Urdu Novel and Short Story*. London: Longmans, Green, 1945.

Syed, Muhammad Aslam. "How Could Urdu Be the Envy of Persian (*rashk-i Fārsī*)! The Role of Persian in South Asian Culture and Literature." In *Literacy in the Persianate World: Writing and the Social Order*, edited by Brian Spooner and William L. Hanaway, 279–310. Philadelphia: University of Pennsylvania Museum of Archaeology and Anthropology, 2012.

Sykes, Percy Molesworth. *A History of Persia*. 2 vols. London: Macmillan, 1921.

Taqī, Yūsuf. *Murshidābād ke Ćār Kilāsīkī Shuʿarāʾ: Qudratullāh Qudrat, Mīr Bāqir Mukhliṣ, Inshāʾallāh Khāṅ Inshā, Mirzā Jān Ṭapish*. Calcutta: Yūsuf Taqī, 1989.

Tavakoli-Targhi, Mohamad. "Orientalism's Genesis Amnesia." *Comparative Studies of South Asia, Africa, and the Middle East* 16, no. 1 (1996): 1–14.

——. *Refashioning Iran: Orientalism, Occidentalism, and Historiography*. Basingstoke: Palgrave, 2001.

Teignmouth, John Shore. *The Private Record of an Indian Governor-Generalship*. Edited by Holden Furber. Harvard Historical Monographs 2. Cambridge, Mass.: Harvard University Press, 1933.

Temple, Richard Carnac. "Preface." In *A Dictionary of Hindustani Proverbs, Including Many Marwari, Panjabi, Maggah, Bhojpuri, and Tirhuti Proverbs, Sayings, Emblems, Aphorisms, Maxims, and Similes*, edited by Richard Carnac Temple and Lala Faqir Chand, i–iii. Banaras, 1886.

Tickell, Alex. "Negotiating the Landscape: Travel, Transaction, and the Mapping of Colonial India." *Yearbook of English Studies* 34 (2004): 18–30.

Todorov, Tzvetan. "The Origin of Genres." In *Modern Genre Theory*, edited by David Duff, 193–209. Harlow: Longman, 2000.

Truschke, Audrey. "Defining the Other: An Intellectual History of Sanskrit Lexicons and Grammars of Persian." *Journal of Indian Philosophy* 40, no. 6 (2012): 635–668.

——. "The Mughal Book of War: A Persian Translation of the Sanskrit Mahabharata." *Comparative Studies of South Asia, Africa, and the Middle East* 31, no. 2 (2011): 506–520.

Turner, T. J., and H. S. Boulderson. "Memorandum from the Sudder Board of Revenue, N.W.P., to the Secy. to the Govt., N.W.P." In *Supplement to the Glossary of Indian Terms*, iv. Agra, 1845.

Tyagi, Om Prakash, and D. P. Yadav. "Publication of 'Farhangi Asafi' Dictionary." *Parliamentary Debates: Official Report* 92, no. 7–12 (1975): 105.

Umar, Muhammad. *Islam in Northern India During the Eighteenth Century*. New Delhi: Munshiram Manoharlal Publishers for Centre of Advanced Study in History, Aligarh Muslim University, 1993.

Versteegh, Kees. *The Arabic Linguistic Tradition*. London: Routledge, 1997.

Vogel, Claus. *Indian Lexicography*. Wiesbaden: Harrassowitz, 1979.

Vogel, J. Ph. "Joan Josua Ketelaar of Elbing, Author of the First Hindūstānī Grammar." *Bulletin of the School of Oriental Studies, University of London* 8, no. 2/3 (1936): 817–822.

Wadūd, Qāẓī ʿAbdul. *ʿAbdul Ḥaq Baḥaiśīyat-i Muḥaqqiq*. Patna: Khuda Bakhsh Oriental Public Library, 1995.

——. *Farhang-i Aṣifiyyah par Tabṣirah*. Patna: Khuda Bakhsh Oriental Public Library, 1981.

——, ed. *Ḳhudā Baḳhsh Saminār: Tadwīn-i Matn ke Masāʾil*. Patna: Khuda Bakhsh Oriental Public Library, 1982.

Wahi, Tripta. "Henry Miers Elliot: A Reappraisal." *Journal of the Royal Asiatic Society of Great Britain and Ireland* 1 (1990): 64–90.

Washbrook, David. " 'To Each a Language of His Own': Language, Culture, and Society in Colonial India." In *Language, History and Class*, edited by P. J. Corfield, 179–203. Oxford: Blackwell, 1991.

Weingrod, Alex. "Patrons, Patronage, and Political Parties." *Comparative Studies in Society and History* 10, no. 4 (1968): 377–400.

Wilensky, H. L. "The Professionalization of Everyone?" *American Journal of Sociology* 70 (1964): 137–158.

Williams, Raymond. *Marxism and Literature*. Oxford: Oxford University Press, 1977.

Winchester, Simon. *The Professor and the Madman: A Tale of Murder, Insanity, and the Making of the Oxford English Dictionary*. New York: HarperCollins, 1998.

Yates, Frances Amelia. *The Art of Memory*. Chicago: University of Chicago Press, 1966.

Zaidi, Ali Jawad. *A History of Urdu Literature*. New Delhi: Sahitya Akademi, 1993.

Zgusta, Ladislav. "Copying in Lexicography: Monier-Williams' Sanskrit Dictionary and Other Cases (Dvaikośyam)." *Lexicographica: An International Annual for Lexicography* 4 (1988): 145–164.

——. *Lexicography Then and Now: Selected Essays*. Edited by Fredric Dolezal and Thomas Creamer. Lexicographica 129. Tübingen: Niemeyer, 2006.

——. *Manual of Lexicography*. Prague: Academia Mouton, 1971.

Ziad, Homayra. "Quest of the Nightingale: The Religious Thought of Khvājah Mīr Dard (1720–1785)." PhD diss., Yale University, 2008.

Ziauddin, M. *A Grammar of the Braj Bhākhā by Mirzā Khān (1676)*. Calcutta: Visva-Bharati Book-Shop, 1935.

INDEX

f denotes figure

ᶜAbdul Wāsĕᶜ Hāṅswī. *See* Hāṅswī, ᶜAbdul Wāsĕᶜ
Abhidhānacintāmaṇi (Hemaćandra), 205n52
'Ābrū', Shāh Mubārak, 95
absolute Encyclopaedia, 207n78
ādāb (modes of comportment), 96, 98, 103, 176, 194, 198
Agha, Asif, 193
Agra (Akbarābād), 29, 34, 35, 63, 59, 62, 63, 69, 73, 90, 95, 98, 163, 179, 218n108
Agrawal, Arun, 185–186
aḥādīṡ. See *ḥadīṡ* (*ḥadīth*)
Ajāy Ćand Nāmah (Book of Ajay Cand), xvii, 14
Akbar, xvii, 45, 64, 227n73
Aḳhbārī Luġhāt (maᶜrūf bĕh Kalīd-i Aḳhbār-Bīnī) (A Newspaper Dictionary also known as The Key to Newspaper Viewing), 1–2, 2f, 7, 9, 12, 26
Alam, Muzaffar, 102
Aligarh, xxi, 14, 191, 192
alphabetical arrangement/order, 2, 3, 14, 15, 17, 21, 22, 58, 66, 73, 74, 76, 82, 87, 106, 120, 194, 197, 198, 199, 207n79
Amarakośa (Amarasiṁha), 14
Amarasiṁha, 14
Amin, Shahid, 66, 67, 164
Anderson, Benedict, 31, 235n25
Anjum, Ḳhāliq, 124, 128, 158
Anjuman-i Taraqqi-yi Urdū (Society for the Advancement of Urdu), xxi, 138, 191
Arabic: as historical language, 5, 37, 38, 40, 41, 53, 61, 74, 101, 166, 192; and lexicography, xvii, 17, 25, 36, 54, 55, 57, 63, 64,89, 164, 202n16, 205n54; 206–207n72; 218n120, 248–49n116, 249n118
Arabic-English Lexicon (Lane), 164
Arabic script, 17, 35, 65, 80, 173, 186
Armaġhān-i Dihlī (Souvenir gift of Delhi) (Sayyid Ahmad), xx, 117, 131, 132, 158
arrangement/order (of terms). *See* alphabetical arrangement/order; macrostructural arrangement; rhyme order; thematic arrangement
artistic spirit, 13
'Ārzū', Sirājuddīn ᶜAlī Khān, xvii, 10, 33, 34, 39, 42, 49, 51–63, 64, 65, 66, 68, 69, 70, 72, 73, 75, 173, 179, 195, 196
'Aṡar', Ḳhwājah Muḥammad Mīr, 95
Āsmān Jāh Bahādur. *See* Bahādur, Āsmān Jāh
assimilation, 31
associational culture, 198, 247n70
Aurangzeb, xvii, 34, 45, 63, 72, 74, 168, 217n100, 220n152

Avicenna (Ibn Sīnā), 14
A Vocabulary of the Names of the Various Parts of the Human Body and of Medical and Technical Terms in English, Arabic, Persian, Hindee, and Sanscrit for the Use of the Members of the Medical Department in India (Breton), 64
Avadh (Oudh), xxi, 35, 79, 92, 98,100, 178, 183, 191, 241n145
Awadhī, 9, 98, 101, 178, 204n35, 206n63
'Aẕfarī', Mirzā ʿAlī Baḳht Bahādur Muḥammad Ẕahīruddīn, xviii, 82, 83, 84–85, 97–99, 102, 103, 105

Bābur, Ẕahīruddīn Muḥammad, 102
Baevskii, Solomon, 14, 119, 193
Bagehot, Walter, 10
Bāġh o Bahār (Mīr Amman), 90
Bahādur, Āsmān Jāh, 132
'Bahār', Tek Ćand, 51, 217n103
Bahār-i ʿAjam ('Bahār'), 51, 217n103
Bailey, T. Grahame, 189, 190
Bakhtin, Mikhail, 5
Banaras. *See* Benares
Barlow, George Hilario, xix, 78, 80, 109, 110
Barnī, Munshī Ẓiyāʾ al-Dīn Aḥmad, 1–3, 7, 9, 10, 26–27
Barthes, Roland, 50
Bate, J. D., xx, 156, 161
Bayley, William Butterworth, 206n67
Bayly, C. A., 46, 50, 103
Beames, John, xx, 66, 67, 70
Benares (Vārāṇasī), xix, 81, 84, 114, 156, 163, 164, 166, 225n31,
Bengal, xvii, 30, 35, 38, 39, 55, 77, 81–82, 85, 92, 95, 98–101, 108–110, 142, 156, 178–179, 183
Bengali, 37, 101, 178, 250n4
Bhojpūrī, 101
Bihar, 55, 67, 76, 100, 108, 113, 123, 149, 158, 161
Bihar Peasant Life (Grierson), 67
Bilgrāmī, Maulvī Auhaduddīn Aḥmad, 241n140
bilingual dictionaries, 4, 8, 14, 25, 37, 56, 182
bin Adam, Hasan, 17
Blochmann, Heinrich Ferdinand, 47, 64, 65, 164
Bose, Rash Behari, 187
Bourdieu, Pierre, 28, 33, 43, 147, 193
Boutros, Felix, 149, 150
Bowrey, Thomas, 19, 20
Braj Bhāṣā, 9, 37, 56, 69, 95, 101, 173
Brass, Paul R., 165, 186, 210n109
Breton, Peter, xix, 42, 64, 67, 70
Brunetière, Ferdinand, 13
Buḳhārī, Mirzā Yūsuf Beg, 80
Burhān-i Qāṭeʿ, 61
Būstān (Saʿdī'), 47

Calcutta, xviii, 8, 15, 17, 19, 30, 39, 64, 76, 78, 80, 84, 85, 99, 105, 109, 110, 112–114, 161, 163, 187, 198, 206n67, 211n19. *See also* College of Fort William
Camac, William, 80
Ćand, Lālā Faqīr, 163
Ćand, Lālah Amīr, 187
Cassiodorus Senator, 21
caste, 23, 66, 183, 230n113, 246n64
catalogue poems, 21
Chatterjee, Partha, 176
Chatterjee, Sunti Kumar, 178
Chinese, folklorists of, 245n54; as historical language, 5; lexicography of, 19, 202n16; population of speakers of Mandarin, 7
chronology, xvii–xxii
Ćirāġh-i Hidāyat (Lamp of wisdom) ('Ārzū'), 10, 51, 61
classic diglossia, 102
Collection of Proverbs and Proverbial Phrases in Persian and Hindustani, with Translations (Hunter), xix, 113
College of Fort William, xix, 19, 35, 110, 112, 122, 206n67, 210–11n8
commensurability: of language, 6–7, 25, 105; linguistic commensurability, 23, 104–105; of modern comprehensive dictionary, 116; representational commensurability, 24–25; of terms, 198. *See also* translation

Comprehensive Persian-English Dictionary (Steingass), 69, 164
Cooke, Theodore, 160
cosmographies, lexicographic works as reflecting, 12,14, 19, 21, 22, 23, 28, 193, 199
courtesan, 60, 100, 176, 179
Cowell, E. B., 65
Croce, Benedetto, 13
Crooke, William, 67, 70
cross-cultural comparison, 4
cultures with dictionaries, 4
Cuomo, Mario, 8

Dakanī Urdu, 9
Dalmia, Vasudha, 165, 166, 168
Daly, Lloyd, 58
'Dard', Ḳhwājah Mīr, 81, 91, 92
Daryā-i Latāfat (Ocean of subtlety) ('Inshā'), xix, 90, 92, 138, 141, 145–146
De, Barun, 79
Declaration of Independence, American (*Ĕʿlān-i Āzādī*), 3
Delbrück, Berthold, 27
democracy, 1–3, 7, 183, 186
De Tassy, Joseph Heliodore Garcin, 41, 42, 44, 71
Deutsch, Karl Wolfgang, 186, 210n109
devanāgarī script, xxi, 35, 173, 186, 191, 199
Dhivehi language, 17, 21
dictionary: academic versus commercial production of, 116–117; corporate production of, 28, 31, 117, 118, 148–149, 198; cultures with, 4; definition of, 210n6; modern standard (comprehensive) dictionary, 25, 27, 31, 116 196, 198; before print, purpose of, 21, 22, 25; relationship with poetry, 8–9, 14, 25, 194; role of in establishing commensurability of language, 6–7, 116, 131; role of in educating and defining bureaucratic and literary classes, 11, 24, 28, 61, 73, 75, 135, 187, 198; role in nationalist projects, 4, 24, 31, 55, 116, 119, 129–131, 150, 153, 154, 166–167, 181, 192. *See also* bilingual dictionaries; Hindustani-English dictionary; Hindustani-Urdu dictionary; Indo-Persian dictionaries; monolingual dictionaries; multilingual vocabularies
A Dictionary, English and Hindoostanee (Gilchrist), 35, 110, 111*f*, 112, 113, 114
A Dictionary, Hindoostanee and English (Taylor), xix
Dictionary of English, Portuguese, Hindostanee, and Malay (Bowrey), 19, 20f
Dictionary of Hindustani Proverbs (Fallon), 161, 163
Dictionary of the English Language (Johnson), 213n41
Dictionary of Urdu, Classical Hindi, and English (Platts), xx, 164, 190
Dictionary, Persian, Arabic, and English (Richardson), xviii, 63
differentiation, 32, 37
diglossia, 5, 22, 94, 101–102
Dihlawī, Mīr Amman, 90, 167, 228n73, 245n57
Dihlawī, Sayyid Aḥmad, xix, xx, xxi, 115–117, 119, 120–122, 123–134, 135–136, 139, 140, 143, 144, 145, 146, 146*f*, 147, 148, 151, 152, 153, 154, 155, 157, 158, 160, 161, 162, 165, 167, 168, 169, 170, 174, 176, 177, 180, 181, 182, 196, 197
Dimaggio, Paul, 43
Discourse Networks 1800/1900 (Kittler), 28
Dīwān-i Reḳhtī ('Rangin'), 138
Dīwān-zādah (Son of the *diwan*) ('Ḥātim'), xviii
Dhaka (Jahāngīr Nagar), xviii, 76, 80, 82, 83, 84, 85
Dodson, Michael, 150
Douglas, Henry, 78, 80
The East and West Khaliq Baree (Munshi Ahmeduddin Khan), xxi

East India Company, 8, 30, 35, 39, 65, 76, 79, 80, 84, 85, 151, 163, 180, 198
Elliot, Henry Miers, xix, xx, 33, 65, 66, 67, 70, 163

Encyclopedia Britannica, 10
encyclopedic information, as included in dictionary entries, 14, 66, 73, 152
English, as replacing Persian in nineteenth century, 6, 8, 25, 30, 36
English Constitution (Bagehot), 10
An English–Hindi Vocabulary in Verse or Vallabhkoṣ (Mishra), xxi, 211n16
equivalents/equivalent terms, 4, 6, 7, 17, 18, 19, 21, 23, 25, 32, 36, 38, 52, 55, 57, 61, 65, 69, 70, 73, 75, 116, 177, 193, 197, 220n155
The Essays of Elia (Bagehot), 10
Everest, George, 164

Fabian, Johannes, 13
'Faiẓ', Faiẓ Aḥmad, 189
Faizabad, 35, 38, 92, 98
Fallon, Samuel William, xix, xx, 118, 120, 131, 144, 149, 151, 152, 153, 154, 155–156, 157–158, 160, 161, 162, 163, 164, 165, 166, 167, 172, 175, 176, 177, 178, 180, 182
Farāhī, Abū Naṣar, xvii
farhang (dictionary, culture), 1, 14, 34, 55, 73, 116, 119, 120, 137–138
Farhang-i Āṣafiyah (Dictionary of the Aṣaf Jāhī dynasty) (Sayyid Ahmad), xx, xxi, 115, 116, 117, 119, 120, 122, 124, 125*f*, 127, 128, 131, 132, 133, 134, 135, 139, 141, 146, 147, 150, 153, 158, 162
Farhang-i Jahāngīrī (Injū Shīrāzī), xvii, 9, 61, 86
Farhang-i Rashīdī (ʿAbdul Rashīd), xvii, 46, 61, 86
Farrell, Gerry, 156
Fārsī Nāmah-i Kalān maʿ Qādir Nāmah-i Ġhālib ('Ġhālib'), 209n93
Faruqi, Shamsur Rahman, 60, 63, 72, 178
Fendall, John, 78, 80
Fishman, Joshua, 102
Fort William Collection, 64, 138
Fort William College. *See* College of Fort William
Frow, John, 13
Fuchs, Barbara, 13

Gellner, Ernest, 4
The General East India Guide and Vade Mecum (Gilchrist), 71
genre: as dynamic, fluctuating "systems," 12; modern comprehensive dictionary as, 116; proliferation of, 195; as set of strategies, 13; as sustained through institutions, 13. See also *ġhazal*; lexicographic genres; *luġhat*; *niṣāb*; prose genres; *qaṣīdah*; royal genre; *tażkirah*
'Ġhālib', Mirzā Asadullāh, xx, 52, 209n93
Ġharāʾib al-Luġhāt (Marvels of words/languages) ('Ārzū'), xvii, 33, 34, 41, 42, 46, 49, 51, 52, 55, 58, 63, 64, 68*f*, 69, 72, 73, 74, 75, 86, 87, 97, 107, 179
Ġhauś, Muḥammad Ġhauś Gwāliyārī, 69
ġhazal, 105, 122, 128, 146
Gilchrist, John Borthwick, 34–36, 37, 38, 39, 40–41, 51, 67, 71, 205n61
Gladwin, Francis, 19, 67
Glossary of Judicial and Revenue Terms (Wilson), xx, 65, 66
Glossary of North Indian Peasant Life (Crooke), 67, 70
glossing, 55, 75, 184, 193, 197
A Grammar of the Hindoostanee Language (Gilchrist), 35
The Grand Master; or, Adventures of Qui Hi? in Hindostan. A Hudibrastic Poem in Eight Cantos by Quiz, 145*f*
"Great Chain of Being," 14. *See also* thematic arrangement
Green, Jonathon, 119
Grierson, George Abraham, 67, 163, 180
Guha, Sumit, 56
Gujrī Urdu, 9
Gulistān-i Suḳhan (Garden of speech) ('Ṣābir'), 137
Gulshan-i Be-Ḳhār (Flowerbed without thorns) ('Sheftah'), 41
Gwalior, 69, 95

ḥadīś (*ḥadīth*), 88, 89, 227n61
Halhed, Nathaniel, 37
'Ḥālī', Alṭāf Ḥusain, 121, 122, 182, 183
Hall, Fitzedward, 241n140, 245n44

Hāṅsī (town), 29, 42, 44–46, 48, 50, 58, 59, 61, 63, 64, 69, 71, 74, 75, 97
Hāṅswī, ʿAbdul Wāsēʿ, xvii, 33, 34, 39, 41, 44, 46, 47, 48, 49–51, 52, 55, 58, 59, 61–63, 67, 69, 70–75, 86, 87, 97, 107, 175, 179, 195
Ḥaq, ʿAbdul, xxi, xxii, 122–123, 134, 135, 151, 152, 153, 154, 181, 190, 191
Hāshmī, Masʿūd, 123, 161
Hastings, Warren, 39
'Ḥātim', Shāh, xviii, 179
Havelock, Eric, 207n78
'Ḥazīn', Mīr Muḥammad Bāqar, 52
Hemaćandra, 205n52
'Hidāyat', Shāh, 81
Hindi: communalization of, 7; 165–166, 168, 184–185, 186; as official or national language, xxi, 7, 56–57, 116, 167, 173, 191, 199; relationship of with other Indian languages, 101–102, 105. *See also* Modern Standard Hindi
Hindi-Urdu debates, 115, 191
Hindoostanee/Hindustani, 9, 15, 19, 26, 35, 36, 37, 38, 39–40, 41, 50, 112, 114, 115, 156, 162, 166, 167, 168–169, 170, 171, 172, 174, 176, 178, 184, 185, 186, 212n30; as national speech, 166–167. See also *A Dictionary, English and Hindoostanee* (Gilchrist); *A Grammar of the Hindoostanee Language* (Gilchrist); *A Vocabulary Persian and Hindoostanee [and Maladivian]* (Leyden)
Hindustan, 64, 116, 165, 166, 168, 171, 178, 182, 184, 185, 212n28
Hindustani-English dictionary, xx, 155, 157, 158, 161, 182. See also *Hindustani-English Law and Commercial Dictionary* (Fallon); *A New Hindustani-English Dictionary* (Fallon)
Hindustani-English Law and Commercial Dictionary (Fallon), 163
Hindustani-Urdu dictionary, 184. See also *Hindūstānī Urdū Luġhat* (Sayyid Ahmad)
Hindūstānī Urdū Luġhat (Sayyid Ahmad), xxi, 115, 116, 117, 119, 131, 158, 184
Hindvī/*hindwī*/Hinduwee, 7, 14, 19, 21, 36, 38, 54, 55, 61, 62, 69, 72, 73, 74, 75, 178, 179, 195, 197
Hisar (Ḥiṣār-i Fīrozah), 45, 46
Histoire de la littérature hindouie et hindoustani (De Tassy), 44
historical languages, 4, 5
Howe, Nicholas, 21
Hunter, William, xix, 110, 111, 112, 113, 114
Hunter, William Orby, 112
Hunter, William Wilson, 126, 164
Ḥusain, Muḥammad Żākir, 136, 139–140, 141, 143
Ḥusainī , Sayyid Ḳhwajah, 121, 161
Hyderabad, xx, xxi, 100, 116, 117, 120, 124, 127, 132, 133, 148, 191
hyperglossia, 5

Ibn Baṭūṭah, 45
Ibn Sīnā (Avicenna), 14
Imperial Gazetteer of India, 164
Indo-Persian dictionaries, xvii, 9, 14, 46–47, 61, 86, 193
Injū Shīrāzī, Mīr Jamāluddīn Ḥusain, xvii, 9
'Inshā', Inshāʾallāh Ḳhāṅ, xix, 89, 91, 93, 94, 95, 96–97, 99, 101, 103, 106, 138, 141–142, 145, 146, 172, 173, 176, 179
Inshā-yi Taqwiyatah al-Ṣibyān (Treatise on the edification of children) (Sayyid Ahmad), 128
Isidore of Seville, 21
Islām, Najmul, 88, 89, 110, 112
isnād (chain of transmission), 86, 89, 117, 182, 193, 196
iṣṭilāh (terminology), 54, 96–97, 129, 138, 160, 168, 169, 172, 174, 175

Jahāndār Shāh, Mirzā Jawān Baḳht, 81, 82
Jahangir, xvii, 9
Jameson, Frederic, 12
Jāmī, Nuruddīn ʿAbdul Raḥmān, 47
Jāmiʿ al-Luġhāt (Majīd), 189
Janssen, Susanne, 33, 42, 43, 47–48, 49, 147
Johnson, Samuel, 121, 122, 213n41
Jones, Sir William, 15, 37, 38, 51, 198

Kākorwī, Nūr al-Ḥasan Nez, 136
Kanz al-Fawāʾid (Treasure of advantages/benefits, also known as *Munāẓarah-i Taqdīr* 'Contest of fates') (Sayyid Ahmad), xx, 131
Karachi, 127, 135, 138, 191
Kashmir, 91, 134, 135, 178
Ketelaar, Joan Josua, 70–71
Al-Ḳhalīl, Abu ʿAbdur Raḥmān, 206–207n72
Ḳhāliq Bārī ('Ḳhusrau'), xvii, 35, 47, 179. See also *niṣāb*
Ḳhān-i Ārzū. *See* 'Ārzū', Sirājuddīn ʿAlī Khān
Ḳhāṅ, Ġhulām Muṣṭafā, 89
Ḳhān, Maḥbūb ʿAlī, 116
Ḳhān, Mirzā, 37
Khan, Munshi Ahmeduddin, xxi, 211n16
Ḳhān, Sayyid Aḥmad, 181, 183
Ḳhān, Wazīr ʿAlī, 79, 107
Khaṛī Bolī/Khaṛī Bolī Hindi, 8, 35, 36, 173
Khattrī, Ayodhyā Prasād, 173
Ḳhudā Baḳhsh Oriental Public Library, 136, 138
'Ḳhusrau', Amīr, 35, 47, 178, 179, 227n69
King, Christopher, 7
Kitāb al-ʿAin (Al-Ḳhalīl), 206–207n72
Kittler, Friedrich, 28

Lahore (Muġhalpūrah), 63, 90, 100, 132, 137, 162, 180, 187
Lāl, Munshī Ćiraṇjī, xx, xxi, 147, 155, 161–163, 165, 166, 167, 168–169, 170–172, 173–174, 175, 176, 177, 178, 180, 181, 182, 184, 185, 186
Lāl Ćandrikā (Lāllū Jī Lāl), 229n88
Lāllū Jī Lāl of Agra, 229n88
Landau, Sidney, 116
Lane, Edward William, 164
language: as central marker capable of motivating political movements, 24; commensurability of, 6–7, 25, 105; diglossic uses of giving way to monolingual ideal, 22; equation of with nation, 191; historical languages, 4, 5; how it comes to be made literary, 6, 8; how it comes to be repositioned as the mother tongue, 6; how it comes to be written down, 6; limited social functions performed by, 22; as medium capable of expressing total social life and political life, 25; mutual coordination of, 193; objectification of into pedagogical materials, 104
Lanson, Gustave, 28
Lawrence, John, 163
Lelyveld, David, 92, 183
L'evolution des genres dans l'histoire de la littérature (Brunetière), 13
lexical cosmography, 14. *See also* cosmography, lexicographic works; preprint lexicographic cosmography
lexical hierarchy, 14. *See also* thematic arrangement
lexicographers: as anthropologists, 117–118, 131; authority of, 27, 78, 118 (*see also* linguistic authority); borrowing/plagiarism of, 26, 31, 115, 135–136, 144; descriptivist lexicographers, 152, 153; as indulging in forms of verbal play, 25; lack of occupational control among, 48; as linguistic gatekeepers, 48; new techniques of, 117–118; overlapping of with poets, 117; prescriptivist lexicographers, 152, 153
lexicographic authority, 27, 28, 48, 67, 78, 114, 117–118, 146–147, 150, 180, 182–183, 193–194, 195, 196
lexicographic genres, 22, 24, 28, 44, 73, 89, 116, 117
lexicographic institutions, rise of, 24, 148–149, 191, 198
lexicographic works: relationship with literature, 14, 25, 43; authority of, 67; use of by historians, 191–192; glossary function of, 73, 106, 196; as guides to acquisition of courtly

culture, 23; as historical archive, 24; as linguistic gatekeepers, 48; as reflecting dominant cosmographies, 12, 23; as serving as significant collections of literature, 194
lexicography: development of under colonial patronage, 27; as documentation of language, 77; double reference function of, 77; as guide to felicitous performance of certain forms of social interaction, 77; metalexicography, 194; as middle-level occupation, 43, 192; Urdu literary culture as developing reflexively in parallel to, 191
Leyden, John, 15–17, 19, 21, 23, 67, 163, 200
Linguarum Totius Orbis Vocabularia Comparativa, 220n162
linguistic authority, 23, 52, 89, 91–93, 96–97, 105, 121, 180, 193
linguistic commensurability, 4, 6, 23, 25, 104–105, 183, 198
Linguistic Survey of India, 163
Listenwissenschaft (list science), 21, 194
Literacy, 8, 9, 19, 22, 24, 34, 77, 104, 105, 117, 157, 169, 180, 184, 193, 195, 197
lithography, 9, 25, 170
Liu, Lydia, 4, 5
Lucknow, xviii, 63, 79, 81, 82, 84, 91, 92, 99, 100, 162, 182, 183, 184. *See also* Avadh (Oudh), Awadhī.
luġhat (word, dictionary), 1, 34, 73, 116, 119, 123, 130, 169
*Luġhāt al-Nisā*ʾ (Dictionary of women) (Sayyid Ahmad), xx, xxi, 131, 133, 158
Lughāt-i Hindī, 19
Luġhat-i Kabīr-i Urdū (Great dictionary of Urdu) (Haq), xxii, 122, 135, 152, 191
Luġhat-i Muḥāwarāt-i Urdū, 139
Luġhāt-i Urdū (Ḳhulāsah-yi Armaġhān-i Dihlī) (Dictionary of Urdu: an abridgment of *Armaġhān-i Dihlī*) (Sayyid Ahmad), xxi, 131
luġhat nawīsh (lexicographer), 57
MacDonnell, Anthony, xxi, 191
MacKenzie, John, 39
macrostructural arrangement, 15, 66, 87, 197. *See also* alphabetical arrangement; thematic arrangement
'Maḥshar', Mirzā ʿAlī Naqī Beg, 91, 92
Maḳhzan al-Muḥāwarāt (Treasury of idioms) (Lāl), xx, xxi, 147, 149, 155, 159*f*, 174, 176, 182, 187
Maḳhzan-i Fawāʾid (Treasury of benefits) ('Nakhat'), xix, 137, 138, 139, 140, 141, 147, 149, 150
Maʿāśir al-Umarā, 45
Majeed, Javed, 71
Majīd, ʿAbdul, 189
Malay, 15, 19, 20*f*
Malcolm, John, 15
Maldives, 17
manuscript production, 10, 15, 17, 19, 28, 53, 64, 65, 68, 82, 85, 86, 88, 106, 117, 139, 140
map, Northern India c. 1783, 81*f*
Maṣdar, Mā-shāʾ Allāh Ḳhān, 92
Maśnavī-yi Bahār-i Dānish (Springtime of knowledge) ('Ṭapish'), xviii, 112
Matthews, D. J., 190
'Maẓhar', Mirzā Jān-i Jānāṅ, 92
McArthur, Tom, 206n65
McGregor, Stuart, 37
mechanical aids, 15, 17, 23, 200
Memoirs on the History, Folk-Lore, and Distribution of the Races of the North Western Provinces of India: Being an Amplified Edition of the Original Supplemental Glossary of Indian Terms (Elliot), xx, 66
metalexicography, 194
Mīnāʾī, Amīr, 136
Minault, Gail, 130
Mirʾāt al-Iṣṭilāḥ ('Muḳhliṣ'), 217n103
'Mīr', Mīr Muḥammad Taqī, xix, 10, 11, 104, 110, 141, 144, 145
Mishra, Pandit Braj Vallabh, xxi, 211n16
Mitchell, Lisa, 6, 104
mnemonic technologies/techniques, 14, 19, 200

modern standard (or comprehensive) dictionary, 25, 27, 31, 116, 196, 198, 199
Modern Standard Hindi, 7, 119, 122, 186
'Mŏhlat', Mirzā ʿAlī, 91
monolingual dictionaries, 32, 55, 120, 123, 150
mother tongue, 4, 6, 7, 9, 11, 94, 118, 157, 158, 170, 171, 172, 180, 182, 184, 186
Mughal Empire, xvii, xviii, 1, 8, 9, 23, 24, 27, 33, 44, 45, 56, 62, 64, 72, 74, 76, 82, 90, 97, 98, 99, 101, 102, 103, 104, 114, 142, 148, 168, 170, 179, 195, 197, 198, 230n104
Muḥammad ʿAlī (Nanko Miyāṅ), Mirzā, 110
Muḥammad Shāh, 45, 141, 142, 219n137, 230n103
muḥāwarah (idiom), 160, 168, 169, 170, 172, 174, 175, 184, 185
'Mukhliṣ', Ānand Rām, 52, 217n103 219n137
multilingual vocabularies, 1, 14, 18, 19, 22, 36, 47, 119, 123, 179, 193
Munīruddīn, Sayyid, 89
Munshī Ćiraṇjī Lāl. *See* Lāl, Munshī Ćiraṇjī
Murray, James, 165
Murshidabad, xviii, xix, 30, 78, 80, 81, 82, 83, 84, 85, 86, 92, 99, 100, 101, 102, 105, 106, 108, 109, 113, 179
'Muṣḥafī', Shaikh Ġhulām Hamadānī, 228n80
Muśmir ('Ārzū'), 53
Muṣṯalaḥāt al-Shuʿarāʾ ('Warastah'), 217n103
Muṣṯalaḥāt-i Urdū (Idioms of Urdu) (Sayyid Ahmad), xx, 131, 132, 158

Nadir Shah, xvii, 45, 51, 142, 143, 144, 232n140
Nafāʾis al-Luġhāt (Bilgrāmī), 241n140
nāgarī script. *See* devanāgarī
Naim, C. M., 10–11
'Nakhat', Niyāz ʿAlī Beg, xix, 137, 139, 140, 141, 143, 145, 146, 147, 149, 150, 177
'Naṣīr', Shāh Naṣīruddīn, 137, 146
National Council for the Promotion of Urdu Language (NCPUL) (India), 24, 135
nationalism, 7, 22, 24, 55, 116, 119, 150, 165, 168, 181, 186, 187
national language, 1, 22, 31, 79, 118, 119, 154, 167, 173, 182, 184, 190, 199
National Language Authority (Pakistan), 24
native assistants, 158, 163, 167
Nawādir al-Alfāẓ (Wonders of words) ('Ārzū'), xvii, xxi, 33, 49, 51, 57, 60, 63, 64, 65, 66, 67, 74, 97, 179
Nets of Awareness (Pritchett), 204n36
A New Hindustani–English Dictionary (Fallon), xx, 120, 155, 156–157, 161, 162, 163, 180, 182
Nicholson, John, 163
Nighaṇṭu, 14
niṣāb (multilingual vocabulary in verse), 6, 14, 25, 35, 47, 48, 71, 75, 119, 123, 195, 200
Niṣāb al-Ṣibyān (Capital-stock of children) (Abū Naṣar Farāhī), xvii

Onomasiological arrangement. *See* thematic arrangement
Opacki, Ireneusz, 12–13
Orientalists, 15, 37, 41, 51, 173, 198
Orsini, Francesca, 233n10
orthography, 19, 22, 29, 61, 68, 74, 193, 197, 220-21, 221n180
Oudh. *See* Avadh
Oxford English Dictionary, 122, 191

pablik (public), 171, 172, 175, 176, 186
Patronage, 6, 11, 23, 112, 114, 116, 117, 121, 124, 130, 135, 137, 147, 148, 150, 151, 158, 170, 179, 181, 241n140
Parekh, Rauf, 191
partition of Indian subcontinent (1947), 8, 46, 127, 154, 191, 221–222n180
Patna (ʿAẓīmābād), xix, 78, 99, 100, 113, 114, 138, 156, 161, 162, 180. *See also* Khudā Bakhsh Oriental Public Library
'Payām' Akbarābādī, Sharafuddīn ʿAlī Khān, 141, 142, 144, 145
Pears Cyclopedia (Bagehot), 10
Pernau, Margrit, 174

Persian: as cosmopolitan language of prestige, 9, 11, 50, 61, 73, 101, 103; effort to de-Persianize language of administration, 56; as historical language, 5; as mother tongue of Central Asian émigrés, 6, 11, 36, 51, 94; as official administrative language, 24, 33, 56, 64; perceived superiority of as classical language, 54; poetry seen as touchstone of, 9; preference for Persian prose over Urdu, 54; replacement of with Urdu as official language, xix, 22, 36; status of as second language, 8
Pincott, Frederick, 173
plagiarism, 26, 31, 115, 135, 136, 144, 209n98. *See also* lexicographers, borrowing/plagiarism
Platts, John T., 155, 156, 163–164, 165, 190
Pliny the Elder, 21
poetry: chain of poetic discipleship, 92, 146; decline in status of professional poets, 10; seen as touchstone of Persian language, 9; veil of (1800), 76–114. *See also* dictionary, relationship with poetry
Pollock, Sheldon, 5, 11
print, 10, 17, 19, 22, 25, 31, 36, 42, 44, 62, 65, 66, 82, 131, 133–136, 138, 147, 150, 156, 158, 160, 168, 173, 176, 180, 191, 195, 198–199. *See also* lithography
print capitalism, 31
Pritchett, Frances, 54, 204n36
prose: citations of within definitions, 10, 30, 160, 163; development of genres of, 9, 10, 35, 41, 52, 77, 93, 94, 101, 105, 106, 122; relation of to poetry, 10, 36, 40, 75, 101, 196
Punjabi, 9, 72, 176

Qādir Nāmah (Book of the Almighty) ('Ġhālib'), xx
Qādirī, Ḥamid Ḥasan, 131, 136, 227n55
qaṣīdah, 14, 25, 128, 137
Qaṣīdah dar Luġhat-i Hindī (An ode on Hindi terms), 6, 36
Qawāʾid-i Luġhāt-I Furs (Grammar of the Persian language) (ʿAbdul Wāsĕʿ), xvii, 46

Raḥmān, Sayyid ʿAbdul, 126
Rai, Alok, 183
Rai, Amrit, 93, 184
'Rangīn', Saʿādat Yār Ḳhān, 138
Rānī Ketakī kī Kahānī (The story of Rānī Ketakī) (Inshāʾ), 105
Rashīd, ʿAbdul, xvii, 46
Ray, Aniruddha, 79
Reid, J. S., 161
reḳhtah (poetic register), 75, 82, 86–88, 93–96, 100–101, 104, 106–107, 141, 144, 147, 173, 179, 229n88
rhyme order, 14, 25
Ricci, Matteo, 14
Richardson, John, xviii, 61, 62, 63
Risālah-i Jān Pahćān (Treatise of the familiar friend) (ʿAbdul Wāsĕʿ), 47
Risālah-i Qawāʿid-i Ṣarf o Naḥw-iUrdū ('Ṣahbāʾī'), 138, 150
Risālah-yi ʿAbdul Wāsĕʿ (Treatise of ʿAbdul Wāsĕʿ) (ʿAbdul Wāsĕʿ), 41–42, 46
Ritter, Valerie, 56
Roebuck, Thomas, xix, 233n159
Roman script, 65, 129, 199, 224–25n23
royal genre, 12–13, 194, 198
Rusūm-i Dihlī (Sayyid Ahmad), 124, 130

'Ṣabīḥ' al-ʿĀlim, Muftī, 109, 110
'Ṣābir', Qādir Baḳhsh Bahādur, 137
Saʿdī', Abū Muḥammad Musliḥuddīn Sherāzī, 47
'Ṣahbāʾī', Imām Baḳhsh, 138, 150, 176
'Sāʾil', Mirzā Yār Beg, 81
Ṣamad Bārī / Jān Pahćān (ʿAbdul Wāsĕʿ), 47, 73
'Sanāʾī', Abū al-Majd Majdūd Ġhaznawī, 53
sanad (deed, diploma, prooftext, authority), 86, 89, 93, 96, 97, 140, 141, 161, 170, 194, 238n98. See also *isnād*
Sanskrit: as language of prestige, 9, 54, 103
Sanskrit cosmopolis, 5, 204n35

Sanskrit–Persian glossaries, 14, 37, 56
Sayyid ʿAbdullāh, 33, 34, 47, 60, 72, 73
Sayyid ʿAbdul Raḥmān. *See* Raḥmān, Sayyid ʿAbdul
Sayyid Aḥmad Dihlawī. *See* Dihlawī, Sayyid Aḥmad
Sayyid al-Luġhāt (Sayyid Ahmad), 132
Scalinger, Joseph Justus, 236n51
Scott, James C., 119
Scott, Sir Walter, 15
Scotland, language in, 38, 39
script: Arabic script, 17, 35, 65, 80, 173, 186; deployment of dictionaries to align symbols of, 32; *devanāgarī* script, xxi, 35, 173, 186, 191, 199; of *hindūstānī*, 185; as a means of organizing dictionaries, 18; relationship of to meaning, 199; Thaana script, 17; Urdu on the Internet, 199
Shādānī, ʿAndalīb, 138
Shah ʿĀlam II, xviii, 81
Shah Jahan, xvii, 1, 45
Shāhjahānābād (Delhi), 29, 30, 34, 60, 62, 63, 73, 90, 92, 96, 97, 98, 99–100, 101, 102, 103, 113, 126, 137, 138, 142, 144, 168, 172, 173, 178, 179
Shams al-Bayān fī Muṣṭalaḥāt al-Hindūstān (The sun of speech, on the idioms of Hindustan) (Shams al-Daulah), xviii, xix, 76, 82, 85, 87, 101, 106, 107, 110, 112, 138, 149, 195, 196
Shams al-Daulah, Nawāb, xviii, xix, 76, 82, 83, 84, 85, 107, 108, 109, 110
Shams al-Mulk, 100
sharīf (elite, noble) culture, 130, 170, 181, 182, 183, 236n55
'Sheftah', Muṣṭafā Ḳhān, 41, 42, 44
Sherānī , Ḥāfiẓ Maḥmūd, 55, 74
Shore, John, 79
ṣifāt allāh (names of Allah), 47, 206n63
al-Simnānī, ʿAlāʾal-Daulah, 14
Singh, Pratāp Nārāyaṇ, 56
Singh, Ranjīt, 137
Singh, Sher, 137
Sirāj Aurangābādī, 88
Smyth, William Carmichael, 112
South Asia: adoption of print in, 19; linguistic diversity of as proverbial, 26; as multilingual society, 22; traditions of compared to European counterparts (at turn of nineteenth century), 19
Spanish, population of speakers of, 7
Standing Commission for Scientific and Technical Terminology, 56
Stark, Ulrike, 198
Steingass, Francis, 60, 61, 62, 69, 70, 164
Subrahmanyam, Sanjay, 102
Sudder Board of Revenue, 66
Sufism, 14, 23, 54, 69, 81, 92, 96, 126, 170, 214n57
sulfite pulping, 9, 25
supplementarity, of premodern Persianate lexicography, 9–10. *See also* dictionary, relationship with poetry
Supplement to the Glossary of Indian Terms (Elliot), xix, xx, 33, 65, 66, 67

taḳhalluṣ (nom de plume, pen name), 41, 42, 224n22
'Ṯapish', Mirzā Jān, xviii, xix, 76, 78, 79, 80–89, 91, 92, 92*f*, 93, 97, 98, 102, 105, 106, 107–110, 112–114, 149, 150, 172, 176, 179, 195, 196, 224n22
Taraqqī-yi Urdū Board, 134, 135, 138
Taylor, Joseph Irwin, xix, 110, 112, 113, 114
taẕkirah (biographical anthology), 41, 44, 88, 117, 137, 140, 141, 146, 147
Taẕkirah-i Hindī ('Muṣḥafī'), 228n80
Telegu lexicography, 248n118
Temple, R. C., 161
terms: alphabetical arrangement of (*see* alphabetical arrangement/order); linguistic equivalents among, 18, 32, 220n155; macrostructural arrangement of (*see* macrostructural arrangement; thematic arrangement)
terminology. See *iṣṯilāh*
Thaana script/writing system, 17
thematic arrangement, 15, 17, 18, 19, 21, 22, 66, 67 194, 206n65
"Third Anniversary Discourse" (Jones), 37

Thomas, George, 42
Ṭiflī nāmah (Book of childhood) (Sayyid Ahmad), 128
Todorov, Tzvetan, 12
Tuḥfat al-Hind (The gift of Hind) (Mirzā Ḳhān), 37
translatio imperii (imposition/transfer of power), 5
translatio studii (transfer of knowledge), 5
translation, 9, 12, 17, 64, 65, 102, 112, 122, 131, 144, 149, 165, 178, 179–180, 183–184. *See also* Vernacular Translation Society
transliteration, xv–xvi, 17, 66, 199, 224–25 n23
Truschke, Audrey, 14
Turkish, 52, 53, 54, 56, 104; as marker of genetic identity and class identity, 99, 101, 102, 103, 105
Twain, Mark, 1, 7
Tyagi, Om Prakash, 134, 135

Uniform Resource Locator (URL), 199
Urdu: decline of in India, 77, 116, 183; as deriving authority from charisma, 27, 30, 31, 42, 83, 104, 105, 117, 120, 170, 180, 182, 183; communalization of, 55; as ethnic marker of political identity, 31–32, 69, 77, 85; formation of in Delhi as literary register, 24 (see also *reḳhtah*); how *hindwī* evolved into, 7; as official or national language, xix, 1,7, 22, 24, 77, 101, 116, 119, 133, 167, 173, 183, 199; preference for Persian prose over Urdu, 54; as replacement for Persian as court language, xix, 22, 36
Urdū Adab (journal), 121
Urdu Dictionary Board, 190
Urdú-Hindí-English Vocabulary, Compiled for the Use of Beginners (Reid), 161
Urdū Luġhat Nawīsī kā Tanqīdī Jāʾizah (A critical analysis of Urdu lexicography) (Hāshmī), 123
Urdū Luġhāt: Tārīḳhī Uṣūl Par (Urdu dictionary: on historical principles) (Abdul Haq), xxii, 191

Varanasi. *See* Benares
vernaculars, 5, 8, 35, 37, 38, 101, 103, 161, 162, 197, 198, 203n27
Vernacular Translation Society, 9, 149, 180, 183–184
A Vocabulary of the Names of the Various Parts of the Human Body and of Medical and Technical Terms in English, Arabic, Persian, Hindee, and Sanscrit for the Use of the Members of the Medical Department in India (Vocabulary) (Breton), xix, 63f, 67
A Vocabulary Persian and Hindoostanee [and Maladivian] (Leyden), 16f, 17, 18*f*, 19

Waqāʿīʾ-i Durāniyah (The Duranian events) (Sayyid Ahmad), xx, 131
Waqār al-Umarā, 132
Wāqiʿāt-i Aẕfarī (‘Aẕfarī’), 105
‘Wārastah’, Lālah Siyālkoṭī Mal, 217n103
Washbrook, David, 25, 210n3
Whittaker's Almanac, 10
Wilson, Horace Hayman, xix, xx, 65, 66, 67, 180, 233n159
Winchester, Simon, 191
word (*lafẕ* or *luġhat*), 169; defining what constitutes, 223n195
word-for-word equivalences, 116. *See also* equivalents/equivalent terms

Yazdānī,Ġhulām, 121
Yūsuf Zulaiḳhā (Jāmī), 47

Żakā Allāh, Munshī Muḥammad, 161
‘Zaṭallī’, Mīr Muḥammad Jaʿfar, 48
Zgusta, Ladislav, 152
Żikr-i Mīr (Memorial of Mir) (‘Mīr’), 10

SOUTH ASIA ACROSS THE DISCIPLINES

EDITED BY MUZAFFAR ALAM, ROBERT GOLDMAN, AND GAURI VISWANATHAN

DIPESH CHAKRABARTY, SHELDON POLLOCK, AND SANJAY SUBRAHMANYAM, FOUNDING EDITORS

Extreme Poetry: The South Asian Movement of Simultaneous Narration by Yigal Bronner (Columbia)

The Social Space of Language: Vernacular Culture in British Colonial Punjab by Farina Mir (California)

Unifying Hinduism: Philosophy and Identity in Indian Intellectual History by Andrew J. Nicholson (Columbia)

The Powerful Ephemeral: Everyday Healing in an Ambiguously Islamic Place by Carla Bellamy (California)

Secularizing Islamists? Jama'at-e-Islami and Jama'at-ud-Da'wa in Urban Pakistan by Humeira Iqtidar (Chicago)

Islam Translated: Literature, Conversion, and the Arabic Cosmopolis of South and Southeast Asia by Ronit Ricci (Chicago)

Conjugations: Marriage and Form in New Bollywood Cinema by Sangita Gopal (Chicago)

Unfinished Gestures: Devadāsīs, Memory, and Modernity in South India by Davesh Soneji (Chicago)

Document Raj: Writing and Scribes in Early Colonial South India by Bhavani Raman (Chicago)

The Millennial Sovereign: Sacred Kingship and Sainthood in Islam by A. Azfar Moin (Columbia)

Making Sense of Tantric Buddhism: History, Semiology, and Transgression in the Indian Traditions by Christian K. Wedemeyer (Columbia)

The Yogin and the Madman: Reading the Biographical Corpus of Tibet's Great Saint Milarepa by Andrew Quintman (Columbia)

Body of Victim, Body of Warrior: Refugee Families and the Making of Kashmiri Jihadists by Cabeiri deBergh Robinson (California)

Receptacle of the Sacred: Illustrated Manuscripts and the Buddhist Book Cult in South Asia by Jinah Kim (California)

Cut-Pieces: Celluloid Obscenity and Popular Cinema in Bangladesh by Lotte Hoek (Columbia)

From Text to Tradition: The Naisadhīyacarita and Literary Community in South Asia by Deven M. Patel (Columbia)

Democracy against Development: Lower Caste Politics and Political Modernity in Postcolonial India by Jeffrey Witsoe (Chicago)

Writing Resistance: The Rhetorical Imagination of Hindi Dalit Literature by Laura R. Brueck (Columbia)

Wombs in Labor: Transnational Commercial Surrogacy in India by Amrita Pande (Columbia)

Culture of Encounters: Sanskrit at the Mughal Court by Audrey Truschke (Columbia)

I Too Have Some Dreams: N. M. Rashed and Modernism in Urdu Poetry by A. Sean Pue (California)

We Were Adivasis: Aspiration in an Indian Scheduled Tribe by Megan Moodie (Chicago)

The Place of Devotion: Siting and Experiencing Divinity in Bengal-Vaishnavism by Sukanya Sarabadhikary (California)

Writing Self, Writing Empire: Chandar Bhan Brahman and the Cultural World of the Early Modern Indo-Persian State by Rajeev Kinra (California)